MODERN RUSSIAN POETRY

MODERN
RUSSIAN POETRY

AN ANTHOLOGY
WITH VERSE TRANSLATIONS
EDITED AND WITH AN INTRODUCTION BY
VLADIMIR MARKOV
AND
MERRILL SPARKS

★

The Bobbs-Merrill Company, Inc.
Publishers · Indianapolis · New York

TO LYDIA

CONTENTS

A list of authors' names and titles or first lines of poems, in Russian and English, will be found on the succeeding pages viii-xlvii.

CONTENTS

I

CONTENTS

THE TIME OF SYMBOLISM

ВЯЧЕСЛАВ ИВАНОВ

АЛЕКСАНДР БЛОК

CONTENTS

II

POST-SYMBOLISTS

III

ВЛАДИСЛАВ ХОДАСЕВИЧ

ГЕОРГИЙ ИВАНОВ

POETRY AND EXILE

MARINA TSVETAEVA

IRINA ODOYEVTSEVA

IV

POETRY AND REVOLUTION

николай клюев

сергей городецкий

V

SOVIET POETRY

ACKNOWLEDGEMENTS

GREAT care has been taken to trace the copyright holders of all poems presented in this anthology. And permission has been asked even in some cases where a claim could hardly be substantiated. For permission to reprint copyright material, the following acknowledgements are made:

To Giangiacomo Feltrinelli for the four original Russian poems by Boris Pasternak from *Dr Zhivago* (Milan, 1957), and to William Collins, Sons & Co., Publishers and Harvill Press, London, publishers of the original English edition, for permission to translate them into English.

To The Clarendon Press, Oxford, for the following poems by Vyacheslav Ivanov: 'Winter, winter, your name is orphanhood', 'These tangling dolphins brought a bivalve out', 'The hunchbacked captives thrown into the clear', *July*, and 'The chiton that the flame consumes hugs him'.

To the Agence Hoffman, Paris, for the four poems by Ivan Bunin.

Special gratitude is expressed to the following poets who permitted their work to be included: Lydia Chervinskaya, Igor Chinnov, Ivan Elagin, Dmitri Klenovsky, Wl. Korvin-Piotrowsky, Nikolai Morshen, Irina Odoyevtseva (for her own and for George Ivanov's poetry), and Vladimir Nabokov, who generously provided not only his poems but also his own translations of them.

ON MODERN RUSSIAN POETRY

I

THIS PREFACE does not aim at presenting a comprehensive and definitive history of modern Russian poetry in a nutshell. For important historical facts and interpretations the reader should turn to other sources, such as the well-known books by Mirsky, Struve, Slonim, Poggioli and others.

From the Western point of view, modern Russian poetry, i.e., in general the poetry of the twentieth century, may look like a curious mixture of modern and nonmodern elements. In Europe, becoming 'modern' largely has meant abandoning the romantic pretensions and rhetorics of the preceding age in favor of the 'naked' realities of the new era with its technology and psychoanalytic revelations. Russia had a different literary history: its Age of Classicism (eighteenth century) was followed by only two decades or so of Romanticism, a movement which never had time to take a clear shape. In Pushkin's work romanticism was only an episode and an almost surface phenomenon; and it is characteristic of the situation that the greatest romantic poet of Russia, Mikhail Lermontov, despite his unusually short life, was responsible for ushering in the Age of Prose and Realism. After this, poetry underwent a gradual decline, and towards the end of the century it was barely tolerated by Russian intelligentsia, preoccupied as it was with social struggles. Much more serious was the deterioration of artistic form, so that even talented poets were doomed to be second-rate even before they began their literary career. This picture is slightly simplified and needs a few corrections, but it is generally true that while in Russian prose of the second part of the nineteenth century one masterpiece appeared after another, giving shape to the image of Russian literature in the rest of the world, poetry, with very few exceptions, was plodding along – the stepdaughter of literature.

All this partly explains why new Russian poetry, when it appeared in the 1890s, wore a neoromantic garb. Historically, however, it was no less radical than its European sisters. In fact, it was a complete and consistent rejection of the preceding era with its utilitarianism, materialism and collective ideals. It also heralded the time of European orientation. But, though borrowing from abroad and assimilating the main tenets of the *fin de siècle*, such as individualism and art for art's sake, the Russians quickly passed the imitative stage and created a poetry which once again, as during Pushkin's time, could be called 'European' as well as 'Russian'. As befits neoromanticism, this Silver Age of Russian poetry (as it was called later) was characterized by a merger of life and art, a metaphysical, religious and mystical search, eschatological expectations and an interest in remote eras and lands. More significantly, it was the time of a new preoccupation with poetic form: attention to the problems of poetic language, investigation of the nature of meter and the enlargement of its area, a refinement of rhyme, and an additional importance attached to verse sound. Still more important was the fact that from, roughly, 1895 to 1930 great poetry was uninterruptedly written by no less than twenty first-rank poets, which is an unusual crop by any standards.

II

Dear friend, what meets our detection
(Don't you see it?) seems to be
Just a shadow, a reflection
Of what our eyes do not see.

                    VLADIMIR SOLOVYEV

The period from 1893 to approximately 1909 is known as the time of symbolism, but some symbolists, especially the earlier ones, were called or called themselves (and occasionally with pride) 'decadents'. It is nearly impossible to separate these two aspects (although there were symbolists with a strongly antidecadent outlook, like Vyachesláv Ivánov); it is even harder to define them. 'Decadence', for example, meant (1) a birth of new consciousness and tragic anticipation of the coming transformation of life, which this generation was perhaps not destined to see, (2) enlargement of the poetic experience, lighting the dark corners of existence and removal of taboos, and (3) certain mannerisms of form, predominance of verbal 'music' at the expense of meaning, and predilection for 'extreme' subject-matters such as sex, illness, evil and death. On the other hand, symbolism could mean many things: poetic technique, similar to that of the French school bearing the same name; poetry of the depths of human spirit and the heights of the Spirit; efforts of poetic seers and prophets to transcend from *realia* of this world to *realiora* of another world; and an attempt to realize the unbelievable synthesis of beauty and religious truth. It was, primarily, the split between the symbolist aesthetes (Bryusov) and symbolist visionaries (V. Ivanov) that led to collapse of the movement, which might have been brought about, too, by overextending and by overstepping the borders of Art.

In this anthology, Russian symbolism is represented by only eight poets, but each one of them is a major figure, historically and/or poetically. Constantíne Balmónt and Valéry Bryúsov were the pioneers of the movement and its recognized leaders. Though they were as different as two poets can be, it is largely to their efforts that modern Russian poetry owed its recognition and its eventual respect. Balmont may pass over too much ground in his jumps from Lucifer to a snowflake, and from Russian folklore (in which he showed little penetration) to Mayan civilization (which he must have understood even less), but he took the Russian reader to corners which the latter never visited. Balmont's colors may be too garish and his melody too jingling, but he drove home to the audiences the fact that hue and sound are important aspects of poetry. Moreover, he was a tireless introducer of new stanzas and other metrical forms, as well as, next to Vyacheslav Ivanov, a supreme master of the sonnet, otherwise so neglected by Russians. A singing bird and a child-poet were the parts that Balmont played to the end of his days, but few, if any, readers and critics followed him all the way. The reasons could be various: poetry-reading Russia might have missed in Balmont the traditional down-to-earth earnestness expected of poets, or the public might have simply become tired of his fireworks and display of sound. Soon after an enormous initial success, everybody suddenly decided that Balmont was washed out and repeated himself; so, for the next forty years of his life, nobody took him seriously. As usual, the contemporaries were in error. Even though he continued to write in the old vein, Balmont was becoming better and better, and his best books are not those of 1900-1905, as is customarily thought, but those of 1914-1917. In his book of sonnets there are about twenty-five poems which deserve a place of honor in any anthology. Judging by his books written in emigration, Balmont went through a creative crisis; he matured and changed. But all this did not matter: no one even tried to read him any more, and he died in an old people's home in France, embittered, in despair and half-mad.

If Balmont for a few years reigned over Russian poetry, it was Bryusov who ruled over it. Bryusov began as a literary revolutionary and almost singlehandedly started the symbolist movement in his teens by publishing in 1894-1895 three booklets containing crude imitations of French *fin de siècle* poetry which he entitled *Russian Symbolists*. From 1904 to 1909 Bryusov was the virtual dictator of Russian modernist forces and managed both to inspire respect in literary conservatives and, from time to time, to shock them with perverse erotic scenes in his verse (such as a necrophiliac breaking into a sepulchre, or two sisters in bed with one man). Though love-passion, modern city and the figures of antiquity were Bryusov's favorite themes, he, like Balmont, wrote about practically everything, from Cleopatra to a boletus mushroom. Like Balmont, Bryusov moved from flower to flower, but as a busy bee rather than a butterfly. A better simile, however, would be a library in which one takes from a shelf one book after another. There probably never was a more consciously bookish poet in Russia, and in one poem he even equated women and books as the two greatest passions of his life. If Balmont liked remote places, Bryusov was attracted by remote epochs of history, and in most of his books (with their French, Greek, but mostly Latin titles) there is always a portion presenting, one after another, real or legendary famous men and women of ancient time – and this portion is a cross between a sculpture gallery and a wax museum. One sometimes gets the impression that this man could write an encyclopedia in verse, describing in equally cold lines anything under the sun (or under the moon, which perhaps fits Bryusov even better). But there is imagination in his dryness and individuality even in his eclecticism, and the frequent present-day dismissal* of Bryusov as practically a mediocrity, who overcame his shortcomings by sheer labor, is unfair and nearsighted, though the poet himself provided such critics with weapons by calling his imagin-

---

* Bryusov's contemporaries would not have agreed: A. Biely said that he gave 'samples of eternal poetry'; Hippius saw in his verse 'blood and brilliance'.

ation, in a poem, a working ox. This man not only 're-established in
Russia the noble art of writing simple and correct verse, lost since the
time of Pushkin' (Gumilev), but he was also, in his own, narrow way,
more of a descendant of Pushkin than many of his contemporaries
who could (and did) make this claim. But actually Bryusov's 'withered'
soul is still an enigma. While being assured by some of his most
penetrating contemporaries that his poetry was guaranteed immortality, he was not sure of it himself, and once said that his greatest
ambition was to remain as a footnote to world literature. Imbued by
this dream, Bryusov all his life wanted to be on the winning side, and
even sponsored ephemeral groups in the hope they would make good
some day and help him to materialize his 'footnote' ideal one way or
the other. Perhaps this was one of the reasons why this inveterate
'decadent' joined the Communist party after the Revolution and even
became a high-ranking literary bureaucrat. The rulers of new Russia
were grateful to him for this, despite the fact that back in 1905 Bryusov
was the most articulate opponent of Lenin's assertion of party-
mindedness in literature. This should have been enough to make him
a villain of Soviet literary history, but it did not happen. On the contrary, together with Blok, he is now the only symbolist who is continu-
ously published after his death. Both are officially labeled 'poets who
overcame symbolism', though there is nothing even in their post-
Revolutionary poetry which could substantiate this point. Even in
Bryusov's late books where he, rather unconvincingly, tried to switch
over to a new quasi-futurist idiom based largely on exclamations,
spondees, sharp enjambments and excessive use of parentheses, one
can find a few good old decadent nightmares smuggled in.

A counterbalance to Balmont and Bryusov, whose poetry aimed at
a thematic expansion, is given in the two symbolist poets who, in
different ways, strike an introspective note and before all things assert
their respective inner worlds. Both walk upon the paths of their spiritual underground (in a Dostoevskian sense), but one of them goes in
God's direction, the other embraces the Devil. They are Hippius and
Sologub.

Zinaída Híppius is still occasionally called a decadent by people
who never read her criticism (in which she consistently fought decadent ideals) and who misunderstand her poetry. This poetry can

only be defined as religious. Future critics may very well some day call Zinaida Hippius the greatest religious poet of Russia because the mainstream of her poetry is nothing but the story of the soul's journey to a complete finding of God. But this road began *de profundis* and, in its initial stages, it was full of various symbols of sin and evil. Some naive critical minds saw in it a predilection for morbidity. And the personal image of Hippius may have distracted many from the intense seriousness of her poetry – especially her sneering attitude and caustic remarks in literary salons, as well as her occasionally devastating literary criticism, which she published under the male pen name of Anton the Extreme. The peak of her religious poetry is, in this opinion, the poem 'Memory', in which she resolutely sweeps aside memory, that primary temptation of semi-religious souls, as a symbol of false immortality. Displaying in her verse both superior intellect and varied emotionality (by the way, she wrote probably the best political poems in Russia), Hippius stood aside from the poetry of her time, almost being ashamed of her poetic gift, and preferred to help her husband, Dmítri Merezhkóvsky, in pursuing his religious and political causes. The discovery of Hippius as a major poet by Russians may also be delayed by the fact that she remained to the end of her life a violent anti-Bolshevik, but this discovery is ultimately inevitable. Her two primary rivals for public attention, Akhmatova and Tsvetayeva, though they may show a more easily appreciable poetic technique, are definitely inferior to Hippius in matters of spiritual penetration and depth. But it is wrong to compare her only with poets of her sex, because this area is consistently transcended in her verse. Hippius is almost forgotten now in Russia, but she herself called memory nothing but 'this ghost of life'.

Fyodor Sologúb's personal universe is somber and exitless in comparison with that of Hippius. If Balmont all his life tried to embrace the world in all its variety, Sologub's was the most consistent effort to limit himself to a definite set of symbols and to a consciously colorless vocabulary for a portrayal of the world in which the false and vulgar variety of the surrounding life, dominated by the evil dragon, the sun, is boldly separated from the immovable, death-beauty produced by the poet's solipsist imagination. Sologub's macrocosm, particularly in its satanist aspects, is not likely to attract many nowadays, but there is grandeur and a peculiar kind of perverse integrity in his poetry. To compare him with Balmont once more, here is the limit of romantic subjectivity as against Balmont's extreme case of romantic objectivity. Unable to leave Russia after the Revolution, in despair after his wife had committed suicide, Sologub tried to divert himself by deceptively simple strains about shepherds and shepherdesses, but ended in complete disgust and depression. Developing one of his favorite images, the zoo-like captivity on this earth, he comes, in one of his late poems, to the picture of being surrounded by beasts and having to eat, without protest, vomit offered him as food.

It is customary to point out a difference between two consecutive stages of Russian symbolism, separating the four poets discussed above from Alexander Blok, Andrei Biely and Vyacheslav Ivánov. The 'older generation' is then labeled predominantly decadent, whereas the latter trio is described as true symbolists. Actually the borderline is not so easy to draw, but there is in the 'younger group' (whose activities were almost synchronic with the 'older' ones) a more pronounced metaphysical trend (all three owe much in their imagery and ideology to the famous philosopher, V. Solovyev), more Russian orientation and a general aversion to art-for-art's-sake ideals. But even after this cautious statement, one can't help seeing that Hippius fits the younger rather than the older set (and it was Hippius who considered Blok a perfect example of a decadent poet).

No one hypnotized his generation more than Alexander Blok. The Russian intelligentsia watched with increased awe his trance-like progression from the worship of the Feminine Idea, through upsurges of carnal passion and drunken despair, to his listening to 'the music of revolution'. One did not have to share Blok's mysticism (which ruled over his poetry long after he broke with his mystical colleagues) to succumb to the broad, emotion-laden melody of his best verse. Many other things contributed to Blok's becoming the most popular figure of the time, 'the tragic tenor of the era' (as Akhmatova was to call him later): prevalence of human content, obvious sincerity, appealing nationalism. Women, or rather the Woman, populate practically every line of Blok's poetry, and reading it is sometimes similar to sitting next to the Russian Don Juan in a restaurant while he goes through the first stages of seduction under the strains of a gypsy violin. (In fact, no one showed more flatteringly than Blok that debauchery could have metaphysical overtones.) It is truly a 'wine, women and song' poetry, and, in addition, a typically Russian version of it, with passion and depression alternating, and with melancholy dominating. The contemporaries also appreciated its mood of the approaching historical cataclysm and the atmosphere of a 'feast during the plague'. In a broader sense, Blok's poetry was also a farewell to the nineteenth century: while being quite up-to-date for his time in terms of technical aspects, he completely lacked the mentality of the twentieth century. All this created a special romantic bouquet which more than compensated for the unevenness of his verse or its intellectual confusion.

Andrei Biely, Blok's friend and foe, was no less the soul of Russian symbolism, but his poetry proved to be of less lasting merit, probably because Biely was too much of a Proteus and lacked inner unity to his verse. Thus the fantastic visions of his early verse do not carry one away anymore, his bewailing of Russia in *Ashes* does not stun, and his later anthroposophic verse leaves one cold. But he was a virtuoso of rhythm and still influences young poets in Russia. Biely's real achievements, however, are in his sometimes unbelievably penetrating literary criticism (especially his Gogol studies) and in his epoch-making prose, which made him a kind of Russian James Joyce.

It is hard to understand the present lack of appreciation of another leader of the symbolists, the erudite Vyacheslav Ivánov, who did more than anyone else in creating an aesthetic foundation for the movement and for elucidating the nature of the poetic symbol. The neglect of his poetry is not a result of its inherent defects. Rather the present-day Russian poetic generation, which lacks a cultural level to appreciate such a poet, is to blame. In this sense, Ivanov belongs to the company of Dante and Goethe, which is not an exaggeration: leaving open evaluation of Ivanov as a poet, one cannot imagine another single Russian literary figure who could, let's say, carry on a conversation with those two poets and not feel ill at ease. The myth-symbols of Ivanov's rite-like poetry do need an approach, and his allusions are not of the kind to be clarified with Bullfinch in your hands (sometimes a Latin footnote in an obscure book by a German scholar can explain everything), but it is irrelevant to accuse Ivanov, as has been done, of lack of spontaneity. In a way he reminds one of T. S. Eliot, only Ivanov is consciously nontragic. From the very start he considered tragedy (in a psychological sense) only a stage in an essentially optimistic process: death is always followed by resurrection in his poetic universe. His verse is a supreme achievement; there is a fullness, roundness and mellowness in it seldom found elsewhere. He does speak with 'gold and honey' as he admonishes a poet to do in one of his works.

Innokénty Ánnensky was a classical scholar like Ivanov, but there is little of his professional erudition in his nervous and compact poetry, which may be roughly described as Baudelaire with an admixture of Dostoyevsky. The ugly world surrounding the poet, and beauty residing somewhere else, may remind us briefly of Sologub, but there is nothing else that these two poets have in common. Annensky is one of the few symbolists who display pity for the suffering of a fellowman, and only Annensky could see in the low aspects of our life a manifestation of a suffering which is essentially a *Sehnsucht* for transcendental beauty. Russian symbolists overlooked Annensky, who began to publish only shortly before his death. Bryusov showed incomprehensible blindness to his poetry and treated it patronizingly; Annensky was, however, appreciated by the younger poets who only a few years after this were to start the movement of Acmeism, which became one of the enemies of symbolism. There is a deceptive concreteness in Annensky's poetry, filled as it is with images of death and with nightmares, but he remains essentially a symbolist in his conviction that our reality is a distortion of higher things. The elliptic quality of his verse made him a poet for only a few, but those few (some of the leading Acmeist poets) built up a real cult of Annensky. His influence was even greater on the Parisian school of Russian poets in exile after the Revolution.

There was no serious opposition to symbolism during the time that it flourished, unless one starts looking for 'realists' in poetry. Such a realist was Ivan Búnin who preserved his hatred and contempt for any kind of Russian modernism to the end of his days, but all he was able to produce in contradistinction was a tourist card poetry of landscape description, admitting a few fine poems. This is not, of course, a reflection on Bunin's prose, which is perhaps the best prose ever written by a Russian, especially in some of his works written in emigration.

III

> No, not the moon, but the dial of a street clock
> Shines for me.
>   MANDELSTAMM

Postsymbolism is as convenient a term to describe the further development of Russian poetry as postimpressionism is for the history of
modern French painting. It took essentially the shape of two different
poetic movements (in fact, practically mutually exclusive), which both
fought symbolism and were not exactly kind to each other, but they
were both in a sense offshoots of symbolism and would be unthinkable
without the latter's enormous achievements in the field of poetic form.
They were called Acmeism and Futurism, names which are hardly
expressive of their nature and aspirations. Both took final shape
around 1913, though their beginnings can be traced to as early as 1909.
Neither of them completely understood the symbolist movement they
attacked nor did they produce aesthetics comparable to the latter's,
but their instinct was correct: one had to do something with Russian
poetry before it lost identity in the quixotic attempt of the symbolists
to realize their ambitious synthesis.

The Acmeists' ideas (which amounted to 'let's switch from Ger-
manic obscurity to Romance clarity' and 'let's concentrate on this
world and forget about metaphysics') were actually expressed before
them by Mikhail Kuzmín, one of the most fascinating poetic figures of
the time. He was both close to (personally and poetically) and remote
from all main poetic schools of the period. He was never a literary
leader, nor did he stand on the periphery. He is of this earth yet elusive; he combines incredible lightness, sometimes almost weightless-
ness, of verse texture with an all-inclusiveness of poetic means. Some
welcomed in him the only twentieth-century heir to Pushkin (which
they saw in Kuzmin's relaxed simplicity and life-affirmation), others
shunned him as a deviate because he wrote about homosexual love as
freely as the ancients, without making it a 'problem'. The primary
importance of Kuzmin was that he drove home the point that art
doesn't have to be heavy to be important (in the way a divertimento by
Mozart is no 'less profound' than a Mahler symphony). Another importance lies in the fact that Kuzmin freely borrowed from all poetic

schools of his time, without becoming eclectic. After him, only Pasternak and, in a sense, Mandelstamm succeeded in this. Lesser figures, like Gorodetsky or Ehrenburg, could never master this, and remained forever literary turncoats. Translating Kuzmin is a despair: he places his words so casually, almost accidentally, and achieves little miracles in every line. He is practically forgotten in Russia now.

Acmeists counted three important poets in their ranks. Nikolái Gumilév was the recognized leader and *maître*. As to his theories and the manifesto, one can only repeat Robert Frost's words about the 'courage to act on limited knowledge', but his instruction in the poetic craft of so many fine poets of his own and the younger generation cannot be dismissed so easily. In a broader sense (and paradoxically), the majority of emigré poets as well as almost all nonfuturist Soviet poets (and that includes so many – from Tíkhonov to Símonov and Vinokúrov), directly or indirectly, owed their poetic technique to Gumilev. His attempt to add a note of virility to Russian verse deserves respect, but on the whole his poetry has been rather overvalued. It is original only in some of its themes, and one may find his predilection for exotic lands and colorful men (conquistadors, captains of sailing boats, explorers of continents) more than slightly adolescent. The most bizarre fact is that in his lines there is little of the Acmeism that he preached. Gumilev's execution by the Communist government made him a hero in some people's eyes, and he *was* a hero in real life, though in an old-fashioned sense. The worst thing about his untimely death was that, judging by his last book of verse, he was just beginning to develop into a really first-rank poet.

Akhmátova, Gumilev's one-time wife, is a much more accomplished poet. Her reputation was firmly established soon after her debut, by poetry of classical economy and precision which makes one think of the best in the Pushkin tradition. Women wrote verse in Russia before Akhmatova, but only after her did they speak with a woman's voice. In a way it was like opening Pandora's box: there has never been an end to the flood of little Akhmatovas in Russian poetry. Later, Akhmatova rose even higher as she spoke about the gruesome events of wars and revolutions from the viewpoint of a Russian wife and mother. During the Soviet time she knew privation, humiliation and, worst of all, forced poetic silence. Her recent honoring at Taormina, Italy, and at Oxford, England, symbolized the fact that real poetry cannot be either ignored or suppressed for a long time by any government. But it was also pathetic that it happened to a seventy-five-year-old woman who was long past her poetic prime. Despite a *succès d'estime* abroad, her recently published *Requiem*, autobiographical poems of a mother who lost her son in Stalin's jails, was a letdown. And it is furthermore pathetic that she was extolled by people who never thought of defending her, and perhaps did not even know her name, when in 1948 she was publicly insulted by the Party as a 'mixture of a whore and a nun'.

It becomes increasingly clear that Ósip Mandelstámm, the third outstanding Acmeist, was a major force in modern Russian poetry, a fact which was hardly clear to his contemporaries. In his early poetry, stone symbolized the Acmeist approach to Art. Architecture, heavy and solid, became the ideal for poetry; this, in its turn, developed into Mandelstamm's favorite theme: empires (Rome, Racine's France, St Petersburg). It was a very individual kind of classicism, a partial result of the poet's flight from what he called 'Judaic chaos'. In the middle of Mandelstamm's poetic life, however, the centrifugal tendencies seemed to predominate and he began to build on verbal association and to use intermixing levels of meaning. In its ideal, it almost looked like poetry of the pure word. Thus Mandelstamm, who, as a critic, tried to camouflage Gumilev's initial flat Acmeist doctrine with symbolist overtones, came as a poet to something which looked suspiciously close to futurism. At any rate, he is probably the poet with the greatest degree of a twentieth-century sensibility who can be mentioned in the same breath with Rilke and T. S. Eliot. After writing an epigram on Stalin, Mandelstamm was sent to a concentration camp where he died. The spectacle of a major poet in rags, half-mad, beaten by his fellow prisoners for stealing bread from them (Mandelstamm suffered from persecution mania and did not eat his own rations from fear of being poisoned) is grisly indeed. Ehrenburg in his memoirs glamorized this into Mandelstamm reading Petrarch at a bonfire in a transfer Siberian camp.

Acmeist aesthetics attracted many minor poets and, as was said before, had a long-range influence. It guaranteed technical perfection and the safety of a well-trodden road, as shown by Zenkévich, Parnók and Shengéli in this book. However, at the beginning Acmeism was

more varied, as demonstrated by the poetry of Vladimir Nárbut with
its stress on ugliness and the grotesque.

Russian futurism was much more exciting as a poetic idea, though
scattered and often inconclusive in poetic practice. The group which
began to call itself 'futurists' in 1913 went first through an impression-
ist and a primitivist stage. Futurists attracted attention mainly through
their antiaestheticism and their rejection of the past ('let's throw
Pushkin, etc., overboard from the ship of modernity'), but their real
significance lay in two slogan-ideas of far-reaching impact and fascinating potentialities. 'Self-oriented word' (*samovitoe slovo*) meant that
the verbal texture of a poetic work became important *per se* and became the real protagonist of poetry. 'Transrational language' (*zaum*)
meant creation of a completely new poetic language which was to
express ideas and emotions directly through sound. Such works are,
naturally, untranslatable. There were four futurist groups, which often
feuded among themselves or made alliances. The most important of
them, known at different times as 'Hylaea' or 'cubo-futurists', was
headed by David Burliúk and included Khlébnikov, Mayakóvsky,
Guró, V. Kaménsky, Lívshits, Kruchénykh (an interesting and active
extremist) and others. Another group, ego-futurists, was created by
Igor Severyánin, whose popularity was brief but incredibly great and
who glorified his own Self and spiced his poetic daydreams with neo-
logisms, but later, in emigration, finally switched to traditional style.
This group also finally went the way of experiment, as seen in the works
of Vasilisk Gnedóv, who wrote not only one-line, one-word, one-letter,
but even wordless poems.* Two other groups, 'Mezzanine of Poetry'
and 'Centrifugue', were less radical in their philosophy and practice,
but they tried to expand the areas of Russian rhyme and metrics as
well as introduce more themes connected with modern city life. Futurism, dismissed by most contemporary critics as either cheap sensation-
alism or gay nonsense, was actually a great fermenting force, whose
influence manifested itself clearly in the Soviet poetry of the '20s and
once again in the works of contemporary youth.

The 'cubo-futurists' proclaimed Velimír Khlébnikov a genius and
called him their leader, but he was actually a lonely figure and a great
poet who outgrew the limits of his own literary group. His importance

* See page 362.

for Russian literature is roughly comparable to that of Ezra Pound, Gertrude Stein and James Joyce for Europe, though his scope and achievement may be even greater than that of the great Irish writer. His bizarre combination of technological utopias with dreams of the prehistoric past was part of his preoccupation with the nature of time, at whose laws he tried to arrive mathematically. In shorter poetic fragments he experimented with all aspects of poetic language, as if poetry were a laboratory, and he hardly left a single possibility undeveloped. In his longer poems he created masterpieces of neoprimitivism, and later portrayed the Russian revolution as a tragic spectacle of historical retribution.

IV

> Emigration is a great evil; but loss of
> freedom is greater.
> MARC ALDANOV

After the Revolution many Russian poets found themselves outside Russia, mainly as the result of the exodus at the end of the civil war. Thus a curious phenomenon of two Russian poetries developing simultaneously in different directions came into existence. Most emigré poets lived in Paris, which became the cultural center of Russian emigration, and their poetry, on the whole, was a continuation of symbolist and postsymbolist traditions; futurist influence, however, was minimal. The ever decreasing reading audience and the virtual impossibility of making a living from literature, except in a few cases, were serious obstacles, but despite this many masterpieces were created by Russians in exile, and now they are slowly becoming a part of the whole Russian literature (for instance, Bunin's *Life of Arsenyev*). Poetry could also boast of many achievements created in this atmosphere of 'loneliness and freedom', as one critic put it, discounting the fact that Hippius, Vyacheslav Ivanov and Balmont wrote some of their best poetry in emigration. The best three poets of Russian exile made their literary debuts in Russia before emigrating, but developed into major figures after leaving their country.

The most influential among them was Vladisláv Khodasévich, who refused to accept the avant-garde 'cancer' which was associated in his mind with the historical cancer of revolution, and he defiantly based his poetry on almost a letter-perfect imitation of Pushkin. The miracle was that he managed to create great and original poetry in this way, a poetry whose mystical content is even more poignantly apparent because of a strict classical form. Khodasevich was, however, a victim of his own symbolism-conditioned eschatological expectations and, as a poet, he finally choked to death in helpless wrath at the world which refused to be internally transformed by beauty.

Khodasevich's most important counterpart in emigré poetry was George Ivánov, a former pupil of Gumilev and a minor Acmeist before the Revolution. Ivanov saved himself as a poet by giving up all hope on the surface. His short, diary-like poems outwardly present the spectacle of a poet for whom the loss of Russia is equivalent to the loss of everything, even poetry. He often reaches the point where the great Nothing begins, and he seems to doubt the very foundations of life and beauty. The hopelessness of this vision is further intensified by Ivanov's refusal to strike the pose of romantically tragic despair, and in his poetry there is the gaiety of a man drowning alone in the middle of the ocean, knowing that no help will reach him. And yet Ivanov, seemingly unintentionally, produces beauty at every step, as if it were residing on his fingertips.

If Khodasevich and Ivanov occupied the center of the arena, Marina Tsvetáyeva was an outcast by nature both in her themes and style. She was another lonely giant of Russian poetry and, moreover, a born nonconformist who praised Germany at the time of World War I and glorified the White Army while living in Red Moscow. The forceful directness of Tsvetayeva's verse went hand-in-hand with a refined culture, and, without ever belonging to futurism, she actually continued its line in her loud and colorful poems with their mixed diction and jagged rhythms. Virtually ostracized by fellow poets in Paris, she went back to Russia (mainly for personal reasons), only to hang herself there in despair.

Next to Khodasevich, and especially after him, the most influential critic of Russian exile was George Adamóvich who found a big following among younger poets with his preaching of honesty, restraint, simplicity and rejection of all multicolored paraphernalia of verse. 'Two lines about the most essential things' became the ideal and slogan of his school, from Steiger and Chervínskaya to Chínnov, and it received the name of 'Parisian tone', which, though dominant and fashionable, did not exhaust the variety of emigré poetry. This poetry also includes surrealistic chains of images by Poplávsky, the dazzling lightness of Odóyevtseva's delirious dreams and the tragic nonsense of Odárchenko, to cite only a few names and styles.

World War II brought about another Russian exodus; this gave some new blood to emigré poetry, by adding a few names, but changing little. The younger poets, such as Elágin, Mórshen and Anstéy, said a few things less nostalgic than their elders, and which were distinctly their own, about Soviet life, war and refugees, but they mostly preferred to say this in the manner of Akhmatova, Pasternak and other greater poets.

At the present time poetry of emigration faces imminent extinction for many obvious reasons. One of the curses of their life has been, of course, lack of attention, natural on the part of critics in Russia, but less forgivable elsewhere. Millions know about Evtushenko whose poetic achievement was never very impressive, though the major poet, George Ivanov, on the other hand, is still known only to a handful (he is not even mentioned in Harkins' dictionary of Russian literature for students), because he is less exploitable by journalists who write about literature. Even more incomprehensible is the lack of attention to this section of Russian poetry on the part of scholars and students. Even if there were no great poets or poetry involved (and the reverse is true), the very fact that more than 250 poets published close to 400 books of verse during this forty-year period, and that this period is at a virtual close and so can be safely studied, entitles it to a modicum of scholastic attention. The time to act is now, because many more leading figures will be dead soon, their archives will be lost and even some of their already out-of-print books will not be easily available.

V

> You are rowing to the land of the future
> With oars of chopped-off arms.
>   SERGEI ESENIN

Traditional division of twentieth-century poetry into pre-Revolutionary and Soviet is both inconvenient and distorting. The Revolution of

1917 was a *historical* event, and in literature it chiefly affected thematic material as well as the destinies of individual writers, but it did not create a new system of poetics. Many poets of post-Revolutionary times had their starting point and formative years before the Revolution, but even those whose debut happened to be after the historic events built on a pre-Revolutionary foundation, be it symbolist, Acmeist or futurist (or even pre-twentieth century). The arguments as to whether Mayakovsky, Mandelstamm, Kluyev and others belong essentially to the pre- or post-Revolutionary period will never stop, but a decision is obligatory, especially in an anthology, even though in each case an important part of their output will remain outside the given period and, if included in the book, will obscure or confuse the picture. It is wrong, however, to consider a poet Soviet only because he happened to create his best work after 1917 in Russia. Pasternak was as Soviet as Pushkin was Tsarist. Length of time doesn't help either: Akhmatova published only for five years before the Revolution, then she lived almost fifty years in Soviet Russia, being more or less active poetically though unpublished for decades. But could one with clean conscience consider her a Soviet poet for that reason?

This is why we separate the period from 1917 to approximately 1930 from the rest of post-1917 poetry and call it 'Poetry and Revolution'. It was the time of great political and social upheavals and of turbulence and torment in individual careers, but it was also the time of constructive mood and great expectations, of efforts to lay a basis for new life. Thus it combines despair (hidden or obvious) with optimism, mysticism with matter-of-factness, and romanticism with naturalistic details. And yet, poetically all this was a continuation of the Silver Age.

Even if Maximilian Volóshin is not the greatest poet of this (or any other) period, he can be considered the most objective poetic chronicler of the Revolution in the sense that he never took either political side and saw in the whole process a tragic fratricidal struggle, 'meaningless and merciless' (as a character in a Pushkin novel once called Russian rebellions). For Voloshin, however, this fight was unmistakably Russian both in temperament and in historical roots, and, true to his anthroposophical philosophy, he saw in it a necessary stage before the final emergence of an ideal, spiritually cleansed Russia. A minor poet before the Revolution, who oscillated between metaphysics and aestheticism and also mastered the art of concrete detail, Voloshin soon acquired a prophetic voice and stature in his poetry during the time of the Revolution.

It is hardly necessary to prove that the towering figure of Maya-kóvsky represents this period best. He was a vassal of the Revolution, loud and direct (but not slackening his craftsmanship in a single line), and he marched with heavy steps through this time, despising traditional beauty and ready to 'tread on the throat of his own song', if it was necessary for the final triumph of new, socialist life. But he was also a lonely, self-centered, sentimental boy who was obsessed with suicide and sang about unrequited love all his life in hysterically nervous poems filled with hyperboles, resounding rhythms and super-original rhymes. His substitution of love for mankind in the place of love for man might have been one of many unresolved conflicts which made him shoot himself in 1930, and the ironic twist to the whole matter was also the fact that this bard of the victorious proletariat fell in love with a White emigré girl in Paris and was refused a visa to go and see her again, this being probably the more direct cause of suicide. There is hardly a city now in Russia which doesn't have a Mayakovsky street after Stalin ordered the Soviet people in 1935 to consider this poet a genius. But here Stalin's decree, for once, had merit, though for the wrong reason, and the new poetic generation of Russia counts Mayakovsky among its idols for his combining of true belief in communism with avant-garde poetic technique.

Another sensational poetic suicide of the '20s was Sergéi Esénin, whose poetry is certainly loved by more Russians and more sincerely than that of Mayakovsky. Even most of the Stalin laureates, in a moment of frankness, would probably admit that they only pay a lip service to the Mayakovsky cult, while adoring Esenin in their hearts. Esenin offers his Russian reader just the right mixture of sentimentality, patriotism, occasional drunken abandon and pleasant melodiousness. Actually, there is little in Esenin that Blok did not have in a greater degree, but Russia traditionally had a soft spot in her heart for 'poets from the people' though they never quite materialized. Here, for the first time, there was not only a genuine peasant and a genuine poet, but a colorful public figure who could, and did, become a Russian Rudolph Valentino. For a time he also symbolized the death of the pre-Revolutionary Russian village, and thus cut a perfect contrast to the 'coarse' and stentorian Muse of Mayakovsky.

It is the opinion of this writer that to understand any literary period it is necessary to find the two contrasting and often mutually excluding figures, one of them usually in the limelight, the other often neglected or not fully appreciated by contemporaries – the two poets who are the poles between which poetic electricity of the time is generated. It is tempting to see such a pair of opposites in Mayakovsky and Esenin, or even in Mayakovsky and Khodasevich, but the right contrast is most likely given us in the juxtaposition of Mayakovsky and Pasternak. Pasternak, branded for most of his life as an apolitical aesthete, was actually more in the mainstream of his age, refusing, as he did, to sacrifice his creative life to the temporary needs of history, standing for the individual person rather than for abstract humanity, and preserving his human dignity against enormous odds. Seen in perspective, his poetry is all about man's looking at nature and finding himself in it; thus nature becomes not a background or surroundings, but a part of his creative self and a symbol of his immortality. In the context of present-day Russia, Pasternak is its future, whereas Mayakovsky is already its past.

The rest of the poets in this varied and dynamic period act as a supporting cast, though one may single out Nikolai Klúyev, who succeeded more than Esenin in creating a poetic myth of peasant Russia and borrowed much of his complex and original imagery from the untapped treasury of mystical symbolism of Russian religious sects. There were other talented poets of the Russian village and countryside: Oréshin, Klychkóv, Radímov and, later, Pável Vasílyev – almost all of them, like Kluyev, victims of Stalin's purges. The proletarian poetry (mainly the group called 'Smithy'), which glorified collectivism, invoked universal revolution and took much of its imagery and themes from factory process, on the whole fared worse and failed to produce original talents despite support from above (Alexandróvsky, Gástev).

The poet-intellectuals of various kinds, many of whom were sympathetic to the revolutionary cause and tried to contribute to it, were more successful than either peasants or workers. Among them one can find Nikolai Aséyev, who managed to merge futurism and folklore in his song-like verse. He followed Mayakovsky to excess and died a Grand Old Man of Soviet poetry. Then there are N. Tíkhonov, who, after his initial success with Gumilev-like ballads of war and revolution, became a literary bureaucrat and a showpiece of the Soviet-sponsored international peace congresses; E. Bagrítsky, who was able, before his untimely death, to capture the romanticism of the Black Sea region and of the Civil War; and P. Antokólsky, who tried to recreate Western history in its revolutionary aspects. The whole picture was, of course, more complex, and the situation of the poetic intelligentsia ranged in reality from the despair-filled scepticism of Sorgenfrei to the sincere (or half-sincere) desire of Gorodétsky to enter the path of new Soviet life irrevocably, his rich pre-Revolutionary background notwithstanding.

The beginning of the '20s was also the time of proliferating small groups, most of them exploiting this or that feature of futurism. Some of them, as represented by the 'nonobjectivist' Nina Habiás, never made it; others had a short-lived popularity, as, for example, the Imagists (Shershenévich, Marienhof) who succeeded in enrolling Esenin in their movement and tried to theorize about the nature of poetic trope, but in practice they were only able to create a more or less interesting mixture of blasphemy and pornography. Mayakovsky's group, 'Lef', on the other hand, tried to be useful to the new Soviet state in proclaiming utilitarian art, but could never persuade the masters to sanction the avant-garde aesthetics. In a similar way, the Constructivists were not successful when they wanted to contribute poetically to a creation of new, businesslike technological Russia. Their leader was I. Selvínsky, one of the most clever poetic tricksters of the time, who had an uncanny ability to reproduce with words the sound of speech or song.

The last splash of futurism was the Dada-like group of 'obereuty' led by Daniel Kharms. This group gave birth to the last really fascinating Russian poet of the twentieth century, Nikolai Zabolótsky, whose debut occurred in 1929. However, he actually belongs to the Revolutionary period because of his primitivism and complex crossing-planes technique (borrowed from Khlebnikov), his grotesque portrayal of city life and his ingenious satire. Mainly because of the critical pressure, he turned finally to a traditional, nineteenth-century idiom in his later explorations of relationships between man and nature, while maneuvering precariously between his own ideas and official prescriptions. His still later poetry, often pastiche-like (and written by the man broken by years spent in jails), belongs to the Soviet period.

V I

> Read it
>   with envy:
>   I'm a citizen
>   of the Soviet Union.
>   MAYAKOVSKY

With Mayakovsky, great poetry may have committed suicide in Russia. After 1930 the bleak desert of the literature of Stalin's time soon begins. It is also known as the literature of socialist realism, although it is certainly not realistic and, strictly speaking, not socialist either. Enforced in the '30s by Stalin as a doctrine on all kinds of artistic activities, it amounts to portraying reality as wishful political thinking. It involved a ban on poetic experiment, closing one's eyes on falsehood and ugliness in the surrounding life, meek acceptance of any policy of the government (even if contradictory or harmful to the country's interests) and limiting oneself to a fixed set of themes: happy life in Soviet Russia (with agricultural, industrial, national and other variations), unhappy life outside Russia and in Russia before the Revolution, glorification of the October revolution and its leaders (i.e., those who were not liquidated in subsequent purges) and several minor themes – antireligious, anti-Western, etc.

There was nothing unusual in this. The history of Russian poetry shows regular alternation of the periods of service (to the state, to the people, or to both) and of those stressing creative freedom: the eighteenth century, the Pushkin period, the Nekrasov period, the Silver Age, the Soviet period. The last mentioned period left poets no freedom of choice whatsoever, as did all of the other 'service' periods; thus service soon degenerated into servility and poetry couldn't help becoming pedestrian, empty, stale and provincial. In fact, this is the time which, least of all, can be modified by the adjective 'modern', poetically speaking.

The two prevalent poetic types are now those of an aged conformist and of a dedicated young communist. A good example of the first is

Samuel Marshák, who wrote sometimes excellent verse for children and made important translations from English (though he distorted the content of Shakespeare's sonnets, he did make them a poetic fact in Russia). His original verse, however, is prose pretending to be poetry, which only demonstrates that no amount of observation and craftsmanship can make nature live in poetic lines. In its extreme this type produces a Lébedev-Kumách, an opportunist without much talent who made a name for himself by accident.

On the other hand, we have Margaríta Aligér, who projects the image of a good and serious girl who writes verse which is not bad. One may even enjoy a poem or two (if it is not outright propaganda), but on reading the third, one gets depressed because of inherent grayness and spiritual mediocrity of this poetry which doesn't even suspect that things like poetic magic exist. A poet is, in this case, nothing but a communist 'schoolmarm'. It is fun to observe Aliger listening to Mozart's C major sonata in one of her poems. The emotions she experiences are a desire to march forward and, even less relevantly, hatred of American militarism. It is a pity that this poem could not be included in the book (it is too long, and the translator flatly refused to waste his precious time), because the playful divinity of Mozart is a perfect foil for the virtues of an Aliger: in front of him it is revealed that her second-rate goodness borders not only on banality, but on stupidity as well. But Aliger is a paragon in comparison with another Stalin laureate, Stepán Shchipachév, who successfully combines mediocrity with pretensions of being profound.

Of course, this does not exclude single instances of genuine values. For example, there is charm in Kirsánov's mildly futuristic verbal play; there is forcefulness in Bergholz's vindictiveness after her husband was shot in a purge (this poetry was printed only in 1964); there is occasional simple humor, but little else, in Tvardóvsky. However, such disjointed sparks do not ignite.

War temporarily saved Russian poetry from final loss of identity, but it resulted only in patriotic sincerity, and no greatness. Moreover, the results of this partial relaxation were completely destroyed in Zhdanov's post-War cultural purge; this was the darkest episode of the Soviet period, whose devastations still have not been completely assessed or (what's worse) sufficiently admitted and repented.

The well-known 'thaw', brought about by Khruschev's 'de-Stalin-ization', resulted in some changes for the better on the literary scene, changes which have been analyzed in the press and even in mono-graphs and need no further discussion here. The most interesting aspect of this thaw was the appearance of a new poetic generation, whose main traits are a reawakening of conscience and a partial return to poetic experiment, branded as formalism under Stalin. This poetic youth, symbolized in Western eyes and immoderately publicized in the figure of Evgény Evtushénko, is actually not so exciting poetically and not so radical in its rebellion, but it is a welcome sign of the slow beginning of liberation of mind and soul. Among them, Voznesénsky is probably closest to the modern Western poetic tradition (though he also learned from Tsvetayeva, Khlebnikov and Mayakovsky), and Vinokúrov the most appealing in his simple honesty. These young men and women violate socialist realism on every step: they betray the existence of underdogs in Soviet society, they are sometimes strangely apolitical, they even attempt something like 'socialist surrealism' (see Akhmadúlina's poem about airplanes), but they are naive, poetically still derivative and actually don't know when they lie (their corrupt fathers at least knew). On the whole, they are more of a new social phenomenon than a true poetic achievement of first order, and the best critical attitude toward them remains a 'wait and see', until they create something worth real attention. They can create it, however, only after they establish normal contact not only with contemporary Western poetry, but with the immediate domestic past as well: after they start discovering poets like Kuzmin, Hippius, Vyacheslav Ivanov, etc. In the Introduction to *Modern German Poetry*, the editors, Christopher Middleton and Michael Hamburger, quoted Hölderlin who said that 'an exploration of the alien and strange ... must be made if the laral domain is to be discovered at all'. The same is true in the contemporary Soviet poetic situation.

The whole truth about present-day Russian poetry is unknown to us. Only occasionally samples of anonymous verse reach us from Soviet Russia: some of it is remarkable, some very poor, some may even be spurious. The recent story of Joseph Brodsky emphasizes the situation: we might never have known his poetry if the account of his trial had not come to us. His poetry is, in some respects, more fascinating or accomplished than that of his over-publicized colleagues. In view of such circumstances, the final verdict about recent developments in Soviet poetry ought to be delayed indefinitely, and so this knowingly incomplete and by necessity superficial survey ends on a semi-hopeful note, instead of a fanfare.

VII

> You pull out your tail, your beak sticks;
> You pull out your beak, your tail sticks.
>
> RUSSIAN PROVERB

An ideal anthology should include the best poetry written by the best poets, and from this viewpoint compiling such an anthology is a test of a compiler's taste. We tried to represent as fully as possible the best verse of the best poets of the twentieth century, not forgetting for a moment the hierarchy of values. This true hierarchy of values had to remain, however, a Russian one; we are aware that some of these 'modern' Russian poets may look old-fashioned to a contemporary Englishman or an American, while others may seem more bizarre than avant-garde. Even when European poetry as a whole develops in the same direction, the details may not coincide or be synchronized in different countries.

But poets do not live in the never-never land of perfection. When one attempts to represent a poet fully, one has to include some secondary works, not quite successful, which more clearly represent the poet's literary position or, for some reason, have become famous and popular. The next step is to open the doors to the anthology for many poets who are not exactly the best, but who convey the atmosphere of the period or add to its understanding. This compromise between quality and historical significance, between pleasure and information immediately brings about a blurring of focus, but it makes the book interesting for a poetry lover as well as for a student of literature. At any rate, a fuller and a more varied picture is achieved in this way, where many sides of the process are represented: beautiful and ugly, profound and stupid, depressing and exalting.

After establishing these general principles, the concrete and painfully exhausting task of specific selection begins: whom and what to include or not to include. It was easy to decide not to include what Russians call *poemy*, i.e., longer poetical works. It is unfair to the poets who had their best achievements in these genres (such as Khlebnikov, Andrei Biely or Bagritsky) and it certainly makes the whole picture rather one-sided, but, on the other hand, there are considerations of room which practically forbid the inclusion of *poemy*, while representing them in excerpts (as done by some anthologists) would be a distortion. We hope, however, that some quixotic publisher will some day venture upon making an anthology of the best Russian *poemy* of modern times.

It was not especially difficult to decide who were the best, or the most important (usually the two coincide) poets, though it did involve some maneuvering between the Scylla of the so-called objectivity and the Charybdis of intuition. There were some surprises, however, in the course of the search. For instance, classifying Benedict Livshits as one of the best poets of the time (or, at least, as a 'borderline case') will cause some raised eyebrows, because even the experts, as a rule, do not know that this interesting poet developed into a star of first magnitude during the later years of his life. For the compilers it was a discovery, too.

Anthologies often give the readers poems rather than present to them poets, i.e., almost impersonal individual examples of poetic gems rather than portraits of men who created them. We chose the latter and tried to show the best in the fullest way. Having selected 'the golden twenty' (with borderline cases, there may be over twenty-five of them) who represent modern Russian poetry at its best (from A to Z: from Akhmatova to Zabolotsky), we exhibited them generously and presented from five to twenty-five poems of each. Some of them are represented by all stages of their poetic development or in most of their themes or poetic forms.

It was different with lesser poetic figures, who were chosen to create atmosphere, to add one more color to the whole picture. They are not represented for their own sake. This is why they may be shown in their less characteristic or successful work or not included at all, even if their names are relatively well-known. Sometimes it is for the good. For instance, it is understandable why Aleksei Surkov is published, rewarded with medals and read (even sung) in the USSR, but it is beyond one's comprehension how he gets into Western anthologies. But some-times omission is regrettable, and the compilers also miss such differ-ent poets as Konevskóy, Baltrusháitis, Komaróvsky, Sásha Chérny, Tretyakóv, Pétnikov, Sergéi Bobróv, Burliúk, Klychkóv, Lugovskói, Guró, Demyán Bédny, Ushakóv, Knut, Kornílov, Anstéy, Lydia Alexéyeva, etc., etc., who can claim originality, historical significance or solidity of achievement, but there is only so much room in the book. On the other hand, one can find in the book such forgotten figures as Habias; there is always the temptation to discover and resurrect.

The assignment of space is another problem. With 'the golden twenty' the number of lines (not poems) is usually, but not always, indicative of the quality or importance of the given poet. Even here, however, the situation is complicated by the fact that poets like Maya-kovsky divide their lines into smaller fragments and thus get more room. The 'atmosphere' poets get the one-two poems treatment, and a two-poem poet is not necessarily better than a one-poem poet (all this is mentioned for reviewers, who almost always start with counting pages in such cases).

The recent Soviet poetic generation received preferential treatment and is represented in the book slightly in excess of its actual impor-tance or achievement, because there is a natural interest in them on the part of the reader now.

Selection is distortion, but anthologies exist and flourish. Trans-lation is an even greater distortion, but translations are a recognized fact of life. The ability of a human being to choose the best, or even the most characteristic, poems in a sometimes prolific output of a poet is limited. To this, one now must add the impossibility of translating all that has been selected. The 'verbal' and the musical poets suffer here most. If some of Khlebnikov's experimental poems seem strained and/or silly to a tradition-minded Russian in the original, a translation (if possible at all) may even strengthen this impression; and his re-petitive strings of images may look not only incoherent but pedestrian in English. On the other hand, melodious nonsense of some of the best poems by Esenin is apt to become nonmelodious nonsense in translation. But even 'simpler' cases are full of traps. To take an ex-ample from another area: so many translators of Pushkin's prose tale *The Queen of Spades* begin their distortions even before they start translating the story itself. They do this by rendering the wheedling snakelikeness of the *taynaya nedobrozhelatelnost* in the epigraph ('deeply-concealed malevolence') with the inappropriate, though semantically precise, 'ill-will', which is a tweedledee-tweedledum kind of word. All that has been said becomes even more important in an anthology like this in which the original faces the translation, so that anyone with enough knowledge of Russian can catch you when you are not precise or when you mistranslate.

Many good poems were considered for inclusion, but rejected on the ground of untranslatability. Actually, the situation is more complex, because some of these poems could be translated, but they would have lost so much of their charm or magic in the process that it was decided to skip them.*

Recently it has been written: 'Collaboration between poets who do not know the original language, and a scholar who does, can be remarkably fruitful' (*Encounter* 115, April 1963, p. 38). Sharing this opinion, the compiler and the translator of this anthology made an alliance and went to work. Having previous experience in anthologizing, the compiler foresaw no great difficulties: he would select, relying on his ear and knowledge, and his partner would translate after being elucidated on the details and subtleties of the original. But while compiling an anthology in one language is a pleasure, to do it in two languages is both pleasure and torture. First of all, the initial compromise between the best and the representative was complicated by the compromise between translatable and untranslatable, and thus the purity of the original designs was spoiled beyond any recognition; in fact, the compiler soon realized that he should forget about his ear and use his mind instead. Secondly, the compiler soon saw that the translator corrects his selection, that he is reluctant to accept what he does not visualize in English, that he, in fact, becomes a compiler too. (On the other hand, the compiler, along the way, found himself in the position of a translator, too, rather than just a preparer of cribs.) At first I tried to oppose this, but gradually I saw in it a blessing, and even learned how to look at the original with different eyes. I saw that a mediocre poem could become a masterpiece in translation: probably any honest

---

* And even Gnedov's 'Poem of the End' needed a translation.

poem is a masterpiece in intention, but this intention can sometimes be fulfilled only in another language. On the contrary, some of your favorite poems begin to look dead and ugly in another language,* and no amount of lecturing the translator as to how the vowels and the consonants are placed in the original will help him reproduce the original miracle: simplicity becomes prose; magic, clumsiness. Here is one illustration. The compiler, being a good Russian, is *ipso facto* an admirer of Alexander Blok. So he naturally delayed the pleasure of introducing his collaborator into Blok's poetry and was quite shocked when his friend declared Blok was a highly overrated poet. In America, with its Free Speech Movement, such blasphemies go unpunished; in Russia, Mr Sparks would be lynched on the spot. Still, I think, he did his best, and some of his Blok translations do sound to my ear faithful copies of the original. I even think that, as a result of this experience, I understood something about Blok, who held me in spell even before I learned to find my way in poetry. Suddenly it dawned on me that Blok, despite all his intoxicating music, was inwardly dead, incapable of loving anything and anybody (including himself), but, unfortunately, capable of loving an idea (The Beautiful Lady, Russia, Revolution). This is a key to his tragedy and to his desire to burn himself alive, together with the world, in the fire of revolution.

But we should come back to our initial discussion of the principles which led us in our work. Of course, our primary intention was to render intact the meaning of the original in precisely the same way it is done in the original. We tried to reproduce the metrics, diction and syntax of the original poem whenever humanly possible; in short, in every single case we began with wanting a good copy and hoping it would sound like poetry in another language. From the very beginning, we rejected what seems a favorite procedure with some translators, namely, to convert the rhymed original written in an identifiable meter into English free verse. But in time we became convinced that trying to achieve precision cuts both ends. There are many examples of this: the relationship of masculine and feminine rhymes is different

* It might be added that a Russian tour de force could be rendered in English (see poems by Khlebnikov, Akhmadulina and Voznesensky), but there is no need to make an English tour de force while trying to be faithful to a standard type of Russian poem.

in English from Russian; an exact copy of Russian iamb would sound monotonous in English, etc. One of the most important things is that, from the Russian viewpoint, English poetry has a great paucity of rhyme. Dactylic rhyme, for instance, which is so widespread in Russian, makes a poem tricky and artificial in English. If a sacrifice had to be made, we often sacrificed the rhyme. We dropped it, say, in odd-numbered lines or even omitted it entirely. But it is better to omit, or reduce the amount of, rhyme than to weaken the poem in its primary aspects, and rhyme is not necessarily one of them. We also used rhymes of the type *hatred: dead*, which is unknown in Russian versification. But on the other hand, in such poetry as that of Mayakovsky, Evtushenko and others, we tried to do justice to their unusual rhymes by inventing unusual rhymes in English, which were not necessarily precise copies of the original. Sometimes we changed the original meter to avoid worse consequences, for example in Sologub, in Pasternak's 'English Lesson', etc. In rare cases, we even had to resort to free verse while translating an original which has both meter and rhyme, as is the case with Steiger and some of Mandelstamm. In short, the compiler regretted many times the fact that he blamed in his reviews other translators who could not do justice to all aspects of their originals.

The poetic individuality of the translator makes itself felt in the translation, and I finally gave up and stopped fighting Mr Sparks' tendency for whimsical enjambments and splits in rhymes (after all, Pasternak modernized his Goethe, too).

In short, things happen to a poem, when it is being translated. Perhaps Robert Lowell is right, and the age of 'imitation' is going to replace the age of translation. Still, we can observe the other extreme in the recent attempt of Vladimir Nabokov (surely the greatest of all translators from Russian into English) to translate Pushkin's *Eugene Onegin* with utmost fidelity and which produced, as a result, only fascinating cribs. There must be a middle ground between translators' padding and *otsebyatiny* (one's own concoctions) and pursuing the translating ideal with a Tolstoyan stubbornness so that finally common sense is sacrificed to Integrity. It must be added, however, that we did follow Nabokov in some of his minor procedures (for instance, lengthening or shortening lines in iambic poems to avoid padding or important omissions), while shunning his general suicidal principles.

In spelling Russian names, we did not aim at a consistency, but mixed tradition (e.g., the final 'y' in names like Mayakovsky) and common sense. Surnames of foreign origin were not given in their Russian form (Mandelstamm, not Mandelshtam). Some first names were slightly changed to avoid unnecessary strangeness (Constantine, not Konstantin). The name, Biely, was spelled with 'ie' to avoid comic associations.

The worst critics of this book will be Russians. To them I could say: I also miss in this book a few poems I love, but this is not an anthology for Russians who know and adore their poetry. This book may irritate some of them by its inclusions as well as by its exclusions. But we had to take that risk.

Many other things could be said (for instance, about the difficulties in translating such Russian words as *toská*, or *glukhói*; or about the excessive usage by Russian poets of the word *nézhnyi*), but this would make this preface even longer and prevent us from including a few more interesting poems.

V. M.

MODERN RUSSIAN POETRY

I

THE TIME OF SYMBOLISM

КОНСТАНТИН ДМИТРИЕВИЧ БАЛЬМОНТ
1867-1942

Я мечтою ловил уходящие тени,
Уходящие тени погасавшего дня,
Я на башню всходил, и дрожали ступени,
И дрожали ступени под ногой у меня.

И чем выше я шел, тем ясней рисовались,
Тем ясней рисовались очертанья вдали,
И какие-то звуки вдали раздавались,
Вкруг меня раздавались от Небес и Земли.

Чем я выше всходил, тем светлее сверкали,
Тем светлее сверкали выси дремлющих гор,
И сияньем прощальным как будто ласкали,
Словно нежно ласкали отуманенный взор.

И внизу подо мною уже ночь наступила.
Уже ночь наступила для уснувшей Земли,
Для меня же блистало дневное светило,
Огневое светило догорало вдали.

Я узнал, как ловить уходящие тени,
Уходящие тени потускневшего дня,
И все выше я шел, и дрожали ступени,
И дрожали ступени под ногой у меня.

(1897)

CONSTANTINE DMITRIEVICH BALMONT
1867 - 1942

In my fancy I clutched at the vanishing shadows,
At the vanishing shadows of the fast-dying day.
I was climbing a tower and the stairway was trembling,
And the stairway was trembling neath my feet all the way.

And the higher I climbed, the more clearly were painted –
The more clearly were painted the far shapes for my eyes.
And I seemed to hear sounds from somewhere in the distance,
From somewhere in the distance, from the earth and the skies.

Yes, the higher I climbed, the more brilliant were shining,
The more brilliant were shining mountain peaks in the sky.
And my misty eyes seemed to be given caresses,
To be given caresses in their tender goodbye.

And far down below me – Night had already fallen,
Night had already fallen upon Earth, now at rest.
But for me there still shone the day's heavenly body,
Fiery heavenly body sinking into the West.

I have learned to hold on to the vanishing shadows,
To the vanishing shadows of the fast-fading day.
Higher, higher I climbed and the stairway was trembling,
And the stairway was trembling neath my feet all the way.

ПОДВОДНЫЕ РАСТЕНЬЯ
Сонет

На дне морском подводные растенья
Распространяют бледные листы,
И тянутся, растут как привиденья,
В безмолвии угрюмой темноты.

Их тяготит покой уединенья,
Их манит мир безвестной высоты,
Им хочется любви, лучей, волненья,
Им снятся ароматные цветы.

Но нет пути в страну борьбы и света,
Молчит кругом холодная вода.
Акулы проплывают иногда.

Ни проблеска, ни звука, ни привета,
И сверху посылает зыбь морей
Лишь трупы и обломки кораблей.

1895

⋆   ⋆   ⋆

Я – изысканность русской медлительной речи,
Предо мною другие поэты – предтечи,
Я впервые открыл в этой речи уклоны,
Перепевные, гневные, нежные звоны.

Я – внезапный излом,
Я – играющий гром,
Я – прозрачный ручей,
Я – для всех и ничей.

THE UNDERWATER PLANTS

The underwater plants spread their pale leaves
Across the bottom of the ocean's tomb.
They stretch, and as they do, they grow like ghosts
In the deep silence of that dark and gloom.

Such quiet solitude depresses them;
They like the world where unknown heights still loom.
They want excitement, the sun's rays and love.
They dream of aromatic flowers in bloom.

No road to that bright, busy land's been found.
The cold water is silent deep at sea.
The sharks go swimming by occasionally.

Not a glimpse, nor greeting, not a sound . . .
And from above – sea ripples send down slips
Of dead men's bodies . . . and fragments of ships.

*   *   *

I'm the exquisite voice of the broad Russian tongue;
Other poets before were precursors who'd sung.
I was first to discover the speech-cadence bounds,
In which vary the angry, melodious sounds.

  I am that – sudden break.
  I am that – thunder shake.
  I am that – limpid lake.
  I am for all and no one.

Переплеск многопенный, разорванно-слитный,
Самоцветные камни земли самобытной,
Переклички лесные зеленого мая,
Все пойму, все возьму, у других отнимая.

Вечно-юный, как сон,
Сильный тем, что влюблен
И в себя и в других,
Я – изысканный стих.

1902

ЗАВЕТ БЫТИЯ

Я спросил у свободного Ветра,
Что мне сделать, чтоб быть молодым.
Мне ответил играющий Ветер:
'Будь воздушным, как ветер, как дым!'

Я спросил у могучего Моря,
В чем великий завет бытия.
Мне ответило звучное море:
'Будь всегда полнозвучным, как я!'

Я спросил у высокого Солнца,
Как мне вспыхнуть светлее зари.
Ничего не ответило Солнце,
Но душа услыхала: 'Гори!'

1903)

Many-foamed, splash on splash, and discordantly fused...
Precious gems that the primeval world has oozed...
And the echoes through woods in the green, green of May...
I shall know. And from others I'll take all away.

> Like a dream (always young),
> I'm in love (so I'm strong)
> With myself, with the throng –
> I'm the exquisite poem.

THE LAW OF LIFE

> I asked of the scattering wind:
> How can I be young always? I spoke,
> And the playing wind fluttered the answer:
> Be airy like wind and like smoke.

> I asked the herculean sea:
> What's the great law of life that you've found?
> And the resonant sea roared, replying:
> Be like me – always mighty with sound.

> I asked the celestial, hot sun:
> To flash brighter than dawn... what to learn?
> And the high, aloof sun gave no answer...
> But my soul heard and said to me: Burn!

СОЛНЕЧНЫЙ ЛУЧ

Свой мозг пронзил я солнечным лучом.
Гляжу на Мир. Не помню ни о чем.
Я вижу свет, и цветовой туман.
Мой дух влюблен. Он упоен. Он пьян.

Как луч горит на пальцах у меня!
Как сладко мне присутствие огня!
Смешалось все. Людское я забыл.
Я в мировом. Я в центре вечных сил.

Как радостно быть жарким и сверкать!
Как весело мгновения сжигать!
Со светлыми я светом говорю.
Я царствую. Блаженствую. Горю.

(1903)

СНЕЖИНКА

Светло-пушистая,
    Снежинка белая,
Какая чистая,
    Какая смелая!

Дорогой бурною
    Легко проносится,
Не в высь лазурную,
    На землю просится.

Лазурь чудесную
    Она покинула,
Себя в безвестную
    Страну низринула.

THE SUNBEAM

I've pierced my brain with this bright beam of sun.
I see the world. Don't know a thing. For I
See only light... mist where all colors run.
My soul's in love... intoxicated... high.

How that beam burns at every fingertip!
How sweet is this presence of fire in me!
All things are mixed. And all things human slip.
I'm with the Whole, core of eternity.

What pleasure to be hot and to shine bright!
What joy consuming each moment in turn!
I speak with Light... for once with help of Light.
I reign. I rise up to the heights. I burn.

SNOWFLAKE

How fluffy and how light
    The snowflake in the cold!
And how pure and white!
    How delicate and bold!

Along the stormy road
    It rushes lightly by.
It wants and seeks the earth
    And not the azure sky.

It left that wondrous blue
    Behind it and has thrown
Itself through winter skies
    Into a land unknown.

В лучах блистающих
    Скользит, умелая,
Средь хлопьев тающих
    Сохранно-белая.

Под ветром веющим
    Дрожит, взметается,
На нем, лелеющем,
    Светло качается.

Его качелями
    Она утешена,
С его метелями
    Крутится бешено.

Но вот кончается
    Дорога дальная,
Земли касается
    Звезда кристальная.

Лежит пушистая,
    Снежинка смелая.
Какая чистая,
    Какая белая!

(1903)

БЕЗГЛАГОЛЬНОСТЬ

Есть в русской природе усталая нежность,
Безмолвная боль затаенной печали,
Безвыходность горя, безгласность, безбрежность,
Холодная высь, уходящие дали.

Приди на рассвете на склон косогора, –
Над зябкой рекою дымится прохлада,

Into the shining rays
      The Knowing One now glides,
And midst the melting flakes
      The White One safely rides.

Borne by a blowing wind
      Caressing it, it sings.
Trembling, it rises up,
      And brilliantly it swings...

And in the swinging sweep
      Seems happy and consoled.
And in the blizzard's blast
      It circles uncontrolled.

But now the long road ends...
      From heights that saw its birth
The star of crystal falls
      Until it touches Earth.

There lies the fluffy one,
      The snowflake bold and light.
How delicate and pure!
      How brilliant and how white!

WORDLESSNESS

A tired tenderness is in our Russian nature –
Concealed melancholy and its speechless pain,
Grief's hopelessness, voicelessness, boundlessness, vastness.
Cold heights and the distances' endless domain.

Come out at the dawn to the slope of a hillock,
Above the cold river hangs the steaming chill.

Чернеет громада застывшего бора,
И сердцу так больно, и сердце не радо.

Недвижный камыш. Не трепещет осока.
Глубокая тишь. Безглагольность покоя.
Луга убегают далеко-далеко.
Во всем утомленье, глухое, немое.

Войди на закате, как в свежие волны,
В прохладную глушь деревенского сада, –
Деревья так сумрачно-странно-безмолвны,
И сердце так грустно, и сердце не радо.

Как будто душа о желанном просила,
И сделали ей незаслуженно-больно.
И сердце простило, но сердце застыло,
И плачет, и плачет, и плачет невольно.

(1903)

КАК Я ПИШУ СТИХИ

Рождается внезапная строка,
За ней встает немедленно другая,
Мелькает третья ей издалека,
Четвертая смеется, набегая.

И пятая, и после, и потом,
Откуда, сколько, я и сам не знаю,
Но я не размышляю над стихом,
И, право, никогда – не сочиняю.

(1905)

The frozen pine forest is one block of blackness;
Your heart is not glad and your pained heart grows ill.

The reeds – motionless. And the sedge does not tremble.
The wordlessness of a peace so absolute.
Deep stillness. The fields run away in the distance;
In all there's a tiredness both muted and mute.

And enter at dusk, as in fresh waves of water,
The cool clumps of orchard trees close by the way;
The trees are so gloomily, so strangely speechless.
Your heart is so sad and it cannot be gay.

As if your own soul has been asking for something,
And needlessly painful were all the replies.
Your heart has forgiven, but your heart has frozen.
It cannot help crying; it cries and it cries.

HOW I WRITE VERSES

A sudden line when all the words occur!
And after it another quickly rises.
The third one flashes from afar for her;
The fourth one, laughing, comes on with surprises.

The fifth, and then . . . later, each intersperses.
From where, how many – only heaven knows.
But I don't pick-pick, worrying my verses,
And I confess to you: I don't compose.

ЛАРЕЦ

Сквозь черную сетку стволов и ветвей,
  И редкое кружево листьев зеленых,
Я вижу, как серый поет соловей,
  И вижу я песню в чуть зримых уклонах.

Всем телом в напев – как изваян, как влит,
  Приподнял головку флейтист затаенный,
То шире, то уже он горлом свистит,
  Ручьями журчанья свирели влюбленной.

Он странно мне близок, угадчик-певец,
  Я помню столетий минувших апрели,
Близь птицы в себе ощутил я ларец,
  В волшебном сокровища звуков звенели.

Широкое А, и глубокое У,
  И смутное М, вместе с Л во влюбленьи,
Сливались, – тебе закричал я 'Ау!'
  И мы целовались, узнав себя в пеньи.

(1916)

КОЛЬЦО

В пиру огней я кравчий был и стольник,
Смотря в алмаз узорного кольца.
Повторный в нем горел восьмиугольник,
И блеск перебегал там без конца.

Люблю многоизменчивость лица,
Перед которым вольный я невольник.
И россыпь грез, кующих круг венца,
И быстрых слов рассыпанный игольник.

THE BOX

Through the dark meshes of branches and trunks
    And the scattered lace of the green leaves
I can see how a gray nightingale sings
    In slight cadences, how his song weaves.

All of his body in song, his small head
    (Concealed flutist) as if sculpted, cast –
Narrowing, widening: his whistling throat,
    Loving pipe with the tones rippling past.

Singer and Seer, he's so close to me.
    I know Aprils of past centuries;
Near to this bird I feel I have a box,
    Magic box, bank of rich melodies.

There is a wide 'A' and there's the deep 'U',
    And the hazy 'M' loving 'L' long.
They blend and I shout 'Ah – Oo, where are you?'
    We kiss, knowing each other in song.

THE RING

Wine-slave and table-master at the feast
Of lights, I saw the patterned diamond ring.
Reflected octagons burnt in it there;
The sparkling danced, an ever-running thing.

I love the constant changes of its face;
I turn involuntary serf before
The scattering dreams that forge the circled crown
And the spilled needles of the words' fast roar.

Четыре есть стихии в Мировом,
А здесь в алмазе дважды есть четыре.
Игла иглу, остря, торопит в мире.

В кольце намек на молнию и гром.
Огни растут. Поток лучей все шире.
И все поют: Идем! Бежим! Блеснем!

(1916)

ЦВЕТ СТРАСТИ

Багряный, нежно-алый, лиловатый,
И белый-белый, словно сон в снегах,
И льющий зори утра в лепестках,
И жаркие лелеющий закаты, –

Пылает мак, различностью богатый,
Будя безумье в пчелах и жуках,
Разлив огня в цветочных берегах,
С пахучей грезой, сонно-сладковатой.

Когда же он роняет лепестки,
Ваяет он кувшинчик изумрудный,
Где семя накопляет, с властью чудной

Сны навевать. В тех снах объем реки.
Дневное – в зыбях, в дали многогудной.
И хмель густой вместил века в цветки.

(1917)

Four elements make up our universe;
The diamond here has two times four of them.
One needle makes another, sharpened fine...

Lightning and thunder lie in the ring's gem.
Lights grow. The rays stream wide as they disperse.
And they all sing: Let's go! Let's run! Let's shine!

POPPY

Deep scarlet, delicate light-red and lilac
And white-white – like a dream the snow begets,
Showing the dawn of morning in its petals,
It flows... and also nurses hot sunsets.

And so a poppy blazes, richly varied,
Arousing madness in beetles and bees,
A flood of fire along flaming embankments,
And with such fragrant dream-sweet reveries.

And when it drops its petals, then it seems
It molds a small green-emerald storage-jar
For saving seeds which have a wondrous power

To bring dreams... a great river in those dreams:
Realities are drowned, dronings fade far,
And this good drunk puts centuries in each flower.

КРОТ

От детских дней я полюбил крота,
За то что ходит в бархатной он шубке,
И белизной его сияют зубки,
И жизнь его, среди существ, не та.

Подземное, ночное, темнота.
Меж тем как в солнце жадные голубки
Глупеют от пригоршни желтой крупки,
Он все один, и там он, где мечта.

Внизу, вглуби, где верно есть аллеи,
И духов черных башни и дворы,
Где странные полночные пиры, –

Где земляные черви точно змеи,
С приказом жить лишь там, а если тут
Покажутся, немедленно умрут.

(1917)

СОН ДЕВУШКИ

Она заснула под слова напева.
В нем слово 'Мой', волнение струя,
Втекало в слово нежное 'Твоя'.
И в жутко-сладком сне застыла дева.

Ей снилось. Нежно у нее из чрева
Росла травинка. Брызгал плеск ручья.
Красивая нестрашная змея
Ласкалась к ней. И стебель вырос в древо.

MOLE

From childhood I have always loved the mole,
Because he wears a coat of velvet fur.
His small teeth shine, could not be pearlier;
His life with creatures has a different role.

The underground, nocturnal, dark extreme...
While in the sun the greedy pigeons reign
And grow dull from handfuls of yellow grain.
But he's alone... and where he is... is Dream.

Down deep, below, where there must be the lanes
And towers and courts of dark spirits at toil,
And where there are strange feasts held at midnight, –

Where earthworms are like snakes beneath the soil.
Their order to live only there explains
That if they show up here, they'll die on sight.

A GIRL'S DREAM

She fell asleep hearing words of a song.
In it, bearing excitement, was that 'Mine'
Which flowed into the tender word called 'Thine'.
The girl froze in a sleep – grisly-sweet and long.

And then she dreamed... Out of her womb softly
A grass blade grew. A stream splashed in a lake.
A beautiful, not terrifying, snake
Stroked her. The stem spread out into a tree.

Ушли густые ветви в небеса.
В них золотились яблоки и птицы.
Качались громы, молнии, зарницы.

И вырос лес. И выросли леса.
И кто-то перстень с блеском огневицы
Надел на палец избранной царицы.

(1917)

ДВА ДОСТИЖЕНИЯ

Два раза человек был в мудром лике змея: –
Когда он приручил к своим делам огонь,
Когда им укрощен был дико ржущий конь, –
И покорить коня гораздо мудренее.

Огонь постигнутый горит, грозя и рдея,
Но подчиняется, лишь в плоть его не тронь.
А сделать, чтобы зверь был бег твоих погонь,
Стократно трудная и хитрая затея.

В сказаньи о Брингильд мы видим, кто сильней.
Оплотом сна ее служил не дуб, не камень,
А зачарованный непогасавший пламень.

Но проскакал Сигурд сквозь изгородь огней.
Был победителем сказаньем званый Грани,
Ведомый духом конь, в сверканьи состязаний.

(1917)

Into the sky thick branches stretched about,
And there birds and gold apples came to linger.
Thunder and lightning, shaking, would not leave her.

More trees would sprout. And then forests grew out...
And someone slipped a ring shiny as fever
Upon the newly-chosen Queen's fourth finger.

TWO ACHIEVEMENTS

Twice Man has shown the wisdom of a snake:
When he adapted fire to his need,
And when he tamed the wildly neighing steed.
Conquering the horse was greater, no mistake.

The fire he grasped burns red and menacing,
But it obeys. (Don't touch its flesh!) But when
A beast is trained to run your errands... then
That's a hundred-times more hard – a clever thing.

Which has more strength? Let Brynhild's tale suggest:
Her sleep was guarded not by oak nor stone,
But by an inextinguishable magic flame.

Sigurd rode through the flames. But not alone:
In legend Grani gained the victor's fame,
The horse by spirit won the bright contest.

БРУСНИКА

Огонь, перебегающий в бруснике,
Сошел с махрово-огненных светил,
Малину и калину расцветил,
Неполно пробежал по землянике.

Отобразился в страстном счастья крике,
У девушки в щеках, играньем сил,
Румянец нежным заревом сгустил,
Ее глаза пугливо стали дики.

И, чувствуя, что в ней горит звезда,
Которой любо всюду видеть алость,
Она влагает искру даже в малость.

Она смеется, а в глазах беда,
Проходит, и пылают города,
Проводит в мире огненную шалость.

(1917)

ОХОТА

Шмели – бизоны в клеверных лугах.
Как бычий рев глухой – их гуд тяжелый.
Медлительные ламы, ноют пчелы.
Пантеры – осы, сеющие страх.

Вверху, на золотистых берегах,
Горячий Шар струит поток веселый.
Залиты светом нивы, горы, долы.
Несчетных крыл везде кругом размах.

LINGONBERRY

The flame that flows inside the lingonberry
Came from the stars – radiant as fire can be.
It burned the raspberry, the snowball tree
And incompletely touched the ripe strawberry.

It shines back with a shout of being merry,
Brushing a girl's cheeks while playing so;
It makes their reds increase with softer glow,
And her eyes, fearful, grow more wild and scary.

And feeling that inside her burns a star
Which loves to see red as the master-stroke,
She puts a spark to everything she spies.

She laughs: a holocaust shines in her eyes.
She passes: cities burn. Like a line far
Across the world she draws her fiery joke.

HUNTING

The bumblebees are bisons in the clover;
Their heavy hum is like a bull's dull bawl.
The honeybees, slow llamas, whine, drone over;
The wasps are panthers terrorizing all.

From gilded shores that burning sphere sends streaming
Downward a gay current for all earthlings.
On fields, hills, valleys – its bright light is gleaming,
And everywhere flutter uncounted wings.

Визг ласточек. Кричат ихтиозавры.
Как острие – стрижей летящий свист.
Гвоздики в ветре, молча, бьют в литавры.

Утайный куст цветочен и тенист.
И выполз зверь. Шуршит о ветку ветка.
Мохнатый мамонт. Жуткая медведка.

(1917)

ЦВЕТА ДРАГОЦЕННОГО

Он жертву облекал, ее сжимая.
У дикого плененного козла
Предсмертная в глазах мерцала мгла,
Покорность, тупость, и тоска немая.

Он жертву умертвил. И, обнимая,
Всю размягчил ее. Полусветла,
Слюна из пасти алчущей текла.
А мир кругом был весь во власти мая.

Насытился. И, сладко утомлен,
Свой двухсаженный рост раскинул мглистый.
Мерцают в коже пятна-аметисты.

Его к покою клонит нежный сон.
И спал. Голубовато-пепелистый,
Яванский аметистовый питон.

(1917)

The swallows scream and ichthyosaurs then shout;
The martins' whistling flows like a sharp blade,
Carnations softly beat their kettledrums.

A screening bush pours out flowers and shade.
Branch rustles branch. A frightening beast crawls out,
A shaggy mammoth: the mole cricket comes.

OF A PRECIOUS COLOR

He hugged his victim with a crunching press,
And (had you looked) the captured wild goat had
That pre-death dark look in his eyes of sad
Melancholy, submission, emptiness.

He killed his victim, softening his prey
With more embraces. From his greedy-lipped
Snake mouth the nebulose saliva dripped.
And all the world bowed to the month of May.

But now he's full. Sated. And sweetly spent,
Lazy, he spreads his dark fourteen-foot length.
The jewel spots on his skin glisten and flash.

A tender dream relaxes his tensed strength;
He sleeps: The amethyst-adorned, blue-ash-
Toned python born in Java is content.

КОВЕР

Я сплю. А на стене моей ковер.
Он плотно всю затягивает стену.
Я вижу нежных красок перемену.
Деревня. Речка. Лес. Весенний хор.

Там дальше город. Сказочный собор.
Душа глядит. Отдаться рада плену.
В саду качает ветерок вервену.
Луна с звездой ведет переговор.

Сбегает в пропасть влага водопада.
Но пропасть – там. Она ушла за край.
Есть златоосень, если кончен май.

Из белых льдов блистательна ограда.
Она моя. Мне разуметь не надо,
Что там за ней. Я жил. Я сплю. Прощай.

(1917)

ТРИНАДЦАТЬ

В тайге, где дико все и хмуро,
Я видел раз на утре дней,
Над быстрым зеркалом Амура
Тринадцать белых лебедей.

О, нет, их не тринадцать было,
Их было ровно двадцать шесть.
Когда небесная есть сила,
И зеркало земное есть.

TAPESTRY

I doze... On my wall there's a tapestry;
It covers all the space from floor to ceiling.
I watch the subtle colors change revealing
A village, stream, woods, vernal choir... See!

A town... A fairy-tale cathedral... far.
My soul looks. Captured so, it wants no pardon.
A breeze shakes the verbena in the garden,
And there – the moon is talking to a star.

The waterfall runs down to an abyss...
That lies somewhere... beyond the borderband.
There'll be a golden fall when May is through.

And this fence, when iced white, is brilliant; this
Is mine. And I don't have to understand
What's back of it. I've lived. I doze. Adieu.

THIRTEEN

In the taiga where it's wild and dark,
In days of youth and early dawns
Above Amur's quick looking-glass
I saw once thirteen pure-white swans.

Oh, no, there weren't thirteen of them,
But twenty-six, all told, of course.
For there's an earthly counterpart
For every known heavenly force.

Все первого сопровождая
И соблюдая свой черед,
Свершала дружная их стая
Свой торжествующий полет.

Тринадцать цепью белокрылой
Летело в синей вышине,
Тринадцать белокрылых плыло
На сребровлажной быстрине.

Так два стремленья в крае диком
Умчалось с кликом в даль и ширь,
А Солнце в пламени великом
Озолотило всю Сибирь...

Теперь, когда навек окончен
Мой жизненный июльский зной,
Я четко знаю, как утончен
Летящих душ полет двойной.

(1930)

And following behind the first,
Keeping in turn, and each turn right,
This closely-bound, harmonious flock
Was making its triumphal flight.

Thirteen in a white wingéd chain
Were soaring in the highest blue.
Thirteen white wingéd birds also
Upon the silver rapids flew.

Two strivings in a savage land
Rushed shouting into vast, far space.
The sun with an enormous flame
Made gold all of Siberia's face.

And now when it, the July heat
Of my life, ends... and no more coals...
I know distinctly how refined
Is the double-flight of soaring souls.

ВАЛЕРИЙ ЯКОВЛЕВИЧ БРЮСОВ
1873-1924

АМАЛТЕЯ

Пустынен берег тусклого Аверна,
Дрожат кругом священные леса,
Уступы гор отражены неверно

И, как завеса, мутны небеса.
Здесь, в тишине, в пещере сокровенной,
Внимая вечно чьи-то голоса,

Живет сибилла. Судьбы всей вселенной
Пред ней проходят; – лица, имена
Сменяются, как сны, в игре мгновенной.

И этой сменой снов потрясена,
Сама не постигая их значенья,
На свитках записать спешит она

И звуки слов, и вещие виденья,
Пророчества, и тайны божества.
И пишет, и дрожит от исступленья,

И в ужасе читает те слова...
Но кончен свиток, и со смехом, злобно,
Она его бросает и, едва

Успев взглянуть, берет другой, подобный,
И пишет вновь, в тревоге, чуть дыша.
А ветер скал лепечет стих надгробный,

Взвивает свитки и влечет, шурша.

1898

VALERY YAKOVLEVICH BRYUSOV
1873-1924

AMALTEA

Nobody lives on dull Avernus' coast;
The sacred forest trembles round the lake;
Rock ledges are reflected blurred and tossed.

The skies are dark like curtains. And awake
In silence here – within this secret den,
Listening all the time as voices speak –

A sibyl lives. The destinies of men
And worlds pass before her; – names, faces, souls
In quick dream-play follow each other then.

And shaken by the way that dreams change roles
(Not knowing what their meaning seems to be),
She speeds to write it all down on the scrolls:

The sounds of words, the prophecies and the
Prophetic visions ... mysteries divine.
And as she writes, she trembles in frenzy.

And in terror she reads those words – each line.
But that one scroll is finished and with laughter
Maliciously she drops it. With no time

To look she takes one more like it thereafter,
And – slight-breathed – writes in anguish most profound.
Wind from the rocks murmurs death verse. The wafter

Sweeps the scrolls up ... off ... with a rustling sound.

Я

Мой дух не изнемог во мгле противоречий,
Не обессилел ум в сцепленьях роковых.
Я все мечты люблю, мне дороги все речи,
    И всем богам я посвящаю стих.

Я возносил мольбы Астарте и Гекате,
Как жрец, стотельчих жертв сам проливал я кровь
И после подходил к подножиям распятий
    И славил сильную, как смерть, любовь.

Я посещал сады Ликеев, Академий,
На воске отмечал реченья мудрецов,
Как верный ученик, я был ласкаем всеми,
    Но сам любил лишь сочетанья слов.

На острове Мечты, где статуи, где песни,
Я исследил пути в огнях и без огней,
То поклонялся тем, что ярче, что телесней,
    То трепетал в предчувствии теней.

И странно полюбил я мглу противоречий,
И жадно стал искать сплетений роковых.
Мне сладки все мечты, мне дороги все речи,
    И всем богам я посвящаю стих...

24 декабря 1899

ПОМПЕЯНКА

'Мне первым мужем был купец богатый,
Вторым поэт, а третьим жалкий мим,
Четвертым консул, ныне евнух пятый,
Но кесарь сам меня сосватал с ним.

I

My spirit does not break in life's dark contradictions,
Nor reason grow more weak in fatal interlocks.
I love all dreams; to me all of the words are precious.
I dedicate my verse to all the gods.

I've lifted up my prayers to Hecate and Astarte...
Priest, pagan, I've shed blood – a hundred calves a breath.
And afterwards I knelt before the crucifixes
And glorified a love which is as strong as death.

I visited the groves: academies, lyceums.
I wrote down on the wax wise speeches that I heard...
A loyal student there, all treated me with kindness,
But I loved only their groupings of words.

On the Isle of Dream where there are songs and statues,
I walked on all the paths – with torch, without torch near.
Sometimes I worshipped these, the bright ones with a body.
Sometimes I trembled, sensing spirits here.

And, strange, I learned to love all life's dark contradictions.
With greed, I learned to look for fatal interlocks.
To me all dreams are sweet, to me all words are precious.
I dedicate my verse to all the gods.

24 December 1899

POMPEIAN WOMAN

'My first husband was quite a wealthy merchant,
My next – a poet, third – a piteous mime,
The fourth – a consul, now "five" is a eunuch,
But Caesar married us himself this time.

Меня любил империи владыка,
Но мне был люб один нубийский раб,
Не жду над гробом: "CASTA ET PUDICA",
Для многих пояс мой был слишком слаб.

Но ты, мой друг, мизиец мой стыдливый!
Навек, навек тебе я предана.
Не верь, дитя, что женщины все лживы:
Меж ними верная нашлась одна!'

Так говорила, не дыша, бледнея,
Матрона Лидия, как в смутном сне;
Забыв, что вся взволнована Помпея,
Что над Везувием лазурь в огне.

Когда ж без сил любовники застыли
И покорил их необорный сон,
На город пали груды серой пыли,
И город был под пеплом погребен.

Века прошли; и, как из алчной пасти,
Мы вырвали былое из земли.
И двое тел, как знак бессмертной страсти,
Нетленными в объятиях нашли.

Поставьте выше памятник священный,
Живое изваянье вечных тел,
Чтоб память не угасла во вселенной
О страсти, перешедшей за предел!

17 сентября 1901

The master of the empire loved me madly,
But I was fond of one Nubian slave.
My belt undid for many. And I never
Dreamed *Casta et Pudica* above my grave.

But you, young friend, my shy one from Mysia,
Forever... ever... I am yours alone.
Love, don't believe that all women are liars;
Among them there was found a faithful one!'

And so she spoke, and she was pale and breathless . . .
Lydia, a matron, as in some vague dream,
Forgetting that all Pompeii was in panic
And that Vesuvius' sky was flame and steam.

And when the lovers tired and became quiet
And they were overcome with potent sleep,
Masses of gray dust fell upon the city,
And it was buried under ashes deep.

Centuries passed, and as from greedy jawbones,
We tore the past from earth here in this place.
We found a symbol of immortal passion:
Two bodies well-preserved in their embrace.

Erect the sacred monument still higher:
Live sculpture of eternal bodies found!
So memory will keep the world reminded
Of passion which transcended every bound.

17 September 1901

РАНЬШЕ УТРА

Я знаю этот свет, неумолимо четкий,
И слишком резкий стук пролетки в тишине,
Пред окнами контор железные решетки,
Пустынность улицы, не дышащей во сне.

Ночь канула в года, свободно и безумно.
Еще горят огни всех вдохновенных сил;
Но свежий утренник мне веет в грудь бесшумно,
Недвижные дома – как тысячи могил.

Там люди-трупы спят, вдвоем и одиноко,
То навзничь, рот открыв, то ниц – на животе.
Но небо надо мной глубоко и высоко,
И даль торжественна в открытой наготе!

Два равных мира есть, две равные стихии:
Мир дня и ночи мир, безумства и ума,
Но тяжки грани их – часы полуночные,
Когда не властен свет и расточилась тьма.

С последним чаяньем, свою мечту ночную
Душа стремится влить в пустые формы дня,
Но тщетно я борюсь и тщетно я колдую:
Ты, день, могучий враг, вновь покоришь меня!

1902

В ДАМАСК

Губы мои приближаются
   К твоим губам,
Таинства снова свершаются,
   И мир как храм.

BEFORE MORNING

I know this clear and unrelenting light...
And coarse coach sounds which through the silence creep...
Before the iron-bars of the office windows lies
The street, deserted in its breathless sleep.

The night sank freely, madly into years.
Lights, all creative fires, still burn and rave.
But the fresh morning breeze breathes on my chest;
The houses stand, dead, like thousands of graves.

There, live-cadavers sleep by twos, alone...
Some, bellies down; some, on their backs – mouths wide.
Distance is solemn in its nakedness,
And over me skies are high and deep-eyed.

There are two equal worlds and elements:
The night – the day; reason – insanity.
And where they meet is heavy, hard to bear...
When light is dim as darkness starts to flee.

With one last hope the soul attempts to pour
Its night dream in the empty mold of day.
I strive in vain, conjure in vain. You, day,
Strong foe, will overcome me anyway.

TO DAMASCUS

My lips are now nearing your lips...
        Your lips and then...
Earth is a temple and mysteries
        Take place again.

Мы, как священнослужители,
   Творим обряд.
Строго в великой обители
   Слова звучат.

Ангелы, ниц преклоненные,
   Поют тропарь.
Звезды – лампады зажженные,
   И ночь – алтарь.

Что нас влечет с неизбежностью,
   Как сталь магнит?
Дышим мы страстью и нежностью,
   Но взор закрыт.

Водоворотом мы схвачены
   Последних ласк.
Вот он, от века назначенный,
   Наш путь в Дамаск!

1903

ОРФЕЙ И ЭВРИДИКА

Орфей

Слышу, слышу шаг твой нежный,
Шаг твой слышу за собой.
Мы идем тропой мятежной,
К жизни мертвенной тропой.

Эвридика

Ты – ведешь, мне быть покорной,
Я должна идти, должна...
Но на взорах – облак черный,
Черной смерти пелена.

Here like the priests, you and I perform
    The ritual round.
In the large cloister exactingly
    The rich words sound.

Angels sing out a troparion...
    Prostrate. And far
Stars are the burning votaries...
    Night – the altar.

What draws us so with such certainty
    Like magnets posed?
We breathe with passion and tenderness;
    Our eyes are closed.

We are engulfed in the whirlpool....
    Caressing thus.
Our destined road from the start of time:
    To Damascus.

ORPHEUS AND EURYDICE

Orpheus

I hear, I hear your soft footsteps,
I hear your footsteps behind.
We walk on a stormy pathway
Toward life from whence dead paths wind.

Eurydice

You lead on; I'll be obedient.
I must follow... walk... I must...
But my eyes – can feel a black cloud,
Black death with its filmy dust.

Орфей

Выше! выше! все ступени,
К звукам, к свету, к солнцу вновь!
Там со взоров стают тени,
Там, где ждет моя любовь!

Эвридика

Я не смею, я не смею,
Мой супруг, мой друг, мой брат!
Я лишь легкой тенью вею,
Ты лишь тень ведешь назад.

Орфей

Верь мне! верь мне! у порога
Встретишь ты, как я, весну!
Я, заклявший лирой – бога,
Песней жизнь в тебя вдохну!

Эвридика

Ах, что значат все напевы
Знавшим тайну тишины!
Что весна, – кто видел севы
Асфоделевой страны!

Орфей

Вспомни! вспомни! луг зеленый,
Радость песен, радость пляск!
Вспомни, в ночи – потаенный
Сладко-жгучий ужас ласк!

Эвридика

Сердце – мертво, грудь недвижна.
Что вручу объятью я?
Помню сны, – но непостижна,
Друг мой бедный, речь твоя.

Orpheus

Higher! Higher! Steps lead upward
To sound, light... the sun again.
Shadows will melt off your eyelids;
Love is waiting for you then!

Eurydice

I don't dare, I don't dare, darling-
Husband, my brother, my friend!
You lead back only a shadow...
As a shadow I ascend.

Orpheus

Please believe me! At the threshold
You like me will meet the Spring.
I who charmed a god with music
Will breathe you life as I sing.

Eurydice

Ah! What does it mean, the music,
To those from where silence dwells!
What is Spring – if you've seen sowings
In the land of asphodels?

Orpheus

Think! Remember! The green meadow
And the joy of dance and song!
... the hidden terror of caresses
Sweetly burning all night long.

Eurydice

My heart's dead; my breath is torpid.
My embrace can't match your own.
I recall the dreams – but cannot,
Poor friend, grasp your speech or tone.

Орфей

Ты не помнишь! ты забыла!
Ах, я помню каждый миг!
Нет, на сможет и могила
Затемнить во мне твой лик!

Эвридика

Помню счастье, друг мой бедный,
И любовь, как тихий сон...
Но во тьме, во тьме бесследной
Бледный лик твой затемнен...

Орфей

– Так смотри! – И смотрит дико,
Вспять, во мрак пустой, Орфей.
– Эвридика! Эвридика! –
Стонут отзвуки теней.

10-11 июня 1904

В ЗАСТЕНКЕ

Кто нас двух, душой враждебных,
Сблизить к общей цели мог?
Кто заклятьем слов волшебных
Нас воззвал от двух дорог?

Кто над пропастью опасной
Дал нам взор во взор взглянуть?
Кто связал нас мукой страстной?
Кто нас бросил – грудь на грудь?

Мы не ждали, мы не знали,
Что вдвоем обречены:
Были чужды наши дали,
Были разны наши сны!

Orpheus

You forgot! You don't remember!
I remember every trace.
No, even the grave can never
Dim for me your fragile face.

Eurydice

Happiness I do remember...
And love... like a quiet dream...
But in this dark, dark so trackless,
Your face is a darkened gleam.

Orpheus

Look! See! (And he looks back wildly
To the empty, dark unknown.)
Eurydice! Eurydice!
(Echoes of the shadows moan.)

10-11 June 1904

TORTURE CHAMBER

Who could merge us for one purpose,
We two, enemies at heart?
Who, conjuring words of magic,
Called us from roads far apart?

Who let us look eye to eye, while
On this perilous abyss?
Who tied us with passion's torment,
Threw us breast to breast like this?

We did not know... nor expect that
Mutual doom was the intent...
For our distances were alien
And our dreams were different.

Долго, с трепетом испуга,
Уклонив глаза свои,
Отрекались друг от друга
Мы пред ликом Судии.

Он же, мудрый, он же, строгий,
Осудил, не облича.
Нас смутил глухой тревогой
Смех внезапный палача.

В диком вихре – кто мы? что мы?
Листья, взвитые с земли!
Сны восторга и истомы
Нас, как уголья, прожгли.

Здесь упав в бессильной дрожи,
В блеске молний и в грозе,
Где же мы: на страстном ложе
Иль на смертном колесе?

Сораспятая на муку,
Давний враг мой и сестра!
Дай мне руку! дай мне руку!
Меч взнесен! Спеши! Пора!

10-11 декабря 1904

В СКЛЕПЕ

Ты в гробнице распростерта в миртовом венце.
Я целую лунный отблеск на твоем лице.

Сквозь решетчатые окна виден круг луны.
В ясном небе, как над нами, тайна тишины.

Frightened, trembling for a long time,
Eyes averted, would not budge...
Each of us denied the other
Before the face of the Judge.

He, the Wise One, He, the Strict One,
Gave us punishment. (What? Why?)
We pained with a muted anguish
When the hangman laughed nearby.

In the whirlwind... (Who, What are we?)
Leaves borne upward from the earth!
Dreams of ecstasy and languor,
Like coals, burnt through us from birth.

Here, fallen in helpless shudders,
Thunderstorms and lightnings' whack.
Where are we: On a bed of passion
Or upon a torture-rack?

Now co-crucified for suffering,
Old enemy and sister mine!
Give me your hand! Give me your hand!
Hurry! The sword's raised! It's time!

10-11 December 1904

IN THE TOMB

You are supine in the tomb's crypt, myrtle wreath in place.
And I kiss the moon's reflection – bright upon your face.

One can see the disk of moon beyond the window bars.
Silent mystery hugs all: us... and the sky's bright stars

За тобой, у изголовья венчик влажных роз,
На твоих глазах, как жемчуг, капли прежних слез.

Лунный луч, лаская розы, жемчуг серебрит,
Лунный свет обходит кругом мрамор старых плит.

Что ты видишь, что ты помнишь в непробудном сне?
Тени темные все ниже клонятся ко мне.

Я пришел к тебе в гробницу через черный сад,
У дверей меня лемуры злобно сторожат.

Знаю, знаю, мне недолго быть вдвоем с тобой!
Лунный свет свершает мерно путь свой круговой.

Ты – недвижна, ты – прекрасна в миртовом венце.
Я целую свет небесный на твоем лице!

1905

ГРЯДУЩИЕ ГУННЫ

Толчи их рай, Атилла!
Вяч. Иванов

Где вы, грядущие гунны,
Что тучей нависли над миром!
Слышу ваш топот чугунный
По еще не открытым Памирам.

На нас ордой опьянелой
Рухните с темных становий –
Оживить одряхлевшее тело
Волной пылающей крови.

Поставьте, невольники воли,
Шалаши у дворцов, как бывало,
Всколосите веселое поле
На месте тронного зала.

Back of you damp roses form a halo at your head;
Drops are on your eyes, pearl drops – of the tears you've shed.

Moonlight hugs each rose and gives the pearls a silver tone,
Moonlight makes its round and passes this old marbled stone.

In such sleep what do you think of? What is it you see?
Dark shadows come lower, lower, bending over me.

I came to your tomb's crypt – through the garden's black.
And malicious lemurs watch me – at the door, in back.

I know, I know it's a brief time with you – underground.
Moonlight, in an endless rhythm, makes its usual round.

You are motionless and lovely, myrtle wreath in place.
And I kiss the bright, celestial light upon your face.

THE COMING HUNS

Tread on their Eden, Atilla!
V. Ivanov

Where are you Huns who are coming,
Who cloud the wide world with your spears?
I hear your pig iron tramping
On the still-undiscovered Pamirs.

Like a drunken horde from dark field-camps
Fall on us in a clamoring flood ...
To revive our too-soon-grown-old bodies
With a fresh surge of burning blood.

Come on, you captives of freedom,
Pitch your tents by the palace wall.
As of old, make a gay field of ripe grain
On the site of the King's throne hall.

Сложите книги кострами,
Пляшите в их радостном свете,
Творите мерзость во храме, –
Вы во всем неповинны, как дети!

А мы, мудрецы и поэты,
Хранители тайны и веры,
Унесем зажженные светы
В катакомбы, в пустыни, в пещеры.

И что, под бурей летучей,
Под этой грозой разрушений,
Сохранит играющий Случай
Из наших заветных творений?

Бесследно все сгибнет, быть может,
Что ведомо было одним нам,
Но вас, кто меня уничтожит,
Встречаю приветственным гимном.

Осень 1904; 30 июля - 10 августа 1905

БЕССОННИЦА

Луна стоит над призрачной горой;
Неверным светом залита окрестность;
Ряд кипарисов вытянулся в строй;
Их тени побежали в неизвестность.

Она проснулась и глядит в окно . . .
Ах, в полночь все странней и идеальней!
Как давит бедра это полотно,
Как мало воздуха в знакомой спальне!

Она молчит, и все молчит вокруг,
Портьеры, дверь, раздвинутые ставни.

Burn all the books in bonfires,
Dance in their lighthearted light.
Be evil and base in the temples.
You are innocent in all you ignite.

And we, thinkers and poets and keepers
Of mysteries and faiths we would save,
Will carry away burning torches
To catacombs, to the desert and cave.

And what of our dear creations
In the wingéd storm's ferment,
In this thunderstorm of destruction,
Will be spared by amused Accident?

Perhaps all that is our own will perish
And leave no trace that men's eyes can see...
Still I welcome with a hymn of greeting
All of you who will destroy me.

Fall 1904; 30 July-10 August 1905

INSOMNIA

The moon stands high above the ghostly mountain
And floods the land with a deceptive light.
The row of cypress trees lines up in one rank
And shadows run to the unknown – this night.

She has awakened now... looks through the window...
All is more strange, ideal – in midnight's bloom!
How heavy on her thighs the blanket presses!
How little air there is in her bedroom!

But she is silent – as is all around her:
The open shutters, the portieres, the door.

И рядом спит ее привычный друг,
Знакомый, преданный, любовник давний.

Он рядом спит. Чернеет борода
И круг кудрей на наволочке белой.
Он равномерно дышит, как всегда;
Под простыней простерто прямо тело.

Луна стоит. Луна ее зовет
В холодные, в свободные пространства.
В окно струится свет, и свет поет
О тайной радости непостоянства...

Встать и бежать... Бежать в лучах луны,
По зелени, росистой, изумрудной,
На выси гор, чтоб сесть в тени сосны,
И плакать, плакать в тишине безлюдной!

Под простыней тревожно дышит грудь,
Мечты влекутся в даль и в неизвестность...
Луна плывет и льет живую ртуть
На сонную, безмолвную окрестность.

8 декабря 1909 - 10 января 1910

*   *   *

Цветок засохший, душа моя!
Мы снова двое – ты и я.

Морская рыба на песке.
Рот открыт в предсмертной тоске.

Возможно биться, нельзя дышать...
Над тихим морем – благодать.

And her habitual friend is sleeping nearby,
Familiar, faithful, lover of years before.

He sleeps beside her ... black beard, with the circle
Of hair in locks on the white pillow case.
And he is breathing – evenly as always;
His body – straight beneath the sheet's clean face.

The moon stands high. And how the moon is calling
Her out to open spaces, cold but free.
Light flows into her window and is singing
About secret joys of inconstancy.

To stand up and to run ... out in the moonlight
Across the emerald and dewy green
To mountain heights. To sit beneath a fir-tree
And cry in silence, cry alone, unseen!

Beneath the sheet her breast breathes on in anguish;
The distant and the unknown claim her dreams ...
And over all the drowsy, silent landscape
The floating moon pours live quick-silver beams.

8 December 1909 - 10 January 1910

★   ★   ★

The dried-up flower, my soul, my own!
We're here again, we two alone.

An ocean fish on the sand again:
The mouth open in pre-death pain.

One can flop; one cannot breathe ...
And paradise lies above calm seas.

Над тихим морем – пустота:
Ни дыма, ни паруса, ни креста.

Солнечный свет отражает волна,
Солнечный луч не достигает дна.

Солнечный свет беспощаден и жгуч...
Не было, нет, и не будет туч.

Беспощаден и жгуч под солнцем песок.
Рыбе томиться недолгий срок.

Цветок засохший, душа моя!
Мы снова двое – ты и я.

1911

НОВЫЙ СИНТАКСИС

Язык изломан? Что ж! – глядите:
Слова истлевшие дотла.
Их разбирать ли, как Эдите
На поле Гастингском тела?

Век взвихрен был; стихия речи
Чудовищами шла из русл,
И ил, осевший вдоль поречий,
Шершавой гривой заскорузл.

Но так из грязи черной встали
Пред миром чудеса Хеми,
И он, как шлак в Иоахимстале, –
Целенье долгих анемий.

Far above calm seas there is emptiness,
No smoke, not even sail or cross.

Sunlight is reflected by the waves;
The rays do not reach the ocean graves.

The sunbeams burn – a merciless crowd...
There were no, are no, will be no clouds.

Merciless, burning... is the sand neath the sun,
And the fish's suffering will soon be done.

The dried-up flower, my soul, my own!
We're here again – we two alone.

NEW SYNTAX

The language fractured? So what! Lookit:
Old words decay. See what I mean?
So should we sort them out like Edith
Did the bodies on Hastings' green?

The age was whirlwinding. Speaking
Crawled, monster-like, from riverbeds.
And slime settled along the bottoms,
Clotted – a mane with shaggy shreds.

Like that the world saw – rising
Kemi miracles from black dirt.
And it – like Joahimstal slag – precious...
Anemias healed which long had hurt.

В напеве первом пусть кричащий
Звук: то забыл про немоту
Сын Креза, то в воскресшей чаще
Возобновленный зов 'ату!'

Над Метценжером и Матиссом
Пронесся озверелый лов, –
Сквозь Репина к супрематистам,
От Пушкина до этих слов.

1922

Let the first lay be only shouting:
It's Croesus' son forgetting so
His being dumb; it's revived thickets
With the resuming 'Tally ho!'

Over the Metzinger and Matisse
The savage hunt blustered in herds –
From Repin to Abstractionism,
From Pushkin on down to these words.

ЗИНАИДА НИКОЛАЕВНА ГИППИУС
1869-1945

ПЕСНЯ

Окно мое высоко над землею,
    Высоко над землею.
Я вижу только небо с вечернею зарею, –
    С вечернею зарею.

И небо кажется пустым и бледным,
    Таким пустым и бледным...
Оно не сжалится над сердцем бедным,
    Над моим сердцем бедным.

Увы, в печали безумной я умираю,
    Я умираю,
Стремлюсь к тому, чего я не знаю,
    Не знаю...

И это желание не знаю откуда,
    Пришло откуда,
Но сердце хочет и просит чуда,
    Чуда!

О, пусть будет то, чего не бывает,
    Никогда не бывает:
Мне бледное небо чудес обещает,
    Оно обещает,

Но плачу без слез о неверном обете,
    О неверном обете...
Мне нужно то, чего нет на свете,
    Чего нет на свете.

1893

ZINAIDA NIKOLAYEVNA HIPPIUS
1869-1945

SONG

My window is high above the earth,
    High above the earth.
I see only the sky with the evening dusk,
    With the evening dusk.

And the sky seems empty and pale,
    So empty and pale.
It will not spare one's poor heart,
    My poor heart.

O, in mad sorrow I am dying,
    I am dying.
I'm striving for something, I don't know what,
    I don't know what.

And this wish I do not know from where,
    Came from where...
But the heart wants, asks for a miracle,
    A miracle!

May it be something that does not occur,
    Never occurs.
The pale sky promises me miracles,
    It promises.

But I cry without tears over vows I can't trust,
    Vows I can't trust.
I need something that is not in this world,
    Something not in this world.

БЕССИЛИЕ

Смотрю на море жадными очами,
К земле прикованный, на берегу...
Стою над пропастью – над небесами, –
И улететь к лазури не могу.

Не ведаю, восстать иль покориться,
Нет смелости ни умереть, ни жить...
Мне близок Бог – но не могу молиться,
Хочу любви – и не могу любить.

Я к солнцу, к солнцу руки простираю,
И вижу полог бледных облаков...
Мне кажется, что истину я знаю –
И только для нее не знаю слов.

1893

ЦВЕТЫ НОЧИ

О, ночному часу не верьте!
Он исполнен злой красоты.
В этот час люди близки к смерти,
Только странно живы цветы.

Темны, теплы тихие стены,
И давно камин без огня...
И я жду от цветов измены, –
Ненавидят цветы меня.

Среди них мне жарко, тревожно,
Аромат их душен и смел, –
Но уйти от них невозможно,
Но нельзя избежать их стрел.

HELPLESSNESS

I'm looking at the sea with greedy eyes,
Chained to the earth above the coastal foam...
I stand on an abyss – above the skies,
Yet cannot fly toward the azure dome.

Should I rebel – or give up all the way?
I lack courage either to live or die...
My God is near me, but I cannot pray.
I want love – and cannot love. And so I

Stretch my arms toward the sun, toward the sun...
A curtain of pale clouds is draped about.
It seems I know the Truth, but I am one
Who cannot find the words to speak it out.

FLOWERS OF NIGHT

O do not trust the night-time
With its beauty where evils thrive.
People are near death at that time;
Only flowers are strangely alive.

The dark walls are warm and quiet;
The hearth-fire died long ago...
I expect the flowers to betray me,
For the flowers hate me so.

Among them I feel hot and anxious;
Their smell is stifling and strong.
But I cannot get away from them
Or escape their arrows for long.

Свет вечерний лучи бросает
Сквозь кровавый шелк на листы...
Тело нежное оживает,
Пробудились злые цветы.

С ядовитого арума мерно
Капли падают на ковер...
Все таинственно, все неверно...
И мне тихий чудится спор.

Шелестят, шевелятся, дышат,
Как враги, за мною следят.
Все, что думаю, – знают, слышат,
И меня отравить хотят.

О, часу ночному не верьте!
Берегитесь злой красоты.
В этот час мы все ближе к смерти,
Только живы одни цветы.

1894

ПЫЛЬ

Моя душа во власти страха
И горькой жалости земной.
Напрасно я бегу от праха –
Я всюду с ним, и он со мной.

Мне в очи смотрит ночь нагая,
Унылая, как темный день.
Лишь тучи, низко набегая,
Дают ей мертвенную тень.

И ветер, встав на миг единый,
Дождем дохнул – и вмиг исчез.

The light of evening is gleaming
Through the blood-red silk onto the leaves...
The evil flowers are awake now!
Tender stems, come alive, interweave.

The poisonous drops of the arum
Fall to the rug measuredly.
All is mystery and treason...
Do I hear hushed conspiracy?

They breathe, they move, they rustle.
Like enemies they watch to see
My deeds, thoughts – (they know and they listen),
And they want to poison me.

O never have faith in the night-time;
Its evil beauty beware!
We are all nearer death at that time;
Only flowers are alive there.

DUST

My soul is gripped by bitter pity,
An earthly pity – and by fear.
I try to flee the dust but vainly;
I'm with it and it's with me here.

And naked night looks into my eyes,
As gloomy as a dark day's light.
Only the clouds that are low-hanging
Give deadly shadows to the night.

The wind, rising for just a moment,
Breathed in with rain ... then hurried by.

Волокна серой паутины
Плывут и тянутся с небес.

Ползут, как дни земных событий,
Однообразны и мутны.
Но сеть из этих легких нитей
Тяжеле смертной пелены.

И в прахе душном, в дыме пыльном,
К последней гибели спеша,
Напрасно в ужасе бессильном
Оковы жизни рвет душа.

А капли тонкие по крыше
Едва стучат, как в робком сне.
Молю вас, капли, тише, тише...
О, тише плачьте обо мне!

1897

ТАМ

Я в лодке Харона, с гребцом безучастным.
Как олово, густы тяжелые воды.
Туманная сырость над Стиксом безгласным.
Из темного камня небесные своды.
Вот Лета. Не слышу я лепета Леты.
Беззвучны удары раскидистых весел.
На камень небесный багровые светы
Фонарь наш неяркий и трепетный бросил.
Вода непрозрачна и скована ленью...
Разбужены светом, испуганы тенью,
Преследуют лодку в бесшумной тревоге
Тупая сова, две летучие мыши,
Упырь тонкокрылый, седой и безногий...
Но лодка скользит не быстрей и не тише.

The fibers of a grayish cobweb
Float out and stretch across the sky.

They crawl like days of earthly doings...
Monotonous, roiled past belief.
The netting from the light thread's pattern
Is heavier than the shroud of death.

And hurrying toward its last perdition,
In dusty smoke, in stifling dust,
The soul in helpless terror batters
The coil of life – with one vain thrust.

And thin drops fall, as in a shy dream,
And pound the roof inaudibly.
O I implore you, drops, fall softly.
O weep more softly over me.

THERE

I'm in Charon's boat with him, passionless oar-man.
The waters are heavy and as thick as lead,
And over the voiceless Styx hangs heavy dampness.
The vaults of the sky are dark stone overhead.
In Lethe... but I hear no lisping of Lethe;
The wide strokes of the oars are soundlessly drawn.
And our lighted lantern, so dull and so trembling,
Throws its dark-red beams on the vaulted sky's stone.
The water is lazy and not clear and bright.
Frightened by shadows, awakened by light,
And following our boat in a noiseless anguish –
The blunt owl and two bats, and behind them much lower:
The thin-wingéd, gray-haired and legless vampire.
But our boat glides on neither faster nor slower.

Упырь меня тронул крылом своим влажным…
Бездумно слежу я за стаей послушной,
И все мне здесь кажется странно-неважным,
И сердце, как там, на земле, – равнодушно.
Я помню, конца мы искали порою,
И ждали, и верили смертной надежде…
Но смерть оказалась такой же пустою,
И так же мне скучно, как было и прежде.
Ни боли, ни счастья, ни страха, ни мира,
Нет даже забвения в ропоте Леты…
Над Стиксом безгласным туманно и сыро,
И алые бродят по камням отсветы.

1900

ЭЛЕКТРИЧЕСТВО

Две нити вместе свиты,
Концы обнажены.
То 'да' и 'нет', – не слиты,
Не слиты – сплетены.
Их темное сплетенье
И тесно, и мертво.
Но ждет их воскресенье,
И ждут они его.
Концов концы коснутся –
Другие 'да' и 'нет',
И 'да' и 'нет' проснутся,
Сплетенные сольются,
И смерть их будет – Свет.

1901

The vampire touched me with its moist wing.
And, thoughtless, I watched where the minding flock went,
And everything here seems strangely unimportant;
My heart, as on Earth, is still indifferent.
I remember sometimes we looked forward to dying
And, waiting, believed what our hope set in store...
But now death has turned out to be just as empty,
And I'm as bored here – as I was bored before.
No pain and no happiness, no fear, no peace,
Not even forgetfulness in Lethe's moans...
Over the voiceless Styx it is damp and foggy,
And scarlet reflections wander among stones.

ELECTRICITY

Two wires are wound together
With their loose endings bare.
One yes, one no – not soldered,
Not melted, but spliced there.
And their dark interlacing
Is narrow, dead, and yet
They wait for resurrection
And are expecting it.
End will touch end – the right
Yes-no *this* yes-no waking...
Those spliced – a fusion making,
And their death will be – Light.

ЧТО ЕСТЬ ГРЕХ?

Грех – маломыслие и малодеянье,
Самонелюбие – самовлюбленность,
И равнодушное саморассеянье,
И успокоенная упоенность.

Грех – легкочувствие и легкодумие,
Полупроказливость – полуволненье.
Благоразумное полубезумие,
Полувнимание – полузабвенье.

Грех – жить без дерзости и без мечтания,
Не признаваемым – и не гонимым.
Не знать ни ужаса, ни упования,
И быть приемлемым, но не любимым.

К стыду и гордости – равнопрезрение...
Всему покорственный привет без битвы...
Тяжеле всех грехов – Богоубьение,
Жизнь без проклятия – и без молитвы.

1902

ПЬЯВКИ

Там, где заводь тихая, где молчит река,
Липнут пьявки черные к корню тростника.

В страшный час прозрения, на закате дней,
Вижу пьявок, липнувших и к душе моей.

WHAT IS SIN?

Sin – Petty thinking and doing the petty thing,
Not having self-love but being in love with self,
Also indifferently being self-scattering,
Enthusiastic with self, satisfied with self.

Sin – Feeling lightly and thinking lightheadedly;
Half-agitated and only half-mischievous;
Prudent and proper – with semi-insanity;
Semi-attention and semi-forgetfulness.

Sin – is to live without courage, without dreaming,
Not recognized, persecuted, nor even moved
To know the sharpness of terror, hope or scheming.
Being completely acceptable – but not loved.

Equal contempt both for shame and for pride, willing
To welcome things slavishly – without a battle's dare.
Heavier than all other sins is this: God-killing –
Life that is without damnation and without prayer.

LEECHES

Where there is a quiet pond,
    Where the stream is mute,
There black leeches fasten to
    Reed and reedy root.

At my life's sunset,
    At that great hour when I KNOW,
I see leeches sticking
    Onto my soul also.

Но душа усталая мертвенно тиха.
Пьявки, пьявки черные жадного греха!

1902

ПАУКИ

Я в тесной келье – в этом мире.
И келья тесная низка.
А в четырех углах – четыре
Неутомимых паука.

Они ловки, жирны и грязны.
И все плетут, плетут, плетут...
И страшен их однообразный
Непрерывающийся труд.

Они четыре паутины
В одну, огромную, сплели.
Гляжу – шевелятся их спины
В зловонно-сумрачной пыли.

Мои глаза – под паутиной.
Она сера, мягка, липка.
И рады радостью звериной
Четыре толстых паука.

1903

But my tired soul no more
   Feels quiet setting in.
Leeches, O black leeches
   Of avaricious sin!

SPIDERS

The cell is narrow and low-ceilinged,
This world's narrow cell I'm in.
And in each one of the four corners
Four never-tiring spiders spin.

They are adroit, fat and dirty.
They spin, spin, spin... And horrendous
Is the manner of their labor:
Nonstopping and monotonous.

And they have woven their four cobwebs
Together, making one large trust.
I look and see their backs are moving
Into the dark and stinking dust.

The web covers my eyes already;
It is soft, sticky and gray.
And four fat spiders with a carnal
Contentedness are glad and gay.

В ЧЕРТУ

Он пришел ко мне, – а кто, не знаю,
Очертил вокруг меня кольцо.
Он сказал, что я его не знаю,
Но плащом закрыл себе лицо.

Я просил его, чтоб он помедлил,
Отошел, не трогал, подождал.
Если можно, чтоб еще помедлил
И в кольцо меня не замыкал.

Удивился Темный: 'что могу я?'
Засмеялся тихо под плащом.
'Твой же грех обвился, – что могу я?
'Твой же грех обвил тебя кольцом.'

Уходя, сказал еще: 'Ты жалок!'
Уходя, сникая в пустоту.
'Разорви кольцо, не будь так жалок!
'Разорви и вытяни в черту.'

Он ушел, но он опять вернется.
Он ушел – и не открыл лица.
Что мне делать, если он вернется?
Не могу я разорвать кольца.

1905

ОНА

В своей бессовестной и жалкой низости,
Она как пыль сера, как прах земной.
И умираю я от этой близости,
От неразрывности ее со мной.

INTO A LINE

He came to me – though I did not know him,
Drew a ring that circled me in space.
Then he told me that I did not know him,
But he pulled his cloak to hide his face.

I asked him to stop for just a moment,
Not to touch me, step aside – waiting...
If he could to dally just a moment
And not to enclose me in the ring.

The Dark One looked startled, 'What can I do?'
(Underneath his cloak came soft laughing.)
'Your sin forms this circle. What can I do?
Your sin closes you within this ring.'

As he left, he added: 'You are wretched.'
Sinking in a void, he gave a sign:
'Tear the ring and do not be so wretched.
Tear the ring, stretch it into a line.'

So he left, but he will be returning.
So he left... and never showed his face.
But what shall I do at his returning?
I can't tear the ring in any place.

SHE

She is as gray as dust, as earthly ashes,
In her shameless, despicable vileness.
And I am perishing from just this nearness,
From this inseparable bond which joins us.

Она шершавая, она колючая,
Она холодная, она змея.
Меня изранила противно-жгучая
Ее коленчатая чешуя.

О, если б острое почуял жало я!
Неповоротлива, тупа, тиха.
Такая тяжкая, такая вялая,
И нет к ней доступа – она глуха.

Своими кольцами она, упорная,
Ко мне ласкается, меня душа.
И эта мертвая, и эта черная,
И эта страшная – моя душа!

1905, СПБ.

ПЕТЕРБУРГ

> Люблю тебя, Петра творенье.

Твой остов прям, твой облик жесток,
Шершавопыльный – сер гранит,
И каждый зыбкий перекресток
Тупым предательством дрожит.

Твое холодное кипенье
Страшней бездвижности пустынь.
Твое дыханье – смерть и тленье,
А воды – горькая полынь.

Как уголь дни, – а ночи белы,
Из скверов тянет трупной мглой.
И свод небесный, остеклелый
Пронзен заречною иглой.

And she is scabrous, yes, and she is prickly,
And she is cold. She is a serpent too.
And her repulsive, searing, overlapping
Snake scales have wounded me as few things do.

If only I could feel a sharp sting twinging!
But she is flaccid, still, with dull veneer.
She is so like a lump, so very sluggish.
One cannot get to her; she cannot hear.

Coiling around me, stubborn, insinuating,
She hugs and strangles me, crushing me whole.
And this thing that's so dead, so black, so frightful –
This wretched, loathesome thing is called my soul.

1905, St Petersburg

PETERSBURG

I love you, Peter's handiwork.

Your skeleton is straight, your outline
Harsh, your rough dusty granite – gray.
And there's a blunt betrayal trembling
At each dim crossroad on the way.

Your boiling cold is more horrendous
Than calms the deserts have withstood.
Your breath is death and putrefaction;
Your waters are bitter wormwood.

Black days. White nights. From public gardens
Drafts of cadaver-darkness fly . . .
The needle's point across the river
Pierces into the glassy sky.

Бывает: водный ход обратен,
Вздыбясь, идет река назад...
Река не смоет рыжих пятен
С береговых своих громад.

Те пятна, ржавые, вкипели,
Их ни забыть, – ни затоптать...
Горит, горит на темном теле
Неугасимая печать!

Как прежде, вьется змей твой медный,
Над змеем стынет медный конь...
И не сожрет тебя победный
Всеочищающий огонь, –

Нет! Ты утонешь в тине черной,
Проклятый город, Божий враг!
И червь болотный, червь упорный
Изъест твой каменный костяк!

1909, СПБ.

А ПОТОМ?

Ангелы со мной не говорят.
Любят осиянные селенья,
Кротость любят и печать смиренья.
Я же не смиренен и не свят:

Ангелы со мной не говорят.

Темненький приходит дух земли.
Лакомый и большеглазый, скромный.
Что ж такое, что малютка – темный?
Сами мы не далеко ушли...

At times the movement stops, reverses:
The stream flows backward, rears and yanks...
The river will not wash off ever
The red spots from the solid banks.

Those spots, the rust ones, settled deeply.
One can't forget or tramp them dim.
The firebrand one can't extinguish
Burns, chars the body dark and grim.

Below, your bronze snake still is writhing;
Your bronze horse freezes – still the same.
And you will never be devoured
By a conquering, purifying flame.

No! You will drown in your black mire,
Vile city! And God's foe – full-blown!
And soon swamp worms, worms ever stubborn
Will eat around your bones of stone.

1909, St Petersburg

AND AFTERWARDS...

Angels do not speak to me.
They like shining, haloed villages...
Meekness and the seal of humbleness,
And I am neither humble nor holy.

Angels do not speak to me.

Earth's dark spirit comes to visit me:
Small, big-eyed and fond of sweets, polite.
If the child is dark, then that's all right.
We have not gone far ourselves, have we?

Робко приползает дух земли.

Спрашиваю я про смертный час.
Мой младенец, хоть и скромен – вещий.
Знает многое про эти вещи.
Что, скажи-ка, слышал ты о нас?

Что это такое – смертный час?

Темный ест усердно леденец.
Шепчет весело: 'и все, ведь, жили.
Смертный час пришел – и раздавили.
Взяли, раздавили – и конец.

Дай-ка мне четвертый леденец.

'Ты рожден дорожным червяком.
На дорожке долго не оставят,
Ползай, ползай, а потом раздавят.
Каждый, в смертный час, под сапогом.

Лопнет на дорожке червяком.

'Разные бывают сапоги.
Давят, впрочем, все они похоже.
И с тобою, милый, будет то же.
Чьей нибудь отведаешь ноги ...

Разные на свете сапоги.

'Камень, нож, иль пуля, все – сапог.
Кровью ль сердце хрупкое зальется,
Болью ли дыхание сожмется,
Петлей ли раздавит позвонок –

Иль не все равно какой сапог?'

Shy, Earth's dark spirit crawls toward me.

I shall ask about the hour of death.
For my child, though shy, knows something too,
Much about these things, more than I do.
Tell me what you've heard for us – and death.

Tell me, what is this, our hour of death?

The dark baby smacks his lollipop,
Whispers gaily: 'All have lived, and then
Death's own hour came to crush all men . . .
Simply crushed them and that's the final stop.

Let me have a fourth lollipop.

'You are born – as worms upon some route.
They won't leave you long there. While they do,
You'll crawl, crawl . . . then they'll crush you.
At death you are all beneath the boot.

To be squashed like worms upon some route.

'There exists every kind of boot . . .
Crushing in the same way, never fear.
It will be the same with you, my dear.
You will bend beneath somebody's boot.

There exists every kind of boot.

'Rocks, knives, bullets. And it still is boots,
Whether weak hearts flood with blood and break,
Or if pain contracts each breath you take,
Or if your neck snaps in tight noose-loops.

Does it matter – just what kind of boots?'

Тихо понял я про смертный час.
Я ласкаю гостя, как родного,
Угощаю и пытаю снова:
Вижу, много знает он о нас!

Понял, понял я про смертный час.

Но когда раздавят – что потом?
Что, скажи? Возьми еще леденчик,
Кушай, кушай, мертвенький младенчик!
Не взял он. И поглядел бочком:

‘Лучше не скажу я, что – потом.’

Январь 1911г., Канн

ВОЗНЯ

Остов разложившейся собаки
Ходит вкруг летящего ядра.
Долго ли терпеть мне эти знаки?
Кончится ли подлая игра?

Все противно в них: соединенье,
И согласный, соразмерный ход,
И собаки тлеющей крученье,
И ядра бессмысленный полет.

Если б мог собачий труп остаться,
Ярко пламенным столбом сгореть!
Если б одному ядру умчаться,
Одному свободно умереть!

Silently I grasped Death's meaning and
I caressed my guest as my own son.
Give him food and ask another one;
There is much he seems to understand.

I grasp Death's meaning; I understand.
But when they have crushed you, what then? Can't
You tell what? Take one more lollipop.
Eat it, eat it, Death-baby, don't stop.
He did not take it. He looked aslant:

'I'd better not say *what then* – and shan't.'

January 1911, Cannes

HUBBUB

Now the skeleton of the rotted dog
Runs around the cannon's flying ball.
How long must I bear such auguries?
Will the cheap play never end at all?

Everything about them gives offense
As the pair moves, unified in rite:
Dog that circles... circles as he rots,
Ball without a meaning to its flight.

If the dog's dead body could stand still
And burn up in flames – pillared, bright, high!
If the ball could fly away somewhere
By itself and being free just die!

Но в мирах надзвездных нет событий,
Все летит, летит безвольный ком
И крепки вневременные нити:
Песий труп вертится за ядром.

Ноябрь 1912, СПБ.

БАНАЛЬНОСТЯМ

Не покидаю острой кручи я,
Гранит сверкающий дроблю.
Но вас, о старые созвучия,
Неизменяемо люблю.

Люблю сады с оградой тонкою,
Где роза с грезой, сны весны
И тень с сиренью – перепонкою
Как близнецы сопряжены.

Влечется нежность за безбрежностью
Все рифмы – девы, – мало жен...
О как их трогательной смежностью
Мой дух стальной обворожен!

Вас гонят... Словно дети малые
Дрожат мечта и красота...
Целую ноги их усталые,
Целую старые уста.

Создатели домов лучиночных,
Пустых, гороховых домов,
Искатели сокровищ рыночных –
Одни боятся вечных слов.

In the upper star-world – no events,
And the will-less mass flies, flies withal...
And the timeless threads cannot be torn.
So the dog's cadaver hounds the ball.

November 1912, St Petersburg

BANALITIES

I shan't leave my steep inclination;
I crush the sparkling granite found.
But with no disloyal deviation,
I love you, old rhymes, and your sound.

I love gardens with fragile fences,
The moon in June, the breeze in trees, –
A glance, romance: like twins united
By the same web are sounds like these.

And being tender hints surrender...
These rhymes are virgins; few are wives.
How my steel spirit is enchanted
By their moving, adjoining lives.

They've been turned out... Like little children
Sunbeams and dreams are trembling now...
But I kiss their tired feet completely,
Their old, retired lips anyhow.

Builders of houses made of shingles,
Of pea-houses – empty, absurd,
And searchers for treasures to market –
Only these fear eternal words.

Я – не боюсь. На кручу сыпкую
Возьму их в каменный приют.
Прилажу зыбкую им зыбку я . . .
Пусть отдохнут! Пусть отдохнут!

Январь 14 г., СПБ.

БЕЗ ОПРАВДАНЬЯ

М. Г-му

Нет, никогда не примирюсь.
        Верны мои проклятья.
Я не прощу, я не сорвусь
        В железные объятья.

Как все, пойду, умру, убью,
        Как все – себя разрушу,
Но оправданием – свою
        Не запятнаю душу.

В последний час, во тьме, в огне,
        Пусть сердце не забудет:
Нет оправдания войне!
        И никогда не будет!

И если это Божья длань –
        Кровавая дорога –
Мой дух пойдет и с Ним на брань,
        Восстанет и на Бога.

Апрель 1916

I don't. I'll take them to my rocky
Shelter, high on my crumbling crest.
I'll stock a rocking cradle for them.
And may they rest! And may they rest!

January 1914, St Petersburg

NO JUSTIFICATION

to M. Gorky

No, I shall never welcome it;
 My just curse has a place.
I won't forgive nor will I rush
 Into the iron embrace.

Like all, I'll go, I'll die, I'll kill.
 Like all, I'll destroy me.
But I shall never stain my soul
 And justifier be.

In my last hours, in fire, in dark,
 Let my heart recall:
There's no reason for any war;
 There'll never be – at all.

And if it is God's handiwork,
 This road of bloodied clod...
My soul will wage war – against Him,
 Opposing even God.

April 1916

ВЕСЕЛЬЕ

Блевотина войны – октябрьское веселье!
От этого зловонного вина
Как было омерзительно твое похмелье,
О бедная, о грешная страна!

Какому дьяволу, какому псу в угоду,
Каким кошмарным обуянный сном,
Народ, безумствуя, убил свою свободу,
И даже не убил – засек кнутом?

Смеются дьяволы и псы над рабьей свалкой,
Смеются пушки, разевая рты...
И скоро в старый хлев ты будешь загнан палкой,
Народ, не уважающий святынь!

29 октября 1917

ЕСЛИ

Если гаснет свет – я ничего не вижу.
Если человек зверь – я его ненавижу.
Если человек хуже зверя – я его убиваю.
Если кончена моя Россия – я умираю.

Февраль 1918

ОТЪЕЗД

До самой смерти... Кто бы мог подумать?
(Санки у подъезда, вечер, снег.)
Знаю. Знаю. Но как было думать,
Что это – до смерти? Совсем? Навек?

JOY

The vomit of the war, this wild joy of October,
That comes from this offensive, stinking wine...
Your hangover disgusts me on this morning after.
O poor and sinful, pitiable land of mine!

What devil and what dog did you attempt to humor?
What nightmare held you helpless in its breath?
Your people in their madness murdered their own freedom,
Not even murdered... but flogged it to death.

Devils and dogs laugh at the mêlées of enslaved men.
The cannons laugh with all mouths opening...
And soon a stick will drive them into some old lean-to,
Those who have lost respect for sacred things.

29 October 1917

IF

If the light goes out – I see nothing.
If a man is a beast – I loathe him.
If a man is worse than a beast – I kill him.
If my Russia is finished – I die.

February 1918

DEPARTURE

Till my own death... Who'd have ever thought it?
(Sleighs at my door, snow, night, chilled breath.)
I know. I know. But who could have thought it?
Completely? Forever? Until my death?

Молчите, молчите, не надо надежды,
(Вечер, ветер, снег, дома...)
Но кто бы мог подумать, что нет надежды...
(Санки. Вечер. Ветер. Тьма.)

МЕРА

Всегда чего-нибудь нет, –
Чего-нибудь слишком много...
На все как бы есть ответ –
Но без последнего слога.

Свершится ли что – не так,
Некстати, непрочно, зыбко...
И каждый не верен знак,
В решеньи каждом – ошибка.

Змеится луна в воде –
Но лжет, золотясь, дорога...
Ущерб, перехлест везде.
А мера – только у Бога.

(1938)

ЛЯГУШКА

Какая-то лягушка (все равно!)
Заботливо, настойчиво, давно
    Свистит под небом черновлажным.

А вдруг она – о самом важном?

И вдруг, поняв ее язык,
Я б изменился, все бы изменилось,
    Я мир иначе бы постиг,
И в мире бы мне новое открылось?

Be silent, be silent. No need now for hoping...
(Night, wind, houses, snow so white.)
But who could have thought it was no use hoping...
(Sleighs and darkness, wind and night.)

THE MEASURING

There is always something lacking,
And some things of too much consist...
Everything seems to have an answer,
But the last syllable is missed.

If something takes place – it's not so,
Not the right time, no substance, no shape.
And every sign is untrue;
Each decision has a mistake.

The moon is a snake on the water,
But the golden road tells a lie...
Everywhere there's too much or too little.
Only God gives the proper supply.

FROG

Some kind of frog (They're all the same to me.)
Is whistling long and loud and thoughtfully.
  Beneath a black damp sky his chatter...

What if it's about things that most matter?

And what if – grasping what he'd say –
All would change and change would move through me?
  I'd see the world in a different way,
And new things in the world would be shown to me?

Но я с досадой хлопаю окном:
Все это – мара ночи южной
С ее томительно-бессонным сном...

Какая-то лягушка! Очень нужно!

(1938)

ПАМЯТЬ

Недолгий след оставлю я
В безбольной памяти людской...
Но память, – призрак бытия,
Неясный, лживый и пустой, –
На что мне он?

　　　　　　Живу в себе,
А если нет – не все ль равно,
Что кто-то помнит о тебе,
Иль всеми ты забыт давно?

Пройдут одною чередой
И долгий век и краткий день...
Нет жизни – в памяти чужой:
И память, как забвенье, – тень.

Но на земле, пока моя
Еще живет и дышит плоть –
Лишь об одном забочусь я:
Чтоб не забыл меня Господь.

1913-1925, СПБ.-Каннэ

But annoyed, I shut the window with a bang.
All this – a southern night's illusion
During a languid, sleepless sleep... Then pang!

Some kind of frog! So what! Big deal intrusion!

MEMORY

I shall not leave too long a trace
In people's painless memory...
This ghost of life is hollow, false
And vague. What good is it for me?

So I exist within myself,
And if not – does it matter so
If someone still remembers you
Or has forgotten long ago?

A brief day or a century
In the same manner come and go...
There is no life in others' memory:
It, like oblivion, is a shadow.

But here on this earth while my flesh
Can still alive and breathing be,
I have but one concern and care:
That God will never forget me.

1913-1925, St Petersburg-Cannes

ФЕДОР СОЛОГУБ
(ФЕДОР КУЗЬМИЧ ТЕТЕРНИКОВ)
1863-1927

Скучная лампа моя зажжена,
Снова глаза мои мучит она.

Господи, если я раб,
Если я беден и слаб,

Если мне вечно за этим столом
Скучным и скудным томиться трудом,

Дай мне в одну только ночь
Слабость мою превозмочь

И в совершенном созданьи одном
Чистым навеки зажечься огнем.

26 августа 1898

ЗВЕЗДА МАИР

Звезда Маир сияет надо мною,
Звезда Маир,
И озарен прекрасною звездою
Далекий мир.

Земля Ойле плывет в волнах эфира,
Земля Ойле,
И ясен свет блистающий Маира
На той земле.

FYODOR SOLOGUB
(FYODOR KUZMICH TETERNIKOV)
1863-1927

Now the dull light in my lamp starts to rise,
And once again it's tormenting my eyes.

Lord, I'm a slave; if it's true,
If I am poor and weak too,

If I am destined forever to pour
Here over petty work, desked by this door,

Let me for one night alone
Conquer each weakness I've shown,

And in one perfect creation, let me
Capture pure fire for eternity.

26 August 1898

MAÏR

The star, Maïr, shines in the sky above me –
    The star, Maïr.
A world is lighted by this star so lovely,
    So far from here.

The land, Oilay, floats on the waves of ether –
    The land, Oilay.
The glittering light of Maïr one can see there
    Is bright as day.

Река Лигой в стране любви и мира,
    Река Лигой
Колеблет тихо ясный лик Маира
    Своей волной.

Бряцанье лир, цветов благоуханье,
    Бряцанье лир
И песни жен слились в одно дыханье,
    Хваля Маир.

15 сентября 1898

        ★ ★ ★

Порой повеет запах странный, –
Его причины не понять, –
Давно померкший, день туманный
Переживается опять.

Как встарь, опять печально всходишь
На обветшалое крыльцо,
Засов скрипучий вновь отводишь,
Вращая ржавое кольцо, –

И видишь тесные покои,
Где половицы чуть скрипят,
Где отсырелые обои
В углах тихонько шелестят,

Где скучный маятник маячит,
Внимая скучным, злым речам,
Где кто-то молится да плачет,
Так долго плачет по ночам.

5 октября 1898

In that calm land of love, the Ligoy river –
The lithe Ligoy –
Makes the bright face of Maïr softly quiver
As waves deploy.

The flowers that smell, the lyres that strum (amazing
Lyres, strumming clear),
And songs of women blend in one breath praising –
Praising Maïr.

15 September 1898

* * *

At times there comes a strange smell wafting;
From whence its source I cannot say.
But I relive what's been dark often,
A kind of smoldering foggy day.

Like then, once more I climb up sadly
The run-down porch at evening
And once again unlatch the creaking
Bolt turning on the rusty ring.

And see the narrow rooms before me,
Where every floorboard squeaks and purrs,
Where the mildewed, damp wallpaper
In the corners slightly stirs,

The dull pendulum dimly swinging
Listens as evil speeches bite,
And for so long someone's been praying
And crying hard throughout the night.

5 October 1898

Когда я в бурном море плавал,
и мой корабль пошел ко дну,
я так воззвал: 'Отец мой Дьявол,
спаси, помилуй, я тону!'

'Не дай погибнуть раньше срока
душе озлобленной моей,
я власти темного порока
отдам остаток черных дней.'

И Дьявол взял меня и бросил
в полуистлевшую ладью.
Я там нашел и пару весел,
и серый парус, и скамью.

И вынес я опять на сушу,
в больное, злое житие,
мою отверженную душу
и тело грешное мое.

И верен я, отец мой Дьявол,
обету, данному в злой час,
когда я в бурном море плавал
и ты меня от смерти спас.

Тебя, отец мой, я прославлю
в укор неправедному дню,
хулу над миром я поставлю
и, соблазняя, соблазню.

1902

My ship began to sink beneath me,
As I sailed on the stormy sea.
I called out thus: My devil, Father,
I'm drowning, have mercy, save me!

Don't let my soul that's grown embittered
Perish before its precise hour,
And I'll give my dark days remaining
Unto your blackest evil's power.

The Devil lifted me and threw me
Into a half-rotting boat where
I found a pair of oars before me
And a gray sail, and a bench there.

I carried back onto the dry land
Into my sick, evil life's mesh
My stranded soul, outcast forever,
And my own sinful body's flesh.

And I've been true, my Father, Devil;
To that pledge I've not been remiss –
When I sailed on that stormy ocean
And you saved me from the abyss.

And I will glorify you, Father,
And blame the wicked Day's abuse.
My curse will stand over the world . . .
And my seducing will seduce.

Змий, парящий над вселенною,
Весь в огне, безумно злой,
Я хвалю тебя смиренною,
Дерзновенною хулой.

Из болотной топкой сырости
Повелел, губитель, ты
Деревам и травам вырасти,
Вывел листья и цветы.

И ползущих и летающих
Ты воззвал на краткий срок.
Сознающих и желающих
Тяжкой жизни ты обрек.

Тучи зыблешь ты летучие,
Ветры гонишь вдоль земли,
Чтоб твои лобзанья жгучие
Раньше срока не сожгли.

Неотменны повеления,
Нет пощады у тебя.
Ты царишь, презрев моления,
Не любя и все губя.

18 июня 1902

* * *

Околдовал я всю природу,
И оковал я каждый миг.
Какую страшную свободу
Я, чародействуя, постиг!

All the world's ruled by the dragon –
Fiery, mad, wicked, perverse.
Let me praise him with a humble,
Daring and ironic curse:

You, destruction-bringer, ordered
The damp swamps to show your power;
You brought forth the trees and grasses
Growing into leaves and flowers.

All things flying, all things crawling
You made – though their time is brief.
Those aware and those ambitious
You doomed to the harshest life.

You moved and clouds started floating...
You chased winds along the land,
So your kisses, deadly scorching,
Would not sear before you planned.

And your orders can't be cancelled;
You have no mercy to bring.
You rule and don't hear our begging.
You don't love. You kill each thing.

18 June 1902

* * *

I have enchanted all of Nature
And forged each moment's quality.
And what a horrifying freedom
I found in such a sorcery!

И развернулась без предела
Моя предвечная вина,
И далеко простерлось тело,
И так разверзлась глубина!

Воззвав к первоначальной силе,
Я бросил вызов небесам,
Но мне светила возвестили,
Что я природу создал сам.

1904

* * *

Мы – плененные звери,
Голосим, как умеем.
Глухо заперты двери,
Мы открыть их не смеем.

Если сердце преданиям верно,
Утешаяся лаем, мы лаем.
Что в зверинце зловонно и скверно,
Мы забыли давно, мы не знаем.

К повторениям сердце привычно, –
Однозвучно и скучно кукуем.
Все в зверинце безлично, обычно.
Мы о воле давно не тоскуем.

Мы – плененные звери,
Голосим, как умеем.
Глухо заперты двери,
Мы открыть их не смеем.

1905

My constant guilt – with no beginning –
Spread till all limit-zones were passed;
The body far away expanded,
And depths opened that were so vast.

Then I called out to the Prime-Mover,
My challenge unto Heaven thrown;
The stars and planets gave the answer:
I made Nature myself, alone.

★   ★   ★

We are all captured beasts,
And we howl – as we might.
We can't open the doors,
For the doors are locked tight.

If our hearts can remember tradition,
When our barking brings solace, we bark.
We don't know. Long ago we've forgotten
That it stinks badly in this zoo-park.

For our hearts can accept repetition;
Bored and weary, we cuckoo our song.
For the zoo is impersonal, habitual;
We've not longed to be free for so long.

We are all captured beasts,
And we howl – as we might.
We can't open the doors,
For the doors are locked tight.

ТИХАЯ КОЛЫБЕЛЬНАЯ

Много бегал мальчик мой.
Ножки голые в пыли.
Ножки милые помой.
Моя ножки, задремли.
Я спою тебе, спою:
Баю-баюшки-баю.

Тихо стукнул в двери сон.
Я шепнула: – Сон, войди. –
Волоса его, как лен,
Ручки дремлют на груди, –
И тихонько я пою:
Баю-баюшки-баю.

– Сон, ты где был? – За горой.
– Что ты видел? – Лунный свет.
– С кем ты был? – С моей сестрой.
– А сестра пришла к нам? – Нет. –
Я тихонечко пою:
Баю-баюшки-баю.

Дремлет бледная луна.
Тихо в поле и в саду.
Кто-то ходит у окна,
Кто-то шепчет: – Я приду. –
Я тихохонько пою:
Баю-баюшки-баю.

Кто-то шепчет у окна,
Точно ветки шелестят:
– Тяжело мне. Я больна.
Помоги мне, милый брат. –
Тихо-тихо я пою:
Баю-баюшки-баю.

LULLABY

Baby, you've run such a lot;
See the dust on your bare feet.
Go and wash them, every spot.
While you do that, doze, my sweet,
I will sing, I'll sing for you:
Bi-Yoo, Bi-Yooshky, Bi-Yoo.

Sleep knocks at the door – soft raps.
I whisper, 'Come in, Sleep. Rest.'
His hair does resemble flax;
His small hands doze on his chest.
Softly-O, I sing to you:
Bi-Yoo, Bi-Yooshky, Bi-Yoo.

'Where have you been, Sleep?' 'The hill.'
'What did you see?' 'The moonglow.'
'Who were you with?' 'Sister, still.'
'Did your sister come too?' – 'No.'
Softly-O, I sing to you:
Bi-Yoo, Bi-Yooshky, Bi-Yoo.

The pale moon is dozing still;
Field and garden no more hum.
Someone's by the window sill,
Whispering, 'Yes, I will come.'
Softly-O, I sing to you:
Bi-Yoo, Bi-Yooshky, Bi-Yoo.

Someone whispers at the sill
As if twigs were rustling here,
'I have had it hard; I'm ill.
Help me, help me, Brother dear!'
Quietly I sing to you:
Bi-Yoo, Bi-Yooshky, Bi-Yoo.

– Я косила целый день.
Я устала. Я больна. –
За окном шатнулась тень.
Притаилась у окна.
Я пою, пою, пою:
Баю-баюшки-баю.

1906

ЧОРТОВЫ КАЧЕЛИ

В тени косматой ели,
Над шумною рекой
Качает чорт качели
Мохнатою рукой.

Качает и смеется,
   Вперед, назад,
   Вперед, назад.
Доска скрипит и гнется,
О сук тяжелый трется
Натянутый канат.

Снует с протяжным скрипом
Шатучая доска,
И чорт хохочет с хрипом,
Хватаясь за бока.

Держусь, томлюсь, качаюсь,
   Вперед, назад,
   Вперед, назад,
Хватаюсь и мотаюсь,
И отвести стараюсь
От чорта томный взгляд.

'I've mowed all day long, and I
Now am tired and I am ill.'
Then her shadow darted by,
Hid below the window sill.
I sing, I sing, sing to you:
Bi-Yoo, Bi-Yooshky, Bi-Yoo.

THE DEVIL'S SWING

Above the noisy river
Where shaggy fir trees stand,
In shade the devil pushes
The swing – with hairy hand.

He pushes, laughter speaking –
    Now to – and fro,
    Now to – and fro...
The board is bending, squeaking,
And the tight rope is creaking,
Rubbing the strong branch so.

The shaky seat-board scurries
Along with grating glides;
The devil guffaws hoarsely
And holds onto his sides.

Hold on, languishing, swinging –
    Now to – and fro,
    Now to – and fro...
Now snatching, catching, clinging,
And try to keep from bringing
My eyes to his eyes' glow.

Над верхом темной ели
Хохочет голубой:
– Попался на качели,
Качайся, чорт с тобой. –

В тени косматой ели
Визжат, кружась гурьбой:
– Попался на качели,
Качайся, чорт с тобой. –

Я знаю, чорт не бросит
Стремительной доски,
Пока меня не скосит
Грозящий взмах руки,

Пока не перетрется,
Крутяся, конопля,
Пока не подвернется
Ко мне моя земля.

Взлечу я выше ели,
И лбом о землю трах.
Качай же, чорт, качели,
Все выше, выше... ах!

1907

*   *   *

Я испытал превратности судеб
и видел много на земном просторе.
Трудом я добывал свой хлеб,
и весел был, и мыкал горе.

Above a dark fir's summit
The Blue One's laugh roared through,
'You got onto the swing, child;
Swing, and the devil with you.'

In shaggy fir trees' shadow
They swarm; the crowd screams too:
'You got onto the swing, child,
Swing, and the devil with you.'

I know he will not let go
Of that swift board till I
Am mowed down by the evil
Gesture his hand strikes by.

Until the hemp that's twisting
Is torn at last in two,
Until my earth comes nearer
To me – this I must do:

I'll fly higher than fir trees...
Bang earth with forehead's crack...
So push, devil, keep swinging
High, higher still! Alack!

★ ★ ★

I've lived through the vicissitudes of fate,
And I've seen much on this terrestrial sphere.
With my labor I earned the bread I ate,
I have been gay – and I've had sorrow here.

На милой, мной изведанной земле
уже ничто меня теперь не держит.
И пусть таящийся во мгле
меня стремительно повержет.

Но есть одно, чему всегда я рад
и с чем всегда бываю светло молод, –
мой труд. Иных земных наград
не жду за здешний дикий холод.

Когда меня у входа в Парадиз
суровый Петр, гремя ключами, спросит:
– Что сделал ты? – меня он вниз
железным посохом не сбросит.

Скажу: – Слагал романы и стихи,
и утешал, но и вводил в соблазны,
и вообще мои грехи,
апостол Петр, многообразны.

Но я – поэт. – И улыбнется он,
и разорвет грехов рукописанье,
и смело в рай войду, прощен,
внимать святое versликованье.

Не затеряется и голос мой
в хваленьях ангельских, горящих ясно,
Земля была моей тюрьмой,
но здесь я прожил не напрасно.

Горячий дух земных моих отрав,
неведомый чистейшим серафимам,
в благоуханье райских трав
вольется благовонным дымом.

1919

Now nothing on this dear earth that I know
So intimately holds me anymore;
Let him who's lurking in the darkness go
And fell me quickly in this mortal war.

But one thing pleases me and I detect
With it I'm always brightly young – all gold:
My work... My work... O, I do not expect
Other rewards here for earth's savage cold.

And when, at those great gates of Paradise,
Peter, clinking the keys, will sternly ask
'What have you accomplished?' He'll be nice;
He will not push me down with his iron staff.

I'll say: I wrote novels and poetry –
And consoled people. Also seduced some.
O yes, my sins show great variety
In general, St Peter – as they come.

But I'm a poet. He will smile and tear
Up that long scroll of sins – the list entire.
Forgiven, I will enter Heaven there
To hear the holy and exalting choir.

And midst angelic praises burning bright –
My voice will not be lost – as one lost strain.
Although earth used to be my jail all right,
I did not live out all my days in vain.

Unknown to purest seraphims – my few,
My earthly poisons' hot essence and spice
Will flow like aromatic smoke into
The fragrance of the flowers of paradise.

★　★　★

Тирсис под сенью ив
Мечтает о Нанетте,
И голову склонив,
Выводит на мюзетте:
Любовью я, – тра, та, там, та, – томлюсь.
К могиле я, – тра, та, там, та, – клонюсь.

И эхо меж кустов,
Внимая воплям горя,
Не изменяет слов,
Напевам томным вторя:
Любовью я, – тра, та, там, та, – томлюсь.
К могиле я, – тра, та, там, та, – клонюсь.

И верный пес у ног
Чувствителен к напасти,
И вторит, сколько мог
Усвоить грубой пасти:
Любовью я, – тра, та, там, та, – томлюсь.
К могиле я, – тра, та, там, та, – клонюсь.

Овечки собрались, –
Ах, нежные сердечки! –
И вторить принялись,
Как могут петь овечки:
Любовью я, – тра, та, там, та, – томлюсь.
К могиле я, – тра, та, там, та, – клонюсь.

Едва от грусти жив
Тирсис. Где ты, Нанетта?
Внимайте, кущи ив!
Играй, взывай, мюзетта:
Любовью я, – тра, та, там, та, – томлюсь.
К могиле я, – тра, та, там, та, – клонюсь.

10 июня 1921

Thyrsis, neath willow shade,
Is dreaming of Nanette,
And lowering his head,
He plays his pipe-musette:
From love – tra-la-la-la – I languish here.
To the grave – tra-la-la-la – I now draw near.

His echo in the brush,
Hearing his mournful cries,
Repeats the same sad rush
Of tunes and languid sighs:
From love – tra-la-la-la – I languish here.
To the grave – tra-la-la-la – I now draw near.

And, faithful at his feet,
His dog, sensing his pain,
Is trying to repeat
With coarse mouth this refrain:
From love – tra-la-la-la – I languish here.
To the grave – tra-la-la-la – I now draw near.

The little sheep, grouping
(Ah, tender little hearts!)
Begin their echoing,
Their sheepish singing starts:
From love – tra-la-la-la – I languish here.
To the grave – tra-la-la-la – I now draw near.

Thyrsis nears death from grief...
O where are you, Nanette?
Listen, yon willow leaf...
Play and entreat, musette:
From love – tra-la-la-la – I languish here.
To the grave – tra-la-la-la – I now draw near.

10 June 1921

Вот подумай и пойми:
В мире ты живешь с людьми, –
Словно в лесе, в темном лесе, –
Где написан бес на бесе, –
Зверь с такими же зверьми.

Вот и дом тебе построен,
Он уютен и спокоен,
И живешь ты в нем с людьми,
Но таятся за дверьми
Хари, годные для боен.

Человек иль злобный бес
В душу, как в карман, залез,
Наплевал там и нагадил,
Все испортил, все разладил
И, хихикая, исчез.

Смрадно скучившись у двери,
Над тобой смеются звери:
– Дождался, дурак, чудес?
Эти чище, чем с небес,
И даются всем по вере.

Дурачок, ты всем не верь, –
Шепчет самый гнусный зверь, –
Хоть блевотину на блюде
Поднесут с поклоном люди,
Ешь и зубы им не щерь.

13 сентября 1926

Think of it and try to understand:
In this world you live with people, and
Just like in a forest, dark or other,
One devil is painted on another –
One beast with a beast like you, firsthand.

Here, you have a house built for you; try it.
It is cozy, comfortable and quiet.
And you live in it with people too.
But behind the doors what mugs you view!
Faces for the butcher! Don't deny it.

And a man or wicked demon, whole,
Gets (like in a pocket) in your soul,
Squats there, where he spits and shits and spoils
All, leaves all disjointed in turmoils...
Disappears then, giggling like a droll.

Crowding at the door and vilely shouting,
All the beasts draw near you with their flouting:
'Fool, here are the miracles you sought!
These are finer than those Heaven brought,
Sent according to one's faith or doubting!'

'Little fool, give no one your belief...'
(This the vilest whispered underneath...)
'Even if the people bow and flatter
You and serve you vomit on a platter,
Eat it, and do not show them your teeth!'

13 September 1926

ИЮЛЬ

Палимая огнем недвижного светила,
Проклятый свой урок отлязгала кирьга
И спящих грабаров с землею сколотила,
Как ливень черные, осенние стога.

Каких-то диких сил последнее решенье,
Луча отвесного неслышный людям зов,
И абрис ног худых меж чадного смешенья
Всклокоченных бород и рваных картузов.

Не страшно ль иногда становится на свете?
Не хочется ль бежать, укрыться поскорей?
Подумай: на руках у матерей
Все это были розовые дети.

1900

СЕНТЯБРЬ

Раззолоченные, но чахлые сады
С соблазном пурпура на медленных недугах,
И солнца поздний пыл в его коротких дугах,
Невластный вылиться в душистые плоды.

И желтый шелк ковров, и грубые следы,
И понятая ложь последнего свиданья,
И парков черные, бездонные пруды,
Давно готовые для спелого страданья...

INNOKENTY FYODOROVICH ANNENSKY
1856-1909

JULY

Scorched by the fire of the sky's unmoving body,
The pick-ax stops clanging out its accursed lesson.
And nailed onto the earth, the piled autumnal haystacks
Of sleeping working-men are black as any downpour.

The last decision of some dark and savage forces,
A vertical ray's call, inaudible to people,
And those lines of lean legs amidst smoky confusion,
Of the disheveled beards, of torn and tattered headgear.

Is not this whirling world many times terrifying?
Does not one want to run away and hide so quickly?
Just think: In the arms of their mothers
All these were once lovely pink children.

SEPTEMBER

The all-dressed-up in gold, consumptive-looking gardens –
Where their slow sickness wears magenta-rich veneers,
The late glow of the sun lingering in its brief arches
Having no power to take the shape of fragrant fruit,

Also the coarse footprints, the yellow silk of carpets,
The comprehended lie of the last rendezvous,
The black, bottomless ponds in parks waiting and ready
(Which have been for some time) for ripened suffering.

Но сердцу чудится лишь красота утрат,
Лишь упоение в завороженной силе;
И тех, которые уж лотоса вкусили,
Волнует вкрадчивый осенний аромат.

(1904)

ТОСКА

По бледно-розовым овалам,
Туманом утра облиты,
Свились букетом небывалым
Стального колера цветы.

И мух кочующих соблазны,
Отраву в глянце затая,
Пестрят, назойливы и праздны,
Нагие грани бытия.

Но, лихорадкою томимый,
Когда неделями лежишь,
В однообразьи их таимый
Поймешь ты сладостный гашиш,

Поймешь, на глянце центифолий
Считая бережно мазки...
И строя ромбы поневоле
Между этапами Тоски.

(1904)

But the heart seems to see just beauty in all losses
And only rapture in the strange and bewitched power,
And those who have already tasted of the lotus
Are roused by autumn's scents which win one's confidence.

ENNUI

There are the delicate pink ovals
On which the mists of morning flood,
And in unique bouquets unwinding
Steel-colored flowers bloom and bud.

For nomad flies they are temptation;
Their gloss hides poisons' virulence...
Intrusive, variegated, idle,
The bare facets of existence.

But when exhausted from a fever
And bed-ridden, as weeks progress,
You understand the pleasant hashish
Concealed within their dull sameness.

You understand – frugally counting
The strokes upon each rose you see...
As you build diamonds, willy-nilly,
Between the stations of ennui.

ЯМБЫ

О, как я чувствую накопленное бремя
Отравленных ночей и грязно-бледных дней!
Вы, карты, есть ли что в одно и тоже время
Приманчивее вас, пошлее и страшней!

Вы страшны нежностью похмелья, и науке,
Любви, поэзии – всему вас предпочтут.
Какие подлые не пожимал я руки,
Не соглашался с чем?... Скорей! Колоды ждут...

Зеленое сукно – цвет малахитов тины,
Весь в пепле туз червей на сломанном мелке...
Подумай: жертву накануне гильотины
Дурманят картами и в каменном мешке.

1906

ЧЕРНАЯ ВЕСНА

Под гулы меди -- гробовой
Творился перенос,
И, жутко задран, восковой
Глядел из гроба нос.

Дыханья, что ли, он хотел
Туда, в пустую грудь?...
Последний снег был темно-бел,
И тяжек рыхлый путь.

И только изморозь, мутна,
На тление лилась,
Да тупо черная весна
Глядела в студень глаз –

IAMBS

Oh, how often I feel the burden I have hoarded
Of smudged, anemic days and many poisoned nights!
You, cards, does anything exist that's more attractive
And at the same time more banal and full of frights!

But you *are* frightful, too, with a hangover's frailty,
Preferred before all things: love, science, poetry.
What sordid hands I have grasped in a friendly handshake!
What I've agreed with!... Come! The deck waits, restlessly.

The green cloth, malachite-like color of the mire –
The ace of clubs is strewed with ashes – broken chalk...
Just think: on the eve of the guillotine, a victim
Is drugged by cards even while in the dungeon's lock.

BLACK SPRING

With blare of brass a funeral
Procession slowly walks...
A wax-like nose sticks gruesomely
Up from the coffin-box.

Did he only want some more air...
Inside his empty chest?
The latest snow was dingy white;
The crumbed road rough – at best.

And only sleet, the turgid sleet,
Poured on the rotting guise.
And stupidly black spring looked at
The jelly of his eyes

С облезлых крыш, из бурых ям,
С позеленелых лиц...
А там, по мертвенным полям,
С разбухших крыльев птиц...

О люди! Тяжек жизни след
По рытвинам путей,
Но ничего печальней нет,
Как встреча двух смертей.

19 марта 1906

О НЕТ, НЕ СТАН

О нет, не стан, пусть он так нежно-зыбок,
Я из твоих соблазнов затаю
Не влажный блеск малиновых улыбок, –
Страдания холодную змею.

Так иногда в банально-пестрой зале,
Где вальс звенит, волнуя и моля,
Зову мечтой я звуки Парсифаля,
И Тень, и Смерть над маской короля...

.   .   .   .

Оставь меня. Мне ложе стелет Скука.
Зачем мне рай, которым грезят все?
А если грязь и низость – только мука
По где-то там сияющей красе...

19 мая 1906, Вологда

From shabby roofs, from brown road-pits,
From faces greenness girds...
And out there along deathly fields
From bloated wings of birds.

O people! Life's footprint is hard
Along our rutted paths.
And there is nothing sadder than
The meeting of two deaths.

19 March 1906

OF ALL THE THINGS WHICH TEMPT ME

Of all the things which tempt me, I'll remember
No, not your body – rippling like a spring,
And not your crimson smile with its wet shimmer
But that cold serpent of your suffering.

So in a ballroom – banal, many-colored,
Sometimes when spirit-stirring waltzes play,
I conjure in my dream Parsifal's music,
The Shadow, Death on the King's mask that day.
.   .   .   .
Leave me. Boredom makes up my bed already.
What's paradise which everyone dreams fair?
What if these dirty depths are painful striving
To gain the Beauty which shines somewhere there?

19 May 1906, Vologda

МАКИ

Веселый день горит... Среди сомлевших трав
Все маки пятнами – как жадное бессилье,
Как губы, полные соблазна и отрав,
Как алых бабочек развернутые крылья.

Веселый день горит... Но сад и пуст и глух.
Давно покончил он с соблазнами и пиром, –
И маки сохлые, как головы старух,
Осенены с небес сияющим потиром.

(1909)

АМЕТИСТЫ

Когда, сжигая синеву,
Багряный день растет неистов,
Как часто сумрак я зову,
Холодный сумрак аметистов.

И чтоб не знойные лучи
Сжигали грани аметиста,
А лишь мерцание свечи
Лилось там жидко и огнисто.

И, лиловея и дробясь,
Чтоб уверяло там сиянье,
Что где-то есть не наша *связь*,
А лучезарное *слиянье*...

(1909)

POPPIES

The gladsome day burns on . . . and mixed with the spent grass,
Patches of poppies shine like greedy impotence,
Like lips, seduction-full, through which poison will pass,
Like opened wings of red butterflies' opulence.

The gladsome day burns on . . . The garden empties, sheds
Its temptations and feasts, is desolate thereby.
And now the dry poppies are like old women's heads
A shining chalice shields and shelters from the sky.

AMETHYSTS

The blood-red day grows rabidly
While burning up the azure mist.
Then often I call up the dusk,
The cool dark of the amethyst . . .

So that no sultry rays would make
The amethyst's clear facets glow,
But just a candle shimmering,
Liquid and fiery, would flow.

Being refracted, lilac-ing,
The shine has power to persuade:
Somewhere not man's own ties exist,
But some radiant fusion is made.

ТОСКА ПРИПОМИНАНИЯ

Мне всегда открывается та же
Залитая чернилом страница.
Я уйду от людей, но куда же,
От ночей мне куда схорониться?

Все живые так стали далеки,
Все небытное стало так внятно,
И слились позабытые строки
До зари в мутно-черные пятна.

Весь я там в невозможном ответе,
Где миражные буквы маячут...
... Я люблю, когда в доме есть дети
И когда по ночам они плачут.

(1909)

'PACE'
Статуя мира

Меж золоченых бань и обелисков славы
Есть дева белая, а вкруг густые травы.

Не тешит тирс ее, она не бьет в тимпан,
И беломраморный ее не любит Пан,

Одни туманы к ней холодные ласкались,
И раны черные от влажных губ остались.

Но дева красотой по-прежнему горда,
И трав вокруг нее не косят никогда.

Не знаю почему – богини изваянье
Над сердцем сладкое имеет обаянье...

ENNUI OF REMEMBERING

Everytime the identical page,
Spilled with ink, opens up before me.
I shall go off from people ... But where,
Where to hide from the night's misery?

All the living ones fade far away,
And what never existed is plain.
The forgotten lines somehow are blurred
Until dawn to a swollen black stain.

One impossible answer: all me –
Where mirage letters loom into sight ...
... I like children around in a house
And I like to hear them cry at night.

THE STATUE OF PEACE

With gilded baths and glory's obelisks to bound her,
A stone-white young girl stands – with tall, thick grass around her.

Her thyrsus gives no joy; her tambourine won't stir;
Even white-marbled Pan is not in love with her.

Only the chilling fogs caress her with embraces,
And on her the moist lips of mist leave their black traces.

But still she is proud of her beauty as before
Though no one mows the grass around her anymore.

The statue of that goddess (I don't know the reason)
Can cast the sweetest spell on me in any season.

Люблю обиду в ней, ее ужасный нос,
И ноги сжатые, и грубый узел кос.

Особенно, когда холодный дождик сеет,
И нагота ее беспомощно белеет...

О, дайте вечность мне, – и вечность я отдам
За равнодушие к обидам и годам.

(1909)

ПЕТЕРБУРГ

Желтый пар петербургской зимы,
Желтый снег, облипающий плиты...
Я не знаю, где *вы* и где *мы*,
Только знаю, что крепко мы слиты.

Сочинил ли нас царский указ?
Потопить ли нас шведы забыли?
Вместо сказки в прошедшем у нас
Только камни да страшные были.

Только камни нам дал чародей,
Да Неву буро-желтого цвета,
Да пустыни немых площадей,
Где казнили людей до рассвета.

А что было у нас на земле,
Чем вознесся орел наш двуглавый,
В темных лаврах гигант на скале, –
Завтра станет ребячьей забавой.

Уж на что был он грозен и смел,
Да скакун его бешеный выдал,
Царь змеи раздавить не сумел,
И прижатая стала наш идол.

I like her being wronged, her terrible nose there,
Her tightened legs and that coarse knot of braided hair.

Especially when a cold, cold drizzle pricks and pelts us
And her own nakedness is very white and helpless.

Give me eternity, I'd give it to the spheres...
For an indifference to all wrongs, to passing years.

PETERSBURG

Yellow mist of the Petersburg winter,
Yellow snow on the walks and the ground...
I don't know where you are – or where we are;
I just know we're inseparably bound.

Did the Tsar's royal fiat invent us?
Swedes forget to drown us in attacks?
In our past, in the place of pure fables,
There are just stones and terrible facts.

All the things that the sorcerer gave us:
Stones, the Neva – the color of fawn,
And the deserts which are the dumb squares
Where the people were hanged before dawn.

And whatever we had in this region,
What raised our double-eagle and sent
The giant in dark laurels on the rock there...
For our children will be merriment.

How courageous he was! Awe-inspiring!
By his violent horse he was betrayed.
For the Tsar could not trample the serpent,
And the snake was the idol we made.

Ни кремлей, ни чудес, ни святынь,
Ни миражей, ни слез, ни улыбки...
Только камни из мерзлых пустынь
Да сознанье проклятой ошибки.

Даже в мае, когда разлиты,
Белой ночи над волнами тени,
Там не чары весенней мечты,
Там отрава бесплодных хотений.

1909

МОЯ ТОСКА

М. А. Кузмину

Пусть травы сменятся над капищем волненья,
И восковой в гробу забудется рука,
Мне кажется, меж вас одно недоуменье
Все будет жить мое, одна моя Тоска...

Нет, не о тех, увы! кому столь недостойно,
Ревниво, бережно и страстно был я мил...
О, сила любящих и в муке так спокойна,
У женской нежности завидно много сил.

Да и при чем бы здесь недоуменья были –
Любовь ведь светлая, она кристалл, эфир...
Моя ж безлюбая – дрожит, как лошадь в мыле!
Ей – пир отравленный, мошеннический пир!

В венке из тронутых, из вянущих азалий
Собралась петь она... Не смолк и первый стих,
Как маленьких детей у ней перевязали,
Сломали руки им и ослепили их.

No shrines, no miracles and no Kremlins,
No mirages, no smiles, tears and ache.
Only stones from frozen, empty spaces
And the knowledge of this cursed mistake.

In the month of May, even when shadows
Of the white nights spread out on the stream,
There's no magic spell spun by the springtime;
There's the poison of each fruitless dream.

MY ANGST

to M. A. Kuzmin

Let the grass change above this agitated temple
And let my waxed hand in the box be no more known,
It seems among you just my perplexity and longing
Will continue to live. Only my angst alone.

And not for those, alas, who hold me dear and special...
Yes, undeservedly, jealously, ardently...
The strength of those who love – gentle even in torment,
This female tenderness has strength one cannot see.

Why should there ever be perplexities within one?
Love has a constant light, is crystal as it were.
But my love has no love – a frothy horse, it trembles.
It is a poisoned feast – and fraudulent – for her!

Bedecked, wearing a wreath of withering azaleas,
Love is prepared to sing... But ere the first verse sighs
The small children of hers have been gathered and tied up,
Their hands broken... They have been blinded in their eyes.

Она бесполая, у ней для всех улыбки,
Она притворщица, у ней порочный вкус –
Качает целый день она пустые зыбки,
И образок в углу – сладчайший Иисус…

Я выдумал ее – и все ж она виденье,
Я не люблю ее – и мне она близка,
Недоумелая, мое недоуменье,
Всегда веселая, она моя тоска.

12 ноября 1909, Царское Село

She is a sexless one – smiling at everybody,
Deceiver-hypocrite, a perverse taste in bloom.
And throughout all the day she rocks the empty cradles;
The sweetest Jesus is her icon in the room.

O! I invented her and still she is a vision.
And I do not love her... still she is always near
Perplexed, ever perplexed – anxiety and longing...
Always she is my angst, forever gay and here.

12 November 1909, Tsarskoe Selo

ВЯЧЕСЛАВ ИВАНОВИЧ ИВАНОВ
1866-1949

АЛЬПИЙСКИЙ РОГ

Средь гор глухих я встретил пастуха,
трубившего в альпийский длинный рог.
Приятно песнь его лилась; но, зычный,
был лишь орудьем рог, дабы в горах
пленительное эхо пробуждать.
И всякий раз, когда пережидал
его пастух, извлекши мало звуков,
оно носилось меж теснин таким
неизреченно-сладостным созвучьем,
что мнилося: незримый духов хор
на неземных орудьях переводит
наречием небес язык земли.
И думал я: 'О гений! как сей рог,
петь песнь земли ты должен, чтоб в сердцах
будить иную песнь. Блажен, кто слышит.'
А из-за гор звучал ответный глас:
'Природа – символ, как сей рог. Она
звучит для отзвука. И отзвук – Бог.
Блажен, кто слышит песнь и слышит отзвук.'

(1901)

УВЛЕЧЕНИЕ

Где цепью розовой, в сияющей дали,
Тянулись облака и в море отражались,
Лазурные валы, горя, преображались
И ризу пурпура прозрачного влекли.

VYACHESLAV IVANOVICH IVANOV
1866-1949

ALPINE HORN

Along the mountain wastes I met a shepherd
Who blew upon a long Alpine horn.
His song flowed pleasantly. But, sonorous,
The horn was just a tool for wakening
A most attractive echo in the mountains.
And each time, after making several sounds,
He waited for the echo to reply.
It travelled up between the gorges in
Such inexpressibly sweet harmony
That one might think: an unseen choir of spirits
With unearthly instruments is translating
The tongue of earth into the speech of heaven.
I thought: 'O, genius, like this horn, you have
To sing a song of earth to wake in hearts
Another song. Blessed is he who hears...'
And from the mountains answered back a voice:
'All Nature is a symbol like this horn...
Sounding just for the answer... which is God.
Blessed is he who hears both song and answer.'

TRANSPORTED

Where as a rosy chain, far in the shining distance,
The clouds stretched out and were reflected in the sea.
The azure waves, burning, were suddenly transfigured
And trailed clear purple robes behind them regally.

Мы ж к пламенным волнам – стремясь – не приближались:
Они бежали нас; чем дале мы гребли,
Пространства бледные за нами умножались,
Где тень и отблеск волн ночной узор плели.

Мы тень с собой несли – и гналися за светом…
Но вдруг опомнились: исчез лукавый сон, –
Внезапно день потух, и потемнело море.

Вставал далекий брег суровым силуэтом,
И безразличен был поблекший небосклон, –
И сердце – гордое свое ласкало горе.

(1901)

ТАОРМИНА

За мглой Авзонии восток небес алей;
Янтарный всходит дым над снеговерхой Этной;
Снег рдеет и горит, и пурпур огнецветный
Течет с ее главы, как царственный елей

На склоны тихие дубрав, на мир полей
И рощей масличных, и берег предрассветный,
Где скоро смутный понт голубизной просветной
Сверкнет в развалинах священных пропилей.

В обломках спит θеатр, орхестра онемела;
Но вечно курится в снегах твоя θимела,
Грядый в востоке дня и в торжестве святынь!

И с твоего кремля, как древле, Мельпомена
Зрит, Эвий, скорбная, волшебный круг пустынь
И Тартар, дышащий под вертоградом плена.

(1901)

And we – though we strove – could not reach the fiery ripples;
They fled away from us. The more we chased their light,
The more were multiplied behind us great pale spaces
Where their shadows and shine wove patterns for the night.

We bore the shadows with ourselves – and chased the glimmer...
But suddenly we stopped: this treacherous dream so brief
Was gone, – and day fast died; the sea grew dark and dimmer.

The distant coast rose up – a severe silhouette,
And the faded horizon was indifferent, yet
My unresisting heart caressed its own proud grief.

TAORMINA

The eastern sky behind Ausonia's dark grows red,
The amber smoke rises above Mount Etna's snows
Which glow and burn... Jewel-like, flowering purple flows
Like regal unction out, down from its fiery head

Onto the groves' calm slopes, onto the peace of fields
And olive trees, onto the predawn coast, where dim
Pontus will soon shine its translucent blue and skim
The ruins which a sacred propylaeum yields.

The theater sleeps in fragments, the orchestra is silent,
But still your thymele smokes in the snows eternal,
You who come at day's east with just such shrines to triumph.

And from your citadel, Evius, Melpomene
Who grieves can see again the deserts' magic circle
And Tartarus breathing gardened captivity.

ИСПЫТАНИЕ

'Что блаженней? Упоений
Раздвигать цветущий полог, –
Истощив ли наслажденья,
Отягченною ногою
Попирать порог увялый?

'Что блаженней? В нежных взорах
Дерзких ласк читать призывы –
Или видеть очи милой,
Утомленные тобою,
Без огня и без желаний?'

Так Эрот, мой искуситель,
Испытал меня коварно,
Осчастливленного милой;
Я ж, подругой умудренный,
Избежал сетей лукавых:

'Вожделенней, сын Киприды,
В угашенных взорах милой,
Без восторга, без призывов, –
Воспалять лобзаньем новым
Жадной страсти едкий пламень...

'Ах, с порога совершений
Вожделенней возвратиться
К исступленьям ненасытным!...'
И, смеясь, Эрот воскликнул:
'Друг, вернись, ты их достоин!'

(1904)

A TEST

'What's the greater joy? To part that
Blooming curtain made for rapture,
Or to tread the withered threshold
With a dragging foot when those sweet
Fleshly pleasures are exhausted?

'What's the greater joy? To read in
Tender eyes the invitations
To forward caresses or to
See the eyes of her you tired
Minus their fire and desire?'

So my tempter, Eros, tested
Me, made glad by my beloved.
He spoke with a shrewd designing.
I, wised up by my good woman,
Brushed aside these sly entrapments.

'It is right, O, son of Venus,
To inflame in her extinguished
Eyes that lack bliss and entreaty,
By new kisses a consuming
Fiery flame of burning passion...

'O, it's better to come back from
Any threshold of fulfillment
To renewed insatiable frenzies!...'
And then Eros cried out, laughing:
'Come back, my friend, you deserve them.'

НАРЦИСС
Помпейская бронза

Кто ты, прекрасный? В лесах, как Сатир одинокий, ты бродишь,
Сам же не чадо дубрав: так благороден твой лик.

Прелесть движений пристойных, убранной обуви пышность –
Все говорит мне: ты – сын вышних иль смертных царей.

Чутко, свой шаг удержав, ты последовал тайному звуку
Стройным склоненьем главы, мерным движеньем перста:

Пана ли внял ты свирель, иль Эхо влюбленные стоны?
Говор ли резвых Наяд? шопот ли робких Дриад?

Праздную руку, едва оперев о бедро, прихотливо
Легким наплечным руном ты перевил, как Лией:

Дивный, не сам ли ты Вакх, лелеемый нимфами Низы,
Ловчий, ленивец нагой, нежных любимец богинь?

Или ты – гордый Нарцисс, упоенный мечтой одинокой,
В томном блуждающий сне, тайной гармонии полн?

К нимфе зовущей иди, ты доселе себя не познавший,
Но не гляди, наклонясь, в зеркало сонной воды!

Ах, если ты не Нарцисс, то свой лик отраженный увидев,
О незнакомец, – дрожу, – новый ты станешь Нарцисс.

(1904)

NARCISSUS

POMPEIAN BRONZE

Who are you, handsome young boy? Like a faun you roam in the
But you're no child of the groves: so noble is your fine face.   [forest.

Movements that flow with a charm, and the richness of your gilded
Show you descend from the gods or are the son of a king.   [sandals

Keen, having slackened your step, you have tagged a mysterious
Gracefully tilting your head, moving your finger in time.   [murmur,

Is it Pan's pipe that you hear – or the amorous moaning of Echo?
The talk of naiads at play? Or shy dryads' whispered speech?

You rest one arm on a hip and over this arm, like Lyaeus,
You have capriciously thrown your light, draping shoulder fleece.

Are you not Bacchus himself, cherished by young nymphs of Nysa?
Hunter, a naked idler, favorite of goddesses all?

Are you the proud Narcissus – carried off, alone, in your fancy –
Wandering in languorous dreams, full of a music not heard?

Go to the nymph who calls you, you who have not known your own
But do not bend, do not look into the stream's sleepy face.   [self,

For seeing you mirrored there – ah, if you are not really Narcissus,
O stranger, I tremble so, you a Narcissus will be.

КОЧЕВНИКИ КРАСОТЫ

Кочевники красоты – вы, художники.
'Пламенники'

Вам – пращуров деревья
И кладбищ теснота!
Нам вольные кочевья
Судила Красота.

Вседневная измена,
Вседневный новый стан:
Безвыходного плена
Блуждающий обман.

О, верьте далей чуду
И сказке всех завес,
Всех весен изумруду,
Всей широте небес!

Художники, пасите
Грез ваших табуны;
Минуя, всколосите –
И киньте – целины!

И с вашего раздолья
Низриньтесь вихрем орд
На нивы подневолья,
Где раб упрягом горд.

Топчи их рай, Атилла, –
И новью пустоты
Взойдут твои светила,
Твоих степей цветы.

(1904)

NOMADS OF BEAUTY

Nomads of beauty, artists, that's what you are.
'Men of Fire'

For you: trees of your forbears
And the graves' narrow ring!
For us: Beauty has destined
Unfettered wandering.

Each new day – a betrayal,
A new camp where we see
A wandering illusion:
Endless captivity.

Have faith in veils of fables,
Distance with its surprise,
The emerald of all springtime,
The total width of skies!

O, artists! Be as shepherds
To droves of your dreams, and
Leave the grain fields you seeded
Which once was virgin land.

And rush from your expanses
In hordes, like winds of smoke
To fields of subjugation,
To slaves proud of their yoke.

Tread on their Eden, Atilla, –
And as to symbolize
The emptiness – stars, flowers
Of your steppeland will rise.

ПЕРЕВОДЧИКУ

Будь жаворонок нив и пажитей – Вергилий,
Иль альбатрос Бодлэр, иль соловей Верлэн
Твоей ловитвою, – все в чужеземный плен
Не заманить тебе птиц вольных без усилий,

Мой милый птицелов, – и, верно, без насилий
Не обойдешься ты, поэт, и без измен,
Хотя б ты другом был всех девяти Камен,
И зла ботаником, и пастырем идиллий,

Затем, что стих чужой – что скользкий бог Протей:
Не улучить его охватом ни отвагой.
Ты держишь рыбий хвост, а он текучей влагой

Струится и бежит из немощных сетей.
С Протеем будь Протей, вторь каждой маске – маской!
Милей досужий люд своей забавить сказкой.

(1904)

СФИНКСЫ НАД НЕВОЙ

Волшба ли ночи белой приманила
Вас маревом в полон полярных див,
Два зверя-дива из стовратных Фив?
Вас бледная ль Изида полонила?

Какая тайна вам окаменила
Жестоких уст смеющийся извив?
Полночных волн немеркнущий разлив
Вам радостней ли звезд святого Нила?

TO THE TRANSLATOR

Whether you hunt Virgil, the meadowlark, –
Or Baudelaire, the albatross, – or Verlaine,
The nightingale – you cannot lure free birds
To strange captivity without hard strain.

My dear bird-catcher, I'm sure you won't spare
Violence or treason, poet – or desist
Though you're shepherd of idylls or a friend
Of all nine muses or evil's botanist.

Since someone else's verse is Proteus,
A slippery god, you can't catch him with grasp
Or courage. You hold the fishtail and it

Pours through the flimsy nets. Be Proteus
With Proteus. Meet each mask with a mask!
Or else amuse them with your own tale's wit.

SPHINXES OVER THE NEVA

Did mirage-like white nights lead you enraptured
By polar wonders to this captive state,
You two beast-marvels from Thebes' hundred gates,
Or was it pale Isis had you so captured?

What mystery made stone out of the acrid
And laughing curve of your merciless lips?
Do these northern, nondarkening waves eclipse
The joy brought by the Nile's stars – Nile so sacred?

Так в час, когда томят нас две зари
И шепчутся лучами, дея чары,
И в небесах меняют янтари, –

Как два серпа, подьемля две тиары,
Друг другу в очи – девы иль цари –
Глядите вы, улыбчивы и яры.

(1911)

УЗЛЫ ЗМЕИ

Триста тридцать три соблазна, триста тридцать три обряда,
Где страстна́я ранит разно многостра́стная услада, –
На два пола – знак Раскола – кто умножит, может счесть:
Шестьдесят и шесть объятий и шестьсот приятий есть.

Триста тридцать три соблазна, триста тридцать три дороги, –
Слабым в гибель, – чьи алмазны светоносные сердца,
Тем на подвиг ярой пытки, риши Гангеса и йоги
Развернули в длинном свитке от начала до конца.

В грозном ритме сладострастий, к чаше огненных познаний
Припадай, браман, заране опаленным краем уст,
Чтоб с колес святых бесстрастий клик последних заклинаний
Мог собрать в единой длани все узлы горящих узд.

(1911)

So, in the hour when that dawn-twilight plagues us
And when they whisper with its beams, beguiling
With spells, and changing ambers in the skies –

Maidens or kings, raising your two tiaras
Like two sickles, you look into the eyes
Of one another, violent and smiling.

SNAKE-KNOTS

Three hundred thirty-three temptations, three-three-three delights
and rites,
Where the Passion-like and many-passioned pleasure wounds and
Whosoever multiplies it – by two sexes – a schism guesses: [bites.
There are sixty-six embraces – and six hundred ready yeses.

Three hundred thirty-three temptations, three-three-three roads, ways
to strike –
(For the weak – perdition) for those whose bright hearts are diamond-
For those, – deeds of ardent pain. Yogis and rishi of the Ganges [like,
Rolled a long scroll out for them – from the beginning to the ending.

In lust's menacing rhythm, to the phial of knowledge's conflagration,
Approach, Brahman, with your lips which are already scorched and
So that from the wheels of holy calms, cries of last incantations   [hot,
Could together bring in one hold all the burning bridles' knots.

СОБОР СВ. МАРКА

Царьградских солнц замкнув в себе лучи,
Ты на порфирах темных и агатах
Стоишь, согбен, как патриарх в богатых
И тяжких ризах кованой парчи,

В деснице три и в левой две свечи
Подъемлющий во свещниках рогатых, –
Меж тем как на галерах и фрегатах
Сокровищниц початки и ключи

В дарохранительный ковчежец Божий
Вселенная несет, служа жезлам
Фригийскою скуфьей венчанных дожей,

По изумрудным Адрии валам;
И роза Византии червленеет,
Где с книгой лев крылатый каменеет.

(1912)

* * *

Твое именованье – Сиротство,
Зима! Зима! Твой скорбный строй – унылость.
Удел – богов глухонемых немилость.
Твой лик – с устами сжатыми вдовство.

Там, в вышних ночи, славы торжество,
Превыспренних бесплотных легкокрылость.
Безвестье тут, беспамятство, застылость, –
А в недрах – Солнца, Солнца рождество!

ST MARK'S

Constantinople sunlight is inlaid,
Locked in the porphyries' and agates' dark,
And so you stand, stooped, like a patriarch
In rich and heavy robes of forged brocade,

With candles raised in horn-shaped chandeliers
(Two in your left hand, three are in your right),
While this world's galleys and frigates bring bright
Treasuries with their keys and samples here

Into the pyx of God inside the apse,
Serving the scepters of aristocratic
Doges crowned by Phrygian skullcaps,

Near emerald waves of the Adriatic;
Byzantium's rose reddens every tone
Where a winged lion with a book is stone.

★   ★   ★

Winter, winter, your name is orphanhood;
Your mournful melody is melancholy.
Your fate: the deaf-mute gods' merciless folly
And your face is a tight-lipped widowhood.

In heights of night there is a glory won.
Light-wingedness of fleshless, higher beings.
But here – forgetfulness, stillness, not seeing –
And in the depths the birth of Sun – the Sun!

Меж пальцев алавастровых лампада
Психеи зябкой теплится едва.
Алмазами играет синева.

Грозя, висит хрустальная громада.
Под кров спасайся, где трещат дрова,
Жизнь темная, от звездных копий хлада!

1920

* * *

Двустворку на хвостах клубок дельфиний
Разверстой вынес; в ней растет Тритон,
Трубит в улиту; но не зычный тон,
Струя лучом пронзает воздух синий.

Средь зноя плит, зовущих облак пиний,
Как зелен мха на демоне хитон!
С природой схож резца старинный сон
Стихийною причудливостью линий.

Бернини, – снова наш, – твоей игрой
Я веселюсь, от Четырех Фонтанов
Бредя на Пинчьо памятной горой,

Где в келью Гоголя входил Иванов,
Где Пиранези огненной иглой
Пел Рима грусть и зодчество Титанов.

1924

And Psyche, freezing in her alabaster,
Can hardly light the lamp she chills to hold.
The blue sky plays with diamonds and each spark

Of crystal heaven hangs, threatening. O dark
Life, hide where firewood crackles faster,
Hide from the starry lances of the cold.

★　★　★

These tangling dolphins brought a bivalve out
Upon their tails. In it Triton is growing.
He plays upon a snail – no loud tones blowing
But beams piercing blue air as fine streams spout.

Midst heated stones that crave the clouds of pines,
The moss forms a green chiton for the creature.
The old dream of the chisel is like Nature
In its primal fancifulness of lines.

Bernini (ours again)! I enjoy still
Your play as I walk where Four Fountains spring
To Pincio along this memorable hill . . .

Where Ivanov entered Gogol's monk-cell home,
Where Piranesi made his needle sing
The architecture and sadness of Rome.

Через плечо слагая черепах,
Горбатых пленниц, нá мель плоской вазы,
Где брызжутся на воле водолазы,
Забыв, неповоротливые, страх, –

Танцуют отроки на головах
Курносых чудищ. Дивны их проказы:
Под их пятой уроды пучеглазы
Из круглой пасти прыщут водный прах.

Их четверо резвятся на дельфинах.
На бронзовых то голенях, то спинах
Лоснится дня зелено-зыбкий смех.

И в этой неге лени и приволий
Твоих ловлю я праздничных утех,
Твоих, Лоренцо, эхо меланхолий.

1924

ИЮЛЬ

Чу, жаркий рык... Созвездье Льва
Уже владычествует в небе.
Как злато, плавятся слова,
Служа поэтовой потребе.

И предопределенный стих
Достиг, еще не прянув, цели:
Так лев следит скачки газели;
Драконов душит так двоих
Алкид-младенец в колыбели.

2 июля 1944

The hunchbacked captives thrown into the clear,
Flat, shallow basin up above their shoulders
(Where the turtles, clumsy ones, grow bolder
And splash in freedom – having lost their fear),

The youths dance on the pug-nosed monsters' sleek,
Wet heads – and wondrous are the pranks they're playing;
Beneath their feet a watery dust is spraying
Out of the round mouth of each bulged-eyed freak.

Four boys are frisking on the dolphins as
The day's greened laughter ripples into flights
And glosses each bronze calf and back that bends so.

In this joy of freedom and laziness
I catch echoes of your festive delights –
And of your melancholy too, Lorenzo.

JULY

Hark! A hot roar ... Starred Leo reigns
Already ... and the heavens show it.
Like gold the words are molten strains
Which serve the rare needs of the poet.

And the predestined verse, it's said,
Before it jumps has gained its reaping:
The lion eyes the gazelle leaping;
The child, Alcides, chokes till dead
Two dragons in his cradle-bed.

2 July 1944

Прилип огнем снедаемый хитон;
Кентавра кровь – как лавы ток по жилам
Геракловым. Уж язвины могилам
Подобятся. Деревья мечет он

В костер... И вихрь багряных похорон
Ползучий яд крылатым тушит пылом.
Так золото очищено горнилом...
Земной любви не тот же ли закон?

Сплетясь, – как дуб с омелой чужеядной ,–
Со Страстию глухонемой и жадной,
Убийцу в ней вдруг узнает она.

Живая плоть бежит от плоти хладной,
И надвое, что было плоть одна,
Рассекла Смерть секирой беспощадной.

1949

The chiton that the flame consumes hugs him.
The centaur's blood is like a lava stream
Inside the veins of Hercules. Wounds seem
Like graves already. He throws each tree's limb

Into the fire ... The dark-red funeral wind
Blows out the creeping poison with a glow.
The furnace smelts pure gold this way, we know ...
And does not earthly love the same law mind?

In an embrace (like mistletoe and oak)
With such a deaf and dumb and greedy passion,
Death sees a murderer here in this wild fashion.

The live flesh from the cold flesh runs askew:
Death cuts what once was one flesh into two
Parts with her ax in one merciless stroke.

АЛЕКСАНДР АЛЕКСАНДРОВИЧ БЛОК
1880-1921

Ужасен холод вечеров,
Их ветер, бьющийся в тревоге,
Несуществующих шагов
Тревожный шорох на дороге.

Холодная черта зари –
Как память близкого недуга
И верный знак, что мы внутри
Неразмыкаемого круга.

Июль 1902

БОЛОТНЫЙ ПОПИК

На весенней проталинке
За вечерней молитвою – маленький
Попик болотный виднеется.

Ветхая ряска над кочкой
        Чернеется
Чуть заметною точкой.

И в безбурности зорь красноватых
Не видать чертенят бесноватых,
        Но вечерняя прелесть
Увила вкруг него свои тонкие руки...
        Предзакатные звуки,
        Легкий шелест.

Тихонько он молится,
Улыбается, клонится,
Приподняв свою шляпу.

ALEXANDER ALEXANDROVICH BLOK
1880-1921

The evening cold is terrible,
The wind anxiously blasting, twisting...
The anguished shuffling of footsteps
Upon the road, steps non-existing.

The cold line of the dawn is like
A memory of a future aching:
A sure sign we are locked inside
A circle whence there's no out-breaking.

July 1902

THE SWAMP PRIEST

On a thawed patch in Spring
At the prayers of evening
A small swamp priest can be seen.

Threadbare cassock on a tufted spot
    Is black
As a hardly discernible dot.

In the calm as the red sunset levels,
One cannot see the wild little devils,
    But the evening enchantment
Wound its thin arms around him...
    And the sounds before sunset
    Lightly rustling...

Softly he prays,
Smiles, kneels,
Adjusting his hat.

153

И лягушке хромой, ковыляющей,
   Травой исцеляющей
Перевяжет болящую лапу.
Перекрестит и пустит гулять:
'Вот, ступай в родимую гать.
   Душа моя рада
   Всякому гаду
   И всякому зверю
   И о всякой вере.'

И тихонько молится,
Приподняв свою шляпу,
За стебель, что клонится,
За больную звериную лапу,
   И за римского папу.

Не бойся пучины тряской –
Спасет тебя черная ряска.

17 апреля 1905

ПОЭТ

Сидят у окошка с папой.
Над берегом вьются галки.

– Дождик, дождик! Скорей закапай!
У меня есть зонтик на палке!

– Там весна. А ты – зимняя пленница,
Бедная девочка в розовом капоре…
Видишь, море за окнами пенится?
Полетим с тобой, дочка, за море.

– А за морем есть мама?

               – Нет.

He would bandage the leg that was hurt
   Of a lame, limping frog in the dirt
With a healing grass-blade, make a brief
Cross on it, let it go, and say, 'Frog,
Here, go back to your own native bog.
     My soul is happy
     For every creature
     And for every beast
     And for every belief.'

Softly he prays,
Adjusting his hat,
For a blade that sways,
For the leg the poor beast cannot hop upon,
    And for the Pope in Rome.

Do not fear the mire's vacillation;
The black cassock will give you salvation.

17 April 1905

POET

She sits at the window with her father.
Over the river the jack-daws are calling.

'Look! I have a pretty umbrella!
Rain, rain, please start falling.'

'There, it's spring. You're a captive of winter
Poor little girl – pink hood,
Do you see the sea foaming from here?
Let's fly overseas, daughter. We could.'

'And is Mama over there?'

       'No.'

– А где мама?

        – Умерла.

             – Что это значит?

– Это значит: вон идет глупый поэт:
Он вечно о чем-то плачет.

– О чем?

        – О розовом капоре.

– Так у него нет мамы?

– Есть. Только ему нипочем:
Ему хочется за море,
Где живет Прекрасная Дама.

– А эта дама – добрая?

        – Да.

– Так зачем же она не приходит?

– Она не придет никогда:
Она не ездит на пароходе.

Подошла ночка,
Кончился разговор папы с дочкой.

Июль 1905

'Where is Mama?'

'Dead.'

What is "dead"?'

'It means: here comes a stupid poet...
Always cries about something in his head.'

'About what?'

'About a pink hood.'

'Doesn't he have a Mother?'
'He has,
Only he doesn't care.
Wants to go overseas somewhere,
Where the Beautiful Lady is.'

'Is the Lady good?'

'Yes, my dear.'

'Won't she visit him on a trip?'

'No, she will never come here:
She doesn't travel by ship.'

The night descended.
The conversation between daughter and father ended.

July 1905

Девушка пела в церковном хоре
О всех усталых в чужом краю,
О всех кораблях, ушедших в море,
О всех, забывших радость свою.

Так пел ее голос, летящий в купол,
И луч сиял на белом плече,
И каждый из мрака смотрел и слушал,
Как белое платье пело в луче.

И всем казалось, что радость будет,
Что в тихой заводи все корабли,
Что на чужбине усталые люди
Светлую жизнь себе обрели.

И голос был сладок, и луч был тонок,
И только высоко, у Царских Врат,
Причастный тайнам, – плакал ребенок
О том, что никто не придет назад.

Август 1905

НЕЗНАКОМКА

По вечерам над ресторанами
Горячий воздух дик и глух,
И правит окриками пьяными
Весенний и тлетворный дух.

Вдали, над пылью переулочной,
Над скукой загородных дач,
Чуть золотится крендель булочной,
И раздается детский плач.

И каждый вечер, за шлагбаумами,
Заламывая котелки,

A girl was singing in the church's choir
About all who were tired in a foreign land,
About all the ships that were sailing the ocean,
About all who'd forgotten their joy once at hand.

Thus her voice was singing, flying to the steeple,
And the sunlight was making her white shoulders gleam.
From the shadows the people were looking and listening
As the white dress was singing in the beam.

And it seemed to all that joy was soon coming,
That all ships found a quiet bay in sight,
That in a foreign land tired people
Had found for themselves a living light.

And the voice was sweet and the beam was slender.
And only on top of the Holy Doors then
A child partaking the mysteries was crying . . .
That none can never return again.

August 1905

THE STRANGER

Above the restaurants on evenings
Wild, heavy air lumbers about.
And on the breath of Spring and rotting things
There rides the sound of drunks who shout.

And farther on, beyond the boredom of
Town houses, dusty alleys – shines
Faintly the modest gilded sign above
The bakery. And a child whines.

And every evening – past the railroad track
Their derby hats cocked rakishly,

Среди канав гуляют с дамами
Испытанные остряки.

Над озером скрипят уключины,
И раздается женский визг,
А в небе, ко всему приученный,
Бессмысленно кривится диск.

И каждый вечер друг единственный
В моем стакане отражен
И влагой терпкой и таинственной,
Как я, смирен и оглушен.

А рядом у соседних столиков
Лакеи сонные торчат,
И пьяницы с глазами кроликов
'In vino veritas!' кричат.

И каждый вечер, в час назначенный
(Иль это только снится мне?),
Девичий стан, шелками схваченный,
В туманном движется окне.

И медленно, пройдя меж пьяными,
Всегда без спутников, одна,
Дыша духами и туманами,
Она садится у окна.

И веют древними поверьями
Ее упругие шелка,
И шляпа с траурными перьями,
И в кольцах узкая рука.

И странной близостью закованный,
Смотрю за темную вуаль,
И вижу берег очарованный
И очарованную даль.

The practiced wits stroll with their ladies back
And forth by ditches – fancy-free.

Upon the lake the creaking oarlocks sing,
A woman shrieks, while in the sky
That disk of moon, inured to everything,
Looks down and leers its stupid eye.

And every evening – this one friend of mine
Is mirrored in the glass he's raised.
Like it does me – the tart, mysterious wine
Leaves him also subdued and dazed.

And by adjoining tables all around
The drowsy waiters stick – like dross.
While drunkards with their rabbit-eyes expound
Their shout, 'In vino veritas!'

And every evening – like a punctual guest
(Is this a dream I entertain?)
The figure of a girl, by silk caressed,
Crosses the misty windowpane.

She edges through the drunks that fill the room,
Is always by herself, unknown.
And breathing scented mists from her perfume,
She picks a windowseat – alone.

Her rich, resilient silks, her black-plumed hat,
Her narrow hands with rings exhale
An atmosphere of wonder such as that
Of some old legendary tale.

Bewitched by this strangeness so near at hand,
I look through her dark veil and see
Appear a most enchanted shoreline and
Enchanted distances for me.

Глухие тайны мне поручены,
Мне чье-то солнце вручено,
И все души моей излучины
Пронзило терпкое вино.

И перья страуса склоненные
В моем качаются мозгу,
И очи синие бездонные
Цветут на дальнем берегу.

В моей душе лежит сокровище,
И ключ поручен только мне!
Ты право, пьяное чудовище!
Я знаю: истина в вине.

24 апреля 1906, Озерки

*   *   *

Ты можешь по траве зеленой
Всю церковь обойти,
И сесть на паперти замшеной,
И кружево плести.

Ты можешь опустить ресницы,
Когда я прохожу,
Поправить кофточку из ситца,
Когда я погляжу.

Твои глаза еще невинны,
Как цветик голубой,
И эти косы слишком длинны
Для шляпки городской.

Vague mysteries are given me to tend;
A sun is left in my control.
And the tart wine has pierced into each bend
And convolution of my soul.

And those black drooping ostrich feathers rise
And fall in my brain evermore...
Together with two blue fathomless eyes
That bloom upon the distant shore.

A treasure lies in my soul – far from sight;
The key to it is only mine.
And you, you drunken monster, you are right.
I know: truth lies in wine.

24 April 1906, Ozerki

* * *

You may go walking round the church
    Upon the fresh green grass,
And sit upon the mossy steps
    And there crochet your lace.

Whenever I pass by and look
    Straight at you, then you go
Lowering your eyelids to adjust
    Your blouse of calico.

And still your eyes are innocent
    Like some blue flower that grows...
And these, your braids, are far too long
    For citified chapeaux.

Но ты гуляешь с красным бантом
И семячки лущишь,
Телеграфисту с желтым кантом
Букетики даришь.

И потому – ты будешь рада
Сквозь мокрую траву
Прийти в туман чужого сада,
Когда я позову.

Октябрь 1906

ПОД МАСКАМИ

А под маской было звездно.
Улыбалась чья-то повесть,
Короталась тихо ночь.

И задумчивая совесть,
Тихо плавая над бездной,
Уводила время прочь.

И в руках, когда-то строгих,
Был бокал стеклянных влаг.
Ночь сходила на чертоги,
Замедляя шаг.

И позвякивали миги,
И звенела влага в сердце,
И дразнил зеленый зайчик
В догоревшем хрустале.

А в шкапу дремали книги.
Там – к резной старинной дверце
Прилепился голый мальчик
На одном крыле.

9 января 1907

But you walk with a bright red bow,
   Eat sunflower seeds, and laugh
With flowers for him with tan-piped cap
   Who works the telegraph.

And therefore, you'll be glad to come
   Across grass wet with dew
Into somebody's garden mist
   When I call out to you.

October 1906

BEHIND THE MASKS

Back behind the mask... eyes sparkling.
Someone's smiling story. Softly
Night was being whiled away.

And the melancholy conscience,
Floating over Chaos, softly
Carried time and all away.

Hands, aloof once, held a goblet
Filled with liquid clear as glass.
Night was falling on the palace;
Steps slowed as she'd pass.

As the minutes ticked and jingled,
Liquor set the heart to singing,
And in the extinguished crystal
... Green reflections pestering.

And in the cupboard ... books were dozing.
And upon an old door's carving,
One small naked boy was clinging...
Clinging there with just one wing.

9 January 1907

Гармоника, гармоника!
Эй, пой, визжи и жги!
Эй, желтенькие лютики,
Весенние цветки!

Там с посвистом да с присвистом
Гуляют до зари,
Кусточки с тихим шелестом
Кивают мне: смотри.

Смотрю я – руки вскинула,
В широкий пляс пошла,
Цветами всех осыпала
И в песне изошла...

Неверная, лукавая,
Коварная – пляши!
И будь навек отравою
Растраченной души!

С ума сойду, сойду с ума,
Безумствуя, люблю,
Что вся ты – ночь, и вся ты – тьма,
И вся ты – во хмелю...

Что душу отняла мою,
Отравой извела,
Что о тебе, тебе пою,
И песням нет числа!...

9 ноября 1907

Accordion! Accordion!
Hey, scream and rage and sing!
Hey-hey, all yellow buttercups,
You flowers of the Spring!

With whistles whistling till the dawn
They have a merry spree.
The brushes rustle in a hush
And nod to me: There! See!

I look. She raises up her arms
And moves her dance along.
She tosses flowers to everyone
And spends herself in song.

Unfaithful one, treacherous one,
And sly one, dance, glide, loll!
And be forever poison to
My atrophying soul.

I'll lose my mind; my mind I'll lose.
I'll love the fact and rant
That you're all darkness, you're all night,
You're all intoxicant...

That you took all my soul away,
Tired it with evilness...
And all I sing is you, is you...
The songs are numberless.

9 November 1907

НА ПОЛЕ КУЛИКОВОМ

Река раскинулась. Течет, грустит лениво
    И моет берега.
Над скудной глиной желтого обрыва
    В степи грустят стога.

О, Русь моя! Жена моя! До боли
    Нам ясен долгий путь!
Наш путь — стрелой татарской древней воли
    Пронзил нам грудь.

Наш путь — степной, наш путь — в тоске безбрежной,
    В твоей тоске, о, Русь!
И даже мглы — ночной и зарубежной —
    Я не боюсь.

Пусть ночь. Домчимся. Озарим кострами
    Степную даль.
В степном дыму блеснет святое знамя
    И ханской сабли сталь...

И вечный бой! Покой нам только снится
    Сквозь кровь и пыль...
Летит, летит степная кобылица
    И мнет ковыль...

И нет конца! Мелькают версты, кручи...
    Останови!
Идут, идут испуганные тучи,
    Закат в крови!

Закат в крови! Из сердца кровь струится!
    Плачь, сердце, плачь...
Покоя нет! Степная кобылица
    Несется вскачь!

7 июня 1908

ON THE FIELD OF KULIKOVO

The river spreads out wide ... Sad, lazy, it is flowing,
    Washing its bare banks, and
Above those yellow clay slopes – haystacks, growing
    Sad, stand on the steppeland.

O Russia! O my wife! Our long and narrow
    Road lies clear though distressed.
Our road with an old Tartar freedom's arrow
    Has deeply pierced our breast.

Our road lies through the steppes, through boundless anguish ...
    Your anguish, Russia dear!
From any dark (foreign or night) I do not languish,
    I do not fear.

Let night come. We'll ride on. We'll light the steppeland's distance
    With campfires' ash.
In smoke the Khan's sabers will show resistance
    As holy banners flash ...

And always war! We only dream of peace through ample
    Blood, dust ... alas! ...
The steppeland mare flies on and on and tramples
    The feather-grass.

And there's no end! The slopes and miles flash clearer
    Past. Stop! The flood
Of frightened clouds is moving nearer, nearer ...
    The sunset's blood.

The sunset's blood! From *my* heart blood is streaming.
    Cry, my heart, cry ...
There is no peace! The steppeland mare flies gleaming,
    Galloping by!

7 June 1908

Я пригвожден к трактирной стойке.
Я пьян давно. Мне все – равно.
Вон счастие мое – на тройке
В сребристый дым унесено...

Летит на тройке, потонуло
В снегу времен, в дали веков...
И только душу захлестнуло
Сребристой мглой из-под подков...

В глухую темень искры мечет,
От искр всю ночь, всю ночь светло...
Бубенчик под дугой лепечет
О том, что счастие прошло...

И только сбруя золотая
Всю ночь видна... Всю ночь слышна...
А ты, душа... душа глухая...
Пьяным пьяна... пьяным пьяна...

26 октября 1908

*   *   *

О доблестях, о подвигах, о славе
Я забывал на горестной земле,
Когда твое лицо в простой оправе
Передо мной сияло на столе.

Но час настал, и ты ушла из дому.
Я бросил в ночь заветное кольцо.
Ты отдала свою судьбу другому,
И я забыл прекрасное лицо.

I'm nailed fast to the tavern counter;
I've been drunk long. And I persist.
My happiness – is on a troika
Sped off into the silver mist...

It rushes with the troika, sinking
In snows of time, as years diffuse...
My soul is swept up by the silver
Darkness beneath the horses' shoes.

Sparks fly up in the lonely darkness;
From them it's light all night, all night...
The sleigh-bells hum beneath the dougas*
That happiness is gone outright.

And now only the golden harness
Is seen all night, is heard all night.
And you, my soul... my soul so lonely,
You're drunk, drunk, drunk... You're drunk all right.

26 October 1908

* dougas – collar yokes for horses

★   ★   ★

On this sorrowful earth I would forget
All valor and heroic deeds and fame
When I would see before me on my desk
Your face which shone out from a simple frame.

But that hour struck: you walked out of the house.
I flung my cherished ring to night and space.
You gave your destiny to someone else
And I forgot your beautiful, fair face.

Летели дни, крутясь проклятым роем…
Вино и страсть терзали жизнь мою…
И вспомнил я тебя пред аналоем,
И звал тебя, как молодость свою…

Я звал тебя, но ты не оглянулась,
Я слезы лил, но ты не снизощла.
Ты в синий плащ печально завернулась,
В сырую ночь ты из дому ушла.

Не знаю, где приют своей гордыне
Ты, милая, ты, нежная, нашла…
Я крепко сплю, мне снится плащ твой синий,
В котором ты в сырую ночь ушла…

Уж не мечтать о нежности, о славе,
Все миновалось, молодость прошла!
Твое лицо в его простой оправе
Своей рукой убрал я со стола.

30 декабря 1908

* * *

Черный ворон в сумраке снежном,
Черный бархат на смуглых плечах.
Томный голос пением нежным
Мне поет о южных ночах.

В легком сердце – страсть и беспечность,
Словно с моря мне подан знак.
Над бездонным провалом в вечность,
Задыхаясь, летит рысак.

The days flew by and whirled in a cursed swarm
When wine and passion racked my life, in truth.
I'd see you at the altar and I'd call
Out to you as I'd call out to my youth.

I called out to you; you did not look back.
I shed my tears, but you did not relent.
You sadly wrapped yourself in your blue cloak,
And from the house to that damp night you went.

I don't know, dear and tender one, where you
Found proper shelter for your pride and plight...
I sleep soundly, dream of the cloak of blue
In which you walked out into that damp night.

Me? No more dreams of tenderness and fame...
It all is ended, youth is over, and
Your face that once shone from a simple frame –
I took it off my desk with my own hand.

30 December 1908

*   *   *

A black raven in snowy darkness,
Black velvet on your dark skin,
A soft song of a southern evening
That your languid voice will spin.

In my light heart: passion, abandon...
Like a sign which the ocean gives me.
'Cross eternity's bottomless chasm,
The horse rushes breathlessly.

Снежный ветер, твое дыханье,
Опьяненные губы мои...
Валентина, звезда, мечтанье!
Как поют твои соловьи...

Страшный мир! Он для сердца тесен!
В нем – твоих поцелуев бред,
Темный морок цыганских песен,
Торопливый полет комет!

Февраль 1910

В РЕСТОРАНЕ

Никогда не забуду (он был, или не был,
Этот вечер): пожаром зари
Сожжено и раздвинуто бледное небо,
И на желтой заре – фонари.

Я сидел у окна в переполненном зале.
Где-то пели смычки о любви.
Я послал тебе черную розу в бокале
Золотого, как небо, аи.

Ты взглянула. Я встретил смущенно и дерзко
Взор надменный и отдал поклон.
Обратясь к кавалеру, намеренно резко
Ты сказала: 'И этот влюблен.'

И сейчас же в ответ что-то грянули струны,
Исступленно запели смычки...
Но была ты со мной всем презрением юным,
Чуть заметным дрожаньем руки...

Ты рванулась движеньем испуганной птицы,
Ты прошла, словно сон мой легка...

The snowy wind, your breathing,
And my lips as drunk as the Spring...
Valentina, my star, my dream-vision!
O how the nightingales sing!

Frightful world! For one heart too narrow!
But in it are your kisses' delights,
The darkness of songs of gypsies
And the comets' hasty flights!

February 1910

IN A RESTAURANT

I shall never forget (Did it all really happen –
That evening?) As the sunset blazed heights,
The pale sky was completely burnt out and stretched farther...
With the yellow sunset... the street lights.

I was there by a window in some crowded hallroom
With the violins singing love's cry.
And I sent you a velvet-black rose in a good glass
Of Aï that was gold as the sky.

You looked up. And then I, insolent and embarrassed,
Met your arrogant glance – bowing low.
And you turned to your date with deliberate sharpness
And said, 'That one there loves me also.'

Then the strings swelled immediately, as if responding,
And the bows started madly to sing.
You were with me – with all the contempt of your young years,
With your hand – now so slightly trembling...

Then you darted away like a bird that is frightened,
And – as light as a dream – you passed me.

MRP I

И вздохнули духи, задремали ресницы,
Зашептались тревожно шелка.

Но из глуби зеркал ты мне взоры бросала
И, бросая, кричала: 'Лови!...'
А монисто бренчало, цыганка плясала
И визжала заре о любви.

19 апреля 1910

УНИЖЕНИЕ

В черных сучьях дерев обнаженных
Желтый зимний закат за окном.
(К эшафоту на казнь осужденных
Поведут на закате таком.)

Красный штоф полинялых диванов,
Пропыленные кисти портьер...
В этой комнате, в звоне стаканов,
Купчик, шулер, студент, офицер...

Этих голых рисунков журнала
Не людская касалась рука...
И рука *подлеца* нажимала
Эту грязную кнопку звонка...

Чу! По мягким коврам прозвенели
Шпоры, смех, заглушенный дверьми...
Разве дом этот – дом в самом деле?
Разве *так* суждено меж людьми?

Разве рад я сегодняшней встрече?
Что ты ликом бела, словно плат?
Что в твои обнаженные плечи
Бьет огромный холодный закат?

Your perfumes were all sighing, your eyelashes dozing
And your silks whispered tormentingly.

From the depths of the mirrors you cast me your glances,
And while casting, you said, 'Catch, my dove!'
And her necklace jingled as the gypsy kept dancing,
Screaming to the sunset about love.

19 April 1910

HUMILIATION

Past the window: a gold winter sunset
In the black branches of the bare trees.
(Those condemned to death always are taken
To the scaffold in sunsets like these.)

Here: the red brocade of faded sofas,
The dusty tassels of the portiere...
In this room midst the clinking of glasses:
Merchant, student, card-shark, officer.

Surely no human hands turn these pages:
Snaps of girls, nude or scantily-clad.
He who presses the bell's dirty button
Must be either depraved or a cad.

There! Across the soft carpet pass ringing
Spurs and laughter that's muffled by doors...
Is this kind of a house a house really?
Must we always be just pigs and boars?

Do I really enjoy today's meeting?
That your face is like linen, so white?
That the huge and the bitter cold sunset
Floods your naked shoulders with its light?

Только губы с запекшейся кровью
На иконе твоей золотой
(Разве *это* мы звали любовью?)
Преломились безумной чертой...

В желтом, зимнем, огромном закате
Утонула (так пышно!) кровать...
Еще тесно дышать от объятий,
Но ты свищешь опять и опять...

Он не весел – твой свист замогильный...
Чу! опять – бормотание шпор...
Словно змей, тяжкий, сытый и пыльный,
Шлейф твой с кресел ползет на ковер...

Ты смела! Так еще будь бесстрашней!
Я – не муж, не жених твой, не друг!
Так вонзай же, мой ангел вчерашний,
В сердце – острый французский каблук!

6 декабря 1911

* * *

Ночь, улица, фонарь, аптека,
Бессмысленный и тусклый свет.
Живи еще хоть четверть века –
Все будет так. Исхода нет.

Умрешь – начнешь опять сначала,
И повторится все, как встарь:
Ночь, ледяная рябь канала,
Аптека, улица, фонарь.

10 октября 1912

Only those lips (like blood which has clotted)
On your golden icon make a sign:
(Was it this we called 'love' – with a label?)
Lips distorted by some insane line...

In the gigantic, gold winter sunset
The bed sinks down so lushly. But then
After all the embracing, I can't breathe...
And you whistle again and again...

It is not gay – your sepulchral whistling...
Hear! Again the spurs murmuring there...
And your gown – a snake heavy, full, dusty –
Drags its train to the rug from the chair.

You are bold! So be even more brazen!
This is no husband-lover-friend deal!
So, my angel of yesterday, do it:
Pierce my heart with your pointed French heel!

6 December 1911

★   ★   ★

The night. The street. Street-lamp. Drugstore.
A meaningless dull light about.
You may live twenty-five years more;
All will still be there. No way out.

You die. You start again and all
Will be repeated as before:
The cold rippling of a canal.
The night. The street. Street-lamp. Drugstore.

10 October 1912

К МУЗЕ

Есть в напевах твоих сокровенных
Роковая о гибели весть.
Есть проклятье заветов священных,
Поругание счастия есть.

И такая влекущая сила,
Что готов я твердить за молвой,
Будто ангелов ты низводила,
Соблазняя своей красотой...

И когда ты смеешься над верой,
Над тобой загорается вдруг
Тот неяркий, пурпурово-серый
И когда-то мной виденный круг.

Зла, добра ли? – Ты вся – не отсюда.
Мудрено про тебя говорят:
Для иных ты – и Муза, и чудо.
Для меня ты – мученье и ад.

Я не знаю, зачем на рассвете,
В час, когда уже не было сил,
Не погиб я, но лик твой заметил
И твоих утешений просил?

Я хотел, чтоб мы были врагами,
Так за что ж подарила мне ты
Луг с цветами и твердь со звездами –
Все проклятье твоей красоты?

И коварнее северной ночи,
И хмельней золотого аи,
И любови цыганской короче
Были страшные ласки твои...

TO MY MUSE

There is present in your secret singing
Fateful news about dying ordained.
There's condemning of sacred traditions,
And in it happiness is profaned.

And it's done with a power so compelling
I agree with the rumors which say
That you brought down the angels from Heaven
And seduced them with Beauty that way . . .

And when you deride Faith and Believing,
Suddenly above you starts to glow
That dull gray-purplish circle on fire
Which I saw once a long time ago.

Are you evil or good? You're not *this* world;
You're profoundly complex, as they tell:
For some souls you are both Muse and Marvel,
But for me you are Torment and Hell.

I don't know why at that hour of sunrise
When I had no more strength left in me,
I did not perish then – but I noticed
Your face there and I asked sympathy.

And I wanted you to be my hostile
Enemy. Then why did you disperse
To me flowery meadows, starred heavens, –
All the sum of your great beauty's curse?

And more treacherous than nights in the Northland,
And more potent than golden Aï,
And more brief than the love of a gypsy
Were your shocking caresses for me.

И была роковая отрада
В попираньи заветных святынь,
И безумная сердцу услада –
Эта горькая страсть, как полынь!

29 декабря 1912

КОРШУН

Чертя за кругом плавный круг,
Над сонным лугом коршун кружит
И смотрит на пустынный луг. –
В избушке мать над сыном тужит:
'На хлеба, на, на грудь, соси,
Расти, покорствуй, крест неси.'

Идут века, шумит война,
Встает мятеж, горят деревни,
А ты все та ж, моя страна,
В красе заплаканной и древней. –
Доколе матери тужить?
Доколе коршуну кружить?

22 марта 1916

And there *was* such a strange, fateful comfort
As you trampled things, holy and good ...
Such a joy for the heart and the spirit:
This mad passion – bitter as wormwood.

29 December 1912

BUZZARD

A buzzard flies the drowsy field,
Smooth circle after circle weaving.
He scans bare lands. A shack's revealed;
A mother for her son is grieving.
'Here, take this bread and suck this tit.
Mind! Grow! Here's your cross; carry it!'

Centuries pass, the war's at hand.
Rebellion came; each village sears.
And you are still the same, my land,
In your old beauty, stained with tears.
O how long must the mother grieve?
How long – the circling buzzard weave?

22 March 1916

АНДРЕЙ БЕЛЫЙ
(БОРИС НИКОЛАЕВИЧ БУГАЕВ)
1880-1934

НА ГОРАХ

Горы в брачных венцах.
Я в восторге, я молод.
У меня на горах
очистительный холод.

Вот ко мне на утес
притащился горбун седовласый.
Мне в подарок принес
из подземных темниц ананасы.

Он в малиново-ярком плясал,
прославляя лазурь.
Бородою взметал
вихрь метельно-серебряных бурь.

Голосил
низким басом.
В небеса запустил
ананасом.

И дугу описав,
озаряя окрестность,
ананас ниспадал, просияв,
в неизвестность,

золотую росу
излучая столбами червонца.
Говорили внизу:
'Это – диск пламезарного солнца ...'

ANDREI BIELY
(BORIS NIKOLAYEVICH BUGAYEV)
1880-1934

ON THE MOUNTAINS

Wedding wreaths crown the mountains.
I'm ecstatic... I'm young.
And all over my mountains
Such a pure chill is hung.

And behold – to my rock
Came a gray-haired hunchback, shuffling-stumbling.
And the gift that he brought
Was pineapples from an underground dungeon.

O he danced – wearing bright crimson-red,
Praised the sky's azure glow.
He swept up with his beard
Whirlwinds of silver-blizzarding snow.

With a cry
Deep as gravel
He threw into the sky
The pineapple.

And then arching a line,
Lighting up its environs,
The pineapple fell – brilliant with shine
Through the unknown,

Radiating a glow
As if dew of gold ducats were falling...
They agreed down below:
'It's a disk of pure flame – a sun shining.'

Низвергались, звеня,
омывали утесы
золотые фонтаны огня –
хрусталя
заалевшего росы.

Я в бокалы вина нацедил
и, подкравшися боком,
горбуна окатил
светопенным потоком.

1903

ХУЛИГАНСКАЯ ПЕСЕНКА

Жили-были я да он:
Подружились с похорон.

Приходил ко мне скелет
Много зим и много лет.

Костью крепок, сердцем прост –
Обходили мы погост.

Поминал со смехом он
День веселых похорон: –

Как несли за гробом гроб,
Как ходил за гробом поп:

Задымил кадилом нос.
Толстый кучер гроб повез.

'Со святыми упокой!'
Придавили нас доской.

Жили-были я да он.
Тили-тили-тили-дон!

1906, Серебряный Колодезь

Golden fountains of fire,
Or else heavenly dew,
Dew like crystal and red as a pyre,
Brightly flew
Down and bathed the rocks too.

Then I poured out some wine in a glass,
Sneaked aside for a moment,
And I drenched the hunchback
With a light, foamy torrent.

A HOOLIGAN'S LITTLE SONG

Once there lived both he and I;
To be friends we had to die.

Skeleton, he'd visit me...
Winters, summers... frequently.

Simple heart and solid bone;
We strolled this graveyard alone.

And with laughter he'd recall
That gay day: our funeral.

How they bore box behind box...
How the priest tagged... over rocks...

Censer smoke filled up the nose.
Fat coachmen made coffin rows.

'Rest with all saints and the Lord!'
They pressed us down with a board.

Once there lived he and I... long...
Til-ly, til-ly, til-ly dong.

1906, Serebryany Kolodez

ДРУЗЬЯМ

Золотому блеску верил,
А умер от солнечных стрел.
Думой века измерил,
А жизнь прожить не сумел.

Не смейтесь над мертвым поэтом:
Снесите ему венок.
На кресте и зимой и летом
Мой фарфоровый бьется венок.

Цветы на нем побиты.
Образок полинял.
Тяжелые плиты.
Жду, чтоб их кто-нибудь снял.

Любил только звон колокольный
И закат.
Отчего мне так больно, так больно!
Я не виноват.

Пожалейте, придите;
Навстречу венком метнусь.
О, любите меня, полюбите –
Я, быть может, не умер, быть может, проснусь –
Вернусь!

1907, Париж

TO MY FRIENDS

He believed in a golden radiance,
And he died from the arrows of the sun.
He measured centuries with his thinking,
But could not live his life – this one.

Don't laugh at the dead poet:
But come, bring him a wreath.
On the cross – winter, summer
There bangs my porcelain wreath.

Its flowers now are broken;
The icon faded gray.
Such heavy stones. I'm waiting
For someone to take them away.

He loved ringing bells and the sunset...
Only this...
Why is it so painful, so painful!
The fault is not his.

Have pity; come – think of me.
I'll rush with my wreath toward you.
O love me – love me.
Perhaps I'm not dead... and I'll wake anew
And come back!

1907, Paris

ОТЧАЯНЬЕ

Довольно: не жди, не надейся –
Рассейся, мой бедный народ!
В пространство пади и разбейся
За годом мучительный год!

Века нищеты и безволья!
Позволь же, о родина мать,
В сырое, в пустое раздолье,
В раздолье твое прорыдать: –

Туда, на равнине горбатой, –
Где стая зеленых дубов
Волнуется купой, подъятой
В косматый свинец облаков,

Где по полю Оторопь рыщет,
Восстав сухоруким кустом,
И в ветер пронзительно свищет
Ветвистым своим лоскутом,

Где в душу мне смотрят из ночи,
Поднявшись над сетью бугров,
Жестокие, желтые очи
Безумных твоих кабаков, –

Туда – где смертей и болезней
Лихая прошла колея, –
Исчезни в пространство, исчезни,
Россия, Россия моя!

1908, Серебряный Колодезь

DESPAIR

Enough: do not wait, do not hope.
Disperse, my poor people, my race!
O torturous years without hope,
Break up, disappear into space!

Long centuries of serfdom and need.
O Motherland, allow me then
Tears for your expanses. I grieve
For your dark empty spaces again: –

Down in the humpbacked valley there,
Where a flock of green oak trees crowd
And stir as a raised thicket, bare
To the shaggy lead-colored clouds,

Where Stupor (a dry-armed bush) roams
Along field and pasture and crag
And piercingly whispers and moans
To winds with its rough, branchy rag,

Where, piercing my soul from the night
(Now risen above hills like moons)
Are cruel yellow eyes leering bright –
The eyes of your crazy saloons.

O follow that hard rut from here,
Where sickness and death are ingrown ...
Go off into space, disappear,
My Russia, O Russia, my own!

1908, Serebryany Kolodez

А С Е

(а – о)

Снеговая блистает роса:
Налила серебра на луга;
Жемчугами дрожат берега;
В светлоглазых алмазах роса.

Мы с тобой – над волной голубой,
Над волной – берегов перебой;
И червонное солнца кольцо:
И – твое огневое лицо.

1913, Христиания

Д У Х

Я засыпал... (Стремительные мысли
Какими-то спиралями неслись;
Приоткрывалась в сознающем смысле
Сознанию не явленная высь) –

И видел духа... Искрой он возник...
Как молния, неуловимый лик
И два крыла – сверлящие спирали –
Кровавым блеском разрывали дали.

Открылось мне: в законах точных числ,
В бунтующей, мыслительной стихии –
Не я, не я – благие иерархии
Высокий свой запечатлели смысл.

Звезда... Она – в непеременном блеске...
Но бегает летучий луч звезды
Алмазами по зеркалу воды
И блещущие чертит арабески.

1914, Арлесгейм

TO ASYA

The dew glows like the snow when it whirls.
It has poured silver over the leas.
And the cold banks are rolling with pearls;
The dew shows diamond sloe-eyes that tease.

Let us sail the blue wave, you and I...
The blue wave as it breaks the bank's base...
The inflamed gold sun framed in the sky
And the blaze of your flamy, fair face.

1913, Christiania

SPIRIT

I was almost asleep... (Swift thoughts came rushing
In on some kind of spiraling express,
And on my realizing mind saw half-opened
Those heights not given to the consciousness):

I saw the Spirit... a spark in its beginning...
With an elusive face – like lightning fine –
And two wings – drilling gyres – which were tearing
The distances with a blood-colored shine.

This revealed: In the laws of precise numbers
And in the rebellious mental element
It was not I but good and kind hierarchies
Which had imprinted their Supreme intent.

. The star... It has a shine that never changes...
But the star's flying beam runs on to bound
In diamonds on the mirror of the water
And dances shining arabesques around.

1914, Arlesheim

ВЯЧЕСЛАВУ ИВАНОВУ

Случится то, чего не чаешь . . .

Ты предо мною вырастаешь –
В старинном, черном сюртуке,
Средь старых кресел и диванов,
С тисненым томиком в руке:
'Прозрачность. Вячеслав Иванов.'

Моргает мне зеленый глаз, –
Летают фейерверки фраз
Гортанной, плачущею гаммой:
Клонясь рассеянным лицом,
Играешь матовым кольцом
С огромной, ясной пентаграммой.

Нам подают китайский чай.
Мы оба кушаем печенье;
И – вспоминаем невзначай
Людей великих изреченья;
Летают звуки звонких слов,
Во мне рождая умиленье,
Как зов назойливых рогов,
Как тонкое, петушье пенье.

Ты мне давно, давно знаком –
(Знаком, быть может, до рожденья) –
Янтарно-розовым лицом,
Власы колеблющим перстом
И – длиннополым сюртуком
(Добычей, вероятно, моли) –
Знаком до ужаса, до боли!

Знаком большим безбровым лбом
В золотокосмом ореоле.

1916, Москва

TO VYACHESLAV IVANOV

What one had not expected happens...

You grow and take shape before me –
In ancient black frock-coat you stand
Among old armchairs and divans,
With a stamped volume in your hand:
'Transparence: Vyacheslav Ivanov.'

A green eye winks at me its blazes,
And then fly fireworks of phrases
In guttural tones of great lament.
Your absent-minded face is bent.
You toy with your tarnished ring –
A huge bright pentagram burning.

Now we are served rare Chinese tea...
Both of us eat the cookies.
And – we recall quite casually
The aphorisms of great men;
The sounds of ringing words are flying,
And they move me time and again
Like constant horn calls in a glen
And like a rooster's slender crying.

I've known you long – long, long ago,
Known you perhaps before my birth:
Your face with its pink-amber glow,
Your fingering your hair... like so,
And your long flapped coat (which I know
Must be booty for moths). And horrid
– Almost – how I know you who wore it,

How I know your large, browless forehead
Encircled by a gold halo.

1916, Moscow

Я – словом так немощно нем...
Изречения мои – маски...
   Рассказываю вам всем,
   Рассказываю сказки,
   Потому что –
   Мне так суждено,
   А почему – не понимаю;
      Потому что все давно
      Ушло во тьму,
      Потому что –
      Все равно,
      Не знаю,
      Или знаю.

(1925)

I'm so feebly mute with my words...
My sayings are all labels...
    I tell you they are absurds,
    Mere masks – I tell you fables.
    Because
    It's my destiny
    And why – I don't understand;
        Because everything long ago
        Left in the dark,
        Because –
        It's all the same
        If I don't know
        Or know.

ИВАН АЛЕКСЕЕВИЧ БУНИН
1870-1953

На высоте, на снеговой вершине,
Я вырезал стальным клинком сонет.
Проходят дни. Быть может, и доныне
Снега хранят мой одинокий след.

На высоте, где небеса так сини,
Где радостно сияет зимний свет,
Глядело только солнце, как стилет
Чертил мой стих на изумрудной льдине.

И весело мне думать, что поэт
Меня поймет. Пусть никогда в долине
Его толпы не радует привет!

На высоте, где небеса так сини,
Я вырезал в полдневный час сонет
Лишь для того, кто на вершине.

1901

ДОННИК

Брат, в запыленных сапогах,
Швырнул ко мне на подоконник
Цветок, растущий на парах,
Цветок засухи — желтый донник.

Я встал от книг и в степь пошел...
Ну да, все поле — золотое,
И отовсюду точки пчел
Плывут в сухом вечернем зное.

IVAN ALEKSEYEVICH BUNIN
1870-1953

I carved a sonnet with a blade of steel
Upon the summit of a snowy peak.
And time has passed. Perhaps the snows reveal
And still preserve my solitary streak.

Upon the summit where the sky is blue
With Winter's light shining like Paradise,
The sun looked on as my stiletto drew
My fourteen lines across the emerald ice.

I like to think a poet here can claim
To understand me – though he be one who
Has never known the valley's fleeting fame!

Upon the summit where the sky is blue
At noon I carved a sonnet – without shame...
Only for him who's on the summit too.

SWEET CLOVER

Wearing his dusty boots, my brother
Tossed in my window a bouquet
From fallow fields: yellow sweet clover...
The flower of the drouth, they say.

I left my books, went to the steppeland...
The whole field was a golden thing!
And everywhere dots of bees floated
In that dry heat of evening.

Толчется сеткой мошкара,
Шафранный свет над полем реет –
И, значит, завтра вновь жара
И вновь сухмень. А хлеб уж зреет.

Да, зреет и грозит нуждой,
Быть может голодом... И все же
Мне этот донник золотой
На миг всего, всего дороже!

(Между 1903 и 1906)

БОГ ПОЛДНЯ

Я черных коз пасла с меньшой сестрой
Меж красных скал, колючих трав и глины.
Залив был синь. И камни, грея спины,
На жарком солнце спали под горой.

Я прилегла в сухую тень маслины
С корявой серебристою корой –
И он сошел, как мух звенящий рой,
Как свет сквозной горячей паутины.

Он озарил мне ноги. Обнажил
Их до колен. На серебре рубашки
Горел огнем. И навзничь положил.

Его объятья сладостны и тяжки.
Он мне сосцы загаром окружил
И научил варить настой ромашки.

12 августа 1908

And like a net the swarms of insects
Hovered above the saffron field...
So: hot and dry again the morrow.
The grain was ripening its yield...

... And threatening want, destitution,
Perhaps famine... And yet to me
That gold sweet clover for one moment
Was more dear than all else could be.

(Between 1903 and 1906)

GOD OF NOON

With my young sister I watched black goats run
Through clay and thorny grasses and red rocks.
The bay was blue. And stones, warming their backs,
Dozed down below the hill in the hot sun.

I lay down in an olive tree's dry shade,
That rough and silvered bark... Before my eyes
He came down like a singing swarm of flies,
Like light that hot, transparent cobwebs made.

He lighted up my legs and bared them to
The knees. He burned my silver shirt awhile.
He laid me down upon my back and threw

Strong arms around me. And with a sweet smile
He rimmed my nipples with sun-tan anew
And taught me how to boil camomile.

12 August 1908

КАДИЛЬНИЦА

В горах Сицилии, в монастыре забытом,
По храму темному, по выщербленным плитам,
В разрушенный алтарь пастух меня привел,
И увидал я там: стоит нагой престол,
А перед ним, в пыли, могильно-золотая,
Давно потухшая, давным-давно пустая,
Лежит кадильница – вся черная внутри
От угля и смолы, пылавших в ней когда-то...

Ты сердце, полное огня и аромата,
Не забывай о ней. До черноты сгори.

25 января 1916

THE CENSER

In the Sicilian hills in a forgotten cloister,
Along dark temple walls and jagged slabs of stone,
A shepherd brought me to the ruins of an altar,
And there I saw a bare communion-stand alone.
Before it, in the dust, golden as tombs we know,
And empty for a long time, extinguished long ago –
A simple censer lay – grown black, inside and back,
From resin and from coal that flamed within it once.

And you, my heart, so full of fire and fragrance,
Do not forget about it. Burn until you're black!

25 January 1916

II
POST-SYMBOLISTS

МИХАИЛ АЛЕКСЕЕВИЧ КУЗМИН
1875-1936

Где слог найду, чтоб описать прогулку,
Шабли во льду, поджаренную булку
И вишен спелых сладостный агат?
Далек закат, и в море слышен гулко
Плеск тел, чей жар прохладе влаги рад.

Твой нежный взор лукавый и манящий, –
Как милый вздор комедии звенящей
Иль Мариво капризное перо.
Твой нос Пьеро и губ разрез пьянящий
Мне кружит ум, как 'Свадьба Фигаро'.

Дух мелочей, прелестных и воздушных,
Любви ночей, то нежащих, то душных,
Веселой легкости бездумного житья!
Ах, верен я, далек чудес послушных,
Твоим цветам, веселая земля!

1906

* * *

Когда мне говорят: 'Александрия',
я вижу белые стены дома,
небольшой сад с грядкой левкоев,
бледное солнце осеннего вечера
и слышу звуки далеких флейт.

206

MIKHAIL ALEKSEYEVICH KUZMIN
1875-1936

Where are the words to sketch a walk that tarries,
Chablis on ice, fried buns, ripe agate-cherries?
Sunset is far away – and from the sea
The hollow sound of splashing bodies carries...
As bodies' heat meets water's cold gladly.

Your glance is tender, sly and captivating,
Like nonsense some light comedy is prating
Or the capricious pen of Marivaux.
Your Pierrot nose, your lips intoxicating
Make me lightheaded like *The Marriage of Figaro*.

The spirit of trifles, airy and delighting –
Of love-filled nights (some cuddling, others stifling),
Of life unthinking in lighthearted mirth!
Ah, though remote from miracles complying,
I'm faithful to your flowers, O gay earth!

* * *

When they say to me, 'Alexandria',
I see the white walls of a house,
A small garden with a bed of stocks,
The pale sun of an autumn evening,
And hear the sounds of far-off flutes.

Когда мне говорят: 'Александрия',
я вижу звезды над стихающим городом,
пьяных матросов в темных кварталах,
танцовщицу, пляшущую 'осу',
и слышу звук тамбурина и крики ссоры.

Когда мне говорят: 'Александрия',
я вижу бледно-багровый закат над зеленым морем,
мохнатые мигающие звезды
и светлые серые глаза под густыми бровями,
которые я вижу и тогда,
когда не говорят мне: 'Александрия!'

(1905-1908)

★　★　★

Не знаю, как это случилось:
моя мать ушла на базар;
я вымела дом
и села за ткацкий станок.
Не у порога (клянусь!), не у порога я села,
а под высоким окном.
Я ткала и пела;
что еще? ничего.
Не знаю, как это случилось:
моя мать ушла на базар.

Не знаю, как это случилось:
окно было высоко.
Наверно, подкатил он камень,
или влез на дерево,
или встал на скамью.

When they say to me, 'Alexandria',
I see stars above a hushing city,
Drunken sailors in dark districts,
A young girl dancing 'The Wasp',
And hear the sound of a tambourine
                and the shouts of a quarrel.

When they say to me, 'Alexandria',
I see a lavender sunset on a green sea,
Shaggy, blinking stars,
And light-gray eyes below thick brows
Which I also see even when
They don't say to me: 'Alexandria!'

              ★   ★   ★

I don't know how it happened:
Mother went to the store;
I swept the house
And sat working the loom.
I didn't sit by the door (I swear), not by the door,
But under the high window.
I wove and sang:
What else? Nothing.
I don't know how it happened:
Mother went to the store.

I don't know how it happened:
The window was high.
He must have rolled up a stone,
Or climbed a tree,
Or stood on a bench.

Он сказал:
'Я думал, это малиновка,
а это – Пенелопа.
Отчего ты дома? здравствуй!'
– Это ты как птица лазаешь по застрехам,
а не пишешь своих любезных свитков
в суде. –
'Мы вчера катались по Нилу –
у меня болит голова.'
– Мало она болит,
что не отучила тебя от ночных гулянок. –
Не знаю, как это случилось:
окно было высоко.

Не знаю, как это случилось:
я думала, ему не достать.
'А что у меня во рту, видишь?'
– Чему быть у тебя во рту?
крепкие зубы да болтливый язык,
глупости в голове.
'Роза у меня во рту – посмотри.'
– Какая там роза! –
'Хочешь, я тебе ее дам,
только достань сама.'
Я поднялась на цыпочки,
я поднялась на скамейку,
я поднялась на крепкий станок,
я достала алую розу,
а он, негодный, сказал:
'Ртом, ртом,
изо рта только ртом,
не руками, чур, не руками!'
Может быть, губы мои
и коснулись его, я не знаю.
Не знаю, как это случилось:
я думала, ему не достать.

He said:
'I thought it was a robin,
But here is Penelope.
Why are you home? Hello there!'
'You're the one who climbs the eaves like a bird,
Not writing his precious scrolls
In court.'
'Yesterday we rode a boat on the Nile –
And I have a headache.'
'Not much of a headache,
Since you still can carouse at night.'
I don't know how it happened:
The window was high.

I don't know how it happened:
I thought he wouldn't get up there.
'And can you see what I have in my mouth?'
'What can you have in your mouth?
Sound teeth and a smooth tongue,
And nonsense in your head.'
'Look, I have a rose in my mouth.'
'Some kind of rose!'
'If you want it,
Reach for it yourself.'
I stood on my toes,
I stood on a bench,
I climbed on the steady loom,
I reached for the scarlet rose,
And that good-for-nothing said:
'With your lips, only from your lips,
Not with your hands, not with your hands.'
It is possible that my lips
Touched his. I don't know.
I don't know how it happened:
I thought he wouldn't get up there.

На знаю, как это случилось:
я ткала и пела;
не у порога (клянусь!), не у порога сидела,
окно было высоко:
кому достать?
Мать, вернувшись, сказала:
'Что это, Зоя,
Вместо нарцисса ты выткала розу?
что у тебя в голове?'
Не знаю, как это случилось.

(1905-1908)

*   *   *

Не похожа ли я на яблоню,
яблоню в цвету,
скажите, подруги?
Не так же ли кудрявы мои волосы,
как ее верхушка?
Не так же ли строен мой стан,
как ствол ее?
Мои руки гибки как ветки.
Мои ноги цепки как корни.
Мои поцелуи не слаще ли сладкого яблока?
Но ах!
Но ах!
хороводом стоят юноши,
вкушая плодов с той яблони,
мой же плод,
мой же плод
лишь один зараз вкушать может!

(1905-1908)

I don't know how it happened:
I wove and sang;
I didn't sit by the door (I swear!), not by the door.
The window was high:
Who could get up there?
Having come home, Mother spoke:
'What's the matter with you, Zoe?
That's no narcissus; you've woven a rose.
What ever got in your head?'
I don't know how it happened.

*   *   *

Am I not like an apple-tree,
An apple-tree in bloom?
Tell me, sweet ladies.
Is not my hair as wavy
As its top?
Is not my form as shapely
As its trunk?
My arms are lithe as branches,
My legs – tenacious roots.
And aren't my kisses sweeter than sweet apples?
But, ah!
But, ah!
The young men stand in a circle
Eating fruit from that apple-tree.
But my fruit,
My fruit,
Only one at a time can eat my fruit!

Из глины голубых голубок
Лепил прилежной я рукой,
Вдыхая душу в них дыханьем.
И шевелилися с шуршаньем,
И жалися одна к другой,
Садяся в круг на круглый кубок.
Клевали алые малины,
Лениво пили молоко,
Закинув горла голубые,
И были как совсем живые,
Но не летали далеко,
И знал я, что они из глины.
И показалось мне бездушным
Таинственное ремесло,
И призрачными стали птицы,
И начала душа томиться,
Чтоб сердце дар свой принесло
Живым голубкам, но послушным.

1913

ХОДОВЕЦКИЙ

Наверно, нежный Ходовецкий
Гравировал мои мечты:
И этот сад полунемецкий,
И сельский дом, немного детский,
И барбарисные кусты.

Пролился дождь; воздушны мысли.
Из окон рокот ровных гамм.
Душа стремится (вдаль ли? ввысь ли?)
А капли на листах повисли
И по карнизу птичий гам.

I tried to breathe a soul into
The blue clay doves I slaved and molded.
They moved, they beat their wings and folded
Them, cuddled to each other through
The rustling of their fresh-formed feathers;
They sat on a round cup together.
They pecked away at red raspberries
And, lazy, drank milk from a jar.
Throwing their blue throats back that way,
They looked a lot alive. Yes, very,
But they could not fly very far,
And I knew they were made of clay.
Such a mysterious craft now seemed
To me as one of soulless bent.
The birds became only illusion...
And my own soul yearned, as it dreamed
My heart would pour gifts in profusion
To doves, alive, obedient.

CHODOWIECKI

I think the gentle Chodowiecki
Engraved my dream landscapes for me.
For here's a German-looking garden,
A rustic house – as if for children –
And here – some clumps of barberry.

The rain's just ended; thoughts are airy
And scales ripple down windowpanes.
The soul aspires (toward heights? toward distance?)
Raindrops cling to the leaves and branches,
And birds quarrel along the drains.

Гроза стихает за холмами,
Ей отвечает в роще рог,
И дядя с круглыми очками
Уж наклоняет над цветами
В цветах невиданных шлафрок.

И радуга, и мост, и всадник, –
Все видится мне без конца:
Как блещет мокрый палисадник,
Как ловит на лугу лошадник
Отбившегося жеребца.

Кто приезжает? кто отбудет?
Но мальчик вышел на крыльцо.
Об ужине он позабудет,
А теплый ветер долго будет
Ласкать открытое лицо.

1916

ПЕЙЗАЖ ГОГЭНА
(второй)

Тягостен вечер в Июле,
Млеет морская медь ...
Красное дно кастрюли,
Полно тебе блестеть!
Спряталась паучиха.
Облако складки мнет.
Песок золотится тихо,
Словно застывший мед.
Винно-лиловые грозди
Спустит небес лоза.
В выси мохнатые гвозди
Нам просверлят глаза.

The thunder dies behind the hillocks,
And from a grove a horn replies.
And now an uncle with round glasses
Already bends above the flowers
In a coat colored with rarest dyes.

A rainbow and a bridge, a rider...
My eyes see this in endless play:
The palisade, still wet, is glistening
As horsemen chase across the meadow
The stallion that has run away.

And who is coming? Who is leaving?
A young boy comes out on a porch
Forgetting all about his supper...
His open face will long be fondled
By the warm wind that wanders Earth.

LANDSCAPE OF GAUGUIN, #2

Evening in July is oppressive.
The copper of the sea melts away...
Reddish bottom of the pan, quit shining!
(You've shone enough today!)
It hid itself – the she-spider.
The cloud is rumpling its folds.
The sand is quietly gilded
Like hardened honey's golds.
The wine-lilac-toned clusters
Will be hung by the vine of the skies.
The shaggy nails of high heaven
Will drill into our eyes.

Густо алеют губы,
Целуют, что овода.
Хриплы пастушьи трубы,
Блеют в разброд стада.
Скатилась звезда лилово...
В траве стрекозиный гром.
Все для любви готово,
Грузно качнулся паром.

1916

* * *

L'ho perduta meschinella...
Le Nozze di Figaro

В такую ночь, как паутина,
Всю синь небесного павлина
Заткали звездные пути.
На башне полночь без пяти,
И спит росистая долина.

Курится круглая куртина.
Как сладко цепь любви нести,
Как сладко сеть любви плести
В такую ночь!

Чуть-чуть приподнята гардина,
Звенит в беседке мандолина...
О, песни вздох, лети, лети!
Тебе булавки не найти,
О маленькая Барбарина,
В такую ночь!

1916

And lips then redden thickly;
They kiss like gadflies do.
The shepherds' hoarse horns echo;
The scattered herds bay too.
A star falls – streaking lilac...
In the grass a cicada talks.
Everything is ready for loving –
The ferry heavily rocks.

★　★　★

L'ho perduta meschinella...
Le Nozze di Figaro

Like webs on such a night and hour,
The stars have woven the blue shower
Of heaven's peacock as they spin.
The dewy valley's sleeping in.
It's five till midnight on the tower.

Mist rises from round beds of flowers.
How sweet the chain of love has been!
How sweet to weave love's net and sin
On such a night!

The window-curtains almost lower,
A mandolin sings in the bower...
O, song's sweet sigh, fly, fly, begin!
You cannot find your little pin,
O, Barbarina, you've no power
On such a night!

ФУЗИЙ В БЛЮДЕЧКЕ

Сквозь чайный пар я вижу гору Фузий,
На желтом небе золотой вулкан.
Как блюдечко природу странно узит!
Но новый трепет мелкой рябью дан.
Как облаков продольных паутинки
Пронзает солнце с муравьиный глаз,
А птицы-рыбы, черные чаинки,
Чертят лазури зыблемый топаз!
Весенний мир вместится в малом мире:
Запахнут миндали, затрубит рог,
И весь залив, хоть будь он вдвое шире,
Фарфоровый обнимет ободок.
Но ветка неожиданной мимозы,
Рассекши небеса, легла на них, –
Так на страницах философской прозы
Порою заблестит влюбленный стих.

1917

ФАУСТИНА

Серебристым рыба махнула хвостом,
Звезда зажелтела в небе пустом –
О, Фаустина!

Все ближе маяк, темен и горд,
Все тише вода плещет о борт –
Тянется тина . . .

Отбившийся сел на руль мотылек . . .
Как день свиданья от нас далек!
Тень Палатина!

FUJIYAMA IN A SAUCER

Through steam from tea I see Mount Fujiyama,
A gold volcano against yellow sky.
A saucer contracts Nature very strangely:
Ripples give new impressions to the eye!
See how the oblong, cobweb clouds are calmly
Pierced by a sun the size of an ant's head.
And how black bits of tea, like birds or fish,
Form lines where that blue topaz sky is spread!
The world of spring is in this microcosm:
The horn will sound, the almond trees will bloom,
The porcelain rim will hold the whole bay in it;
With twice as much water, there'd still be room.
An unexpected branch of light mimosa,
Cleaving the sky, lays down its graceful line...
So sometimes on philosophy's prose pages
A quick line of love poetry will shine.

FAUSTINA

A fish waves a silver tail, passing by.
A star starts to yellow in the empty sky.
O Faustina!

Dark, proud, the lighthouse grows more near.
Water laves the boat more gently here
In dragging slime.

A strayed butterfly alights on the wheel...
When will our day of reunion be real!
Dim Palatine!

Ветром запах резеды принесло.
В розовых брызгах мое весло.
О, Фаустина!

(1917-1918)

ВЕНЕЦИЯ

Обезьяна распростерла
Побрякушку над Ридотто,
Кристалличной сонатиной
Стонет дьявол из Казотта.
Синьорина, что случилось?
Отчего вы так надуты?
Рассмешитесь: словно гуси,
Выступают две бауты.

Надушенные сонеты,
Мадригалы, триолеты,
Как из рога изобилья
Упадут к ногам Нинеты...
А Нинета в треуголке
С вырезным, лимонным лифом –
Обещая и лукавя,
Смотрит выдуманным мифом.

Словно Тьеполо расплавил
Теплым облаком атласы...
На террасе Клеопатры
Золотеют ананасы.
Кофей стынет, тонкий месяц
В небе лодочкой ныряет,
Под стрекозьи серенады
Сердце легкое зевает.

Треск цехинов, смех проезжих,
Трепет свечки нагоревшей.
Не бренча стряхает полночь
Блестки с шали надоевшей.

Mignonette flavors the wind from the shore.
The rosy spray sparkles around my oar.
O Faustina!

VENICE

Then the monkey spread a rattle
Over the Ridotto scene. A
Devil from Cazotte is moaning
In a crystal sonatina.
Signorina, what's the matter?
Why do your two lips so pucker?
Laugh, my lady, laugh: like ganders
Two proud dominoes are strutting.
Now the perfumed madrigals,
Triolets and sonnets sigh there,
Fall as from a horn of plenty
To Ninetta's feet and lie there...
In three-cornered hat, with cut-out
Lemon blouse, Nina, sweet-scented,
Slyly and affording promise,
Seems a myth someone invented.
Did Tiepolo's brush fashion
With a warm cloud these rich satins...
Gold pineapples on the terrace
That was named for Cleopatra.
And the coffee cools. The slender
Moon dives in the sky: parading
Little boat. My light heart yawning...
Cicadas are serenading.
Gold coins crackle. Transients' laughter...
And the wax-bound candle sputters.
Midnight sheds her sparkling spangles
From her dull shawl – no sound mutters.

Молоточки бьют часочки...
Нина – розочка, на роза...
И секретно, и любовно
Тараторит Чимароза.

(1919-1920)

МУЗА

В глухие воды бросив невод,
Под вещий лепет темных лип,
Глядит задумчивая дева
На чешую волшебных рыб.

То в упоении зверином
Свивают алые хвосты,
То выплывут аквамарином,
Легки, прозрачны и просты.

Восторженно не разумея
Плодов запечатленных вод,
Все ждет, что голова Орфея
Златистой розою всплывет.

Февраль 1922

ПОРУЧЕНИЕ

Если будешь, странник, в Берлине,
у дорогих моему сердцу немцев,
где были Гофман, Моцарт и Ходовецкий
(и Гете, Гете, конечно), –
кланяйся домам и прохожим,
и старым, чопорным липкам
и окрестным плоским равнинам.

No rose... but a small rose: Nina...
Hours strike with tiny hammers...
And the clever Cimarosa
Secretly, lovingly chatters.

MUSE

She threw her net in hidden water.
Under the lisped, prophetic swish
Of dark lindens, the thoughtful daughter
Looks at the scales of magic fish.

In animal intoxication
Sometimes they weave their scarlet tails,
Sometimes – aquamarine lustration –
They flash their light, transparent trails.

Ecstatically not comprehending
The fruits these sealed waters disclose,
She looks for Orpheus' head ascending,
Emerging like a golden rose.

February 1922

A MESSAGE

If you should be a wanderer
In Berlin, in the Deutschland I cherish,
Land of Hoffmann, Mozart and Chodowiecki
(And certainly Goethe, Goethe),
Greet the houses and passersby for me,
And also its old prim lindens
And the flat plains around the city.

Там, наверно, все по-другому, –
не узнал бы, если б поехал,
но я знаю, что в Шарлоттенбурге,
на какой-то, какой-то штрассе,
живет белокурая Тамара
с мамой, сестрой и братом.
Позвони не очень громко,
чтоб она к тебе навстречу вышла
и состроила милую гримаску.
Расскажи ей, что мы живы, здоровы,
часто ее вспоминаем,
не умерли, а даже закалились,
скоро совсем попадем в святые,
что не пили, не ели, не обувались,
духовными словами питались,
что бедны мы (но это не новость:
какое же у воробьев именье?),
занялись замечательной торговлей:
все продаем и ничего не покупаем,
смотрим на весеннее небо
и думаем о друзьях далеких.
Устало ли наше сердце,
ослабели ли наши руки,
пусть судят по новым книгам,
которые когда-нибудь выйдут.
Говори не очень пространно,
чтобы, слушая, она не заскучала.
Но если ты поедешь дальше
и встретишь другую Тамару, –
вздрогни, вздрогни, странник,
чтобы тебе не умереть на месте,
слыша голос незабываемо крылатый,
следя за движеньями вещей Жар-Птицы,
смотря на телесное, летучее солнце.

Май 1922

I think everything now is different;
I'd not know it if I went there.
But I know in the Charlottenburg section
On some kind, some kind of strasse,
There lives a blonde Tamara –
With her mother, sister and brother.
Ring the bell, but not very loudly,
To bring her out to the doorway,
And make a nice, pleasant grimace.
Tell her we're alive and healthy
And that we remember her often,
That we aren't dead. We've even grown tougher,
That soon we'll be saints completely,
That we don't drink, we don't eat, we're shoeless,
That we live on the things of the spirit,
That we're poor (but this is no new news:
Since when have sparrows owned something?)
That we're all in a fantastic business,
We sell everything and buy nothing,
We look at the sky in Springtime
And think of our friends who are distant.
Whether our hearts are exhausted,
Whether our hands have grown weaker
Let them judge by our new publications
Which will someday be appearing.
Don't speak and be too long-winded
So that you wear her out while she listens.
But if you should travel farther
And meet another Tamara...
O Wanderer, shudder, O shudder...
Or else you die there that instant
When you hear a voice – wingéd, unforgetable,
And watch movements of that wise Firebird,
And look at the flying embodied sun.

May 1922

КОНЕЦ ВТОРОГО ТОМА

Я шел дорожкой Павловского парка,
Читая про какую-то Элизу
Восьмнадцатого века ерунду.
И было это будто до войны,
В начале Июня, жарко и безлюдно.
'Элизиум, Элиза, Елисей',
Подумал я, и вдруг мне показалось,
Что я иду уж очень что-то долго:
Неделю, месяц, может быть года.
Да и природа странно изменилась:
Болотистые кочки все, озерца,
Тростник и низкорослые деревья, –
Такой всегда Австралия мне снилась,
Или вселенная до разделенья
Воды от суши. Стаи жирных птиц
Взлетали невысоко и садились
Опять на землю. Подошел я близко
К кресту высокому. На нем был распят
Чернобородый ассирийский царь.
Висел вниз головой он и ругался
По матери, а сам весь посинел.
Я продолжал читать, как идиот,
Про ту же все Элизу, как она
Забыв, что ночь проведена в казармах,
На утро удивилась звуку труб.
Халдей, с креста сорвавшись, побежал
И стал точь в точь похож на Пугачева.
Тут сразу мостовая проломилась,
С домов посыпалася штукатурка,
И варварские буквы на стенах
Накрасились, а в небе разливалась
Труба из глупой книжки. Целый взвод
Небесных всадников в персидском платьи
Низринулся, – и яблонь зацвела.

THE END OF THE SECOND VOLUME

I walked along a path in Pavlovsk Park
Reading about a heroine, Elise,
Some nonsense of the eighteenth century.
And all of that was just before the war –
The first of June. Hot. And no one in view.
'Elyseum, Elise, and Eli too.'
I thought. And suddenly it seemed to me
That I had been a long time on my way:
A week, a month, perhaps a year or more.
Suddenly Nature changed – as by caprice:
Around were swampy tufts and little lakes,
Reeds and low-growing trees, – I always used
To dream that Australia looked just this way,
Or Earth before the separation of
The water and dry land. And fat birds flew
In flocks, up (not so very high), again
Alighted on the land. I came close then
To a tall cross. And there was crucified
On it a black-bearded Assyrian king.
Hanging there upside down, he cursed and cried
Obscenely, and his flesh had all turned blue.
An idiot, I read on stupidly
About the same Elise, about how she,
Forgetting she had spent the night inside
The barracks, heard (surprised) the bugle sing.
Having got off the cross, the Chaldean ran
– And looked exactly then like Pugachov.
Immediately here the sidewalk broke;
The stucco fell from houses and the scrawls
Of the barbarian letters on the walls
Filled up with color. Wide across the skies
The bugle in the stupid book caroused.
A whole platoon of heaven-riders, dressed
Like Persians, rushed down. Apple trees began

На персях у персидского Персея
Змея свой хвост кусала кольцевидно,
От Пугачева на болоте пятка
Одна осталась грязная. Солдаты
Крылатые так ласково смотрели,
Что показалось мне, – в саду публичном
Я выбираю крашеных мальчишек.
'Ашанта бутра первенец Первантра!'
Провозгласили, – и смутился я,
Что этих важных слов не понимаю.
На облаке ж увидел я концовку,
Гласящую: конец второго тома.

1922

ПЕРВЫЙ УДАР

Стояли холода, и шел 'Тристан'.
В оркестре пело раненое море,
Зеленый край за паром голубым,
Остановившееся дико сердце.
Никто не видел, как в театр вошла
И оказалась уж сидящей в ложе
Красавица, как полотно Брюллова.
Такие женщины живут в романах,
Встречаются они и на экране...
За них свершают кражи, преступленья,
Подкарауливают их кареты
И отравляются на чердаках.
Теперь она внимательно и скромно
Следила за смертельною любовью,
Не поправляя алого платочка,
Что сполз у ней с жемчужного плеча,
Не замечая, что за ней упорно
Следят в театре многие бинокли...
Я не был с ней знаком, но все смотрел

To bloom. Upon the Persian Perseus' breast
The snake was biting its own tail – ringwise.
All that remained of Pugachov was one
Lone dirty heel upon the swamp. The band
Of wingéd soldiers looked so kind I thought
That I was in a public garden – and
Choosing young boys with make-up from the lot.
'Ashanta, butra, Firstantros' first son!'
It was announced. I was ashamed, not proud,
I could not comprehend these solemn words.
And then I saw the 'FINIS' on a cloud
Which said the second book had reached its end.

THE FIRST THRUST

The cold stayed on. TRISTAN was playing now:
The wounded sea sang in the orchestra,
The rich green land behind the azure mist,
And then his wildly beating heart – stopped.
No one saw her enter the theater,
But she was found (already) in the box –
As lovely as a painting by Briullóv.
This type of woman lives of course in novels,
And you can find her, too, on movie-screens...
Because of her, thefts and crimes are committed,
Her carriage is awaited at each turn,
And people take poison up in the attic.
Here now intently and most modestly
She watched this play of love that would bring death,
With no adjusting of the scarlet scarf
Which had slipped off, down from her pearl shoulder,
Not seeing she was watched persistently
By opera glasses in the theater...
I didn't know her but I kept on looking

На полумрак пустой, казалось, ложи...
Я был на спиритическом сеансе,
Хоть не люблю спиритов, и казался
Мне жалким медиум – забитый чех.
В широкое окно лился свободно
Голубоватый леденящий свет.
Луна как будто с севера светила:
Исландия, Гренландия и Тулэ,
Зеленый край за паром голубым...
И вот я помню: тело мне сковала
Какая-то дремота перед взрывом,
И ожидание, и отвращенье,
Последний стыд и полное блаженство...
А легкий стук внутри не прерывался,
Как будто рыба бьет хвостом о лед...
Я встал, шатаясь, как слепой лунатик,
Дошел до двери... Вдруг она открылась...
Из аванложи вышел человек
Лет двадцати, с зелеными глазами;
Меня он принял будто за другого,
Пожал мне руку и сказал: 'покурим!'
Как сильно рыба двинула хвостом!
Безволие – преддверье высшей воли!
Последний стыд и полное блаженство!
Зеленый край за паром голубым!

1927

Through semi-darkness of her (empty?) loge ...
I went once to a spiritual seance
(Though I don't like spiritualists. And that
Downtrodden Czech, the medium, seemed awful.)
And there the bluish and the chilling light
Was flowing freely in through a wide window.
The moon seemed to be shining from the North,
From Iceland and from Greenland and from Thule.
The rich green land behind the azure mist ...
And I recall my body was forged rigid
By logginess as before an explosion;
Both present: expectation and disgust,
The last shame coupled with the fullest bliss ...
And a light knocking never stopped inside
As if some fish's tail beat on the ice ...
Unsteadily I stood – a blind sleepwalker –
And reached the door ... Then suddenly it opened ...
And from the avant-loge a man came out
– About twenty years old – who had green eyes.
Mistaking me, it seemed, for someone else,
He shook my hand and said, 'Let's have a smoke.'
And then how strangely the fish flapped its tail!
The door to greater will is lack of will!
The last shame coupled with the fullest bliss!
The rich green land behind the azure mist!

НИКОЛАЙ СТЕПАНОВИЧ ГУМИЛЕВ
1886-1921

КАПИТАНЫ

На полярных морях и на южных,
По изгибам зеленых зыбей,
Меж базальтовых скал и жемчужных
Шелестят паруса кораблей.

Быстрокрылых ведут капитаны,
Открыватели новых земель,
Для кого не страшны ураганы,
Кто изведал мальстремы и мель;

Чья не пылью затерянных хартий, –
Солью моря пропитана грудь,
Кто иглой на разорванной карте
Отмечает свой дерзостный путь

И, взойдя на трепещущий мостик,
Вспоминает покинутый порт,
Отряхая ударами трости
Клочья пены с высоких ботфорт,

Или, бунт на борту обнаружив,
Из-за пояса рвет пистолет,
Так что сыплется золото с кружев,
С розоватых брабантских манжет.

Пусть безумствует море и хлещет,
Гребни волн поднялись в небеса, –
Ни один пред грозой не трепещет,
Ни один не свернет паруса.

NIKOLAI STEPANOVICH GUMILEV
1886-1921

THE CAPTAINS

On the ridges of rippling green waves
In the arctic and southern seas,
Among reefs of basalt and pearl
Rustle sails of the ships in the breeze.

These swift-wingéd are captained by men
Who discover new lands and new goals,
And for whom hurricanes hold no dread,
Who have known many maelstroms and shoals –

With their breasts soaked with salt of the sea,
Not the dust of a long mislaid chart,
Who with needles can mark their bold course
On a torn map that's crumbling apart,

And who, climbing the shuddering bridge,
Still recall their lost port with no pain
As they slash off the fragmented foam
On their jack boots with whacks of a cane,

Or discovering a mutiny on board
Tear the gun from the belt with such pace
That the gold scatters off of their cuffs
Which are made of a pink Brabant lace.

Let the waves lift their crests to the skies,
Let the seas rage and lash at the rails,
Not one captain will quake in the storm,
Not one captain will roll down his sails.

Разве трусам даны эти руки,
Этот острый, уверенный взгляд,
Что умеет на вражьи фелуки
Неожиданно бросить фрегат,

Меткой пулей, острогой железной
Настигать исполинских китов
И приметить в ночи многозвездной
Охранительный свет маяков?

(1908)

ВОЙНА

Как собака на цепи тяжелой,
Тявкает за лесом пулемет,
И жужжат шрапнели, словно пчелы,
Собирая ярко-красный мед.

А 'ура' вдали, как будто пенье
Трудный день окончивших жнецов.
Скажешь: это – мирное селенье
В самый благостный из вечеров.

И воистину светло и свято
Дело величавое войны,
Серафимы, ясны и крылаты,
За плечами воинов видны.

Тружеников, медленно идущих
На полях, омоченных в крови,
Подвиг сеющих и славу жнущих,
Ныне, Господи, благослови.

Как у тех, что гнутся над сохою,
Как у тех, что молят и скорбят,

Cowards never are given such hands
And such confident eyes with keen glow,
That know how and can suddenly hurl
Frigates against a felucca foe

And can strike giant whales – with well-aimed
Bullets or with an iron harpoon's flight,
And can spot in the star-spangled night
Guardian gleams of the lighthouse's light.

WAR

The machine gun barks behind the thicket
Like a dog upon a heavy chain,
And the shrapnel buzzes like bees, busy,
Bringing bright red honey home again.

Far off the hurrahing is like singing
Reapers whose hard daily work is done.
You must say that it's a peaceful village
As the most becalming night's begun.

And, O, verily war, this majestic
Enterprise, is sacred and all light;
Wingéd seraphim behind the warriors'
Shoulders can be witnessed shining bright.

And O, dear Lord grant your gracious blessing
To the workers slowly walking there
On the fields that blood has sprinkled, sowing
Heroes' deeds, reaping a glory rare,

As you would to those whose necks are bending
Over plows and those who mourn and pray;

Их сердца горят перед Тобою,
Восковыми свечками горят.

Но тому, о Господи, и силы
И победы царский час даруй,
Кто поверженному скажет: – Милый,
Вот, прими мой братский поцелуй.

1914

РАБОЧИЙ

Он стоит пред раскаленным горном,
Невысокий старый человек.
Взгляд спокойный кажется покорным
От миганья красноватых век.

Все товарищи его заснули,
Только он один еще не спит:
Все он занят отливаньем пули,
Что меня с землею разлучит.

Кончил, и глаза повеселели.
Возвращается. Блестит луна.
Дома ждет его в большой постели
Сонная и теплая жена.

Пуля, им отлитая, просвищет
Над седою, вспененной Двиной,
Пуля, им отлитая, отыщет
Грудь мою, она пришла за мной.

Упаду, смертельно затоскую,
Прошлое увижу наяву,
Кровь ключом захлещет на сухую,
Пыльную и мятую траву.

Their hearts come and kneel and burn before you
Like candles of wax which melt away.

But, O, Lord, give victory and vigor
To him who at the light armistice
Will say to the one he's just defeated:
Dear friend, please accept your brother's kiss.

THE WORKER

There he stands before the red-hot furnace,
Just a small old man – (not much in size),
And the way his red eyelids keep blinking
Gives a humble air to his calm eyes.

All his friends have gone to sleep, and only
He is still awake – earning his worth,
Busy with his work casting the bullet
Which will separate me from the earth.

Now he's finished and his eyes grow lighter.
He is going home. The moon shines dim.
At his house his wife is warm and sleepy,
Waiting in a big bed there for him.

And the bullet he has made will whistle
Over the Dviná – gray-haired with foam.
Seeking out my heart, that very bullet
Cast by him will come and find its home.

Then I shall fall down in mortal anguish,
I shall see the truth of my life pass,
And my blood will gush out like a fountain
On the dry, dusty and trampled grass.

И Господь воздаст мне полной мерой
За недолгий мой и горький век.
Это сделал, в блузе светло-серой,
Невысокий старый человек.

1916

* * *

Оглушенная ревом и топотом,
Облеченная в пламень и дымы,
О тебе, моя Африка, шопотом
В небесах говорят серафимы.

И твое раскрывая Евангелье,
Повесть жизни ужасной и чудной,
О неопытном думают ангеле,
Что приставлен к тебе, безрассудной.

Про деянья свои и фантазии,
Про звериную душу послушай,
Ты, на дереве древнем Евразии
Исполинской висящая грушей.

Обреченный тебе, я поведаю
О вождях в леопардовых шкурах,
Что во мраке лесов за победою
Водят полчища воинов хмурых;

О деревнях с кумирами древними,
Что смеются улыбкой недоброй,
И о львах, что стоят над деревнями
И хвостом ударяют о ребра.

And the Lord will pay me full measure
For my brief and bitter lifetime span.
This is what a small old man in light-gray
Blouse has worked and done, – A small old man.

*   *   *

You are dazed by the roar and the trampling;
You are dressed up in smoke and in flame.
O, my Africa, – up there in heaven
All the seraphim whisper your name.

As they open your gospel, your story
Full of terror – and wonder too,
They think of the novitiate angel
Who is carelessly assigned to you,

Hear about your own deeds and your fancies,
And your animal soul now laid bare;
On the old spreading tree of Eurasia
You hang down like a gigantic pear.

I, your vassal, will tell you your story –
How the chieftains in leopard-skins stood
Leading hordes of their own gloomy warriors
Seeking victory in the dark wood,

About villages with ancient idols
Who, while smiling, let cruel scowls prevail,
About villages lions stand over
Whipping their ribs with their bushy tails.

Дай за это дорогу мне торную
Там, где нету пути человеку,
Дай назвать моим именем черную
До сих пор неоткрытую реку.

И последнюю милость, с которою
Отойду я в селенья святые, —
Дай скончаться под той сикоморою,
Где с Христом отдыхала Мария.

1918

ЛЕС

В том лесу белесоватые стволы
Выступали неожиданно из мглы,

Из земли за корнем корень выходил,
Точно руки обитателей могил.

Под покровом ярко-огненной листвы
Великаны жили, карлики и львы,

И следы в песке видали рыбаки
Шестипалой человеческой руки.

Никогда сюда тропа не завела
Пэра Франции иль Круглого Стола,

И разбойник не гнездился здесь в горах,
И пещерки не выкапывал монах.

Только раз отсюда в вечер грозовой
Вышла женщина с кошачьей головой,

Но в короне из литого серебра,
И вздыхала и стонала до утра,

For this service give me a smooth pathway
Which a man cannot travel or see,
Or else grant me a black, unknown river
Which will someday be named after me.

One more favor is all I beg of you,
And I'll reach holy camp blessed and spiced:
Let me die neath a sycamore's branches –
That tree where Mary rested with Christ.

THE FOREST

In the forest tree trunks with their whitish bark
Stood out unexpectedly in that deep dark.

Rank root after root came crawling from the earth,
Like the arms of those stretched out in their grave's berth.

Giants, dwarfs and even lions lived beneath
Its bright flaming cover of branch, bloom, and leaf.

And the fishermen discovered on the sand
The strange print of a six-fingered human hand.

Good King Arthur's men had never borne the lance
Through those pathways; neither had the Knights of France.

Robbers never lurked behind the underbrush;
Hermits never dug caves in its lonely hush.

But one time upon a stormy night appeared
Some mysterious woman with her cat-head reared...

And she had a crown of casted silver on!
She continued moaning, sighing until dawn

И скончалась тихой смертью на заре
Перед тем, как дал причастье ей кюрэ.

Это было, это было в те года,
От которых не осталось и следа,

Это было, это было в той стране,
О которой не загрезишь и во сне.

Я придумал это, глядя на твои
Косы, кольца огневеющей змеи,

На твои зеленоватые глаза,
Как персидская больная бирюза.

Может быть, тот лес – душа твоя,
Может быть, тот лес – любовь моя, –

Или может быть, когда умрем,
Мы в тот лес направимся вдвоем.

(1921)

СЛОВО

В оный день, когда над миром новым
Бог склонял лицо Свое, тогда
Солнце останавливали словом,
Словом разрушали города.

И орел не взмахивал крылами,
Звезды жались в ужасе к луне,
Если, точно розовое пламя,
Слово проплывало в вышине.

And with morning peaceful death came and she went,
Went before the priest gave the last sacrament.

All of this took place, took place in years long past,
So long past that not a trace remained to last.

All of this took place, took place within a land
Which one would not dream in dreams – or understand.

I made it all up, while looking at your braids,
Two flamboyant snakes – in fiery glissades.

Looking deep into your sick-green turquoise eyes,
Like a pair of Persian gems which hypnotize.

Perhaps this is true: that forest is your soul.
Or that forest is our love which I extoll.

Or, perhaps that forest is where you and I
Will go, both of us, at that hour when we die.

THE WORD

In those primal days when God Almighty
Bent His face over the fresh world – then
The word made the sun stand still in heaven,
The word tore apart the towns of men.

And when the word – like a pink flame burning –
Floated freely in the highest flight,
Eagles did not stir their wings or flutter
And the stars crouched toward the moon in fright.

А для низкой жизни были числа,
Как домашний, подъяремный скот,
Потому что все оттенки смысла
Умное число передает.

Патриарх седой, себе под руку ·
Покоривший и добро и зло,
Не решаясь обратиться к звуку,
Тростью на песке чертил число.

Но забыли мы, что осиянно
Только слово средь земных тревог,
И в Евангельи от Иоанна
Сказано, что слово это Бог.

Мы ему поставили пределом
Скудные пределы естества,
И, как пчелы в улье опустелом,
Дурно пахнут мертвые слова.

(1921)

ШЕСТОЕ ЧУВСТВО

Прекрасно в нас влюбленное вино
И добрый хлеб, что в печь для нас садится,
И женщина, которою дано,
Сперва измучившись, нам насладиться.

Но что нам делать с розовой зарей
Над холодеющими небесами,
Где тишина и неземной покой,
Что делать нам с бессмертными стихами?

Ни съесть, ни выпить, ни поцеловать.
Мгновение бежит неудержимо,

Those on lower planes were given numbers –
Like domestic cattle under yoke;
For all shades of meaning can be rendered
By sagacious numbers at one stroke.

And the hoary patriarch is bringing
Both evil and good neath his command;
Not prone to turn to the sound, he sketches
Numbers with his cane upon the sand.

We forget that just the word is haloed
Here where earthly cares leave us perplexed.
In the Gospel of St John is written
That the word is God: that is the text.

We have put a limit to its meaning:
Only to *this* life, this shallow shell.
And like bees in an abandoned beehive,
Dead, deserted words have a bad smell.

SIXTH SENSE

O beautiful the wine in love with us!
The good bread in the oven – for us baking!
And that woman, who gave torment and fuss,
Whom now we can enjoy – for just the taking!

But what to do with this rose sunset over
A sky becoming cold as hues disperse,
Where silence and unearthly calm still hover,
What should we do with our immortal verse?

You can't eat, drink, or kiss sunsets or lines...
The moment runs unchecked and we, hand-wringing,

И мы ломаем руки, но опять
Осуждены идти все мимо, мимо.

Как мальчик, игры позабыв свои,
Следит порой за девичьим купаньем
И, ничего не зная о любви,
Все ж мучится таинственным желаньем;

Как некогда в разросшихся хвощах
Ревела от сознания бессилья
Тварь скользкая, почуя на плечах
Еще не появившиеся крылья, –

Так век за веком – скоро ли, Господь? –
Под скальпелем природы и искусства
Кричит наш дух, изнемогает плоть,
Рождая орган для шестого чувства.

(1921)

ЗАБЛУДИВШИЙСЯ ТРАМВАЙ

Шел я по улице незнакомой
И вдруг услышал вороний грай,
И звоны лютни, и дальние громы –
Передо мною летел трамвай.

Как я вскочил на его подножку,
Было загадкою для меня,
В воздухе огненную дорожку
Он оставлял и при свете дня.

Мчался он бурей темной, крылатой,
Он заблудился в бездне времен...
'Остановите, вагоновожатый,
Остановите сейчас вагон!'

Are still condemned to overlook the signs
And somehow miss the mark – with our wide swinging.

Just as a boy sometimes watching girls bathing
(Having forgotten all about his games,
Yet innocent of love and love's behaving)
Is tortured by a strange desire's flames;

Just as that slippery creature at one time,
Feeling still-unformed wings upon his shoulders,
Roared out his sense of helplessness through slime
And geologic giant ferns and boulders –

So century on century (Lord, quickly?)
Beneath nature and art's knife our intense
Spirit cries out, our flesh grows faint and sickly –
Trying to birth organs for our sixth sense.

THE LOST STREETCAR

I was walking along the street as a stranger
And suddenly heard the cawing of crows,
The playing of lutes and distant thunder...
Before me a rushing streetcar arose.

How I managed to jump on the step as it passed me
Has remained a riddle to this day,
For it left a path in the air that was flaming
Even in daylight as it went its way.

It rushed like a storm that was dark and wingéd,
Lost in the depths of time somehow.
Stop the streetcar! Stop, stop, driver!
Stop the streetcar! Stop right now!

Поздно. Уж мы обогнули стену,
Мы проскочили сквозь рощу пальм,
Через Неву, через Нил и Сену
Мы прогремели по трем мостам.

И, промелькнув у оконной рамы,
Бросил нам вслед пытливый взгляд
Нищий старик, – конечно, тот самый,
Что умер в Бейруте год назад.

Где я? Так томно и так тревожно
Сердце мое стучит в ответ:
'Видишь вокзал, на котором можно
В Индию Духа купить билет?'

Вывеска... кровью налитые буквы
Гласят – зеленная, – знаю, тут
Вместо капусты и вместо брюквы,
Мертвые головы продают.

В красной рубашке, с лицом как вымя,
Голову срезал палач и мне,
Она лежала вместе с другими
Здесь, в ящике скользком, на самом дне.

А в переулке забор дощатый,
Дом в три окна и серый газон...
'Остановите, вагоновожатый,
Остановите сейчас вагон!'

Машенька, ты здесь жила и пела,
Мне, жениху, ковер ткала,
Где же теперь твой голос и тело,
Может ли быть, что ты умерла!

Как ты стонала в своей светлице,
Я же с напудренной косой

Too late. We had passed the wall already,
Slipped through the grove where the palm trees toss,
The Neva, the Nile, the Seine beneath us,
Three bridges we thundered across.

The face of an old beggar flashed past the window,
And his glance studied us, following us from the rear . . .
The same man, of course, the very same beggar,
Who died in Beirut sometime last year.

Where am I? My heart beats in replying
(Filled with a languor and care past control).
Do you see a station in which one can purchase
A ticket to the India of the soul?

Signboard . . . And the VEGETABLE SHOP letters
Are painted with blood. I know here instead
Of cabbages, instead of rutabagas,
They sell only heads that are dead.

A man in a red shirt, face like an udder,
Cuts my head off too on the blocks.
It is lying together with the others
On the very bottom in a slippery box.

And there is a board fence in the alley,
A house with three windows and a lawn grown gray.
Stop the streetcar! Stop, stop, driver!
Stop the streetcar right away!

Now, Mashenka, you lived and sang here,
Wove carpets for me, the man you would wed.
Where now then is your voice and body?
Is it conceivable you are dead?

How you cried in your room so tiny!
And I in a powdered wig at the door

Шел представляться Императрице,
И не увиделся вновь с тобой.

Понял теперь я: наша свобода
Только оттуда бьющий свет,
Люди и тени стоят у входа
В зоологический сад планет.

И сразу ветер знакомый и сладкий,
И за мостом летит на меня
Всадника длань в железной перчатке
И два копыта его коня.

Верной твердынею православья
Врезан Исакий в вышине,
Там отслужу молебен о здравье
Машеньки и панихиду по мне.

И все ж навеки сердце угрюмо,
И трудно дышать, и больно жить...
Машенька, я никогда не думал,
Что можно так любить и грустить.

(1921)

МОИ ЧИТАТЕЛИ

Старый бродяга в Аддис-Абебе,
Покоривший многие племена,
Прислал ко мне черного копьеносца
С приветом, составленным из моих стихов.
Лейтенант, водивший канонерки
Под огнем неприятельских батарей,
Целую ночь над южным морем
Читал мне на память мои стихи.
Человек, среди толпы народа

Was going to be presented to the Empress.
And I never saw you anymore.

I understand it now: Our freedom
Is only a light striking us from out-there.
People and spirits stand at the entrance
To a zoological garden of planets somewhere.

The sweet and familiar wind comes swiftly –
And across the bridge toward me full force
Flies the iron-gloved hand of the rider
– And two hoofs of his rearing horse.

The faithful fortress of orthodoxy,
Saint Isaac's, rises heavenly.
There I'll say a prayer for the health of Mashenka
And a simple 'Rest in peace' for me.

To breathe is hard; to live is painful...
My desolate heart is forever sad.
Mashenka, I never thought it possible
To love one so much and to feel so bad.

MY READERS

The old vagabond in Addis Ababa,
Who conquered many tribes,
Sent me one of his black lancers
Greeting me with my own poetry.
A lieutenant, who used to lead gunboats
Under enemy fire,
Recited my poems to me all through the night
Upon the southern sea.
A man, who midst a crowd had shot

Застреливший императорского посла,
Подошел пожать мне руку,
Поблагодарить за мои стихи.

Много их, сильных, злых и веселых,
Убивавших слонов и людей,
Умиравших от жажды в пустыне,
Замерзавших на кромке вечного льда,
Верных нашей планете,
Сильной, веселой и злой,
Возят мои книги в седельной сумке,
Читают их в пальмовой роще,
Забывают на тонущем корабле.

Я не оскорбляю их неврастенией,
Не унижаю душевной теплотой,
Не надоедаю многозначительными намеками
На содержимое выеденного яйца.
Но когда вокруг свищут пули,
Когда волны ломают борта,
Я учу их, как не бояться,
Не бояться и делать, что надо.
И когда женщина с прекрасным лицом,
Единственно дорогим во вселенной,
Скажет: 'Я не люблю вас', –
Я учу их, как улыбнуться,
И уйти, и не возвращаться больше.

А когда придет их последний час,
Ровный красный туман застелет взоры,
Я научу их сразу припомнить
Всю жестокую, милую жизнь,
Всю родную, странную землю,
И, представ перед ликом Бога
С простыми и мудрыми словами,
Ждать спокойно Его суда.

(1921)

The Emperor's ambassador,
Came up to shake my hand,
To thank me for my verse.

Many of them – strong, wicked and gay –
Who killed elephants and people,
Who died of thirst in the desert,
Who froze on a polar ice-floe,
Loyal to our planet
(Strong, gay and wicked),
Carry my books in a saddlebag,
Read them in groves of palm trees
And abandon them with the ship.

I don't offend them with hypertensions,
Or humiliate them with too much heart,
Don't bug them with vital allusions
To the contents of an empty shell.
But when bullets whistle by,
When waves break the sides of the ship,
I teach them not to fear,
Not to fear and to do their job.
And when a woman with a beautiful face,
The only dear face in the world,
Says, 'I don't love you',
I teach them to smile,
To leave her and never go back.

And when the last hour comes,
When the red, even mist films their eyes,
I will teach them to recall quickly
Their entire pleasant-cruel life
And all their own, strange earth...
And when standing before God's face
To await calmly His Judgement
With simple, wise words.

АННА АХМАТОВА
(АННА АНДРЕЕВНА ГОРЕНКО)
1889 - 1966

ПУШКИН

Смуглый отрок бродил по аллеям
У озерных глухих берегов.
И столетие мы лелеем
Еле слышный шелест шагов.

Иглы сосен густо и колко
Устилают низкие пни...
Здесь лежала его треуголка
И растрепанный том Парни.

1911

ПЕСНЯ ПОСЛЕДНЕЙ ВСТРЕЧИ

Так беспомощно грудь холодела.
Но шаги мои были легки.
Я на правую руку надела
Перчатку с левой руки.

Показалось, что много ступеней,
А я знала – их только три!
Между кленов шопот осенний
Попросил: 'Со мною умри!

Я обманут моей унылой,
Переменчивой, злой судьбой.'

ANNA AKHMATOVA
(ANNA ANDREYEVNA GORENKO)
1889 - 1966

PUSHKIN

A swarthy young boy lolled down pathways
By himself at the edge of the lake.
For a hundred long years we have cherished
The slight rustle his far footsteps make.

The thick, prickly fir-needles pile up
Above the low stumps of each tree...
Here's his three-cornered hat and a dog-eared
Volume of verse by Parny.

SONG OF THE LAST MEETING

I was helpless and my breast was freezing,
But I walked and my footsteps were light.
And the glove that was meant for my left hand
I unthinkingly put on my right.

And it seemed there were so many steps then,
But I knew there were only three!
In the maple trees there was the whisper
Of autumn that said, 'Die with me.

For I've been deceived by a whimsy
Called Fate – sad, wicked, untrue.'

Я ответила: 'Милый, милый!
И я тоже. – Умру с тобой . . . '

Это песня последней встречи.
Я взглянула на темный дом.
Только в спальне горели свечи
Равнодушно-желтым огнем.

1911

МУЗЕ

Муза сестра заглянула в лицо,
Взгляд ее ясен и ярок,
И отняла золотое кольцо,
Первый весенний подарок.

Муза! ты видишь, как счастливы все –
Девушки, женщины, вдовы,
Лучше погибну на колесе,
Только не эти оковы.

Знаю: гадая, не мне обрывать
Нежный цветок маргаритку,
Должен на этой земле испытать
Каждый любовную пытку.

Жгу до зари на окошке свечу
И ни о ком не тоскую,
Но не хочу, не хочу, не хочу
Знать, как целуют другую.

Завтра мне скажут, смеясь, зеркала:
'Взор твой не ясен, не ярок . . . '
Тихо отвечу: 'Она отняла
Божий подарок.'

(1911)

I answered, 'I've been deceived also,
My dear, and I'll die with you.'

This: the song of our last meeting...
I looked back at the dark house's frame;
In the bedroom the candles were burning
An indifferent, yellowed flame.

TO MY MUSE

My sister Muse peered into my face;
Her eyes were clear and bright-shining.
And she took back the ring of pure gold –
Spring's first gift thereby reclaiming.

Muse, see how happy everyone is –
Young girls and women and widows.
Better to suffer and die on the rack
Rather than here in these shackles.

I know I can't know what's going to be:
Petals from daisies won't clue us.
And we all have to experience pain
That love on this earth brings to us.

I burn a light in my window till dawn,
And there is no one I'm missing.
But I don't want, I don't want to know how
Another is kissed or is kissing.

Mirrors tomorrow will laughingly say:
'Your eyes are not clear and bright, dear...'
I'll answer softly, 'She took away
God's gift I prized dear.'

ОН ЛЮБИЛ

Он любил три вещи на свете:
За вечерней пенье, белых павлинов
И стертые карты Америки.
Не любил, когда плачут дети,
Не любил чая с малиной
И женской истерики.
. . . А я была его женой.

(1912)

* * *

Слаб голос мой, но воля не слабеет.
Мне даже легче стало без любви.
Высоко небо, горный ветер веет,
И непорочны помыслы мои.

Ушла к другим бессонница-сиделка,
Я не томлюсь над серою золой,
И башенных часов кривая стрелка
Смертельной мне не кажется стрелой.

Так прошлое над сердцем власть теряет.
Освобожденье близко. Все прощу,
Следя, как луч взбегает и сбегает
По влажному весеннему плющу.

1912

HE DID LOVE...

He did love three things in this world:
Choir chants at vespers, albino peacocks,
And worn, weathered maps of America.
And he did not love children crying,
Or tea served with raspberries,
Or woman's hysteria.
... And I was his wife.

* * *

My voice is weak, but my will does not weaken;
And without love I somehow feel relieved.
The sky is high, the wind blows from the headlands,
My thoughts and plans are chaste, purely conceived.

Insomnia, my bed-nurse, went to others.
Gray ashes... But no sighs for 'used to be'.
And those curved hands on that clock in the tower
Do not seem poisoned arrows aimed at me.

So in my heart the past loses its power;
I'm almost free; I'll forgive anything
Watching the sunrays leaping helter-skelter
Along the dew-damp ivy in the Spring.

Все мы бражники здесь, блудницы.
Как невесело вместе нам!
На стенах цветы и птицы
Томятся по облакам.

Ты куришь черную трубку,
Так странен дымок над ней.
Я надела узкую юбку,
Чтоб казаться еще стройней.

Навсегда забиты окошки.
Что там – изморозь иль гроза?
На глаза осторожной кошки
Похожи твои глаза.

О, как сердце мое тоскует!
Не смертного ль часа жду?
А та, что сейчас танцует,
Непременно будет в аду.

1 января 1913

★　★　★

Не любишь, не хочешь смотреть?
О, как ты красив, проклятый!
И я не могу взлететь,
А с детства была крылатой.
Мне очи застит туман,
Сливаются вещи и лица,
И только красный тюльпан,
Тюльпан у тебя в петлице.

1913

CABARET ARTISTIQUE

We are all here carousers and harlots.
What a dismal and unhappy crowd!
On the walls the birds and the flowers
Seem to yearn and strain for a cloud.

You are smoking away on a black pipe
With the hovering smoke strange and dim.
And I wear a skirt that is narrow
To make *me* seem even more slim.

The windows are covered completely.
What's outside – frost or storm? Tell me that.
Your eyes seem to have the appearance
Of the eyes of a cautious cat.

Oh, my heart is so sad in its anguish!
Am I here waiting for the death bell?
And that woman right there who is dancing
Is certainly going to hell.

1 January 1913

★   ★   ★

You don't love me, you don't look at me!
Oh, you devil, you're a handsome thing!
And I simply can soar no more –
Though from childhood I've had wings.
A mist overfloods my eyes;
Things and faces blur and swell...
And only the red tulip,
The red tulip in your lapel.

Вижу выцветший флаг над таможней
И над городом желтую муть.
Вот уж сердце мое осторожней
Замирает, и больно вздохнуть.

Стать бы снова приморской девчонкой,
Туфли на босу ногу надеть,
И закладывать косы коронкой,
И взволнованным голосом петь.

Все глядеть бы на смуглые главы
Херсонесского храма с крыльца,
И не знать, что от счастья и славы
Безнадежно дряхлеют сердца.

1913

*   *   *

Вечерние часы перед столом.
Непоправимо белая страница.
Мимоза пахнет Ниццей и теплом,
В луче луны летит большая птица.

И, туго косы на ночь заплетя,
Как будто завтра нужны будут косы,
В окно гляжу я, больше не грустя,
На море, на песчаные откосы.

Какую власть имеет человек,
Который даже нежности не просит!
Я не могу поднять усталых век,
Когда мое он имя произносит.

Лето 1913

Faded flag on the customs building
And the town's yellow haze lazing by . . .
And my heart stops, grown suddenly cautious,
Much too pained to make even a sigh.

O, to be a small girl by the seaside,
To wear shoes on bare feet as my choice,
And to put up my braids in a chignon,
And to sing in an excited voice.

And to look and look long at the swarthy
Chersonese temple tops from my door,
And not know being happy and famous
Only ages the heart even more.

* * *

The hours of evening . . . I am at my desk:
An uncorrectable page – blank and white.
Mimosa smells of Nice and southern warmth,
And a big bird flies on a beam of light.

And having wound my braids tight for the night
(As if I needed any braids tomorrow),
I look out through the window at the sea
And sandy slopes – with no more ache or sorrow.

How powerful a man is who does not
Demand even tenderness for his claim . . .
For I . . . I cannot raise my tired eyelids
Whenever I hear his voice speak my name.

Summer 1913

Цветов и неживых вещей
Приятен запах в этом доме.
У грядок груды овощей
Лежат, пестры, на черноземе.

Еще струится холодок,
Но с парников снята рогожа.
Там есть прудок, такой прудок,
Где тина на парчу похожа.

А мальчик мне сказал, боясь,
Совсем взволнованно и тихо,
Что там живет большой карась
И с ним большая карасиха.

1913

* * *

Я с тобой не стану пить вино,
Оттого что ты мальчишка озорной.
Знаю я – у вас заведено
С кем попало целоваться под луной.

А у нас тишь да гладь,
Божья благодать.

А у нас светлых глаз
Нет приказу подымать.

Декабрь 1913

The smell of objects not alive
And flowers brighten up this home.
Near flower-beds heaped vegetables
Lay different colors on black loam.

A slight chill still floats on the air;
The hotbed straw feels rake and spade.
There is a pond, a little pond,
Where algae scum spreads its brocade.

With fearful face a small boy told
Me these words, hushed and feverish:
'A great big carp lives down in there . . .
And with him is his big she fish.'

* * *

No, I will not drink wine with you,
Because you are such a wild and reckless son.
I know how you are and what you do:
In the moonlight you kiss any-, everyone.

At our place, peace reigns true,
Peace of God too.

And there none – commands one
To raise placid eyes to you.

December 1913

УЕДИНЕНИЕ

Так много камней брошено в меня,
Что ни один из них уже не страшен,
И стройной башней стала западня,
Высокою среди высоких башен.
Строителей ее благодарю,
Пусть их забота и печаль минует.
Отсюда раньше вижу я зарю,
Здесь солнца луч последний торжествует.
И часто в окна комнаты моей
Влетают ветры северных морей,
И голубь ест из рук моих пшеницу...
А недописанную мной страницу –
Божественно-спокойна и легка,
Допишет Музы смуглая рука.

1914

* * *

Лучше б мне частушки задорно выкликать,
А тебе на хриплой гармонике играть,

И уйдя, обнявшись, на ночь за овсы,
Потерять бы ленту из тугой косы.

Лучше б мне ребеночка твоего качать,
А тебе полтинник в сутки выручать,

И ходить на кладбище в поминальный день,
Да смотреть на белую Божию сирень.

1914

SOLITUDE

So many rocks have been hurled at me
That no one scares me now with hidden powers.
The trap became a graceful tower to see,
A tall one even here among tall towers.
I thank those who assisted in its making;
May care and sorrow pass them, every one.
Here I am with the first who see dawn breaking;
I triumph with the last rays of the sun.
And oftentimes winds from a northern sea
Fly through the windows of my room to me;
A dove eats wheat from my extended hand . . .
And as for those blank pages on my stand –
Divinely calm and delicate and light,
The dusky hand of my Muse comes to write.

★   ★   ★

I would rather shout out – a street-song quick and gay
And have you grab your grunty – accordion and play.

And go into the oat fields – and hold you through the night
And somehow lose a ribbon – from hair I've braided tight.

I'd rather rock your baby – my livelong life away
And wish that you were making – fifty cents a day.

And to the cemetery – on All Saints' Day we'd plod
And be content to look at – the white lilacs of God.

МОЛИТВА

Дай мне долгие годы недуга,
Задыханья, бессонницу, жар,
Отыми и ребенка, и друга,
И таинственный песенный дар.
Так молюсь за твоей литургией
После стольких томительных дней,
Чтобы туча над скорбной Россией
Стала облаком в славе лучей.

(1915)

*　*　*

Есть в близости людей заветная черта,
Ее не перейти влюбленности и страсти, –
Пусть в жуткой тишине сливаются уста,
И сердце рвется от любви на части.

И дружба здесь бессильна, и года
Высокого и огненного счастья,
Когда душа свободна и чужда
Медлительной истоме сладострастья.

Стремящиеся к ней безумны, а ее
Достигшие – поражены тоскою . . .
Теперь ты понял, отчего мое
Не бьется сердце под твоей рукою.

1915

PRAYER

Give me fever, insomnia, short-windedness,
Years of malady – bitter and long.
Take away my own child and my sweetheart
And the cryptic, divine gift of song.
During Thy Liturgy this I pray, Lord,
After so many harrowing days,
So that clouds which are darkening Russia
Will grow white in a burst of sun-rays.

★ ★ ★

With closest friends there is a secret line . . .
Passion and love can't cross it or deny it,
Although in anxious silence lips combine
And hearts are torn to pieces by love's riot.

Friendship is helpless here . . . So are the years
Of even a supreme, bright happiness . . .
When these, our souls, are free and foreigners
To the lazy languor of voluptuousness.

Those who strive for it are mad . . . And those who
Gain it are stricken by anguish and yearning.
Now you know why my heart which still loves you
Can never tremble under your hand's turning.

Под крышей промерзшей пустого жилья
Я мертвенных дней не считаю,
Читаю посланья Апостолюв я,
Слова Псалмопевца читаю.
Но звезды синеют, но иней пушист,
И каждая встреча чудесней, –
А в Библии красный кленовый лист
Заложен на Песни Песней.

1915

★ ★ ★

По твердому гребню сугроба
В мой белый, таинственный дом
Такие притихшие оба
В молчании нежном идем.
И слаще всех песен пропетых
Мне этот исполненный сон,
Качание веток задетых
И шпор твоих легонький звон.

Январь 1917

★ ★ ★

Теперь никто не станет слушать песен,
Предсказанные наступили дни.
Моя последняя, мир больше не чудесен,
Не разрывай мне сердца, не звени.

Еще недавно ласточкой свободной
Свершала ты свой утренний полет,
А ныне станешь нищенкой голодной,
Не достучишься у чужих ворот.

1917

Though roof is iced and house is empty
I do not count these lifeless days.
I read the books of the Apostles
And words of David's Psalms of praise.
The stars are blue, the frost is fluffy,
Each meeting marvelous to see...
And in *The Bible* one red maple
Leaf marks the Song of Songs for me.

* * *

Along the hard crest of a snowdrift,
Into my mysterious white house,
We two walk... grown suddenly quiet
In a tenderness such calm allows.
And sweeter than songs of my singing
Is this fulfilled dream that occurs:
The branches we brush by still swaying,
The soft, crystal clink of your spurs.

January 1917

* * *

Now no one listens to the songs or singing;
The days the prophets told about have come.
The world no more is wonderful. My last poem, ringing,
Don't tear my heart. Don't even dare to hum.

Till recently you were a swallow darting
Unfettered, free, across the morning air.
Now you'll become a beggar-woman, starving,
Knocking at gates, and no one will be there.

Когда в тоске самоубийства
Народ гостей немецких ждал,
И дух суровый византийства
От русской Церкви отлетал,
Мне голос был. Он звал утешно,
Он говорил: 'Иди сюда,
Оставь свой край глухой и грешный,
Оставь Россию навсегда.

Я кровь от рук твоих отмою,
Из сердца выну черный стыд,
Я новым именем покрою
Боль поражений и обид.'
Но равнодушно и спокойно
Руками я замкнула слух,
Чтоб этой речью недостойной
Не осквернился скорбный дух.

1917

* * *

И мнится – голос человека
Здесь никогда не прозвучит,
Лишь ветер каменного века
В ворота черные стучит.
И мнится мне, что уцелела
Под этим небом я одна, –
За то, что первая хотела
Испить смертельного вина.

1917

When in a suicidal anguish
People expected German guests
And that austere Byzantine spirit
Flew from the Russian Church, once blessed . . .
I heard a voice. It called to soothe me.
Consolingly, it said, 'Come here.
Leave your remote and sinful country.
Leave Russia now for good, my dear.

I'll wash your hands free of all bloodstains,
I'll rid your heart of this black shame.
And I'll conceal the pain of insults
And your defeats with a new name.'
But not caring to hear, I calmly
Shut my ears tight, a hand on each,
So that my saddened soul would not be
Profaned by this unworthy speech.

* * *

It seems no human voice will ever
Utter a sound here anymore.
Only the wind from some far Stone Age
Is knocking now at the black door.
It seems I am the last survivor
Beneath a sky incarnadine,
Because I was the first who wanted
To drink deeply this deadly wine.

Для того ль тебя носила
Я когда-то на руках,
Для того ль сияла сила
В голубых твоих глазах!
Вырос стройный и высокий,
Песни пел, мадеру пил,
К Анатолии далекой
Миноносец свой водил.

На Малаховом Кургане
Офицера расстреляли.
Без недели двадцать лет
Он глядел на Божий свет.

1918, Петербург

* * *

Чем хуже этот век предшествующих? Разве
Тем, что в чаду печали и тревог
Он к самой черной прикоснулся язве,
Но исцелить ее не мог.

Еще на западе земное солнце светит,
И кровли городов в его лучах блестят,
А здесь уж белая дома крестами метит
И кличет воронов, и вороны летят.

1919

Was this why I used to carry
You in my arms as my prize?
Was this why your strength and courage
Shone out of your bright blue eyes?
You grew up so tall and slender,
Sang songs, drank madeira toasts.
Your torpedo-boat sailed far-off
To the Anatolian coast.

On Malakhov hill there were
Shots that killed this officer.
He looked at God's world so old:
Less than twenty years all told.

1918, Petersburg

★   ★   ★

What makes this century worse than those that came before?
In fumes of care and sorrow that we feel
It penetrated to our deepest sore,
A wound so black it could not heal.

And still Earth's brilliant sun is shining in the West;
There, city roofs glisten with every ray.
Here, Death marks crosses on our homes. Obsessed,
She calls the ravens... and they're on their way.

Не бывать тебе в живых,
Со снегу не встать,
Двадцать восемь штыковых,
Огнестрельных пять.

Горькую обновушку
Другу шила я.
Любит, любит кровушку
Русская земля.

1914

МУЗА

Когда я ночью жду ее прихода,
Жизнь, кажется, висит на волоске.
Что почести, что юность, что свобода
Пред милой гостьей с дудочкой в руке.
И вот вошла. Откинув покрывало,
Внимательно взглянула на меня.
Ей говорю: 'Ты ль Данту диктовала
Страницы Ада?' Отвечает: 'Я.'

1924

You will no more be alive,
Rising from the snow;
Twenty-eight bayonet and five
Rifle holes now show.

Friend, I sewed with my own hand
Your last uniform.
Bitter cloth ... But Russia's land
Treasures blood still warm.

MUSE

When in the night I wait for her arrival,
My life seems hanging by the smallest hair.
For what are honors, youth, freedom, survival,
When such a guest, Pan's pipe in hand, is there!
And here she enters. Unveiled, she engages
Me with her eyes most scrutinizingly.
I speak to her: '*You* gave Dante the pages
Of the *Inferno*?' And she answers: 'Me.'

Мне ни к чему одические рати
И прелесть элегических страстей.
По мне в стихах все быть должно некстати,
Не так, как у людей.

Когда б вы знали, из какого сора
Растут стихи, не ведая стыда,
Как желтый одуванчик у забора,
Как лопухи и лебеда.

Сердитый окрик, дегтя запах свежий,
Таинственная плесень на стене...
И стих уже звучит задорен, нежен,
На радость вам и мне.

1940

ЭПИГРАММА

Могла ли Биче словно Дант творить,
Или Лаура жар любви восславить?
Я научила женщин говорить,
Но, Боже, как их замолчать заставить?

1960

I have no use for elegiac passion
Or for the grandeur of a classic ode.
In verse put things in some free, inapt fashion
And not by custom's code.

If you but knew from what trivial nonsense
Our poems grew... not knowing any shame,
Like yellow dandelions lining the fence,
Like burdock, goosefoot... Thus, they came.

A mad shout, the fresh smell of tar, mysterious
Mildew upon the wall... And poetry
Already sounds in lines – tender, delirious,
A joy to you and me.

EPIGRAM

Could Beatrice fashion such a work as Dante's,
Or Laura praise love's fever and love's chill?
I showed woman her voice and how to use it,
But, God, how can one teach her to be still?

ОСИП ЭМИЛЬЕВИЧ МАНДЕЛЬШТАМ
1891-1938

Звук осторожный и глухой
Плода, сорвавшегося с древа
Среди немолчного напева
Глубокой тишины лесной...

1908

* * *

Дано мне тело – что мне делать с ним,
Таким единым и таким моим?

За радость тихую дышать и жить
Кого, скажите, мне благодарить?

Я и садовник, я же и цветок,
В темнице мира я не одинок.

На стекла вечности уже легло
Мое дыхание, мое тепло.

Запечатлеется на нем узор,
Неузнаваемый с недавних пор.

Пускай мгновения стекает муть –
Узора милого не зачеркнуть.

1909

OSIP EMILYEVICH MANDELSTAMM
1891-1938

The cautious and the muffled sound
Of fruit – fresh fallen from a tree
Midst the unending melody
Of silence that the woods compound...

★　★　★

A body has been given me. Define,
What I should do with it, so whole, so mine.

For such a quiet joy – to breathe, to live,
Tell me, to whom should I my 'thank you' give?

A gardener, I, too, am flower grown.
In this world's dungeon I am *not* alone.

My breath, my warmth have settled certainly
Upon the great glass of eternity.

Lately unrecognizable, the bit
Of pattern will be imprinted on it.

And let the moment's muddledness expire –
That precious pattern cannot lose its fire.

О небо, небо, ты мне будешь сниться!
Не может быть, чтоб ты совсем ослепло
И день сгорел, как белая страница:
Немного дыма и немного пепла!

1911

* * *

Образ твой, мучительный и зыбкий,
Я не мог в тумане осязать.
'Господи!' – сказал я по ошибке,
Сам того не думая сказать.

Божье имя, как большая птица,
Вылетело из моей груди.
Впереди густой туман клубится,
И пустая клетка позади.

1912

NOTRE DAME

Где римский судия судил чужой народ –
Стоит базилика, и радостный и первый,
Как некогда Адам, распластывая нервы,
Играет мышцами крестовый легкий свод.

Но выдает себя снаружи тайный план:
Здесь позаботилась подпружных арок сила,
Чтоб масса грузная стены не сокрушила,
И свода дерзкого бездействует таран.

O Heaven-Sky, you'll come, you'll come returning!
You're not forever blind to sunlight's flashes,
Nor has day, like one white page, finished burning –
And left a little smoke, a little ashes!

★   ★   ★

I could not make out your vague and terror-
Bringing image in the fog's thick pall.
'Lord!' I spoke, but I spoke so in error,
Not intending to say that at all.

God's name, like a giant bird ascending,
Flew out of my chest – free, unconfined.
Before me the fog rolls – dense, unending...
And an empty cage remains behind.

NOTRE DAME

Where Roman judges tried an alien people
A basilica stands. Being first and joyful
(As Adam was once), stretching out its nerve-endings,
The vault, shaped like a cross, plays with its muscles.

Outside, the secret plan betrays its purpose:
For here the tightening arches' strength took measures
So walls would not be crushed by heavy masses,
So that the bold vault's rams would be more static.

Стихийный лабиринт, непостижимый лес,
Души готической рассудочная пропасть,
Египетская мощь и христианства робость,
С тростинкой рядом – дуб, и всюду царь – отвес.

Но чем внимательней, твердыня Notre Dame,
Я изучал твои чудовищные ребра,
Тем чаще думал я: из тяжести недоброй
И я когда-нибудь прекрасное создам.

1912

АМЕРИКАНКА

Американка в двадцать лет
Должна добраться до Египта,
Забыв 'Титаника' совет,
Что спит на дне мрачнее крипта.

В Америке гудки поют,
И красных небоскребов трубы
Холодным тучам отдают
Свои прокопченные губы.

И в Лувре океана дочь
Стоит, прекрасная как тополь;
Чтоб мрамор сахарный толочь,
Влезает белкой на Акрополь;

Не понимая ничего,
Читает 'Фауста' в вагоне
И сожалеет, отчего
Людовик больше не на троне.

1913

A primal labyrinth, an unknown forest,
A reasoned chasm of the Gothic Spirit,
Egyptian power with a Christian shyness,
Next to oaks, reeds – and the plumb, the king always.

And so the more attentively I studied
Your monstrous ribs, O Notre Dame, O fortress,
The more often I thought: I, too, from ugly
Harsh heaviness shall build a shining Beauty.

AN AMERICAN GIRL

American, twenty years old,
(Forgot what the *Titanic* told,
Sleeping below, dark as a crypt)
She's bound that she must reach Egypt.

America. The factory-whistles
Are singing. And the red skyscrapers
Watch their rising chimney tips
Give to the cold clouds their smudged lips.

The Louvre. Our daughter of the sea
Stands lovely as a poplar tree.
She climbs the Acropolis – a squirrel
That grinds away the sugared marble.

No meaning penetrates her brain,
But still she reads *Faust* on the train.
And she is sorry she must own
Louis is not now on the throne.

О временах простых и грубых
Копыта конские твердят
И дворники в тяжелых шубах
На деревянных лавках спят.

На стук в железные ворота
Привратник, царственно-ленив,
Встал, и звериная зевота
Напомнила твой образ, скиф!

Когда с дряхлеющей любовью,
Мешая в песнях Рим и снег,
Овидий пел арбу воловью
В походе варварских телег.

1914

*   *   *

Природа – тот же Рим и отразилась в нем.
Мы видим образы его гражданской мощи
В прозрачном воздухе, как в цирке голубом,
На форуме полей и в колоннаде рощи.

Природа – тот же Рим, и, кажется, опять
Нам незачем богов напрасно беспокоить:
Есть внутренности жертв, чтоб о войне гадать,
Рабы, чтобы молчать, и камни, чтобы строить!

1914

The hoofs of horses keep recalling
A time – rough, simple and remote...
So do the porters on their wooden
Benches, asleep in thick furcoats.

One, regal, lazy, hearing knocking
At an iron gate, got up. This man,
So animal-like in his yawning,
Brought back your image, Scythian,

When – full of aging love and mixing
Our snow and Rome in his song's parts –
Old Ovid sang of one ox-wagon
In campaigns with barbarian carts.

⋆   ⋆   ⋆

Nature equates with Rome – and is reflected in it.
We see its images of civic power revealed
In the transparent air as in blue Colosseums,
In columnades of groves, in the forum of a field.

Nature equates with Rome and it would seem to follow
We have no reason now to bother gods: from spilled
Entrails of sacrifices there is war predicted,
There are slaves to be silent – and stones from which to build!

Бессонница. Гомер. Тугие паруса.
Я список кораблей прочел до середины:
Сей длинный выводок, сей поезд журавлиный,
Что над Элладою когда-то поднялся.

Как журавлиный клин в чужие рубежи –
На головах царей божественная пена –
Куда плывете вы? Когда бы не Елена,
Что Троя вам одна, ахейские мужи?

И море, и Гомер – все движется любовью.
Кого же слушать мне? И вот Гомер молчит,
И море черное, витийствуя, шумит
И с тяжким грохотом подходит к изголовью.

1915

*　*　*

На розвальнях, уложенных соломой,
Едва прикрытые рогожей роковой,
От Воробьевых гор до церковки знакомой
Мы ехали огромною Москвой.

А в Угличе играют дети в бабки,
И пахнет хлеб, оставленный в печи.
По улицам меня везут без шапки,
И теплятся в часовне три свечи.

Не три свечи горели, а три встречи –
Одну из них сам Бог благословил,
Четвертой не бывать, а Рим далече, –
И никогда он Рима не любил.

Insomnia. Homer. And sails drawn tight.
I've read half-through the catalog of ships:
That long-extended flock, that flight of cranes
Which once rose over Hellas to the sky.

O, wedge of cranes, pointing to far-off lands
(These kings, heads covered with the gods' own foam),
Where are you sailing to? Were there no Helen,
Achaeans, then what would Troy be to you?

Both sea and Homer – all is moved by love.
Which one should I hear? Homer now is silent,
And the dark sea, declaiming, roars and comes
Close to my pillow with all thunder crashing.

★ ★ ★

Upon a wide sled full of fateful litter,
And hardly covered by matting and straw,
From Sparrow Hills to the familiar chapel
We ride along and enter great Moscow.

Children are playing knucklebones in Uglitch;
There is the smell of bread left in the stove.
They carry me along the street bareheaded,
And three candles burn in a church alcove.

Not three candles, but three meetings are burning;
And *one* was blessed by God Himself one day.
There'll be no fourth . . . and as to Rome Eternal,
He never liked it, and it's far away.

Ныряли сани в черные ухабы,
И возвращался с гульбища народ.
Худые мужики и злые бабы
Переминались у ворот.

Сырая даль от птичьих стай чернела
И связанные руки затекли;
Царевича везут, немеет страшно тело –
И рыжую солому подожгли.

1916

*　*　*

Мне холодно. Прозрачная весна
В зеленый пух Петрополь одевает,
Но, как медуза, невская волна
Мне отвращенье легкое внушает.
По набережной северной реки
Автомобилей мчатся светляки,
Летят стрекозы и жуки стальные,
Мерцают звезд булавки золотые,
Но никакие звезды не убьют
Морской волны тяжелый изумруд.

1916

TRISTIA

Я изучил науку расставанья
В простоволосых жалобах ночных.
Жуют волы, и длится ожиданье,
Последний час вигилий городских,

The sleigh dives in, out of black ruts and pitholes,
And people are returning home from fetes.
And scrawny men with their malicious women
Are fidgeting at doors and gates.

The distant, damp sky fills with flocks of black birds;
My tied hands have already gone to sleep.
The czarevitch is moved, my body deadens –
The red-haired straw ignites and the flames leap.

★ ★ ★

I'm cold. And everywhere transparent Spring
Clothes all Petropolis with fluffy green,
But these waves of the Neva only sting
Me with disgust – like jellyfish I've seen.
The fire-flies of cars dart flickeringly
Beside this northern stream along the quay.
Here dragonflies and steely beetles skimmer
And here the golden stickpins of stars glimmer,
But never can stars kill and put to grave
The heavy emerald of the sea-wave.

TRISTIA

I've learned the science of farewells – at night
When those unloosened-hair laments are wept.
The oxen chew; the waiting lasts – till light
Ends those long vigil hours the city kept.

И чту обряд той петушиной ночи,
Когда, подняв дорожной скорби груз,
Глядели вдаль заплаканные очи,
И женский плач мешался с пеньем муз.

Кто может знать при слове – расставанье,
Какая нам разлука предстоит,
Что нам сулит петушье восклицанье,
Когда огонь в акрополе горит,
И на заре какой-то новой жизни,
Когда в сенях лениво вол жует,
Зачем петух, глашатай новой жизни,
На городской стене крылами бьет?

И я люблю обыкновенье пряжи:
Снует челнок, веретено жужжит.
Смотри, навстречу, словно пух лебяжий,
Уже босая Делия летит!
О, нашей жизни скудная основа,
Куда как беден радости язык!
Все было встарь, все повторится снова,
И сладок нам лишь узнаванья миг.

Да будет так: прозрачная фигурка
На чистом блюде глиняном лежит,
Как беличья распластанная шкурка,
Склонясь над воском, девушка глядит.
Не нам гадать о греческом Эребе,
Для женщин воск, что для мужчины медь.
Нам только в битвах выпадает жребий,
А им дано гадая умереть.

1918

And I revere those night rites with cocks crowing,
When tear-red eyes, raising their load of long
Road sorrow, looked into the distance – flowing
A woman's weeping with the Muses' song.

Who knows what lies ahead with that 'farewell',
What kind of separation, and what this
First rooster's exclamation may foretell,
When the fire burns on the acropolis;
And at the dawn of some new life, new way,
While the ox chews lazily in his stall,
Why this same cock, herald of the new day,
Flaps loud his wings upon the city wall?

I love the regular routine of spinning:
The shuttle moves to, fro; the spindle hums...
Look, there is Delia – barefooted and grinning!
She flies toward you. And like swans down she comes!
O, how poor the language of joy and laughter,
That meager basic thread our lives invite!
All was before; all will repeat hereafter.
Only moments of knowing bring delight.

So be it: like a squirrel skin distending,
A small transparent figure lies
Upon a clean, clay platter. And there bending
Above the wax, a girl probes with her eyes.
We can't predict for the Greek Erebus;
Wax is for women what bronze is for men.
But where in battle our lot falls to us,
They die telling fortunes time and again.

Прославим, братья, сумерки свободы, –
Великий сумеречный год.
В кипящие ночные воды
Опущен грузный лес тенет.
Восходишь ты в глухие годы,
О солнце, судия, народ.

Прославим роковое бремя,
Которое в слезах народный вождь берет.
Прославим власти сумрачное бремя,
Ее невыносимый гнет.
В ком сердце есть, тот должен слышать, время,
Как твой корабль ко дну идет.

Мы в легионы боевые
Связали ласточек – и вот
Не видно солнца; вся стихия
Щебечет, движется, живет;
Сквозь сети – сумерки густые –
Не видно солнца и земля плывет.

Ну что ж, попробуем: огромный, неуклюжий,
Скрипучий поворот руля.
Земля плывет. Мужайтесь, мужи.
Как плугом, океан деля,
Мы будем помнить и в летейской стуже,
Что десяти небес нам стоила земля.

Май 1918, Москва

Brothers, let's glorify the twilight of freedom,
The great crepuscular year.
A heavy forest of nets has been dropped
Into the seething waters of the night.
You are rising during gloomy years,
O sun and judge, O people.

Let's glorify the destined burden
Which the people's leader tearfully assumes.
Let's glorify the sombre burden of power,
Its unbearable yoke.
He who has a heart, O time,
Must hear your ship sinking to the depths.

We have bound swallows
Into fighting legions, and now
We cannot see the sun; this entire element
Is chirping, stirring, living;
Through the mesh, the thick twilight,
We cannot see the sun and the land floats away.

Well then, let's try: an enormous, clumsy,
Creaking turn of the rudder.
The land floats away. Courage, men.
Cleaving the ocean as with a plow,
We shall remember even in Lethe's cold
That Earth cost us as much as ten heavens.

May 1918, Moscow

Сестры – тяжесть и нежность – одинаковы ваши приметы.
Медуницы и осы тяжелую розу сосут.
Человек умирает, песок остывает согретый
И вчерашнее солнце на черных носилках несут.

Ах, тяжелые соты и нежные сети,
Легче камень поднять, чем имя твое повторить!
У меня остается одна забота на свете:
Золотая забота, как времени бремя избыть.

Словно темную воду я пью помутившийся воздух.
Время вспахано плугом, и роза землею была.
В медленном водовороте тяжелые нежные розы,
Розы тяжесть и нежность в двойные венки заплела!

Март 1920, Коктебель

⋆ ⋆ ⋆

Веницейской жизни мрачной и бесплодной
Для меня значение светло.
Вот она глядит с улыбкою холодной
В голубое дряхлое стекло.

Тонкий воздух кожи. Синие прожилки.
Белый снег. Зеленая парча.
Всех кладут на кипарисные носилки,
Сонных, теплых вынимают из плаща.

И горят, горят в корзинах свечи,
Словно голубь залетел в ковчег.
На театре и на праздном вече
Умирает человек.

Sisters – heaviness and tenderness – your markings are the same.
Bees and wasps suck the heavy rose.
Man dies, the hot sand cools, and yesterday's sun
Is borne on a black stretcher to its repose.

O, heavy honeycomb and tender meshes –
It's easier to lift a stone than repeat your name!
How to free myself from the burden of time
Is my only aim in this world, a golden aim.

I drink the air as if it were dark water.
Time has been plowed; rose is earth underneath.
In slow whirlpools love weaves heavy and tender roses,
The heaviness and tenderness of the rose, into a double wreath!

March 1920, Koktebel

* * *

For me the meaning of Venetian life,
Sombre and sterile, is a flood of light.
Here she is – with a cool smile
Looking into the aged, blue glass.

The thin air of skin. Blue capillaries.
White snow. Green brocade.
And everyone is placed on cypress stretchers –
Warm and sleepy, taken out of a cloak.

And candles in the baskets are burning, burning –
As if a dove fluttered into the ark.
On the stages of theaters, in idle discussions –
Man dies.

Ибо нет спасенья от любви и страха:
Тяжелее платины Сатурново кольцо!
Черным бархатом завешанная плаха
И прекрасное лицо.

Тяжелы твои, Венеция, уборы,
В кипарисных рамах зеркала.
Воздух твой граненый. В спальне тают горы
Голубого дряхлого стекла.

Только в пальцах роза или склянка –
Адриатика зеленая, прости!
Что же ты молчишь, скажи, венецианка,
Как от этой смерти праздничной уйти?

Черный Веспер в зеркале мерцает.
Все проходит. Истина темна.
Человек родится. Жемчуг умирает.
И Сусанна старцев ждать должна.

1920

* * *

Чуть мерцает призрачная сцена,
Хоры слабые теней,
Захлестнула шелком Мельпомена
Окна храмины своей.
Черным табором стоят кареты,
На дворе мороз трещит,
Все космато – люди и предметы,
И горячий снег хрустит.

Понемногу челядь разбирает
Шуб медвежьих вороха.

For there is no escape from love and fear:
Saturn's ring is heavier than platinum!
The block draped with black velvet,
A beautiful face.

Venice, your garments are heavy,
Mirrors in cypress frames.
Your faceted air. Mountains of the aged,
Blue glass melt in the bedroom.

But your fingers hold a rose or a phial –
Farewell, green Adriatic!
Why then, Maid of Venice, are you silent?
How can one leave this festive death?

Black Hesperus glimmers in the mirror.
Everything passes. Truth is dark.
Man is born. Pearls die,
And Susanna must wait for the old men.

* * *

Now the ghostlike stage glows ever dimmer;
Feeble choirs of phantom-shapes...
And Melpomene swept out to trim her
Temple windows with silk drapes.
Black cabs stand like carts of gypsies camping;
Frost snaps up and down the street.
All is shaggy – objects, people, tramping,
Crunching hot snow neath their feet.

Slowly servants hand back furs, piled high there,
Bearskin coats warm for the snows.

В суматохе бабочка летает,
Розу кутают в меха.
Модной пестряди кружки и мошки,
Театральный легкий жар,
А на улице мигают плошки
И тяжелый валит пар.

Кучера измаялись от крика,
И храпит и дышит тьма.
Ничего, голубка Эвридика,
Что у нас студеная зима.
Слаще пенья итальянской речи
Для меня родной язык,
Ибо в нем таинственно лепечет
Чужеземных арф родник.

Пахнет дымом бедная овчина,
От сугроба улица черна,
Из блаженного певучего притина
К нам летит бессмертная весна,
Чтобы вечно ария звучала:
– Ты вернешься на зеленые луга,
И живая ласточка упала
На горячие снега.

1920

* * *

В Петербурге мы сойдемся снова,
Словно солнце мы похоронили в нем,
И блаженное бессмысленное слово
В первый раз произнесем.

In the bustle flies a butterfly there
And some furs enfold a rose.
Well-styled motley, insect-patterns splashing.
In the theater ... fevered air.
Outside in the dark are lanterns, flashing,
And the heavy fog floats everywhere.

Drivers are worn-out from shouts and snarling,
While the black night sleeps and snores.
O what care we, Eurydice, my darling,
If the wind of winter blows?
Sweeter than Italia's liquid singing
Is my own, my native tongue,
For in it the lisp of foreign harps comes springing,
Rippling strangely as it's sung.

In poor sheepskin wraps the smoke-smells grovel;
Streets grow dingy from the piled snow's muss.
From a far-off sacred and melodious hovel
Spring, eternal, faithful, flies to us.
To keep the aria forever ringing
You will come back when the green, green meadows grow.
For the swallow, once alive and winging,
Now lies on the white-hot snow.

★　★　★

We shall meet again in Petersburg,
As if that is where the sun's interred.
We shall utter then for the first time –
The blesséd, meaningless word.

В черном бархате советской ночи,
В бархате всемирной пустоты
Все поют блаженных жен родные очи,
Все цветут бессмертные цветы.

Дикой кошкой горбится столица,
На мосту патруль стоит,
Только злой мотор во мгле промчится
И кукушкой прокричит.
Мне не надо пропуска ночного,
Часовых я не боюсь:
За блаженное бессмысленное слово
Я в ночи советской помолюсь.

Слышу легкий театральный шорох
И девическое 'ах' –
И бессмертных роз огромный ворох
У Киприды на руках.
У костра мы греемся от скуки,
Может быть века пройдут,
И блаженных жен родные руки
Легкий пепел соберут.

Где-то хоры сладкие Орфея
И родные темные зрачки
И на грядки кресел с галлереи
Падают афиши-голубки.
Что ж, гаси, пожалуй, наши свечи,
В черном бархате всемирной пустоты
Все поют блаженных жен крутые плечи,
А ночного солнца не заметишь ты.

25 ноября 1920 – (1928)

In the black velvet of the Soviet night,
In the velvet of the world's empty room,
Dear eyes of the blesséd women are still singing.
Everlasting flowers are still in bloom.

The capital arches like a savage cat.
A patrol stands on the bridge nearby.
And an evil car speeds through the darkness,
Making its cuckoo-ing cry.
I don't need a pass this evening –
Sentries do not bring me fright:
For the sake of the blesséd, meaningless word,
I shall pray in the Soviet night.

I hear a light rustling in the theater
And a girl's excited 'Ah' – and then
A huge bunch of everlasting roses
Fills the arms of Venus once again.
Bored, we warm ourselves at some bonfire;
Maybe ages will pass, and the dear
Hands of the blesséd women
Will collect the light ashes here.

The sweet choirs of Orpheus and the dear, dark
Pupils of their eyes exist somewhere.
And the doves, programs, fall from the gallery
To the flower-beds of the parterre.
Well, blow out our candles if you want;
In the black velvet of the world's oblivion
Shoulders of the blesséd women are still singing;
But you will not notice the night sun.

25 November 1920 – (1928)

Editors' note: The second version of the poem is chosen here, but 'the Soviet night' is from the first version. Later, because of censorship, Mandelstamm changed it to 'the January night'.

Возьми на радость из моих ладоней
Немного солнца и немного меда,
Как нам велели пчелы Персефоны.

На отвязать неприкрепленной лодки,
Не услыхать в меха обутой тени,
Не превозмочь в дремучей жизни страха.

Нам остаются только поцелуи,
Мохнатые как маленькие пчелы,
Что умирают, вылетев из улья.

Они шуршат в прозрачных дебрях ночи,
Их родина – дремучий лес Тайгета,
Их пища – время, медуница, мята.

Возьми ж на радость дикий мой подарок,
Невзрачное сухое ожерелье
Из мертвых пчел, мед превративших в солнце.

Ноябрь 1920

*   *   *

Кому зима, арак и пунш голубоглазый,
Кому душистое с корицею вино,
Кому жестоких звезд соленые приказы
В избушку дымную перенести дано.

Немного теплого куриного помета
И бестолкового овечьего тепла;
Я все отдам за жизнь – мне так нужна забота –
И спичка серная меня б согреть могла.

O, joyfully take out of my palms
A little sun and honey as the bees
Of strict Persephone would bid you to.

One cannot untie the non-fastened boat,
One cannot hear the shadow shod in furs,
Nor overcome fear in this tangled life.

And only kisses still remain for us,
As fuzzy as the buzzing bees which die
As soon as they have left their warm beehive.

They rustle in the lucid groves of night;
Their homeland: the thick woods of Taygetos;
Their food consists of mint, lungwort and time.

So joyfully take my wildwood gift:
A simple, unpretentious dried necklace
Of dead bees that turned honey into sun.

November 1920

★　★　★

Some are given winter, arak and blue-eyed punch.
Others: fragrant wine with currants.
Still others, the salty decrees of cruel stars
Enforced even in smoky huts.

A little warm chicken droppings
And the heat of stupid sheep;
I would give everything for life; I need care so much;
Even a sulfur match could warm me.

Взгляни: в моей руке лишь глиняная крынка,
И верещанье звезд щекочет слабый слух,
Но желтизну травы и теплоту суглинка
Нельзя не полюбить сквозь этот жалкий пух.

Тихонько гладить шерсть и ворошить солому,
Как яблоня зимой в рогоже голодать,
Тянуться с нежностью бессмысленно к чужому
И шарить в пустоте, и терпеливо ждать.

Пусть заговорщики торопятся по снегу
Отарою овец, и хрупкий наст скрипит,
Кому зима – полынь и горький дым – к ночлегу,
Кому – крутая соль торжественных обид.

О если бы поднять фонарь на длинной палке,
С собакой впереди итти под солью звезд,
И с петухом в горшке прийти на двор к гадалке.
А белый, белый снег до боли очи ест.

1922

НАШЕДШИЙ ПОДКОВУ

Глядим на лес и говорим:
Вот лес корабельный, мачтовый,
Розовые сосны
До самой верхушки свободные от мохнатой ноши,
Им бы поскрипывать в бурю
Одинокими пиниями
В разъяренном безлесном воздухе;
Под соленою пятою ветра устоит отвес, пригнанный к пляшущей
                                                                палубе.
И мореплаватель,
В необузданной жажде пространства,
Влача через влажные рытвины хрупкий прибор геометра,

Look: In my hand is only a clay jar.
And the squeaking of stars tickles my failing ears.
But one cannot help loving, through this miserable fluff,
The yellow of grass and the warmth of clay.

To caress the wool softly and ted the straw,
To starve like an apple tree in winter wrapped in mattings,
To stretch tenderly and meaninglessly toward the alien,
To grope in the emptiness and to wait patiently.

Let the conspirators hurry along the snow
Like a herd of sheep, and the fragile crust crunches.
For some winter is wormwood and bitter smoke for refuge.
For others it is the hard salt of solemn offenses.

Oh, if I could raise a lantern on a long pole
And walk preceded by a dog beneath the salt of stars
And drop in – with a rooster in a pot – on a fortune-teller!
But the white white snow eats my eyes till they smart.

THE HORSESHOE FINDER

We look at a forest and we say:
Here is a forest – for ships, for masts,
Pink pine trees,
Free to the very top from their shaggy burden.
They should creak in a storm
As lonely piñons
In the angry, unforested air.
Under the salty heel of the wind the plumb remains adjusted to the
dancing deck...
And the seafarer,
In an unbridled thirst for space,
Dragging the delicate apparatus of a geometrist through the water-
troughs,

Сличит с притяженьем земного лона
Шероховатую поверхность морей.

А вдыхая запах
Смолистых слез, проступивших сквозь обшивку корабля,
Любуясь на доски
Заклепанные, слаженные в переборки
Не вифлеемским мирным плотником, а другим –
Отцом путешествий, другом морехода, –
Говорим:
И они стояли на земле,
Неудобной, как хребет осла,
Забывая верхушками о корнях,
На знаменитом горном кряже,
И шумели под пресным ливнем,
Безуспешно предлагая небу выменять на щепотку соли
Свой благородный груз.

С чего начать?
Все трещит и качается.
Воздух дрожит от сравнений.
Ни одно слово не лучше другого,
Земля гудит метафорой,
И легкие двуколки,
В броской упряжи густых от натуги птичьих стай,
Разрываются на части,
Соперничая с храпящими любимцами ристалищ.

Трижды блажен, кто введет в песнь имя;
Украшенная названьем песнь
Дольше живет среди других –
Она отмечена среди подруг повязкой на лбу,
Исцеляющей от беспамятства, слишком сильного одуряющего
Будь то близость мужчины,   [запаха –
Или запах шерсти сильного зверя,
Или просто дух чобра, растертого между ладоней.

Compares the gravity of the rough surface of the sea
With that of the lap of the earth.

And inhaling the smell
Of the resin tears seeping through the hull of the ship,
Admiring the boards,
Riveted, put into bulkheads,
Not by the peaceful carpenter of Bethlehem, but by another one,
Father of travels, friend of sailors,
We say:
They also stood on the land
(Uncomfortable as a donkey's backbone),
Their tops forgetting their roots,
On a celebrated mountain range,
And they moaned under the saltless downpour,
Unsuccessfully offering the sky their exalted load –
In exchange for a pinch of salt.

Where to begin?
Everything cracks and rocks.
The air trembles with similes.
No word is better than another;
The earth hums with metaphor.
And light, two-wheeled carts,
Swift-harnessed with thick-straining flocks of birds,
Break themselves to pieces,
Rivaling the hippodrome's snorting prancers.

Thrice-blessed is he who puts a name on a song!
The name-adorned song
Lives longer amid the others . . .
Among its companions it is marked by a headband,
Which heals the unconsciousness, from a stench which is too strong
Whether from the nearness of a man,   [and stultifying –
Or the smell of the fur of a strong beast,
Or simply the aroma of thyme rubbed between the palms.

Воздух бывает темным как вода, и все живое в нем плавает как
Плавниками расталкивая сферу,   [рыба,
Плотную, упругую, чуть нагретую –
Хрусталь, в котором движутся колеса и шарахаются лошади,
Влажный чернозем Нееры, каждую ночь распаханный заново
Вилами, трезубцами, мотыгами, плугами.
Воздух замешан так же густо, как земля, –
Из него нельзя выйти, в него трудно войти.
Шорох пробегает по деревьям зеленой лаптой;
Дети играют в бабки позвонками умерших животных.
Хрупкое летоисчисление нашей эры подходит к концу.
Спасибо за то, что было:
Я сам ошибся, я сбился, запутался в счете.
Эра звенела, как шар золотой,
Полая, литая, никем не поддерживаемая,
На всякое прикосновение отвечала 'да' и 'нет'.
Так ребенок отвечает:
'Я дам тебе яблоко', или: 'Я не дам тебе яблока.'
И лицо его точный слепок с голоса, который произносит эти
                                                    слова.

Звук еще звенит, хотя причина звука исчезла.
Конь лежит в пыли и храпит в мыле,
Но крутой поворот его шеи
Еще сохраняет воспоминание о беге с разбросанными ногами –
Когда их было не четыре,
А по числу камней дороги,
Обновляемых в четыре смены
По числу отталкиваний от земли пышущего жаром иноходца.

Так,
Нашедший подкову
Сдувает с нее пыль
И растирает ее шерстью, пока она не заблестит,
Тогда
Он вешает ее на пороге,

At times the air is muddled like water, and all living things swim in it
With fins elbowing the environment,   [like fish,
Dense, elastic, slightly heated –
A crystal in which wheels move and horses shy,
The moist loam of Neaira, tilled anew every night
By forks, tridents, hoes and plows.
The air is kneaded until thick as earth;
You cannot leave it, and entering it is difficult.
A rustle runs through the trees like a green ball game;
The children play knucklebones with the vertebrae of dead animals.
The fragile chronology of our time comes to an end.
Thanks for what once was:
I myself made a mistake, I am confused, I lost my count.
The era rang, like a golden globe,
Hollow, cast, supported by no one,
Responding to every touch with 'yes' and 'no' . . .
As a child answers:
'I'll give you an apple', or: 'I won't give you an apple.'
And his face is a precise mold of the voice that said these words.

The sound still rings, though the source of the sound is lost.
A horse lies in dirt and snorts in his foam.
But the sharp arch of his neck
Still keeps the memory of a race, with scattered legs,
When there were not four of them,
But as many as there were rocks on the road,
Refreshed in four shifts,
According to the number of the heat-glowing ambler's pushings-off
                                        from the ground

So
The horseshoe finder
Blows off the dust from it,
Rubs it with wool till it shines,
And then
Hangs it over the threshold,

Чтобы она отдохнула,
И больше уж ей не придется высекать искры из кремня.

Человеческие губы,
                    которым больше нечего сказать,
Сохраняют форму последнего сказанного слова,
И в руке остается ощущение тяжести,
Хотя кувшин
            наполовину расплескался,
                                пока его несли домой.
То, что я сейчас говорю, говорю не я,
А вырыто из земли, подобно зернам окаменелой пшеницы.
Одни
        на монетах изображают льва,
Другие –
        голову;
Разнообразные медные, золотые и бронзовые лепешки
С одинаковой почестью лежат в земле.
Век, пробуя их перегрызть, оттиснул на них свои зубы.
Время срезает меня, как монету,
И мне уж не хватает меня самого.

1923, Москва

ВЕК

Век мой, зверь мой, кто сумеет
Заглянуть в твои зрачки
И своею кровью склеит
Двух столетий позвонки?
Кровь-строительница хлещет
Горлом из земных вещей,
Захребетник лишь трепещет
На пороге новых дней.

So that it can rest
And no more have to strike the flint.

Human lips,
      which have nothing more to say,
Keep the shape of the last-said word,
And the hand retains the feeling of weight,
Though the pitcher
      is half-splashed away
          while being brought home.
What I now say, *I* do not say,
But it is grubbed out of the earth, like the grains of fossil wheat.
Some
     depict a lion on a coin,
Others –
     a head;
Various copper, gold and bronze tablets
With like honors lie in the earth.
The era, trying to gnaw them in two, left the marks of its teeth on them.
Time cuts *me* like a coin,
And I, even now, have not enough of myself.

1923, Moscow

MY AGE

My age, my beast, who will be able
To look into the pupils of your eyes –
And with his own blood cement
The vertebrae of two centuries?
Blood that builds gushes through the throat
Of things upon the earth;
Only a parasite trembles
On the threshold of new days.

Тварь, покуда жизнь хватает,
Донести хребет должна,
И невидимым играет
Позвоночником волна.
Словно нежный хрящ ребенка –
Век младенческой земли,
Снова в жертву, как ягненка,
Темя жизни принесли.

Чтобы вырвать жизнь из плена,
Чтобы новый мир начать,
Узловатых дней колена
Нужно флейтою связать.
Это век волну колышет
Человеческой тоской,
И в траве гадюка дышит
Мерой века золотой.

И еще набухнут почки,
Брызнет зелени побег,
Но разбит твой позвоночник,
Мой прекрасный жалкий век.
И с бессмысленной улыбкой
Вспять глядишь, жесток и слаб,
Словно зверь, когда-то гибкий,
На следы своих же лап.

1923

АРИОСТ

Во всей Италии приятнейший, умнейший,
Любезный Ариост немножечко охрип –
Он наслаждается перечисленьем рыб
И перчит все моря нелепицею злейшей.

A creature, as long as it has enough
Life left, must carry its backbone;
And any wave plays
With an invisible spine.
This age of the infant earth
Is like a baby's tender cartilage,
And once again the cranium of life
Has been sacrificed like a lamb.

In order to tear life out of captivity
And start a new world,
One must tie the knotty elbows
Of days together with a flute.
It is the age that rocks
The wave with human anguish,
And a viper in the grass
Breathes in gold measures of the age.

The buds will swell again,
And the green sprouts will burst.
But your spine has been shattered,
My beautiful, pitiful age.
And you look back, cruel and weak,
With a senseless smile,
Like a beast that was once supple,
At the tracks of your own paws.

ARIOSTO

The most intelligent, and the most pleasant man
In Italy, dear Ariosto has become
A little hoarse: he likes enumerating fish,
And peppers all seas with the worst absurdities.

И словно музыкант на десяти ццмбалах,
Не уставая рвать повествованья нить,
Ведет туда-сюда, не зная сам, как быть,
Запутанный рассказ о рыцарских скандалах.

На языке цикад – пленительная смесь
Из грусти пушкинской и средиземной спеси –
Он завирается, с Орландом куралеся,
И содрогается, преображаясь весь.

И морю говорит: шуми без всяких дум.
И деве на скале: лежи без покрывала.
Рассказывай еще – тебя нам слишком мало.
Покуда в жилах кровь, в ушах покуда шум...

О, город ящериц, в котором нет души –
Когда бы чаще ты таких мужей рожала,
Феррара черствая, – который раз с начала,
Покуда в жилах кровь, рассказывай, спеши.

В Европе холодно, в Италии темно,
Власть отвратительна, как руки брадобрея,
А он вельможится все лучше, все хитрее
И улыбается в крылатое окно

Ягненку на горе, монаху на осляти,
Солдатам герцога, юродивым слегка
От винопития, чумы и чеснока,
И в сетке синих мух уснувшему дитяти.

А я люблю его неистовый досуг –
Язык бессмысленный, язык солено-сладкий
И звуков стакнутых прелестные двойчатки,
Боюсь раскрыть ножом двустворчатый жемчуг.

And like a musician with ten cymbaloms to play,
Not being tired of tearing any story's thread,
Not knowing what to do, he leads us here and there
Through involved narratives about scandals of knights.

In the language of cicadas (a Pushkin sadness
Mixed charmingly with Mediterranean arrogance),
Forever telling lies, he plays pranks with Orlando,
And – being all transfigured – shudders afterwards.

And then he tells the sea: 'Roar on, but have no thoughts.'
And to the maiden on the rock: 'Lie there uncovered.'
Come, tell us more. We have too little of you, Sir,
While blood runs through the veins and sound rings in the ears . . .

O, city of lizards, that doesn't have a soul,
Hard Ferrara, if only you could birth such men
More often – Come, tell the story for the umpteenth time
From the beginning; hurry – while blood runs through the veins!

It is cold in Europe, dark in Italy.
Power is disgusting like a barber's hands,
And he grandees, better and shrewder, all the time
Smiling into the winged window, smiling then

At the lamb on the hill, at a monk on an ass,
At the Duke's hired mercenaries, slightly crazed
From bouts of wine-drinking and garlic and the plague,
And at the child asleep in a net of blue flies.

How I adore his furious pastime, yes, love
The nonsense language and the sweet and salty speech
And his enchanting doublets of colliding sounds, –
I'm afraid to pry the two-shelled pearl with my knife.

Любезный Ариост, быть может, век пройдет –
В одно широкое и братское лазорье
Сольем твою лазурь и наше черноморье...
... И мы бывали там. И мы там пили мед...

4-6 мая 1933, Старый Крым

* * *

Мы живем, под собою не зная страны,
Наши речи за десять шагов не слышны,
А где хватит на полразговорца, –
Там помянут кремлевского горца.

Его толстые пальцы, как черви, жирны,
А слова, как пудовые гири, верны.
Тараканьи смеются усища,
И сияют его голенища.

А вокруг его сброд толстокожих вождей,
Он играет услугами полулюдей,
Как подковы кует за указом указ –
Кому в лоб, кому в бровь, кому в пах, кому в глаз.

Что ни казнь у него, – то малина
И широкая грудь осетина.

1934

Dear Ariosto – maybe a whole century
From now, your azure and our own black sea-ness will
Dissolve into one broad and brotherly blueness
... Of course we were there, too. And there we all drank mead ...

4-6 May 1933, Old Crimea

* * *

We exist in a country grown unreal and strange;
No one ten steps away hears the talk we exchange.
But when chances for half-conversations appear,
We will never omit the Kremlin mountaineer.

Each thick finger, a fattened worm, gesticulates,
And his words strike you like they were many-pound weights.
His full cockroach mustache hints a laughter benigning,
And the shafts of his boots: always spotlessly shining.

And the gang of thick-skinned leaders near him obeys;
Semi-humans are at his disposal always.
Decree after decree he incessantly coins
Which hit people on foreheads, eyebrows, eyes and groins.

He possesses the broad chest, a Georgian perfection,
And each new death for him is a berry confection.

Не сравнивай: живущий несравним.
С каким-то ласковым испугом
Я согласился с равенством равнин,
И неба круг был мне недугом.

Я обращался к воздуху – слуге,
Ждал от него услуги или вести,
И собирался в путь, и плавал по дуге
Неначинающихся происшествий.

Где больше неба мне – там я бродить готов,
И ясная тоска меня не отпускает
От молодых еще воронежских холмов
К всечеловеческим – яснеющим в Тоскане.

16 марта 1937, Воронеж

Do not compare: the one alive is peerless,
Incomparable. With certain pleasant fright
I agreed with the plains' equality;
The sky's circle was my illness and blight.

I often turned to my servant, the air –
Awaiting news – or service on his part.
Preparing for a trip, I swam the arch
Of those adventures which would never start.

I'm set to roam where I'll have much more sky,
But that bright longing does not permit me,
To go from these still-young hills of Voronezh
To bright, all-human ones in Tuscany.

16 March 1937, Voronezh

ВЕЛИМИР ХЛЕБНИКОВ
(ВИКТОР ВЛАДИМИРОВИЧ ХЛЕБНИКОВ)
1885-1922

ТРУЩОБЫ

Были наполнены звуком трущобы,
Лес и звенел и стонал,
Чтобы
Зверя охотник копьем доканал.
Олень, олень, зачем он тяжко
В рогах глагол любви несет?
Стрелы вспорхнула медь на ляжку,
И не ошибочен расчет.
Сейчас он сломит ноги о земь
И смерть увидит прозорливо,
И кони скажут говорливо:
'Нет, не напрасно стройных возим.'
Напрасно прелестью движений
И красотой немного девьего лица
Избегнуть ты стремился поражений,
Копьем искавших беглеца.
Все ближе конское дыханье,
И ниже рог твоих висенье,
И чаще лука трепыханье,
Оленю нету, нет спасенья.
Но вдруг у него показалась грива
И острый львиный коготь,
И беззаботно и игриво
Он показал искусство трогать.
Без несогласья и без крика
Они легли в свои гробы,
Он же стоял с осанкою владыки –
Были созерцаемы поникшие рабы.

(1910)

VELIMIR KHLEBNIKOV
(VICTOR VLADIMIROVICH KHLEBNIKOV)
1885-1922

THICKET

The thickets were filled with sound thereat;
The woods were ringing – moaning near
So that
The hunter could do in the beast with his spear,
O deer, nice deer, why do you carry
The weight of love on your antlers?
The arrow's copper sought the haunch . . .
Yes, calculation never errs.
His legs will break beneath him shortly –
And he will sense his soon death plainly.
Horses will chatter, 'No, not vainly
Do we transport men, fine and portly.'
In vain but with such charming motion
And with the beauty of your virgin's face
You tried to dodge defeat – whose lance each place
Hunted you, fugitive, with such devotion.
Your antlers hang ever more low;
The horses' breathing comes still closer,
And there's more trembling of the bow . . .
The deer has no escape now. No, sir.
But all of a sudden a mane grew on him,
Each paw a lion's claw.
As if playing, nonchalantly,
He showed how touch is art and law.
With no discord and with no shout
They lay in coffins in their graves;
With sovereign's stance he stood about . . .
One could see almost everywhere the crest-fallen slaves.

ЗАКЛЯТИЕ СМЕХОМ

О, рассмейтесь, смехачи!
О, засмейтесь, смехачи!
Что смеются смехами, что смеянствуют смеяльно.
О, засмейтесь усмеяльно!
О, рассмешищ надсмеяльных – смех усмейных смехачей!
О, иссмейся рассмеяльно, смех надсмейных смеячей!
Смейево, смейево,
Усмей, осмей, смешики, смешики,
Смеюнчики, смеюнчики,
О, рассмейтесь, смехачи!
О, засмейтесь, смехачи!

(1910)

★ ★ ★

Слоны бились бивнями так,
Что казались белым камнем
Под рукой художника.
Олени заплетались рогами так,
Что, казалось, их соединял старинный брак
С взаимными увлечениями и взаимной неверностью.
Реки вливались в море так,
Что казалось: рука одного душит шею другого.

1911

INCANTATION BY LAUGHTER

O you laughniks, laugh it out!
  O you laughniks, laugh it forth!
You who laugh it up and down, laugh along so laughily;
  Laugh it off belaughingly!
Laughters of the laughing laughniks, overlaugh the laughathons!
Laughiness of the laughish laughers, counterlaugh the Laughdom's
  Laughio! Laughio!   [laughs!
  Dislaugh, relaugh, laughlets, laughlets,
    Laughulets, laughulets.
  O you laughniks, laugh it out!
  O you laughniks, laugh it forth!

             ★ ★ ★

The elephants were fighting with their tusks
And were white stone
Beneath a sculptor's hand.
The deer intertwined their antlers
United by an ancient marriage
With mutual attraction and unfaithfulness.
Flowing into the sea,
The hand of one river strangles the neck of another.

Бобэоби пелись губы
Вээоми пелись взоры
Пиээо пелись брови
Лиэээй пелся облик
Гзи-гзи-гзэо пелась цепь.
Так на холсте каких-то соответствий
Вне протяжения жило Лицо.

(1912)

* * *

Чудовище – жилец вершин,
С ужасным задом,
Схватило несшую кувшин,
С прелестным взглядом.
Она качалась точно плод
В ветвях косматых рук.
Чудовище, урод
Довольно, тешит свой досуг.

(1912)

* * *

Из отдыха и вздоха
Веселый мотылек
На край чертополоха
Задумчиво прилег.

Bo-bay-o-be, lips were singing.
Vay-ay-o-me, eyes were singing.
Pee-ay-ay-o, sang the forehead.
Lee-ay-ay-ay, sang the figure.
Gzee-gzee-gzay-o, sang the chain.
So on the canvas of some similitudes,
Beyond all spatial bounds there lived the FACE.

* * *

A monster with a horrid butt
Came from his peak to snitch her;
He seized the charming-eyed young girl
Packing a water pitcher.
On branches of his hairy arms
She dangles like a fruit,
And he is glad, enjoying himself,
That grotesque monster-brute.

* * *

All rest, all air, all flutter,
A merry butterfly,
Absorbed in thought, alighted
Close to a thistle's eye.

Летит его подруга
Из радуги и блеска,
Два шелковые круга,
Из кружева нарезка.
И юных два желанья,
Поднявшихся столбом,
Сошлися на свиданье
И тонут в голубом.
На закон меча намек
Этот нежный мотылек.
Ах, юнак молодой,
Дай тебе венок надену!
Ты забудешь разбой,
Ты забудешь измену.

(1912)

МРАЧНОЕ

Когда себе я надоем,
Я брошусь в солнце золотое,
Крыло шумящее одем,
Порок смешаю и святое.
Я умер, я умер, и хлынула кровь
По латам широким потоком.
Очнулся я, иначе, вновь
Окинув вас воина оком.

(1914)

КУРГАН

Копье татар чего бы ни трогало –
Бессильно все на землю клонится.
Раздевши мирных женщин догола,
Летит в Сибирь – Сибири конница.

His ladylove comes flying –
All color, rainbow, shine;
Two double silken circles
With laced escalloped line.
And then two youthful longings
Rise in a curlicue
And mating with each other
Vanish into the blue.
Does not the sword's law apply
To this gentle butterfly?
Let me crown you with wreaths,
O my good young man,
You'll forget your evil deeds,
You'll forget your evil plan.

SOMETHING GLOOMY

When I am fed up with myself,
I'll throw me to the golden sun,
I'll put on me a rustling wing,
I'll make sacred and evil one.
I'm dead, I'm dead, and like a wide stream
My blood is gushing on the armor.
I've woke up – I'm different, anew,
Scanning you with the eye of a warrior.

MOUND

All things that the Tartar lances touch
Sink down to the ground more sad and wearier.
Stripping the women bare they clutch,
The Siberian horsemen fly to Siberia.

Курганный воин, умирая,
Сжимал железный лик Еврея.
Вокруг земля, свист суслика, нора и –
Курганный день течет скорее.

Семья лисиц подъемлет стаю рожиц,
Несется конь, похищенный цыганом,
Лежит суровый запорожец
Часы столетий под курганом.

1915

            ★   ★   ★

Ни хрупкие тени Японии,
Ни вы, сладкозвучные Индии дщери,
Не могут звучать похороннее,
Чем речи последней вечери.
Пред смертью жизнь мелькает снова,
Но очень скоро и иначе.
И это правило – основа
Для пляски смерти и удачи.

(1916)

            ★   ★   ★

Весеннего Корана
Веселый богослов,
Мой тополь спозаранок
Ждал утренних послов.

The warrior, dying long ago,
Hugged the iron face of the Hebrew Master.
Round him dirt, burrows, whistling marmots, so
The day in the mound goes by faster.

Small muzzles of a pack of foxes rise;
A horse a gypsy stole tramples the ground;
The buried, stern cossack lies
For long centuries' hours beneath the mound.

* * *

Neither sweet-sounding maidens of India
Nor the fragile shadows of Japan
Can ever sound more funereal
Than the talk of one's last supper can.
Life flashes by before our dying,
But in a rapid, different glance.
And this rule is the base applying
When death and luck combine in dance.

* * *

The merry theologian
Of the Koran of Spring,
My poplar, was awaiting
The envoys of morning.

Как солнца рыболов,
В надмирную синюю тоню
Закинувши мрежи,
Он ловко ловит рев волов
И тучу ловит соню,
И летней бури запах свежий.
О тополь рыбак,
Станом зеленый,
Зеленые неводы
Ты мечешь столба.
И вот весенний бог
(Осетр удивленный)
Лежит на каждой лодке
У мокрого листа.
Открыла просьба: 'Небо дай' –
Зеленые уста.
С сетями ловли бога
Великий Тополь
Ударом рога
Ударит о поле
Волною синей водки.

1919

ЕДИНАЯ КНИГА

Я видел, что черные Веды,
Коран и Евангелие
И в шелковых досках
Книги монголов,
Сами из праха степей,
Из кизяка благовонного,
Как это делают
Калмычки каждой зарей, –
Сложили костер
И сами легли на него.

A fisher of the sun,
He throws nets to high fisheries,
Above the world,
And, clever, catches calls of oxen,
A cloud (that lazy girl),
And fresh smells of a summer storm.
O fisherman-poplar
With your green form,
You cast your green nets high
And far with your pole.
And here! A god of Spring
(A sturgeon in surprise)
Lies in the trembling boat
Of each wet leaf afloat.
The simple asking: 'give me sky'
Has opened your green lips.
With nets for god-hunting,
The Supreme Poplar,
With one horn bunting,
Will whack the field
With a wave of blue vodka.

THE ONE BOOK

I saw the black Veda,
The Koran and the Gospels,
And the book of the Mongols
Inside silk boards
Make themselves a bonfire
From the dust of the steppes,
From the incense cow-dung
(Which Kalmuk women fix at dawn)
And lie down on the flames.

Белые вдовы в облаке дыма скрывались,
Чтобы ускорить приход
Книги единой,
Чьи страницы большие моря,
Что трепещут крылами бабочки синей,
А шелковинка – закладка,
Где остановился взором читатель.
Реки великие синим потоком:
Волга, где Разину ночью поют,
Желтый Нил, где молятся солнцу,
Янцзекиянг, где жижа густая людей,
И ты, Миссиссипи, где янки
Носят штанами звездное небо,
В звездное небо окутали ноги,
И Ганг, где темные люди – деревья ума,
И Дунай, где в белом белые люди
В белых рубахах стоят над водой,
И Замбези, где люди черней сапога,
И бурная Обь, где бога секут
И ставят в угол глазами
Во время еды чего-нибудь жирного,
И Темза, где серая скука.
Род человечества – книги читатель.
И на обложке – надпись творца,
Имя мое, письмена голубые.
Да, ты небрежно читаешь,
Больше внимания,
Слишком рассеян и смотришь лентяем.
Точно уроки закона божия,
Эти горные цепи и большие моря.
Эту единую книгу
Скоро ты, скоро прочтешь.
В этих страницах прыгает кит,
И орел, огибая страницу угла,
Садится на волны морские, груди морей,
Чтоб отдохнуть на постели орлана.

1920

These white widows – flying off in smoke clouds
To speed the coming
Of the one book
Whose pages are large seas
Trembling like wings of a blue butterfly,
And a silken thread is the bookmark
Where the reader stopped his eyes.
Great rivers with their blue streams:
The Volga, where they sing nightsongs to Razin;
The yellow Nile, where they worship the sun;
The Yangtze, with its thick wash of people;
And you, Mississippi, where the Yankees
Wear the starry sky for their pants,
Wrapping their legs with that starry sky.
The Ganges, where brown people are trees of the mind;
The Danube, where white men
In white shirts stand over the water.
The Zambesi, with natives more black than a boot;
The stormy Ob, where they flog their gods
And put them with eyes facing the corner
When they eat something fattening.
And the Thames, where there is gray boredom.
The Breed of Man reads this book;
On the cover is an inscription by the creator:
My name in blue letters.
Yes, you have been reading carelessly.
Please pay more attention.
You are too absent-minded, and lazy, young man,
As if mountain-chains and large seas
Were your catechism lessons.
Soon, very soon you will read
This one book.
In its pages a whale leaps . . .
And an eagle, circumventing the page of the angle,
Alights on the waves, the breasts of the sea,
To rest on the sea-eagle's bed.

ИРАНСКАЯ ПЕСНЯ

Как по речке по Ирану,
По его зеленым струям,
По его глубоким сваям,
Сладкой около воды
Ходят двое чудаков
Да стреляют судаков.
Они целят рыбе в лоб,
Стой, голубушка, стоп!
Они ходят, приговаривают.
Верю, память не соврет.
Уху варят и поваривают.
'Эх, не жизнь, а жестянка!'
Ходит в небе самолет,
Братвой облаку удалой,
Где же скатерть-самобранка,
Самолетова жена?
Иль случайно запоздала,
Иль в острог погружена?
Верю сказкам наперед:
Прежде сказки – станут былью,
Но когда дойдет черед,
Мое мясо станет пылью.
И когда знамена оптом
Пронесет толпа, ликуя,
Я проснуся, в землю втоптан,
Пыльным черепом тоскуя.
Или все свои права
Брошу будущему в печку?
Эй, черней, лугов трава!
Каменей навеки, речка!

1921

IRANIAN SONG

All along the Iran River,
And along its greenish current,
All along piles deeply driven...
Loafing near by the sweet water,
Two eccentrics shoot at fish,
Wanting fried carp for a dish.
They aim right between the eyes.
Hold still, Lovely; you're a prize!
As they walk, they talk and whoop.
Sure, my memory prevails...
Then they boil their fish soup.
'Isn't this a lousy life?'
Now the magic rug (a plane,
Buddy to the clouds) flies by.
Where's the magic tablecloth,
Carpet-airplane's faithful wife?
Is it simply late in coming
Or is she somewhere in jail?
I believe each fairy tale;
Former fable: future fact.
But when life fulfills each pact,
My flesh will be dust and shale.
And when crowds in jubilation
Pass with flags, en masse, wholesale,
They'll wake me, in grave's depression,
Trampling on my dusty skull.
Since we're just fuel for the furnace
Of a future that will burn us,
Dry up, grasses of the meadow!
River, turn to stone forever!

Э - - э! ы - ым! весь в поту
Понукает вола серорогого,
И ныряет соха выдрой в топкое логово,
Весенний кисель жевали и ели зубы сохи.
Бык гордился дородною складкой на шее,
И рога перенял у юного месяца.
Жабы молились, работая в пузыри,
Толстый священник сидел впереди,
Глаза золотые на выкате,
И книгу погоды читал.
Черепахи вытягивали шеи, точно удивленные.
Весенних запахов и ветров пулемет
В нахмуренные лбы и ноздри
Стучал проворно ту-ту-ту.
Билися битвами запахов,
Цветы сражались пыльцой,
Кто медовее – будет тот победитель.
И давали уроки другой войны,
И запахов весенних пулемет,
И вечер точно первосвященник зари.
Битвами запаха бились цветы,
Летали душистые пули,
И было согласное и могучее пение жаб
В честь ясной погоды.
Люди, учитесь новой войне,
Где выстрелы сладкого воздуха,
Окопы из брачных цветов,
Медового неба стрельба, боевые приказы.
И вздымались молитвенниками
Богослужебные пузыри
У лягушек
Набожных тихой погоде.

(1921)

Eh! Eh! Oo - Oom! All covered with sweat,
He prods the gray-horned ox there,
And the plow dives like an otter in the swampy lair.
And the plow-teeth chew and eat the Spring pudding.
The ox was proud of his neck's bulky fold,
And he took his horns from a young moon.
The toads were in prayer, making bubbles;
A fat priest sat in the front
With his bulging gold eyes
Reading the weather-book.
Turtles stretched their necks, as if they were surprised.
The machine gun of Spring smells and winds
Rattled rapidly *ta-ta-ta-tat*
Into frowning foreheads and nostrils.
Flowers fought with their pollen...
Waging war in battles of fragrances
– And the most honeyed one the victor.
Here were lessons for a different war:
The machine gun of Spring perfumes,
With evening a high priest of the dusk.
The flowers fought battles of fragrances;
Aromatic bullets flew.
There were toads with concordant, strong singing
In praise of bright weather.
People, learn a new war –
Where the shots are those of sweet air,
Trenches dug from nuptial flowers.
Where cannonades and military orders
Bark from the honeyed sky,
And liturgical bubbles
Of frogs,
Worshipping the quiet weather,
Rise like psalters.

ИГОРЬ-СЕВЕРЯНИН
(ИГОРЬ ВАСИЛЬЕВИЧ ЛОТАРЕВ)
1887-1941

СОНАТЫ В ШТОРМ

На Ваших эффектных нервах звучали всю ночь сонаты;
А Вы возлежали в башне на ландышевом ковре...
Трещала, палила буря, и якорные канаты,
Как будто титаны – струны, озвучили весь корвет.
Но разве Вам было дело, что где-то рыдают и стонут,
Что бешеный шторм грохочет, бросая на скалы фрегат.
Вы пили вино мятежно, Вы брали монбланную ноту!
Сверкали агаты брошек, но ярче был взоров агат!

Трещала, палила буря. Стонала дворцовая пристань.
Кричали и гибли люди. Корабль набегал на корабль.
А вы, семеня гранаты, смеясь, целовали артиста...
Он сел за рояль, как гений, – окончил игру, как раб.

(1912)

ЮГ НА СЕВЕРЕ

Я остановила у эскимосской юрты
Пегого оленя, – он поглядел умно.
А я достала фрукты
И стала пить вино.

IGOR-SEVERYANIN
(IGOR VASILYEVICH LOTAREV)
1887-1941

SONATAS IN THE STORM

All night the sonatas sounded – upon your spectacular psyche.
You lounged in a tower on a rug where lilies of the valley were set.
The tempest was booming, cracking; the anchor ropes, stretched
tightly,
Resembling titanic strings, echoed back from the whole corvette.
But were you concerned that somewhere were moaning and sobs,
hand-wringing,
That there was a wild storm raging, crashing frigate against the shoals?
With passion you drank your wine and you hit a Mont Blanc note
singing!
Your broaches' bright agates shone but your dark agate eyes flamed
coals.

The storm kept on rumbling, thrashing. The palace wharf moaned in
submission.
And people were shouting, drowning. A ship jammed a ship
mid-wave.
De-seeding a ripe pomegranate, you laughed as you kissed the
musician...
He had started his piece – a genius; he had finished it your slave.

SOUTH IN THE NORTH

I stopped my piebald deer, who looked very astute,
Outside the igloo of an Arctic Eskimo,
And I took out some fruit
And began to drink Bordeaux.

343

И в тундре – вы понимаете? – стало южно...
В щелчках мороза – дробь кастаньет...
И захохотала я жемчужно,
Наведя на эскимоса свой лорнет.

(1912)

ШАМПАНСКИЙ ПОЛОНЕЗ

Шампанского в лилию! Шампанского в лилию! –
Ее целомудрием святеет оно.
Mignon с Escamillio! Mignon с Escamillio!
Шампанское в лилии – святое вино.

Шампанское, в лилии журчащее, искристо –
Вино, упоенное бокалом цветка.
Я славлю восторженно Христа и Антихриста
Душой, обожженною восторгом глотка!

Голубку и ястреба! Рейхстаг и Бастилию!
Кокотку и схимника! Порывность и сон!
В шампанское лилию! Шампанского в лилию!
В морях Дисгармонии – маяк Унисон!

Октябрь 1912

ДЫМ ЛЬДА

Под ветром лед ручья дымится,
Несутся дымы по полям.
Запорошенная девица
Дает разгон своим конькам.

And, you know, the tundra southerned then soon after...
In the frost clicks was the sound of exotic castanets,
     And with my pearled laughter
     I looked at the Eskimo through my lorgnette.

CHAMPAGNE POLONAISE

A lily filled with champagne! A lily filled with champagne!
How holy it becomes from the lily's chastity.
Mignon and Escamillo! Mignon with Escamillo!
A lily filled with champagne. A holy wine for me.

Light champagne is sparkling, bubbling in the lily –
The wine intensified by the flower's chaliced cup.
I praise ecstatically both dear Christ and Devil
With my soul scorched by the rapture of my gulp.

Together: dove and hawk! The Reichstag and the Bastille!
A hermit and a cocotte! Stupor and Elan!
A lily filled with champagne! Champagne in the lily!
In oceans of Dissonance – the lighthouse: Unison.

October 1912

SMOKE OF ICE

Beneath the wind the brook's ice smoking...
Along the field the smoke gyrates.
A girl covered all white with snowdust
Starts going faster on her skates.

Она несется по извивам
Дымящегося хрусталя,
То припадая к белым гривам,
То в легком танце воскрыля.

На белом белая белеет –
Вся вихрь, вся воздух, вся полет.
А лед все тлеет, тлеет, тлеет, –
Как будто вспыхнет этот лед!

1923

She scurries on – along the windings
Of the smoking crystal expanse.
Sometimes she crouches toward the white manes,
Sometimes wings up in a light dance.

Her white whitens on white. Behold her:
All swirling wind, all air, all flight.
And the ice smolders, smolders, smolders –
As if its glass would soon ignite.

БЕНЕДИКТ КОНСТАНТИНОВИЧ ЛИВШИЦ
1886-1939

ТЕПЛО

Вскрывай ореховый живот,
Медлительный палач бушмена:
До смерти не растает пена
Твоих старушечьих забот.

Из вечно-желтой стороны
Еще не додано объятий –
Благослови пяту дитяти,
Как парус, падающий в сны.

И, мирно простираясь ниц,
Не знай, что за листами канув,
Павлиний хвост в ночи курганов
Сверлит отверстия глазниц.

1911

ФОНТАНКА

Асфальтовая дрожь и пена
Под мостом – двести лет назад
Ты, по змеиному надменна,
Вползла в новорожденный град.

И днесь не могут коноводы
Сдержать ужаленных коней:
Твои мучительные воды
Звериных мускулов сильней.

BENEDICT KONSTANTINOVICH LIVSHITS
1886-1939

THE WARMTH

O, open up his nut-brown belly,
Slow killer of the bush-man, you.
Till death comes nothing will undo
The foam of your old-woman's worry.

And from the side with yellow streaming,
More huggings must be given yet –
So bless the foot of this child-pet,
Who like a sail sinks into dreaming.

And, calmly, prostrate, try ignoring
The peacock tail (Past trees' background)
Falling into the night of mounds,
Into the deep eye-sockets boring.

THE FONTANKA CANAL

Below the bridge the froth and asphalt-
Like shudder. Arrogant serpent,
Two-hundred years ago you entered
This new-born city, insolent.

Stung stallions still resist their trainers
And bolt against the pulls and calls,
Because your pain-inflicting waters
Outdo muscles of animals.

Что – венетийское потомство
И трубачей фронтонных ложь,
Когда, как хрия вероломства,
Ты от дворцов переползешь

Под плоскогорьем Клодта Невский
И сквозь рябые черныши
Дотянешься, как Достоевский,
До дна простуженной души?

1914

КАЗАНСКИЙ СОБОР

И полукруг, и крест латинский,
И своенравца римский сон
Ты перерос по исполински –
Удвоенной дугой колонн.

И вздыбленной клавиатуре
Удары звезд и лет копыт
Равны, когда вдыхатель бури
Жемчужным воздухом не сыт.

В потоке легком небоската
Ты луч отвергнешь ли один,
Коль зодчий тратил, точно злато,
Гиперборейский травертин?

Не тленным камнем – светопада
Опоясался ты кольцом,
И куполу дана отрада
Стоять колумбовым яйцом.

1914

What is this legacy from Venice
Or lies of pediment trumpeteers,
If (like a timeless trick of treason)
From palaces your crawling veers

Beneath Klodts' plateau at the Nevsky,
Along pock-marked boletic poles,
Stretching to reach like Dostoyevsky
The bottom of our freezing souls?

KAZAN CATHEDRAL

The Latin cross, the semi-circle,
The Roman sleep of a willful man,
You outgrew all this like a giant:
With columns' double arching span.

The blows of stars, the flight of horse-hoofs
Equate with rearing keyboards there,
When the inhaler of a tempest
Is not sated with pearl-like air.

In that light-flood of slopes celestial
Would you reject one ray you've seen –
When, like gold, the architect squandered
Such Hyperborean travertine?

You are not girt by stones which perish,
But by such rings as lightfalls beg;
The cupola gained this great pleasure:
To stand like a Columbus egg.

И вот умолк повествователь жалкий,
Прародины последняя заря,
Не догорев, погасла в орихалке...
Беспамятство. Саргасские моря.

Летейский сон. Летейская свобода.
Над паматью проносятся суда
Да в простодушном счете морехода
Двух-трех узлов не хватит иногда.

Да вот еще... Когда, смежая очи,
Я Саломее говорю: пляши! –
В морях веков, в морях единой ночи
Ты оживаешь, водоросль души.

О, танцовщица! Древняя русалка,
Опознаю сквозь обморок стиха
В твоих запястьях отблеск орихалка
И в имени – все три подводных 'а'.

А по утрам, когда уже тритона
Скрываются под влагой плавники,
Мне в рукописи прерванной Платона
Недостает всего одной строки.

1924

At last the sorry storyteller's finished.
And without burning up, the setting sun
In our First Land went out in orichalcum...
Sargasso Sea. Complete oblivion.

A Lethean sleep. A Lethean freedom.
With ships rushing above the memory...
And sometimes there are two or three knots missing
As sailors make their naive counts at sea.

And here's another thing... With my eyes closing
I say to Salomé: Dance, dance your rite!
Then, seaweed of my soul, again you flourish
In seas of centuries, seas of one night.

O ever-dancing girl! O ancient mermaid!
Through poetry's unconsciousness I claim
And know the copper shining in your bangles
And three subaqueos a's within your name.

And in the morning when the fins of Triton
Vanish into the ocean's liquid crypt,
Just one short line is all there is that's lacking
In Plato's interrupted manuscript.

Когда у вас дыханья не хватает,
Земных ветров кузнечные меха,
И даже магистерий в тиглях тает,
Не превращаясь в золото стиха,

Я не хочу добычи беззаконной:
Пусть лира задыхается в дыму –
Над умирающею Персефоной
Я покрывала не приподыму.

Что плакальщиц заломленные руки
Пред этой бездною глухонемой:
Земной ли голос плачет о разлуке,
Айдесский ли ответствует на мой?

Повремени, повремени, о лира,
Не торопись судить, не суесловь:
Мерило слова и мерило мира –
Играющая временем любовь.

И в тишине, где нас никто не слышит,
Где пеньем сфер мы сражены в упор,
Не нашу ль жизнь, как легкий пар, колышет
Карбункулом пылая атанор?

1926

When you, the bellows of the winds of earth,
Are short of breath, and even when the rolled
Magisterium melts in crucibles
And is not turned into poetry's gold,

I shall not ever want an unearned prize.
So let the lyre choke in the smoke for me;
I shall not stoop to raise a covering
Over the dying, dear Persephone.

What good are wringing hands of wailers here
Before this deaf-mute chasm's fragile line:
Is it a mortal voice crying goodbye
Or that of Hades now answering mine?

O linger, linger longer, lovely lyre.
Don't judge too quick or let vain words outpour:
The yardstick of the word and of the world
Is love playing with time – and nothing more.

And in the silence when no one hears us,
Where we're struck, point-blank, with the sphere's sung theme,
Does not the carbuncle-red athanor
Move our lives the same way it does light steam.

ВАСИЛИЙ ВАСИЛЬЕВИЧ КАМЕНСКИЙ
1884-1961

Я – В ЦИРКЕ

В Тифлисе – в Цирке Бр. Есиковских
мои 7 гастролей с 19 октября 1916 г.

Бумм – трали – лля.
Чудо.
Сегодня экстра – гастрольное
Сверх – представление:
Василий Каменский
Верхом на коне
Исполнит стихи –
Грянет речь о Поэзии Цирка.

(И снова как в Детстве:
Музыка. Блестки. Огни.
Карусельная красота.)

Я – Первый из Поэтов Мира
Кто на арене Цирка
Величественно выступил
В кафтане из парчи
Верхом на вороном коне –
Под куполом с трапециями
Себе поставил Памятник.
О 19-е октября –
Когда восславил я:
Наездниц Верину и Викторию Харини
Акробатов Китая Чин-ху –
Рыжих клоунов Мишель и Этардо –
Эквилибриста Джиовани –
Дрессировщика лошадей Афанасьева
Гладиаторов греков Трояно
Ловких эксцентриков Донато и Поло

VASILY VASILYEVICH KAMENSKY
1884-1961

ME – AND THE CIRCUS

In Tiflis, in the Esikovsky Brothers' Circus,
my seven guest appearances, starting October
19, 1916.

Boom – tra-la-la.
A miracle.
Today – an extraordinary
Super – performance:
Vasily Kamensky
On horseback
Will perform his poetry –
Will stun you with his speech, the Poetry of a Circus.

(And again as in my Childhood:
Music. Glitter. Lights.
The merry-go-round marvel.)

I – the First Poet of the World
Who majestically appeared
In a Circus arena
In a kaftan made of brocade
On the back of a raven horse –
Built himself a Monument
Under the Top with trapezes.
O, 19th of October –
When I glorified:
The bareback riders Verina and Victoria Harini
The Chinese acrobat Chin-Hu –
The red-haired clowns Michel and Etardeau –
The equilibrist Giovanni –
The horse-trainer Afanasyev
The Greek Gladiators Trayanos
The clever comics Donato and Paolo

357

На трапеции Элеонору
Джигитовщиков Вано и Тамару
Музыкальных клоунов Андро
Дерби жокея Феррони
Шута – дрессировщика Дурова
Кор-де-балет и сестер Арнольди
Директора Есиковского
Режиссеров Харини и Льва Хундадзе.
Восславил всех яркоцветно
Моих цирковых друзей.
О – 19-е октября.
Толпа. Лошади. Аттракционы.
Ловкость. Быстрота. Риск.
Бумм-трали-ля. Бумм.
(И снова как в Детстве.)

1916

On the trapeze Leonora
The trick-riders Vano and Tamara
The musical clowns Les Andreaux
The derby jockey Ferroni
The animal trainer and clown Durov
The Arnoldi Sisters with a corps de ballet
The producer Esikovsky
The directors Harini and Leo Hundadze.
Now I've glorified in a multicolored way
All my circus friends.
O – 19th of October.
Crowd. Horses. Attractions.
Agility. Speed. Daring.
Boom – tra-la-la. Boom.
(And again as in my Childhood.)

АЛЕКСЕЙ ЕЛИСЕЕВИЧ КРУЧЕНЫХ
р. 1886

ВЫСОТЫ
(вселенский язык)

```
      е у ю
      и а о
       о а
   о а е е и е я
       о а
      е у и е и
       и е е
  и и ы и е и и ы
```

1913

ALEKSEI ELISEYEVICH KRUCHENYKH
b. 1886

HEIGHTS
(UNIVERSAL LANGUAGE)

```
        e u w
        i a o
          o a
    o a e e i e w
          o a
        e u i e i
         i e e
    i i y i e i i y
```

ВАСИЛИСК ГНЕДОВ
(ВАСИЛИЙ ИВАНОВИЧ ГНЕДОВ)
р. 1890

ПОЭМА КОНЦА

(1913)

VASILISK GNEDOV
(VASILY IVANOVICH GNEDOV)
b. 1890

POEM OF THE END

See page lxiii

МИХАИЛ АЛЕКСАНДРОВИЧ ЗЕНКЕВИЧ
р. 1891

МЯСНЫЕ РЯДЫ

А. Ахматовой

Скрипят железные крючки и блоки,
И туши вверх и вниз сползать должны.
Под бледною плевой кровоподтеки,
И внутренности иссиня-черны.

Все просто так. Мы – люди, в нашей власти
У этой скользкой смоченной доски
Уродливо-обрубленные части
Ножами рвать на красные куски.

И чудится, что в золотом эфире
И нас, как мясо, вешают Весы,
И также чашки ржавы, тяжки гири,
И также алчно крохи лижут псы.

И как и здесь, решающим привеском
Такие ж жилистые мясники
Бросают на железо с легким треском
От сала светлые золотники...

Прости, Господь! Ужель с полдневным жаром,
Когда от туш исходит тяжко дух,
И там, как здесь, над смолкнувшим базаром,
Лишь засверкают стаи липких мух?

(1912)

MIKHAIL ALEXANDROVICH ZENKEVICH
b. 1891

ROWS OF MEAT

to A. Akhmatova

The iron hooks and the blocks with pulleys squeak;
The carcasses crawl up, down, forth, back.
The bruises show beneath the pallid tissues,
And the insides are shining, bluish-black.

We are people and it is in our power
To cut into red chunks of flesh and fat
These ugly chopped parts on this slippery board.
And everything is as simple as that.

I sometimes think that in a golden heaven
We are all weighed by that Scale just like meat.
The plates there are as rusty, weights as heavy;
The dogs, as greedy, pounce on scraps to eat.

And sinewy butchers, just like these here,
Toss golden-shiny, greasy *zolotnicks*
As a decisive, counterweight onto
The iron making identical light clicks.

Forgive us Lord! Is it in the noon's heat,
When these thick, rancid carcass odors rise,
That there, like here, over a silenced market
Will flash only dark swarms of sticky flies?

ВЛАДИМИР ИВАНОВИЧ НАРБУТ
1888-1944

ПОРТРЕТ

Мясистый нос, обрезком колбасы
Нависший на мышастые усы,
Проросший жилками (от ражей лени), –
Похож был вельми на листок осенний.
Подстриженная сивая щетина,
Из-под усов срывалась – в виде клина;
Не дыней ли (спаси мя от греха!),
Глянь, подавилась каждая щека?
Грубее и сонливей лопухов,
Солонки сочные из-за висков,
Ловя, ховая речи, вызирали
Печурками (для вкладки в них миндалин).
И в ямках-выбоинах под бровями
Два чернослива с белыми краями,
Должно быть, в масле (чтоб всегда сиять),
Полировали выпуклую гладь.
И лоб, как купол низенький извне,
Обшитый загорелой при огне,
Потрескавшейся пористою кожей,
Проник заходиной в волосьев ложе.
И взмылила главы обсосок сальный
Полсотня лет, глумясь над ним нахально:
Там – вошь сквозная, с точкою внутри,
Впотьмах цепляет гнид, как фонари.

(1912)

VLADIMIR IVANOVICH NARBUT
1888-1944

PORTRAIT

The fleshy, vein-shot nose (of the lazy phony),
Above the mouse moustache, hangs like baloney;
But then again, this bulbous piece of beef
Resembles, too, a languid autumn leaf.
The trimmed yellow-gray bristle of his beard
Falls down below the moustache – wedge-shaped, weird.
Look at those cheeks – See how puffed out and swollen
(Ora pro nobis!) Choking with a melon?
Like burdocks – only coarser, sleepier,
Catching and hiding speeches, as it were,
Peering out both sides, those two fat-filled dishes,
Or places to roast almonds – oven niches.
In ruts beneath the brows – hard at their toil
(As if completely coated there with oil)
Two ever-shining plums floating in white
Polish the bulging surfaces with light.
A low-set cupola (the forehead's spire)
Is wrapped in skin tanned darkened-red by fire.
Covered with crackles and yet always porous,
It thrusts its spear forth into the hair's forest.
And half-a-hundred years shoot to the top,
Jeering that head, that lardy lollipop.
There lucid lice with black dots on dark nights
Clutch scattered nits like they were lantern lights.

СОФЬЯ ЯКОВЛЕВНА ПАРНОК
1885-1933

В земле бесплодной не взойти зерну,
Но кто не верил чуду в час жестокий? –
Что возвестят мне Пушкинские строки?
Страницы милые я разверну.

Опять, опять 'Ненастный день потух',
Оборванный пронзительным 'но если'!
Не вся ль душа моя, мой мир не весь ли
В словах теперь трепещет этих двух?

Чем жарче кровь, тем сердце холодней,
Не сердцем любишь ты, – горячей кровью.
Я в вечности, обещанной любовью,
Не досчитаю слишком многих дней.

В глазах моих веселья не лови:
Та, третья, уж стоит меж нами тенью.
В душе твоей не вспыхнуть умиленью,
Залогу неизменному любви, –

В земле бесплодной не взойти зерну,
Но кто не верил чуду в час жестокий? –
Что возвестят мне Пушкинские строки?
Страницы милые я разверну.

(1916)

SOPHIA YAKOVLEVNA PARNOK
1885-1933

No grain will sprout within a barren land,
But in harsh moments who does not believe in
A miracle? And how will Pushkin help me?
I'll open up this cherished book and see.

Again, again: 'The dreary day has died',
Abruptly ending with that piercing, 'But if'!
Does not all of my soul, all of my world
Start trembling in these last two words of his?

The hotter blood comes with the colder heart.
You don't love with your heart, but with hot blood.
I'll lack too many days at that last counting,
In that eternity promised by love.

Don't try to catch a lightness in my eyes;
Another casts a shadow in between us.
Your soul will flash its tenderness no longer
And tenderness is always proof of love, –

No grain will sprout within a barren land,
But in harsh moments who does not believe in
A miracle? And how will Pushkin help me?
I'll open up this cherished book and see.

Паук заткал мой темный складень
И всех молитв мертвы слова,
И обезумевшая за день
В подушку никнет голова.

Вот так она придет за мной, –
Не музыкой, не ароматом,
Не демоном темнокрылатым,
Не вдохновенной тишиной, –

А просто пес завоет, или
Взовьется взвизг автомобиля
И крыса прошмыгнет в нору.
Вот так! Не добрая, не злая,
Под эту музыку жила я,
Под эту музыку умру.

(1923)

Cobwebs on my dark folding icon...
The words of all my prayers are dead;
My head, maddened throughout the daytime,
Falls on a pillow on a bed.

That is how she will come for me...
O, not as music, not as fragrance,
Not as a dark, winged demon, no,
And not as an inspired silence...

Simply a dog will howl his cries up;
The screeching of a car will rise up;
A rat will dart toward a hole.
Like that! O, neither good nor evil.
I lived with this music and I will
With this music give up my soul.

ГЕОРГИЙ АРКАДЬЕВИЧ ШЕНГЕЛИ
1894-1956

Худенькие пальцы нижут бисер, –
Голубой, серебряный, лимонный;
И на желтой замше возникают
Лилии, кораблик и турчанка.

Отвердел и веским стал мешочек.
Английская вдернута бичевка;
Загорелым табаком наполнить, –
И какой ласкающий подарок!

Но вручен он никому не будет:
Друга нет у старой институтки;
И в глазах, от напряженья красных,
Тихие слезинки набегают.

И кисет хоронится в шкатулку,
Где другие дремлют вышиванья,
Где отцовский орден и гравюра:
Кудри, плащ и тонкий росчерк: Байрон.

1919

GEORGE ARKADYEVICH SHENGELI
1894-1956

Slender fingers string the glass beads, colored
Shiny silver and light blue and lemon;
And there springs upon the yellow chamois:
Lilies, a small ship, a Turkish woman.

And the little bag grows hard and heavy.
Last, the English drawstring is inserted;
Now to fill it with sun-tanned tobacco,
And it will become a touching present.

But it will be handed to nobody:
For she has no friends, this genteel spinster.
Quietly small teardrops form and well-up
In her eyes, eyes red from too much straining.

And the pouch is put away and hidden
In a box where her embroideries slumber,
Near her father's medal and an old etching:
Hairlocks, cloak and that thin flourish, 'Byron'.

III

POETRY AND EXILE

ВЛАДИСЛАВ ФЕЛИЦИАНОВИЧ ХОДАСЕВИЧ
1896-1939

В ПЕТРОВСКОМ ПАРКЕ

Висел он, не качаясь,
На узком ремешке.
Свалившаяся шляпа
Чернела на песке.
В ладонь впивались ногти
На стиснутой руке.

А солнце восходило,
Стремя к полудню бег,
И перед этим солнцем,
Не опуская век,
Был высоко приподнят
На воздух человек.

И зорко, зорко, зорко
Смотрел он на восток.
Внизу столпились люди
В притихнувший кружок.
И был почти невидим
Тот узкий ремешок.

1916

БЕЗ СЛОВ

Ты показала мне без слов,
Как вышел хорошо и чисто
Тобою проведенный шов
По краю белого батиста.

VLADISLAV FELITSIANOVICH KHODASEVICH
1896-1939

IN PETROVSKY PARK

He hung there without swaying
By his belt's narrow band;
His hat had fallen, making
A dark spot on the sand;
His fingernails were denting
The palm of his clenched hand.

Meanwhile the sun came, rising
To run toward noon's full glare.
And in that sun's bright morning
With eyes' wide-opened stare,
A man was raised, was being
Suspended in the air.

And far and far and farther...
He scanned the eastern sky.
Below him people crowded,
And talking seemed to die...
And one could hardly see it,
The small belt he hung by.

WITHOUT A WORD

Without a word you showed to me
How very neat and well-begotten
The stitching was you skilfully
Made on the hem of the white cotton.

А я подумал: жизнь моя,
Как нить, за Божьими перстами
По легкой ткани бытия
Бежит такими же стежками.

То виден, то сокрыт стежок,
То в жизнь, то в смерть перебегая...
И, улыбаясь, твой платок
Перевернул я, дорогая.

1918

ВАРИАЦИЯ

Вновь эти плечи, эти руки
Погреть я вышел на балкон.
Сижу, – но все земные звуки –
Как бы во сне или сквозь сон.

И вдруг, изнеможенья полный,
Плыву: куда – не знаю сам,
Но мир мой ширится, как волны,
По разбежавшимся кругам.

Продлись, ласкательное чудо!
Я во второй вступаю круг
И слушаю, уже оттуда,
Моей качалки мерный стук.

1919

I thought: My life is, in a sense,
A thread with God's own fingers sewing.
The light fabric of existence
Has running stitches like these showing.

The stitch is now seen, now concealed:
Now life, now death . . . a threading rover . . .
My dear, with thoughts in such a field,
I smile and turn your kerchief over.

A VARIATION

To warm again these hands, these shoulders,
I come out to the balcony.
I sit – and all the sounds of earth come
As in, or through, a sleep – to me.

And suddenly, dead from exhaustion,
I float or drift to who-knows-where.
My world in wave-like circles widens
To other circles far out there.

Stop! Stop this miracle which hugs me!
I'm entering the second sphere . . .
I listen . . . From this realm already:
My rocker's knock . . . knock . . . knock . . . I hear.

ОБЕЗЬЯНА

Была жара. Леса горели. Нудно
Тянулось время. На соседней даче
Кричал петух. Я вышел за калитку.
Там, прислонясь к забору, на скамейке
Дремал бродячий серб, худой и черный.
Серебряный тяжелый крест висел
На груди полуголой. Капли пота
По ней катились. Выше, на заборе,
Сидела обезьяна в красной юбке
И пыльные листы сирени
Жевала жадно. Кожаный ошейник,
Оттянутый назад тяжелой цепью,
Давил ей горло. Серб, меня заслышав,
Очнулся, вытер пот и попросил, чтоб дал я
Воды ему. Но чуть ее пригубив, –
Не холодна ли, – блюдце на скамейку
Поставил он, и тотчас обезьяна,
Макая пальцы в воду, ухватила
Двумя руками блюдце.
Она пила, на четвереньках стоя,
Локтями опираясь на скамью.
Досок почти касался подбородок,
Над теменем лысеющим спина
Высоко выгибалась. Так, должно быть,
Стоял когда-то Дарий, припадая
К дорожной луже, в день когда бежал он
Пред мощною фалангой Александра.
Всю воду выпив, обезьяна блюдце
Долой смахнула со скамьи, привстала
И – этот миг забуду ли когда? –
Мне черную, мозолистую руку,
Еще прохладную от влаги, протянула...
Я руки жал красавицам, поэтам,
Вождям народа – ни одна рука

THE MONKEY

The day was hot, the woods on fire. And time
Dragged tediously. In the dacha next to mine
A rooster crowed. I left my yard. Outside
The garden gate, leaning against the fence,
A thin, dark, wandering Serbian dozed on
A bench. His heavy silver cross hung low
On his half-naked chest. The drops of sweat
Rolled down. A little higher on the fence
A monkey in a red shirt sat and chewed
The dusty lilac leaves with lusty greed.
A leather collar, with a heavy chain
That pulled it back, pressed tight against its throat.
Hearing my steps, the old man roused, wiped off
His sweat and asked me for some water. Then
His lips tested to see how cold
It was; he placed the saucer on the bench.
At once the monkey, fingers in the water,
Picked up the saucer with both hands and stood
On all fours, elbows on the bench, and drank . . .
Its chin almost touching the boards, its back
Hunching an arch above the balding pate.
In such a posture Darius long ago
Bent, pressing to a puddle in the road
The day the mighty phalanxes of young
Alexander sent him and his men fleeing.
The monkey drank up all the water there
And brushed away the saucer off the bench.
And stood up! And – (Will I ever forget
This moment?) – how its black and calloused hand,
Still cool and moist from the water, stretched . . .
Stretched out to me! Though I have shaken hands
With lovely women, poets, heads of states,
No other hand had such a noble shape!
And never had another single hand

Такого благородства очертаний
Не заключала! Ни одна рука
Моей руки так братски не коснулась!
И видит Бог, никто в мои глаза
Не заглянул так мудро и глубоко,
Воистину – до дна души моей.
Глубокой древности сладчайшие преданья
Тот нищий зверь мне в сердце оживил,
И в этот миг мне жизнь явилась полной,
И мнилось – хор светил и волн морских,
Ветров и сфер мне музыкой органной
Ворвался в уши, загремел, как прежде,
В иные незапамятные дни.
И серб ушел, постукивая в бубен.
Присев ему на левое плечо,
Покачивалась мерно обезьяна,
Как на слоне индийский магараджа.
Огромное малиновое солнце,
Лишенное лучей,
В опаловом дыму висело. Изливался
Безгромный зной на чахлую пшеницу.

В тот день была объявлена война.

1919

ГОСТЮ

Входя ко мне, неси мечту,
Иль дьявольскую красоту,
Иль Бога, если сам ты Божий.
А маленькую доброту,
Как шляпу, оставляй в прихожей.

Touched mine with such a clasp of brotherhood!
And God knows no one ever looked so deep
Into my eyes – or with such wisdom! Yes,
Or saw the very bottom of my soul!
The handshake of that beggar animal
Revived the sweetest legend in my heart,
A kinship from a far antiquity.
And at that very moment all of life
Became fulfilled and realized for me.
It seemed – a choir, of stars and ocean waves,
Of winds and spheres with organ music, swelled
Again ... as something I had heard before
In landscapes almost lost from memory.
The Serbian left – thumping his tambourine.
The monkey bounced on his left shoulder, swaying
In rhythm like an Indian maharajah
Upon an elephant. And in the sky
The wild, enormous, red-raspberry sun
Without a single beam
Hung in the opal smoke. No thunder spoke.
Heat poured onto the pale, consumptive wheat.

That was the very day war was declared.

TO MY GUEST

When you come to my place, bring me
A dream ... or Hell's beauty set free ...
Or God ... if *you* are God's, the All-Way.
But leave each sweet amenity
With your hat, outside, in the hallway.

Здесь, на горошине земли,
Будь или ангел, или демон.
А человек – иль не затем он,
Чтоб забыть его могли?

1921

ИЗ ОКНА

I

Нынче день такой забавный:
От возниц, что было сил,
Конь умчался своенравный;
Мальчик змей свой упустил;
Вор цыпленка утащил
У безносой Николавны.

Но – настигнут вор нахальный,
Змей упал в соседний сад,
Мальчик ладит хвост мочальный,
И коня ведут назад:
Восстает мой тихий ад
В стройности первоначальной.

II

Все жду: кого-нибудь задавит
Взбесившийся автомобиль,
Зевака бледный окровавит
Торцовую сухую пыль.

И с этого пойдет, начнется:
Раскачка, выворот, беда,
Звезда на землю оборвется,
И станет горькою вода.

Here on this little pea called Earth
Be either angel or a demon.
Don't be just Man. For is not he, Man,
Here for us to forget his worth?

THROUGH THE WINDOW

I

All today has been amusing:
First, a wild horse ran away,
Then the boy outside was losing...
Lost his kite. And then a stray
Thief snatched from Nick's noseless, gray
Girl a chicken worth the choosing.

But the thief's been apprehended,
And the kite fell down next door –
Where the tail is being mended.
Now the horse comes home once more.
My mute hell flames as before,
Its first harmony unended.

II

I wait. A car will hit somebody,
Some crazy car – hellbound or bust!
The fear-struck, car-struck man will bloody
His pale self and the street's dry dust.

And from this will start: quakes, roaring,
Upset, turned inside-out, all waste;
Each star will crash loose from its mooring;
Water will take a bitter taste.

Прервутся сны, что душу душат.
Начнется все, чего хочу,
И солнце ангелы потушат,
Как утром – лишнюю свечу.

1921

ЛАСТОЧКИ

Имей глаза – сквозь день увидишь ночь,
Не озаренную тем воспаленным диском.
Две ласточки напрасно рвутся прочь,
Перед окном шныряя с тонким писком.

Вон ту прозрачную, но прочную плеву
Не прободать крылом остроугольным,
Не выпорхнуть туда, за синеву,
Ни птичьим крылышком, ни сердцем подневольным.

Пока вся кровь не выступит из пор,
Пока не выплачешь земные очи –
Не станешь духом. Жди, смотри в упор,
Как брызжет свет, не застилая ночи.

1921

БАЛЛАДА

Сижу, освещаемый сверху,
Я в комнате круглой моей.
Смотрю в штукатурное небо
На солнце в шестнадцать свечей.

Кругом – освещенные тоже,
И стулья, и стол, и кровать.

Such foul dreams which choke souls with warning
Will end and my wish be begun,
And, like we douse candles at morning,
The angels will put out the sun.

THE SWALLOWS

Have eyes. Then through the day you'll see the night
Not lighted by that inflamed disk. Two swallows
Try now in vain to get away. Their flight
Speeds past my window, their thin squeaking follows.

That solid, clear membrane suspended there
Cannot be pierced by any wing's sharp angles.
One cannot fly beyond that azure air
With small bird wings – or hearts that serfdom strangles.

Until your blood seeps out through every pore,
Until you cry – and cry your earthly eyes out,
You won't become spirit. So wait before
That light which sprays but does not put night's skies out.

BALLAD

I sit in my circular attic;
A brilliance beams down from on high.
My sun is a sixteen-watt lightbulb;
The plaster I see is my sky.

And also around me are lighted
My table, my bed and my chair.

Сижу – и в смущеньи не знаю,
Куда бы мне руки девать.

Морозные белые пальмы
На стеклах беззвучно цветут.
Часы с металлическим шумом
В жилетном кармане идут.

О, косная, нищая скудость
Безвыходной жизни моей!
Кому мне поведать, как жалко
Себя и всех этих вещей?

И я начинаю качаться,
Колени обнявши свои,
И вдруг начинаю стихами
С собой говорить в забытьи.

Бессвязные, страстные речи!
Нельзя в них понять ничего,
Но звуки правдивее смысла,
И слово сильнее всего.

И музыка, музыка, музыка
Вплетается в пенье мое,
И узкое, узкое, узкое
Пронзает меня лезвие.

Я сам над собой вырастаю,
Над мертвым встаю бытием,
Стопами в подземное пламя,
В текучие звезды челом.

И вижу большими глазами –
Глазами, быть может, змеи –
Как пению дикому внемлют
Несчастные вещи мои.

I sit here, self-conscious, and can't find
A place for my hands anywhere.

The white palms of frost on the window
Are blooming without any sound;
My watch moves inside my vest-pocket,
Metallically ticking each round.

O poverty (present, unpretty)
Of my life from which there's no out!
To whom can I tell how I pity
Myself and these things hereabout?

And then, with my knees clasped before me,
I start in to sway, and I fall
Into a deep trance . . . and I'm speaking
In verse to myself through it all.

Mad, rambling and passionate speeches
Whose meaning is totally blurred!
But sounds are more truthful than meaning,
And nothing's as strong as the word.

And music and music and music
Weaves into my song's poetry.
And narrow and narrow and narrow:
The blade that is passing through me.

And then I grow out of my own self,
Rise above an existence so dead:
The underworld's fire feels my two feet,
Flowing stars touch the top of my head.

I see with enormous, enlarged eyes
(Perhaps with the eyes of a snake)
My pitiful bed, chair and table
Give ear to the wild song I make.

И в плавный, вращательный танец
Вся комната мерно идет,
И кто-то тяжелую лиру
Мне в руки сквозь ветер дает.

И нет штукатурного неба
И солнца в шестнадцать свечей:
На гладкие черные скалы
Стопы опирает Орфей.

1921

* * *

Леди долго руки мыла,
Леди крепко руки терла.
Эта леди не забыла
Окровавленного горла.

Леди, леди! Вы как птица
Бьетесь на бессонном ложе.
Триста лет уж вам не спится –
Мне лет шесть не спится тоже.

1922

УЛИКА

Была туманной и безвестной,
Мерцала в лунной вышине,
Но воплощенной и телесной
Теперь являться стала мне.

The whole room starts swaying in rhythm;
It dances round ... gyre ... after gyre.
Someone in the wind comes and hands me
A massive, well-tuned, heavy lyre.

There's no plaster sky any longer,
No sixteen-watt sun overhead;
The feet of Orpheus are touching
The smooth, black rocks with their tread.

★ ★ ★

Lady washed her hands and rubbed them
For a long time ... not forgetting ...
Lady scoured her hands and scrubbed them ...
Bloody throat ... and bad blood-letting.

Lady, Lady, bird who shan't sleep,
Quiver in your bed and lie there.
These three hundred years you can't sleep ...
And for six years I can't either.

EVIDENCE

She sparkled like an apparition
High in the moonlight ... and unknown.
But then she started her transition,
Personified, to flesh and bone.

И вот – среди беседы чинной,
Я вдруг с растерянным лицом
Снимаю волос, тонкий, длинный,
Забытый на плече моем.

Тут гость из-за стакана чаю
Хитро косится на меня.
А я смотрю и понимаю,
Тихонько ложечкой звеня:

Блажен, кто завлечен мечтою
В безвыходный, дремучий сон,
И там внезапно сам собою
В нездешнем счастье уличен.

1922

* * *

Перешагни, перескачи,
Перелети, пере- что хочешь –
Но вырвись: камнем из пращи,
Звездой, сорвавшейся в ночи...
Сам затерял – теперь ищи...

Бог знает, что себе бормочешь,
Ища пенснэ или ключи.

1922

Now, midst a proper conversation,
I quickly spot a long, thin hair...
Embarrassed by the situation,
I pick it off my shoulder. There!

Behind his teacup, my guest, thinking,
Eyes me. But I look... understand...
And stir, making the slightest tinkling
With the teaspoon I hold in my hand.

Blessed is he, lured by his daydream
To that sleep where no paths lie curled.
And there he traps himself and may dream,
Caught in a joy not of this world.

*   *   *

Step over, past! Jump over, through!
Fly over, out! Attempt all passes,
But 'Out!' A slingshot's hurling stone,
A star plummeting outward... You
Lost it... Now find it on your own.

While looking for our keys or glasses,
God knows what mutterings we do!

Было на улице полутемно.
Стукнуло где-то под крышей окно.

Свет промелькнул, занавеска взвилась,
Быстрая тень со стены сорвалась –

Счастлив, кто падает вниз головой:
Мир для него хоть на миг – а иной.

1922

AN MARIECHEN

Зачем ты за пивною стойкой?
Пристала ли тебе она?
Здесь нужно быть девицей бойкой, –
Ты нездорова и бледна.

С какой-то розою огромной
У нецелованных грудей, –
А смертный венчик, самый скромный,
Украсил бы тебя милей.

Ведь так прекрасно, так нетленно
Скончаться рано, до греха.
Родители же непременно
Тебе отыщут жениха.

Так называемый хороший,
И в правду – честный человек
Перегрузит тяжелой ношей
Твой слабый, твой короткий век.

Уж лучше бы – я еле смею
Подумать про себя о том –
Попасться бы тебе злодею
В пустынной роще, вечерком.

Over the dull street a half-darkness hangs;
Under a roof somewhere a window bangs.

Flash goes a light, out fly curtains and all...
Then the fast shadow breaks loose from the wall.

Lucky the man falling headfirst, for he
Sees for one moment the world differently.

AN MARIECHEN

Why are you there behind the beer-bar?
It fits you – serving beer and ale?
Here girls are bolder and more brazen,
And you look rather sick and pale

With that enormous rose you're wearing
Between your unkissed virgin breasts...
A funeral wreath (and one most modest)
Would make you, dear, the loveliest.

Look, it is beautiful and lasting
To die early before we sin.
But your parents will find a bridegroom
For you – and so it will begin:

For then that so-called nice and pleasant
And (I admit) an honest man
With heavy loads will overburden
Your fragile, fleeting lifetime span.

It would be better (and I hardly
Dare think of it myself outright)
To meet a fiend by chance encounter
In some deserted grove one night.

Уж лучше в несколько мгновений
И стыд узнать, и смерть принять,
И двух истлений, двух растлений
Не разделять, не разлучать.

Лежать бы в платьице измятом
Одной, в березняке густом,
И нож под левым, лиловатым,
Еще девическим соском.

1923

ДАЧНОЕ

Уродики, уродища, уроды
Весь день озерные мутили воды.

Теперь над озером ненастье, мрак,
В траве – лягушачий зеленый квак.

Огни на дачах гаснут понемногу,
Клубки червей полезли на дорогу,

А вдалеке, где все затерла мгла,
Тупая грамофонная игла

Шатается по рытвинам царапин,
И из трубы еще рычит Шаляпин.

На мокрый мир нисходит угомон…
Лишь кое-где, топча сырой газон,

Блудливые невесты с женихами
Слипаются, накрытые зонтами,

А к ним под юбки лазит с фонарем
Полуслепой, широкоротый гном.

1923

For that brief time it would be better
Both to accept death, to know shame...
And not to sever or split ever
Two deflowerings which are the same.

It would be better: small dress crumpled,
Alone... the birch grove, thick and tall.
And his knife under your left nipple,
Turned purple – but still virginal.

IN THE SUBURBS

Small freaks, gigantic freaks, and just plain freaks
Have roiled the lake all day to muddy streaks.

Now, overhead, dark skies foretell bad weather;
Frogs in the grass grunt their green croaks together.

The lights in houses gradually go out,
And worms in paths begin to crawl about.

And in the distance where the deep dark swaggers,
An ancient gramophone's blunt needle staggers...

Through every pitted scratch it goes exploring,
While from the horn Chaliapin still comes roaring.

A quiet settles over all the town...
Just here and there trampling the wet grass down,

Lusting boys glue to sweethearts, each a lover,
Beneath a damp umbrella used for cover.

And now, beneath the skirts, with lantern bright,
A half-blind, broad-mouthed gnome crawls with delight.

ХРАНИЛИЩЕ

По залам прохожу лениво.
Претит от истин и красот.
Еще невиданные дива,
Признаться, знаю наперед.

И как-то тяжко, больно даже
Душою жить – который раз?
В кому-то снившемся пейзаже,
В когда-то промелькнувший час.

Все бьется человечий гений:
То вверх, то вниз. И то сказать:
От восхождений и падений
Уж позволительно устать.

Нет! Полно! Тяжелеют веки
Пред вереницею Мадон, –
И так отрадно, что в аптеке
Есть кисленький пирамидон.

1924

ПЕРЕД ЗЕРКАЛОМ

Nel mezzo del cammin di nostra vita

Я, я, я. Что за дикое слово!
Неужели вон тот – это я?
Разве мама любила такого,
Желтосерого, полуседого
И всезнающего, как змея?

Разве мальчик, в Останкине летом
Танцовавший на дачных балах, –

REPOSITORY

I stroll through halls of the museum,
Fed up with Truths and Beauties – all.
I know their looks before I see them,
These marvels hanging on each wall.

It's difficult and even painful
To let one's soul – How well I know! –
Live in a landscape someone's brain, full
Of one quick flash, dreamed long ago.

The human genius, never steady,
Leaps – spurting upward, downward still.
Permit us to grow tired already
From climbing up and down each hill.

Enough! The long line of madonnas
Makes eyelids heavier than lead;
It's good drugstores have mercy on us ...
With piquant bromides for one's head.

BEFORE THE MIRROR

Nel mezzo del cammin di nostra vita

I – I – I, weird word, stupid reflection!
Is that one, staring there at me, me?
Did my mother adore this perfection,
Now grown half-gray, with sallow complexion,
The all-wise, eyeing serpent I see?

And the boy at Ostánkino dancing
At the balls in the summer each year ...

Это я, тот, кто каждым ответом
Желторотым внушает поэтам
Отвращение, злобу и страх?

Разве тот, кто в полночные споры
Всю мальчишечью вкладывал прыть, –
Это я, тот же самый, который
На трагические разговоры
Научился молчать и шутить?

Впрочем – так и всегда на средине
Рокового земного пути:
От ничтожной причины – к причине,
А глядишь заплутался в пустыне,
И своих же следов не найти.

Да, меня не пантера прыжками
На парижский чердак загнала.
И Виргилия нет за плечами, –
Только есть одиночество – в раме
Говорящего правду стекла.

1924

ОКНА ВО ДВОР

Несчастный дурак в колодце двора
Причитает сегодня с утра,
И лишнего нет у меня башмака,
Чтобы бросить его в дурака.

.　　.　　.　　.　　.

Кастрюли, тарелки, пьянино гремят,
Баюкают няньки крикливых ребят.
С улыбкой сидит у окошка глухой,
Зачарован своей тишиной.

.　　.　　.　　.　　.

Am I he? I, the critic, whose lancing
Puts the green, tender poets to prancing
With disgust, with real anger, with fear?

And the one with a boy's animation
Who would argue beyond midnight's stroke . . .
Am I he? I, who've learned limitation,
And reply to a grave conversation
With a silence or else with a joke?

But it always is so in the middle
Of this doomed way on Earth, where we've strayed
From this reason to that one . . . both, little.
Look, you're lost in a desert. The riddle
Is to find the old footprints *you* made.

Not a panther, pursuing, consigned me
To this attic in Paris, this roof.
And no Virgil is standing behind me.
Only loneliness looks out to find me
From the mirror's frame telling the truth.

WINDOWS ONTO THE YARD

That wretched moron in the well of the yard
Has been sobbing since morning – so hard.
There isn't an extra shoe on the spot
I can throw at the cursed idiot.

.   .   .   .   .   .

Pans, plates, and a piano thundering wild.
And there: a wet nurse lullabying a child.
A deaf man sits at the window with a smile,
Seems enchanted by silence meanwhile.

.   .   .   .

Курносый актер перед пыльным трюмо
Целует портреты и пишет письмо, –
И честно гонясь за правдивой игрой,
В шестнадцатый раз умирает герой.

. . . . . .

Отец уж надел котелок и пальто,
Но вернулся, бледный как труп:
– Сейчас же отшлепать мальчишку за то,
Что не любит луковый суп!

. . . . . .

Небритый старик, отодвинув кровать,
Забивает старательно гвоздь,
Но сегодня успеет ему помешать
Идущий по лестнице гость.

. . . . . .

Рабочий лежит на постели в цветах.
Очки на столе, медяки на глазах.
Подвязана челюсть, к ладони ладонь.
Сегодня в лед, а завтра в огонь.

. . . . . .

Что верно, то верно! Нельзя же силком
Девчонку тащить на кровать!
Ей нужно сначала стихи почитать,
Потом угостить вином . . .

. . . . . .

Вода запищала в стене глубоко:
Должно быть, по трубам бежать не легко,
Всегда в тесноте и всегда в темноте,
В такой темноте и в такой тесноте!

. . . . . .

1924

An actor, pug-nosed, by a vanity stand
Kisses portraits and answers a letter by hand, –
And trying to make his realism sublime,
Our hero dies this sixteenth time.

.   .   .   .

Father donned overcoat, derby hat on his head,
But came back – as pale as the dead:
'Immediately paddle that boy! Nincompoop –
For not liking his onion soup!'

.   .   .   .

An unshaven old man moved his bed away
And is diligently driving a nail today,
But he'll be prevented from his macabre affair
By a guest who is climbing the stair.

.   .   .   .

Midst flowers, in bed – a workingman lies:
His specs on the table, copper coins on his eyes.
His jaw is tied up, palm to palm on his frame.
Today into ice; tomorrow into flame.

.   .   .   .

What's true is true! One should not, of course,
Drag any dear girl into bed by force.
One should first read her poetry, line after line,
And then lovingly give her some wine . . .

.   .   .   .

The water inside of the wall squeaks and gripes: –
It must not be easy to run in the pipes,
Always in narrowness, always in night . . .
And such a dark night . . . and so narrow and tight.

.   .   .   .

ЗВЕЗДЫ

Вверху – грошовый дом свиданий.
Внизу – в грошовом 'казино'
Расселись зрители. Темно.
Пора щипков и ожиданий.
Тот захихикал, тот зевнул...
Но неудачник облыселый
Высоко палочкой взмахнул.
Открылись темные пределы,
И вот – сквозь дым табачных туч –
Прожектора зеленый луч.
На авансцене, в полумраке,
Раскрыв золотозубый рот,
Румяный хахаль в шапокляке
О звездах песенку поет.
И под двуспальные напевы
На полинялый небосвод
Ведут сомнительные девы
Свой непотребный хоровод.
Сквозь облака, по сферам райским
(Улыбочки туда-сюда)
С каким-то веером китайским
Плывет Полярная Звезда.
За ней вприпрыжку поспешая,
Та пожирней, та похудей,
Семь звезд – Медведица Большая –
Трясут четырнадцать грудей.
И до последнего раздета,
Горя брильянтовой косой,
Вдруг жидколягая комета
Выносится перед толпой.
Глядят солдаты и портные
На рассусаленный сумбур,
Играют сгустки жировые
На бедрах Etoile d'Amour,

STARS

Upstairs – a cheap house for sweet meetings.
Downstairs – a cheap casino where
The spectators are seated. There
It's dark... pinches and expectations,
With now a giggle, now a yawn...
A balding failure as his greeting
To the house raises his baton.
And opening everywhere: dark.
The green beam of the spotlight crowds
Down through the tobacco-smoke clouds.
In half-dark at the footlights arc
A pink Don Juan with opera hat
Opens his gold-toothed mouth and croons
A silly song about the stars.
Accompanied by boudoir tunes
Against a faded firmament,
The dubious virgins count the bars –
Their dance obscenely diffident.
Through clouds, along celestial spheres
(Smiles here and there; smiles as per plan)
With some kind of a Chinese fan
The North Star floats out. Then appears
Following her – the Big Bear-Dipper:
The Seven Stars who skip and scatter
(Some of them thinner, some are fatter.)
And shake their jellied fourteen breasts.
Then, suddenly, almost undressed,
Spiraling with her diamond braid,
The thin-legged comet spins and veers
To show the crowd what God has made.
Soldiers, shopkeepers peer and pour
At this next chaos – gaudy, gay:
Clusters and rolls of fine fat play
On the thighs of Etoile d'Amour.

Несутся звезды в пляске, тряске,
Звучит оркестр, поет дурак,
Летят алмазные подвязки
Из мрака в свет, из света в мрак.
И заходя в дыру все ту же,
И восходя на небосклон, –
Так вот в какой постыдной луже
Твой День Четвертый отражен!...
Не легкий труд, о Боже правый,
Всю жизнь воссоздавать мечтой
Твой мир, горящий звездной славой
И первозданною красой.

1925

ПАМЯТНИК

Во мне конец, во мне начало.
Мной совершенное так мало!
Но все ж я прочное звено:
Мне это счастие дано.

В России новой, но великой,
Поставят идол мой двуликий
На перекрестке двух дорог,
Где время, ветер и песок...

1931

Stars rush in dancing, shaking, swinging;
The band goes wild; the fool keeps singing.
And how the diamond garters fly
From light to dark, from dark to light;
They set in the same hole and rise
Again in these celestial skies.
This is a puddle – shame perfected
In which Thy Fourth Day is reflected!...
O Righteous God, it is not easy
Through life to rebuild in one's dreams
Your world which burns in starry glory
Where Your created beauty gleams.

MONUMENT

In me are both End and Beginning...
What I have won hardly worth winning!
But still I am a solid link:
This joy is mine; this joy I drink.

In that great Russia coming at you
They will erect my two-faced statue.
Where two roads meet, there I shall stand...
Where there is Time... and wind... and sand...

ГЕОРГИЙ ВЛАДИМИРОВИЧ ИВАНОВ
1894-1958

Медленно и неуверенно
Месяц встает над землей.
Черные ветки качаются
Пахнет весной и травой.

И отражается в озере
И холодеет на дне
Небо, слегка декадентское,
В бледно-зеленом огне.

Все в этом мире попрежнему
Месяц встает как вставал,
Пушкин именье закладывал
Или жену ревновал –

И ничего не исправила,
Не помогла ничему
Смутная, чудная музыка,
Слышная только ему.

(1930)

★ ★ ★

Хорошо что нет Царя.
Хорошо что нет России.
Хорошо что Бога нет.

Только желтая заря.
Только звезды ледяные.
Только миллионы лет.

GEORGE VLADIMIROVICH IVANOV
1894-1958

Slowly and almost uncertainly
The moon rises over the earth.
There's a fragrance of grass and of springtime;
Black branches sway back and forth.

Skies are reflected within the lake,
Chilled on the bottom below;
Cooling, they seem slightly decadent,
Pale with a greenish glow.

Things in this world are as they have been –
The moon rises now as before.
Pushkin was mortgaging his estate
Or was jealous of his wife once more.

Nothing has ever been rectified,
Nothing has been made less grim
By that indistinct, wonderful music,
Audible only to him.

★   ★   ★

It is good there is no Czar.
It is good there is no Russia.
It is good there is no God.

Only icy light from stars.
Only yellow sunsets blushing.
Only years in endless flood.

409

Хорошо что – ничего,
Хорошо что – никого,
Так черно и так мертво –

Что мертвее быть не может
И чернее не бывать,
Что никто нам не поможет
И не надо помогать.

(1930)

*　*　*

Россия счастие. Россия свет.
А, может быть, России вовсе нет.

И над Невой закат не догорал,
И Пушкин на снегу не умирал,

И нет ни Петербурга, ни Кремля –
Одни снега, снега, поля, поля...

Снега, снега, снега... А ночь долга
И не растают никогда снега.

Снега, снега, снега... А ночь темна
И никогда не кончится она.

Россия тишина. Россия прах.
А может быть Россия – только страх.

Веревка, пуля, ледяная тьма
И музыка сводящая с ума.

Веревка, пуля, каторжный рассвет,
Над тем, чему названья в мире нет.

(1931)

Good – there's nothing to be found.
Good – that no one is around.
And blackness and death abound.

Life could not be more dead – ever.
There could be no blacker day.
And no one will help us. Never.
But who needs help anyway?

★   ★   ★

Russia, our happiness. Russia, our light.
And what if there is no Russia in sight,

No Neva with the sunset's fading glow,
No Pushkin – wounded, dying in the snow,

No Petersburg, no Kremlin on Earth's face,
Nothing but snow and snow – and open space?

Snow, snow, it is all snow. And night goes on,
And it will never end, never be gone.

Snow, snow, it is all snow . . . And dark, dark night
Will never end nor yield to dawn's bright light.

Russia is dust. And silence – crisp and clear.
And what if all that Russia is is fear?

A rope, a bullet, icy dark – and add
A music that is driving you half-mad,

A rope, a bullet, a dawn which pain inflamed
Over things that the world has not yet named?

Тихим вечером в тихом саду
Облака отражались в пруду.

Ангел нес в безконечность звезду
И ее уронил над прудом...

И стоит заколоченный дом,
И молчит заболоченный пруд,
Скоро в нем и лягушки умрут.

И лежишь на болотистом дне
Ты, сиявшая мне в вышине.

(1950)

★   ★   ★

Теперь тебя не уничтожат,
Как тот безумный вождь мечтал.
Судьба поможет, Бог поможет,
Но – русский человек устал...

Устал страдать, устал гордиться,
Валя куда-то напролом.
Пора забвеньем насладиться,
А может быть – пора на слом...

... И ничему не возродиться
Ни под серпом, ни под орлом!

(1950)

Quiet evening – a quiet park place;
Clouds, mirrored in a pond's dark face.

Taking the star into far, far space,
An angel dropped it over the pond...

And a boarded-up house stands beyond,
And the bog-pond is silent nearby –
Even frogs in it soon will die,

And down deep on the slushy slime:
You, my star, once celestial, sublime.

* * *

They will not now annihilate you
As that insane leader aspired.
Both destiny and God will aid you,
But – the Russian man is tired...

Of being proud, of new pain daily
While rushing, breaking all enroute.
It's time to claim oblivion gaily,
To quit perhaps, *machine kaput*...

And no new life will flow or even trickle –
Beneath the eagle or the hammer-sickle.

Что-то сбудется, что-то не сбудется.
Перемелется все, позабудется...

Но останется эта вот, рыжая,
У заборной калитки трава.

...Если плещется где-то Нева,
Если к ней долетают слова —
Это вам говорю из Парижа я
То, что сам понимаю едва.

Апрель 1950

* * *

Где прошлогодний снег, скажите мне?...
Нетаявший, почти альпийский снег,
Невинной жертвой отданный весне,
Апрелем обращенный в плеск и бег,
В дыханье одуванчиков и роз,
Взволнованного мира светлый вал,
В поэзию,
                В бессмысленный вопрос,
Что ей Виллон когда-то задавал?

(1950)

Certain things will come true, certain things will not.
Everything will pass by, it will be forgot...

But there still will remain: growing, rusty-red-
Colored grass by the garden-door – there!

... If the Neva is splashing somewhere,
If my words fly to it – across air,
Then from Paris to you they are said,
Things that I myself scarcely find clear.

April 1950

★ ★ ★

Tell me, where are the snows of yesteryear?
The still-unmelted, almost-Alpine snows,
A pure sacrifice to Spring, changed here
By April into brooks, into the rose
And dandelion's breath, into the bright
Waves of the trembling world one views.
Into poetry.
          Even into the quite
Senseless question Villon once asked his Muse.

А люди? Ну на что мне люди?
Идет мужик, ведет быка.
Сидит торговка: ноги, груди,
Платочек, круглые бока.

Природа? Вот она природа –
То дождь и холод, то жара.
Тоска в любое время года,
Как дребезжанье комара.

Конечно, есть и развлеченья:
Страх бедности, любви мученья,
Искусства сладкий леденец,
Самоубийство, наконец.

(1950)

★ ★ ★

В награду за мои грехи,
Позор и торжество,
Вдруг появляются стихи –
Вот так... Из ничего.

Все кое-как и как-нибудь,
Волшебно на авось:
Как розы падают на грудь...
– И ты мне розу брось!

Нет, лучше брось за облака –
Там рифма заблестит,
Коснется тленного цветка
И в вечный превратит.

(1950)

And people? I should care for people?
A peasant walks; he guides an ox.
A peddler woman sits: small kerchief,
Legs, breasts, round hips and display box.

And Nature? Look! Here is your Nature: –
Now rain and cold. And now heat here.
And, like the buzz from a mosquito,
Ennui at any time of year.

Of course, there are also amusements:
The lollipop of Art, the fright
Of Poverty, the pain of Loving...
Then, if you want it, Suicide.

★ ★ ★

Here is reward for all my sins,
This triumph and disgrace:
A poem suddenly begins
From nothing, from no place.

The words come magically half-dressed,
Wearing haphazard clothes,
Like roses falling on my chest...
– And you, toss me a rose!

No, throw it past that cloud that towers...
A rhyme shines there and runs
To touch and transform mortal flowers
Into eternal ones.

На грани таянья и льда
Зеленоватая звезда.

На грани музыки и сна
Полу-зима, полу-весна,

К невесте тянется жених
И звезды падают на них,

Летят сквозь снежную фату,
В сияющую пустоту.

Ты – это я. Я – это ты.
Слова нежны. Сердца пусты.

Я – это ты. Ты – это я
На хрупком льду небытия.

(1950)

* * *

В дыму, в огне, в сияньи, в кружевах,
И веерах и страусовых перьях!...
В сухих цветах, в бессмысленных словах
И в грешных снах и в детских суеверьях –

Так женщина смеется на балу,
Так беззаконная звезда летит во мглу...

(1950)

Twixt ice and melting, in between,
On that border – a star grown green.

Twixt dream and music, bordering,
A line half-wintertime, half-spring.

A bridegroom stretches toward his bride,
And stars fall on them at their side.

They fall into her snowy dress,
Into a shining emptiness.

You, you are me and I am you.
Hearts are empty; words – tender, few.

I, I am you and you are me
On the thin ice of not-to-be.

       ★   ★   ★

In smoke, in fire, in luster and in laces,
The fans and ostrich feathers flowing wild,
Amidst dry flowers and the senseless phrases,
Sinful dreams, superstitions of a child.

... A woman laughing at a formal ball.
A no-law star in its abysmal fall.

> А от цево? Никто не ведает притцыны.
>
> Фонвизин

По улице уносит стружки
Ноябрьский ветер ледяной.
– Вы русский? – Ну, понятно, р у ш к и й .
Нос бесконечный. Шарф смешной.

Есть у него жена и дети,
Своя мечта, своя беда...
Как скучно жить на этом свете,
Как неуютно, господа!

Обедать, спать, болеть поносом.
Немножко красть. – А кто не крал?
... Такой же Гоголь с длинным носом
Так долго, страшно умирал...

(1950)

★　★　★

Эмалевый крестик в петлице
И серой тужурки сукно...
Какие печальные лица
И как это было давно.

Какие прекрасные лица
И как безнадежно бледны –
Наследник, императрица,
Четыре великих княжны...

1950

And who can tell me why?
Nobody knows the reason.
                                    Fonvizin

Along the street the scraps are scattered
By the iced November wind that blows.
'Are you Russian?' 'Of course I'm Rooshian.'
Outlandish scarf. Endless nose.

He has a wife, he has his children,
His dream, his cross – time and again...
'How tedious living in this world,
And such a trouble, gentlemen!' *

To die, sleep, run with diarrhea,
To steal a bit. 'And who does not?'
... And Gogol with a long nose like him,
Ghastly, long-dying on his cot...

★   ★   ★

Enameled cross in the buttonhole,
The gray fabric of his coat.
Their faces – how very sad!
The time – how remote!

What lovely faces, and yet how pale
In utter hopelessness!
The Czarevitch, the Empress,
Four Grand-Duchesses...

* A paraphrase of a famous conclusion to one of Gogol's tales. Tr.

Мелодия становится цветком,
Он распускается и осыпается,
Он делается ветром и песком,
Летящим на огонь весенним мотыльком,
Ветвями ивы в воду опускается ...

Проходит тысяча мгновенных лет
И перевоплощается мелодия
В тяжелый взгляд, в сиянье эполет,
В рейтузы, в ментик, в 'Ваше благородие',
В корнета гвардии – о, почему бы нет? ...

Туман ... Тамань ... Пустыня внемлет Богу.
– Как далеко до завтрашнего дня! ...

И Лермонтов один выходит на дорогу,
Серебряными шпорами звеня.

1950

*　*　*

Еще я нахожу очарованье
В случайных мелочах и пустяках –
В романе без конца и без названья,
Вот в этой розе, вянущей в руках.

Мне нравится, что на ее муаре
Колышется дождинок серебро,
Что я нашел ее на тротуаре
И выброшу в помойное ведро.

1950

The music is transformed into a flower;
It opens up and shakes its petals free.
It turns to wind and sand, a spring-moth flying
To the flame. It droops into the water sighing
With the bent branches of a willow tree.

One thousand years pass like a single moment...
The melody is metamorphosed (caught
Now as a heavy look, an epaulet shining)
To riding breeches, a cape with fur-lining,
To 'Your Grace', 'Lieutenant of the Guards'. And why not?

Fog, fog... Taman... The desert hears the Lord.
How long until tomorrow's day occurs...

And Lermontov, alone, comes down the road
Clinking his silver spurs.

★   ★   ★

I still am able to find some enchantment
In trifles I meet quite by accident:
A book with title and the ending missing,
This rose I hold, withering, without scent.

It pleases me that drops of rain are trembling
Silver and pure upon its moire velours,
That I found this rose on a dirty sidewalk,
That I'll toss it into the trash, for sure.

Я хотел бы улыбнуться,
Отдохнуть, домой вернуться...
Я хотел бы так немного,
То, что есть почти у всех,
То, что мне просить у Бога
И бессмыслица и грех.

1950

* * *

Я научился понемногу
Шагать со всеми – рядом, в ногу
По пустякам не волноваться
И правилам повиноваться.

Встают – встаю. Садятся – сяду,
Стозначный помню номер свой
Лояльно благодарен Аду
За звездный кров над головой.

1950

I would like to smile, to jest,
To go home, to have some rest.
Just what everybody has
(Is that much?) I want for me.
Still to pray to God for this
Is nonsense and blasphemy.

★ ★ ★

Little by little, I've learned to run
And keep in step with everyone,
To toss aside small irritations,
And to obey all regulations.

Stand up! I stand. Sit down! I sit.
I've learned my number very well.
And for that roof of stars – admit
My humble gratitude to Hell.

Я люблю безнадежный покой,
В октябре – хризантемы в цвету,
Огоньки за туманной рекой,
Догоревшей зари нищету...

Тишину безымянных могил,
Все банальности 'Песен без слов',
То, что Анненский жадно любил,
То, чего не терпел Гумилев.

1954

I like things which are calm and forlorn:
Lights that shine through the stream's foggy gloom,
The long-dying sunset's poverty,
The October chrysanthemum bloom,

The triteness of 'Songs Without Words',
Quiet graves with no names at their side –
All that Annensky avidly loved,
All that Gumilev couldn't abide.

МАРИНА ИВАНОВНА ЦВЕТАЕВА
1892-1941

МОЛИТВА

Христос и Бог! Я жажду чуда
Теперь, сейчас, в начале дня!
О дай мне умереть, покуда
Вся жизнь как книга для меня.

Ты мудрый. Ты не скажешь строго:
– 'Терпи, еще не кончен срок.'
Ты сам мне подал – слишком много!
Я жажду сразу – всех дорог!

Всего хочу: с душой цыгана
Идти под песни на разбой,
За всех страдать под звук органа
И амазонкой мчаться в бой;

Гадать по звездам в черной башне,
Вести детей вперед, сквозь тень...
Чтоб был легендой – день вчерашний,
Чтоб был безумьем – каждый день!

Люблю и крест, и шелк, и каски,
Моя душа мгновений след...
Ты дал мне детство – лучше сказки
И дай мне смерть – в семнадцать лет.

26 сентября 1909 г., Таруса

MARINA IVANOVNA TSVETAYEVA
1892-1941

PRAYER

O Christ and God, I thirst for a miracle
At this day's dawn. Now, let such be!
O let me die while all existence
Is opening like a book for me.

You're wise. You will not say severely:
'Be calm. Your time is not yet up!'
You Yourself gave to me, O, too much!
I thirst for all roads – in one cup.

I want all things: the soul of gypsies –
To walk with songs and rob someone.
To hurt for all midst organ-playing.
To rush to war – an Amazon.

To read the stars from some black tower.
To lead small children through the lane . . .
So yesterday would be a legend,
So every day would be insane!

I like a cross and silks and helmets.
My soul's a trace of moments seen . . .
You gave me youth – fairer than fable,
So give me death – at seventeen!

26 September 1909, Tarusa

Четвертый год.
Глаза, как лед,
Брови уже роковые,
Сегодня впервые
С кремлевских высот
Наблюдаешь ты
Ледоход.

Льдины, льдины
И купола.
Звон золотой,
Серебряный звон.
Руки скрещены,
Рот нем.
Брови сдвинув – Наполеон! –
Ты созерцаешь – Кремль.

– Мама, куда – лед идет?
– Вперед, лебеденок.
Мимо дворцов, церквей, ворот –
Вперед, лебеденок!
Синий
Взор озабочен.
– Ты меня любишь, Марина?
– Очень.
– Навсегда?
– Да.

Скоро – закат,
Скоро – назад:
Тебе в детскую, мне –
Письма читать дерзкие,
Кусать рот.

А лед
Все
Идет.

24 марта 1916

The four-year old.
Eyes icy cold,
Eyebrows, fated already...
Today for the first time
You see the ice-floe
From the Kremlin heights;
Look below.

The ice-floe, ice-floe
And cupolas.
Ringing of gold, gold
And silvery tone.
With your arms crossed so,
Mouth still.
Eyebrows knitted... – Napoleon,
You study Kremlin hill.

'Mama – where does the ice go?'
'Forward – little swan,
Past churches, and palaces, gates below,
Forward, little swan.'
Lovely
Blue eyes now worry:
'O Marina, you love me?'
'Surely.'
'For always?'
'Yes.'

Sunset – and then
Soon home – again.
And you to the nursery, me –
Me, I shall read – rude letters,
And bite lips – so...

And the ice-floe
Still
Moves below.

24 March 1916

MRP R

Имя твое – птица в руке,
Имя твое – льдинка на языке.
Одно-единственное движенье губ.
Имя твое – пять букв.
Мячик, пойманный на лету,
Серебряный бубенец во рту.

Камень, кинутый в тихий пруд,
Всхлипнет так, как тебя зовут.
В легком щелканье ночных копыт
Громкое имя твое гремит.
И назовет его нам – в висок
Звонко щелкающий курок.

Имя твое – ах, нельзя! –
Имя твое – поцелуй в глаза,
В нежную стужу недвижных век,
Имя твое – поцелуй в снег.
Ключевой, ледяной, голубой глоток.
С именем твоим – сон глубок.

15 апреля 1916

* * *

Зверю – берлога,
Страннику – дорога,
Мертвому – дроги.
Каждому – свое.

Женщине – лукавить,
Царю – править,
Мне – славить
Имя твое.

2 мая 1916 г.

Your name – a bird in my hand,
Your name – an icicle on my tongue.
One and just one – forming of lips.
Your name – four letters... done.
A ball that's caught in flight,
A silver bell inside the mouth.

A stone thrown in a quiet pond
Will gulp as your name sounds.
In the light clatter of hoofs at night
Thunders your loud name.
And the trigger crashing into the temple
Will echo it for us.

Your name – oh! – but one can't!
Your name – the kiss upon the eyes,
On the fragile frost of still eyelids.
Your name – a kiss on the snow,
A well-like, light-blue, icy swallowing.
With your name, the sleep is deep.

15 April 1916

★   ★   ★

For a beast – an abode,
For a pilgrim – a road,
For a corpse – a hearse.
And for each – his own claim.

A woman – betrays,
A czar – rules his days,
As for me – I shall praise
Always your name.

2 May 1916

Кавалер де Гриэ! – Напрасно
Вы мечтаете о прекрасной,
Самовластной – в себе не властной –
Сладострастной своей Manon.

Вереницею вольной, томной
Мы выходим из ваших комнат.
Дольше вечера нас не помнят.
Покоритесь, – таков закон.

Мы приходим из ночи вьюжной,
Нам от вас ничего не нужно,
Кроме ужина – и жемчужин,
Да быть может еще – души!

Долг и честь, Кавалер, – условность.
Дай Вам Бог целый полк любовниц!
Изъявляя при сем готовность...
Страстно любящая Вас.
М.

Декабрь 1917

ДОН

Кто уцелел – умрет, кто мертв – воспрянет.
И вот потомки, вспомнив старину:
– Где были *вы*? – Вопрос как громом грянет,
Ответ как громом грянет: – На Дону!

– Что делали? – Да принимали муки,
Потом устали и легли на сон.
И в словаре задумчивые внуки
За словом: долг напишут слово: Дон.

17 марта 1918 г.

Chevalier de Grieux, Sir, vainly
Do you dream of your lovely, insanely
Capricious (not controlling self mainly),
Your voluptuous Manon.

We leave your rooms like a procession,
A free, langorous line, for possession.
We're forgot after one evening's session.
SUBMIT is the law we must own.

We come from the night with snow blowing,
Needing nothing from you – but the bestowing
Of supper . . . and pearls for showing . . .
And a small bit of soul now and then.

Duty and honor, Sir, is a convention.
God give you regiments of mistresses. I mention
Herewith my readiness to give you attention.
Passionately loving you.
                                        M.

December 1917

THE DON

Those who survived will die; those dead will waken.
And lo! their sons recalling days long gone:
'Where were you?' The question as by thunder shaken,
The answer likewise thunders back: 'On the Don!'

'What did you do?' Accepted suffering, tired,
Lay down to sleep a little later on . . .
And in dictionaries the young your children sired
Will write down next to 'duty' the word, 'Don'.

17 March 1918

АНДРЕЙ ШЕНЬЕ

Андрей Шенье взошел на эшафот.
А я живу – и это страшный грех.
Есть времена – железные – для всех.
И не певец, кто в порохе – поет.

И не отец, кто с сына у ворот
Дрожа срывает воинский доспех.
Есть времена, где солнце – смертный грех.
Не человек – кто в наши дни – живет.

4-го апреля 1918 г.

*   *   *

Все великолепье
Труб – лишь только лепет
Трав – перед Тобой.

Все великолепье
Бурь – лишь только щебет
Птиц – перед Тобой.

Все великолепье
Крыл – лишь только трепет
Век – перед Тобой.

23 апреля 1921 г.

ANDRÉ CHÉNIER

André Chénier climbed up the scaffolding.
I live – and this is the great sin I've done.
There are times hard as iron for everyone.
And midst gunpowder, who's the bard who'd sing?

And, tell me, at the gate what father can
Tremblingly tear the armor off his son?
There are times when the sun's a sin for one.
In such days he who lives is not a man.

4 April 1918

★   ★   ★

All the magnificence
Of trumpets – is only a whisper
Of grasses – before you.

All the magnificence
Of storms – is only a twitter
Of birds – before you.

All the magnificence
Of wings – is only a flutter
Of eyelids – before you.

23 April 1921

ВОЗВРАЩЕНИЕ ВОЖДЯ

Конь – хром,
Меч – ржав.
Кто – сей?
Вождь толп.

Шаг – час,
Вздох – век,
Взор – вниз.
Все – там.

Враг. – Друг.
Терн. – Лавр.
Все – сон...
– Он. – Конь.

Конь – хром.
Меч – ржав.
Плащ – стар.
Стан – прям.

3 июля 1921 г.

ДИАЛОГ ГАМЛЕТА С СОВЕСТЬЮ

– На дне она, где ил
И водоросли... Спать в них
Ушла, – но сна и там нет!
– Но я ее любил
Как сорок тысяч братьев
Любить не могут!
          – Гамлет!

RETURN OF THE LEADER

Horse – lame,
Sword – rusty.
Who – he?
Crowd's boss.

A step – an hour,
A sigh – an age,
Eyes – down.
People – there:

Foe. – Friend.
Thorn. – Laurel.
All – dreams...
He. – Horse.

Horse – lame.
Sword – rusty.
Cloak – old.
Back – straight.

3 July 1921

DIALOGUE – HAMLET/CONSCIENCE

'She's on the bottom where
There's muck and algae... Deep there
She went... to sleep, no sleep there
For her! But I loved her
Like forty thousand brothers
Could never love!'
                              – Hamlet!

На дне она, где ил:
Ил!... И последний венчик
Всплыл на приречных бревнах...
– Но я ее любил
Как сорок тысяч...
                              – Меньше,
Все ж, чем один любовник.

На дне она, где ил.
– Но я ее –
            (*недоуменно*)
                        – любил??

5-го июня 1923 г.

ПОПЫТКА РЕВНОСТИ

Как живется вам с другою, –
Проще ведь? – Удар весла! –
Линией береговою
Скоро ль память отошла

Обо мне, пловучем острове
(По небу – не по водам!)
Души, души! быть вам сестрами,
Не любовницами – вам!

Как живется вам с *простою*
Женщиною? *Без* божеств?
Государыню с престола
Свергши (с оного сошед),

Как живется вам – хлопочется –
Ежится? Встается – как?
С пошлиной бессмертной пошлости
Как справляетесь, бедняк?

She's on the bottom where
There's muck! muck!... Her lost little
Wreath floated past the river
Logs... 'But I did love her
Like forty thousand...
                              – Less, yes,
Even less than one lover.

'She's on the bottom where...
There's muck... But I...
                    (*perplexedly*)
                              loved her??'

5 June 1923

AN ATTEMPT AT JEALOUSY

How is your life with another?
Easier? A stroke of oars!
Did all memory so quickly
(Like a coastline's sinking shores)

Fall away from me, an island
Floating (on the sky, not sea!)?
Souls, Souls! You were meant for sisters,
Not lovers... your destiny!

How is your life with a *simple*
Woman? All divines unknown?
Having overthrown the Empress,
You yourself stepped from the throne.

What's your life like? Do you hurry
Still, with cringing? Who wakes you?
What happens when that eternal
Tax of commonness is due?

'Судорог да перебоев –
Хватит! Дом себе найму.'
Как живется вам с любою –
Избранному моему!

Свойственнее и съедобнее –
Снедь? Приестся – не пеняй . . .
Как живется вам с подобием –
Вам, поправшему Синай!

Как живется вам с чужою,
Здешнею? Ребром – люба?
Стыд Зевесовой возжою
Не охлестывает лба?

Как живется вам – здоровится –
Можется? Поется – как?
С язвою бессмертной совести
Как справляетесь, бедняк?

Как живется вам с товаром
Рыночным? Оброк – крутой?
После мраморов каррары
Как живется вам с трухой

Гипсовой? (Из глыбы высечен
Бог – и начисто разбит!)
Как живется вам с стотысячной –
Вам, познавшему Лилит!

Рыночною новизною
Сыты ли? К волшбам остыв,
Как живется вам с земною
Женщиною, без шестых

'Stop! Enough breakdowns and shudders!
I'll rent a house – and have done.'
Can you live with *any* person,
Tell me, my selected one!

Tastier and better food? If
You are fed-up, blame none... sigh...
How is your life with a copy,
You who trampled Mount Sinai?

How is your life with a stranger,
One from *here*? Her rib suits you?
Does not shame whip round your forehead
Like the reins of Zeus? How do

You live? How's your health? What's doing
With you these days? Can you sing?
What happens when that eternal
Conscience (Poor man!) starts to sting?

How's life with goods from a market?
Are the taxes much too high?
After marble from Carrara –
How is your life with the dry

Dust, plaster of Paris? (Chiseled
Block was once a God: our myth
Crashed!) One of the hundred thousands
Is yours. You, who knew Lilith.

Does the market kind of plaything
Please you? Doffing magic tricks,
How's your life with just a mortal
Woman, without the extra sixth

Чувств?
    Ну, за голову: счастливы?
Нет? В провале без глубин –
Как живется, милый? Тяжче ли,
Так же ли как мне с другим?

19-го ноября 1924 г.

⋆ ⋆ ⋆

Емче органа и звонче бубна
Молвь – и одна для всех:
Ох, когда трудно, и ах, когда чудно,
А не дается – эх!

Ах с Эмпиреев и ох вдоль пахот,
И повинись, поэт,
Что ничего кроме этих ахов,
Охов у Музы нет.

Наинасыщеннейшая рифма
Недр, наинизший тон.
Так, перед вспыхнувшей Суламифью –
Ахнувший Соломон.

Ах: разрывающееся сердце,
Слог, на котором мрут.
Ах, это занавес – вдруг – разверстый.
Ох: ломовой хомут.

Словоискатель, словесный хахаль,
Слов неприкрытый кран,
Эх, слуханул бы разок – как ахал
В ночь половецкий стан!

Sense?
     So hold your head. Well, happy?
No. Endless abyss in view.
How is your life, darling? Harder
Or like mine with one not you?

19 November 1924

*   *   *

Larger than organs, more ringing than tambourines –
Speech: one for everyone.
Oh! – difficult. Ah! – marvelous.
Uh! – when a thing's not done.

Ah! – empyrean. Oh! – from the furrow.
Admit it, poets; it's so:
There is no sound that your Muse possesses,
Save for this 'Ah!' and this 'Oh!'

From the deep womb – the rhyme that is richest,
Deepest tone and fullest one . . .
So, before the Shulamite's flash of fire:
The ah-ing Solomon.

Ah! is the heart that bursts with rapture,
Syllable to greet death's stroke.
Ah! is the curtain, suddenly opened.
Oh! is the drayman's yoke.

Uh! the word-searcher, unsated word-necker,
Unturned-off faucet of words.
Uh! I should like to have heard once at night-time
Ah's from those Polovetsian herds.

И пригибался, и зверем прядал...
В мхах, в звуковом меху:
Ах – да ведь это ж цыганский табор
– Весь! – и с луной вверху!

Се жеребец, на аршин ощерясь,
Ржет, предвкушая бег.
Се, напоровшись на конский череп,
Песнь заказал Олег –

Пушкину. И – раскалясь в полете –
В прабогатырских тьмах –
Неодолимые возгласы плоти:
Ох! – эх! – ах!

23-го декабря 1924 г.

*   *   *

Тоска по родине! Давно
Разоблаченная морока!
Мне совершенно все равно,
Где – совершенно одинокой

Быть, по каким камням домой
Брести с кошелкою базарной
В дом, и не знающий, что – мой,
Как госпиталь или казарма.

Мне все равно, каких среди
Лиц – ощетиниваться пленным
Львом, из какой людской среды
Быть вытесненной – непременно –

How they crouched down ... like animals, leaping,
Mossed in the murmur's moist fur.
Ah! But this is a camp of gypsies,
Complete! With the moon astir!

Lo! A stallion with yard-long mouth open
Neighs and wants to be racing soon.
Lo! Having run straight into the horse's
Skull, Oleg orders a tune

To Pushkin. And fired red-hot in flight,
In pre-epic times, shapelessly raw,
Flesh in a flush of unconquerable crying:
Oh! Uh! Ah!

23 December 1924

*   *   *

This thing called homesickness! A fable
That was exploded long ago!
Because for me it does not matter
Where to be completely so

Alone, and with my bag from the market
To plod home on who cares *what* stone –
To some house (like hospital, barracks)
That doesn't know it is my own.

It doesn't matter whose – the faces,
Midst which to bristle like a pure,
Caged lion – or which human setting
To be shoved out of soon – for sure –

В себя, в единоличье чувств.
Камчатским медведем без льдины
Где не ужиться (и не тщусь!),
Где унижаться – мне едино.

Не обольщусь и языком
Родным, его призывом млечным.
Мне безразлично – на каком
Непонимаемой быть встречным!

(Читателем, газетных тонн
Глотателем, доильцем сплетен . . .)
Двадцатого столетья – он,
А я – до всякого столетья!

Остолбеневши, как бревно,
Оставшееся от аллеи,
Мне все – равны, мне все – равно,
И, может быть, всего равнее

Роднее бывшее – всего.
Все признаки с меня, все меты,
Все даты – как рукой сняло:
Душа, родившаяся – где-то.

Так край меня не уберег
Мой, что и самый зоркий сыщик
Вдоль всей души – всей поперек! –
Родимого пятна *не* сыщет!

Всяк дом мне чужд, всяк храм мне пуст,
И все – равно, и все – едино.
Но если по дороге куст
Встает, особенно – рябина . . .

1934

Into myself and my own feelings
(Kamchatka bear without his ice).
It's all the same: *where* not to get on?
Or *where* not to be treated nice?

And this about one's native language:
I'll not be fooled ... though it's milk-sweet.
Who cares which mother-tongue is spoken
If not understood by those you meet!

(By readers, by the gossip milkers,
By those who gulp each paper's word ...)
They're of this century, the twentieth,
And I – ere centuries occurred!

Having grown wooden like an old log
Remaining here from some park lane.
Each person, *every* thing's the same thing,
And that, perhaps, which seems again

More same than all else *was* the dearest:
All marks, all dates, all signs of *me* –
Vanish as by hand-flicking magic:
A soul born – somewhere: that simply.

My native land did not sustain me
Enough so that on all my soul
Even the most thorough detective
Could find a birthmark or a mole!

Each house is strange; each church means nothing.
It's all one and the same to me.
But if a bush looms by my pathway
Especially a rowan tree ...

ИРИНА ВЛАДИМИРОВНА ОДОЕВЦЕВА
р. 1901

Он сказал: 'Прощайте, дорогая,
Может быть, я больше не приду.'
По аллее я пошла, не зная,
В Летнем я саду или в аду.

Тихо, пусто. Заперты ворота,
Но зачем теперь итти домой?
Меж деревьев черных – белый кто-то
Бродит, спотыкаясь, как слепой.

Вот подходит ближе. Встала рядом
Статуя, сверкая при луне,
На меня взглянула белым глазом,
Голосом глухим сказала мне:

'Хочешь, поменяемся со мною?
Каменное сердце не болит.
Каменной ты станешь, я – живою.
Встань сюда, возьми мой лук и щит.'

'Хорошо, – согласно я сказала, –
Вот мое пальто и башмаки.'
Статуя меня поцеловала.
Я взглянула в белые зрачки.

Губы шевелиться перестали
И в груди не слышу теплый стук.
Я стою на белом пьедестале,
Щит в руках и за плечами лук.

Утро ... С молоком проходят бабы;
Дети и чиновники спешат;

IRINA VLADIMIROVNA ODOYEVTSEVA
b. 1901

He had said, 'Goodbye, my darling. Maybe
I won't come back – ever. Time will tell.'
And I walked off, down the lane, not knowing
If this was the Summer Park – or Hell.

Silent. Empty. And the gate is fastened.
But why should I now ever go home?
Stumbling like a blind man, by the black trees,
Somebody in white begins to roam.

She comes closer ... till she stands beside me:
It's a statue, bright in the moonglow.
She looks at me with her white eyes staring,
And she asks me in a voice turned low:

'What do you think of our trading places?
If a heart is stone, it doesn't ache.
You will become stone; I'll be the live one.
Stand there. Here's my bow and shield. So take.'

'All right,' I say – in a good agreement.
'Here's my coat and shoes; they're just your size.'
Then the statue turns her head to kiss me;
I see the white pupils of her eyes.

Then I notice my lips stop their moving.
My heart's warm beat doesn't sound at all.
Shield in hand and bow behind my shoulders,
I'm standing on a white pedestal.

Morning ... and the early shuffle of the milkmaids.
Children and officials hurry ... Add

Звон трамваев, дождь и ветер слабый
И такой обычный Петроград.

Господи!... И вдруг мне стало ясно:
Мне любимого не разлюбить,
Каменною стала я напрасно,
Камень будет дольше сердца жить.

А она уходит, напевая,
В рыжем клетчатом пальто моем.
Я стою, холодная, нагая,
Под осенним проливным дождем.

(1922)

* * *

– В этом мире любила ли что-нибудь ты?...
– Ты должно быть смеешься! Конечно, любила.
– Что? – Постой. Дай подумать! Духи, и цветы,
И еще зеркала... Остальное забыла.

1950

Rain and weak wind, and the streetcars ringing:
All the usual world of Petrograd.

Lord!... O Lord, I realize this instant:
I can't stop loving my love, my man.
All in vain I turned into a statue;
Stone can last longer than one's heart can.

And she's leaving now – in my red-checkered
Coat – and humming a melodic strain,
While I still stand here – frozen and naked
In the dismal, pelting, autumn rain.

★   ★   ★

'Did you love anything in this wide universe?'
'Well, of course I did! Why do you make such a jest?',
'What?' 'O, wait, let me think! There were perfume and flowers,
Also mirrors ... and ... I have forgotten the rest.'

По набережной ночью мы идем.
Как хорошо – идем, молчим вдвоем.

И видим Сену, дерево, собор
И облака...
                    А этот разговор
На завтра мы отложим, на потом,
На после-завтра...
                    На когда умрем.

(1951)

How nice to walk the quay at night! No fuss.
We stroll and we are silent, both of us.

We see the Seine, a tree, and there's the rising stone
Of a cathedral, and clouds...
                                        We'll postpone
Our talking till tomorrow, later, aye,
Till day after tomorrow,
                                        till we die.

НИКОЛАЙ АВДЕЕВИЧ ОЦУП
1894-1958

Всю комнату в два окна,
С кроватью для сна и любви,
Как щепку несет волна,
Как хочешь волну зови.

И если с небом в глазах
Я тело твое сожму,
То знай: это только страх –
Чтоб не тонуть одному.

(1923)

NIKOLAI AVDEYEVICH OTSUP
1894-1958

The whole room with two windows,
With a bed for sleep and love,
Is borne on a wave like driftwood –
Call the wave what you think of.

And if I press your body
With sky in my eyes, I own
That I do so from fear only –
So as not to drown alone.

ЭМИГРАНТ

Как часто я прикидывал в уме,
Какая доля хуже:
Жить у себя, но как в тюрьме,
Иль на свободе, но в какой-то луже.

Должно быть, эмиграция права,
Но знаете конечно сами:
Казалось бы – 'Вот счастье, вот права':
Европа с дивными искусства образцами.

Но изнурителен чужой язык,
И не привыкли мы к его чрезмерным дозам,
И эта наша песнь – под тряпкой вскрик,
Больного бормотанье под наркозом.

Но под приказом тоже не поется
И может быть в потомстве отзовется,
Не их затверженный мотив,
А наш полузадушенный призыв.

(1952)

EMIGRÉ

How often I have pondered in my mind
Which choice by lot is worse: to be
At home but live as in jail,
Or live in such a hole (although I'm free).

Perhaps, living in exile is all right.
But then, of course, you know the part:
You think: 'Here there are rights and happiness.' *
Europe – with wonderful examples of great art.

But strange language leaves us tired;
We're not used to large doses of it – in such mass.
And this, our song: a shout beneath a rag,
The muttering of a patient under gas.

But neither can one sing by the decree,
And what will echo in posterity
May not be their parroted themes –
But something of our own half-strangled plea.

* A quotation from one of Pushkin's late poems. Tr.

БОРИС ЮЛИАНОВИЧ ПОПЛАВСКИЙ
1903-1935

СТОИЦИЗМ

В теплый час над потемневшим миром
Желтоносый месяц родился.
И тотчас же выстиранный с мылом,
Вдруг почувствовал осень сад.

Целый день жара трубила с башни,
Был предсмертный сон в глазах людей.
Только поздно улыбнулся влажно
Темноалый вечер чародей.

Под зеленым сумраком каштанов
Высыхал гранит темнолиловый.
Хохотали дети у фонтана,
Рисовали мелом город новый.

Утром птицы мылись в акведуке,
Спал на голых досках император.
И уже средь мрамора и скуки
Ад дышал полуденный с Эфрата.

А над замком под смертельным небом,
Распростерши золотые крылья,
Улыбалась мертвая победа
И солдат дремал под слоем пыли.

Было душно. В неуютной бане
Воровали вещи, нищих брили.
Шевеля медлительно губами,
Мы в воде о сферах говорили.

BORIS YULIANOVICH POPLAVSKY
1903-1935

STOICISM

The yellow-nosed moon was born at twilight,
The warm hour when darkness covers all.
And as if laundered with soap that instant,
Suddenly the park felt it was fall.

Pre-death sleep was in the eyes of people –
After heat had tooted from a tower.
And the dark-red sorcerer of evening
Smiled late in the day with his moist power.

Under the green dusk of shady chestnuts,
Lilac granite dried and became cool.
Children with some chalk drew a new city,
And laughed, playing near the fountain's pool.

Birds bathed in the aqueduct with morning.
On the bare boards slept the emperor.
And already midst marble and boredom,
Noon's hell breathed from the Euphrates' shore.

Under lethal sky above the castle,
With her spreading golden wings out–thrust,
The dead victory was smiling, and a
Soldier dozed beneath a film of dust.

Air was stifling. In the bath's discomfort
Things were being stolen, beggars shaved.
Moving our lips slowly in the water,
We discussed the spheres, how they behaved,

И о том, как отшумев прекрасно
Мир сгорит, о том что в Риме вечер,
И о чудной гибели напрасной
Мудрецов, детей широкоплечих.

Надсмехались мокрые атлеты,
Разгоралась желтая луна,
Но Христос, склонившийся над Летой,
В отдаленьи страшном слушал нас.

В море ночи распускались звезды,
И цветы спасались от жары,
Но уже проснувшись шли над бездной
В Вифлеем индусские цари.

И слуга у спящего Пилата
Воду тихо в чашу наливал,
Центурион дежурный чистил латы
И Иосиф хмуро крест стругал.

1950

* * *

На мраморе среди зеленых вод
Ты спишь, душа, готовая проснуться,
Твой мерно дышит розовый живот
И чистый рот, готовый улыбнуться.

Сошло в надир созвездие живых
Судьба молчит, смеясь железным ликом,
На бронзовую шляпу снег летит,
На черный лоб садится птица с криком.

How the world will burn up, having grandly
Roared away, – its being night in Rome,
And the lovely, senseless deaths of wise-men
And broad-shouldered youths here and at home.

And the yellow moon burned more, more brightly
As wet athletes made their mocking fuss.
And the Christ, bending down over Lethe,
In the dire distance was hearing us.

In the sea of night stars were unfolding,
And the flowers sought refuge from heat;
And over chasms, wakened kings from India
Marched toward Bethlehem on guided feet.

Sleeping Pilate's servant poured a basin
Full of water – very quietly.
One centurion polished his armor;
Joseph, sad, planed a cross from a tree.

★   ★   ★

You sleep, my soul, on marble midst the green,
Green waters, ready for another waking;
Your pink belly breathes rhythmically; your clean,
Pure mouth has a slight smile already breaking.

Fate is silent, a laughing iron face that
Sees constellations of the living reaching
Down to the nadir. Snow tops the bronze hat;
A bird sees the black forehead, lights there screeching.

Она прошла, возлюбленная жизнь,
Наполнив своды запахом фиалок.
Издали двери незабвенный визг,
И снег пошел на черный край фиала.

Крадется ночь, как ледяная рысь,
По улицам, где в камне стынут воды.
И зорко смотрит птица сверху вниз,
Куда укрыться ей от непогоды.

(1935)

O, it has passed, our life's dear silhouette;
The violet's fragrance fills the vaults' ledges;
The doors closed with a clank one can't forget;
It started snowing on the vial's black edges.

The night steals like an icy lynx on each
Street where the stones' caught waters freeze together,
A bird looks high and low, sharply, to reach
A place to hide from this inclement weather.

АНАТОЛИЙ СЕРГЕЕВИЧ ШТЕЙГЕР
1907-1944

Мы верим книгам, музыке, стихам,
Мы верим снам, которые нам снятся,
Мы верим слову... (Даже тем словам,
Что говорятся в утешенье нам,
Что из окна вагона говорятся)...

1933, Марсель

* * *

Слабый треск опускаемых штор,
Чтобы дача казалась незрячей,
И потом, точно выстрел в упор, –
Рев мотора в саду перед дачей.

... И еще провожающих взор
Безнадежный, тоскливый, собачий.

(1944)

* * *

У нас не спросят: вы грешили?
Нас спросят лишь: любили ль вы?
Не поднимая головы,
Мы скажем горько: – Да, увы,
Любили... как еще любили!...

(1944)

ANATOLY SERGEYEVICH STEIGER
1907-1944

We believe books, music, poetry;
We believe dreams that we see in our sleep.
We believe words . . . (Even those words
Which are spoken to console us,
Spoken from the window of a train) . . .

1933, Marseilles

* * *

The weak rattling of lowered blinds
Made the dacha itself seem un-seeing,
And then like a shot, point-blank, – the roar
Of the car in the dacha's front garden.

. . . And the eyes of the ones left behind –
So dog-like, hopeless, sad, unbelieving.

* * *

We won't be asked then: Did you sin?
We'll be only asked: Did you love?
And without raising up our heads,
We'll say bitterly: Yes, alas.
We loved . . . and how we loved!

467

АНТОНИН ПЕТРОВИЧ ЛАДИНСКИЙ
1896-1961

ОХОТА

В парнасских чащах голубых
Затравленный, как зверь опасный,
Взлетев, изнемогает стих,
Слабеет в рощах голос ясный.

В переполохе жарких свор
Твой одинокий голос тонет,
Когда летит во весь опор
Неумолимая погоня.

И в этом роковом кругу,
Под градом стрел и в трубном хоре
Рычит звереныш! На бегу
Клыком собаке брюхо порет!

А Муза в синеве дубов
Ломает руки в исступленьи:
Все чудится ей медь рогов,
Пернатых стрел густое пенье –

Шлют братский взор издалека
Ее глазам огромным синим
Два мутных маленьких глазка
В колючей яростной щетине.

(1930)

ANTONIN PETROVICH LADINSKY
1896-1961

HUNTING

In those blue thickets of Parnassus
The dangerous beast is brought to bay:
The clear-voiced verse that soared to heaven
Falls in the grove – fading away.

The lone voice drowns amidst the hustle
Of packs of heated hounds which race
And rush at top speed while pursuing
With no mercy their frantic chase.

And centered in that fateful circle,
Midst trumpeting and arrow stabs,
The young beast roars! Running, he slashes
The dog bellies with his tusk jabs.

The muse in the blue of the oak trees,
Who wrings her hands in frenzy, seems
To hear the horns' brass and the heavy
Song of the feathered arrow-streams.

And two small, troubled eyes, ignited
In that fierce, prickling bristle, stood
And sent her large blue eyes so distant
A desperate glance of brotherhood.

ВЛАДИМИР АЛЕКСЕЕВИЧ СМОЛЕНСКИЙ
1901-1961

СТАНСЫ

Закрой глаза, в виденьи сонном
Восстанет твой погибший дом –
Четыре белые колонны,
Над розами и над прудом.

И ласточек крыла косые
В небесный ударяют щит,
А за балконом вся Россия,
Как ямб торжественный звучит.

Давно был этот дом построен,
Давно уже разрушен он,
Но, как всегда, высок и строен,
Отец выходит на балкон.

И зоркие глаза прищуря,
Без страха смотрит с высоты,
Как проступают там, в лазури,
Судьбы ужасные черты.

И чтоб ему прибавить силы,
И чтоб его поцеловать,
Из залы, или из могилы,
Выходит улыбаясь мать.

И вот, стоят навеки вместе
Они среди своих полей,
И, как жених своей невесте,
Отец целует руку ей.

VLADIMIR ALEKSEYEVICH SMOLENSKY
1901-1961

STANZAS

Close your eyes tight. And in your dreaming
Your vanished house, somewhere beyond,
Will rise with four white columns gleaming
Above the roses and the pond.

And then the wings of swallows slanting
Will strike that shield of sky. And all
Beyond the balcony is chanting...
Russia's an iamb festival.

Built long ago... this house with hallways.
Long since... destroyed totally.
But tall and shapely, now as always,
Father comes to the balcony.

With his far-seeing, keen eyes squinting
He boldly looks down from on high
At the dire features of fate glinting
Their outlines in the azure sky.

To give him more strength to renew him,
To give him kisses later on,
My mother smilingly comes to him
Back from the grave or the salon.

And so they stand together through life,
Surrounded by their fields and land.
And, as a bridegroom with his new wife,
My father bends to kiss her hand.

А рядом мальчик черноглазый
Прислушивается, к чему –
Не знает сам, и роза в вазе
Бессмертной кажется ему.

(1953)

And nearby is a dark-eyed boy,
Listening to what – nobody knows.
He thinks this an immortal joy:
The vase before him with a rose.

ЛИДИЯ ДАВЫДОВНА ЧЕРВИНСКАЯ
р. 1907

Хочется Блоковской, щедрой напевности
(Тоже рожденной тоской),
Да, и любви, и разлуки, и ревности,
Слез, от которых покой.

Хочется верности, денег, величия,
Попросту – жизни самой.
От бесприютности, от безразличия
Тянет в чужую Россию – домой...

Лучше? Не знаю. Но будет иначе –
Многим беднее, многим богаче,

И холоднее зимой.

(1937)

LYDIA DAVYDOVNA CHERVINSKAYA
b. 1907

One would like much lilting Blokian melody
(Born, too, from longing's release).
Yes, also love, separation and jealousy,
Even the tears which bring peace.

One would like greatness and money and faithfulness
And simply life: joy and pain.
So from indifference or just being shelterless
One is drawn home, to strange Russia, again.

Better? Who knows? But different... yes, brothers!
Poorer in some ways, richer in others,

And in the winters more cold.

АННА СЕМЕНОВНА ПРИСМАНОВА
1898-1960

КРОВЬ И КОСТЬ

I

В моей природе два начала,
и мать, баюкая меня,
во мне двух близнецов качала:
кость трезвости и кровь огня.

Но кровь и кость, два равных рвенья,
вступив с младенчества в борьбу,
отметили мою судьбу
печальным знаком раздвоенья.

II

О музыка, тебя ли слышу
я над собою по утрам?
Ты крест в мою вставляешь крышу –
и дом – не дом уже, а храм!

Всесильная, одна ты можешь
и кровь и кость в себя вобрать.
Ты мне едва ли жить поможешь,
зато поможешь умирать.

(1946)

ANNA SEMYONOVNA PRISMANOVA
1898-1960

BLOOD AND BONE

I

Two elements are in my nature;
And humming lullabies to me,
My mother rocked twins: blood of fire
And bone of staid sobriety.

And blood and bone, equally mine,
Have marked since childhood all my living;
My destiny has been one, giving
Always this sad and dual sign.

II

O poetry, are you above me
On mornings giving me new proof
My house is no house but a temple,
Putting a cross upon my roof?

Omnipotent, you and you only
Blend bone and blood as one ally –
You'll hardly help me in my living;
But you will help me when I die.

ВЛАДИМИР ВЛАДИМИРОВИЧ НАБОКОВ
р. 1899

Каким бы полотном батальным ни являлась
советская сусальнейшая Русь,
какой бы жалостью душа ни наполнялась –
не поклонюсь, не примирюсь

со всею мерзостью, жестокостью и скукой
немого рабства... Нет, о, нет,
еще я духом жив, еще не сыт разлукой –
увольте – я еще поэт!

1944, Cambridge, Mass.

* * *

Какое сделал я дурное дело,
и я ли развратитель и злодей,
я, заставляющий мечтать мир целый
о бедной девочке моей?

О, знаю я: меня боятся люди,
и жгут таких как я за волшебство,
и как от яда в полом изумруде
мрут от искусства моего.

Но как забавно, что в конце абзаца,
корректору и веку вопреки,
тень русской ветки будет колебаться
на мраморе моей руки.

1959, San Remo

478

VLADIMIR VLADIMIROVICH NABOKOV
p. 1899

No matter how the Soviet tinsel glitters
Upon the canvas of a battle piece;
No matter how the soul dissolves in pity,
I will not bend, I will not cease

Loathing the filth, brutality and boredom
Of silent servitude. No, no, I shout,
My spirit is still quick, still exile-hungry,
I'm still a poet, count me out!

(Translated by the author)

* * *

What is the evil deed I have committed?
Seducer, criminal – is this the word
For me who set the entire world a-dreaming
Of my poor little girl?

Oh, well I know that people do not love me:
They burn the likes of me for wizard wiles
And as of poison in a hollow smaragd
Of my art die.

Amusing, though, that at the last indention,
Despite proofreaders and my age's ban,
A Russian branch's shadow shall be playing
Upon the marble of my hand.

(Translated by the author)

ВЛ. КОРВИН-ПИОТРОВСКИЙ
(ВЛАДИМИР ЛЬВОВИЧ КОРВИН)
1901-1966

РОЗЫ НА СНЕГУ

Дымятся розы на снегу,
Их вьюга заметает пылью, –
Проворный попик набегу
Трет белый нос епитрахилью.

Трескучий холод кости ест, –
Все разошлись мороза ради, –
И только – розы, снег и крест,
Приваленный к чужой ограде.

И двое пьяниц, – землю бьют,
Тяжелым заступом ломают,
Продрогнув, крепко водку пьют
И что-то грешное поют,
Отроковицу поминают.

И во хмелю своем, гордясь
Ее невинной красотою,
Уж не робея, не стыдясь,
От ветра лишь отворотясь,
Нечистой тешатся мечтою –

Железная земля тяжка, –
Гроб гулко ахает и стонет,
Под грудой мерзлого песка
Никто не смеет и не тронет.

WL. KORVIN-PIOTROWSKY
(VLADIMIR LVOVICH KORVIN)
1901-1966

ROSES IN THE SNOW

The roses smoke upon the snow,
The blizzard sweeps the snowdust o'er them.
The brisk, small priest, still on the go,
Rubs his nose with his stole before them.

The crackling cold chills bones with frost;
Now all have left this freezing weather.
The roses, snow, the leaning cross
On that strange fence – alone together.

And two drunks chopping at the ground, –
They break it with a heavy shovel.
For warmth they gulp more vodka down
And sing some kind of sinful round
Naming the young girl as they grovel.

Delighting in her virgin state
And loveliness, feeling their drinking,
Not shy but shameless, talking great,
They duck the wind, turn toward the gate,
Amuse themselves, do dirty thinking.

The earth is hard-as-iron land;
The coffin echoes and moans there too.
Beneath the mound of frozen sand
No one will touch her, no one dare to.

Она лежит, снегов бледней,
На смертном иль на брачном ложе,
И небо низкое над ней
На вечность мутную похоже.

Дымится куст, дымится твердь,
Земля во власти мглы летучей,
Безлюдье в темноте скрипучей, —
Лишь ночь и ночь. Лишь смерть и смерть.

1944

Whether marriage or death her bed,
She lies more pale than snow upon it.
And that low sky above her head
Is like eternity's dark bonnet.

The bush is smoking... and the sky.
Winged darkness holds Earth in its breath.
This cracking dusk. No one nearby...
Just night and night. Just death and death.

ЮРИЙ ПАВЛОВИЧ ОДАРЧЕНКО
1890-1960

Как бы мне в стихах не сбиться
Лишь на то, что ночью снится.

Солнца, солнца, солнца луч,
Озари из темных туч
В голове моей больной
Твой прекрасный рай земной:

Я прикован к гильотине,
Голова моя в корзине,
И от солнечных лучей
Кровь немного горячей.

(1949)

★ ★ ★

Той дорогой, которой иду,
Я наверное в ад попаду.

Но оттуда по шелковой лесенке,
Напевая веселые песенки,
Я обратно на землю вернусь
И на крыше в кота воплощусь.

Буду жить я у девочки маленькой
В ее розовой чистенькой спаленке.
Буду нежно мурлыкать опять –
Но о чем, никому не понять.

(1949)

YURI PAVLOVICH ODARCHENKO
1890-1960

How can I keep from my verse
Nightmares that are so perverse?

Sunbeam, sunbeam, send a ray
Through the dark clouds in my gray,
Morbid head; light up the skies
Of Earth's lovely paradise:

Chained. A guillotine. I'm dead.
And a basket holds my head.
The sunrays splash in a flood,
Slightly warming up my blood.

* * *

On the path that I walk I can tell
I'll most certainly end up in hell.

But from there – on a silky rope ladder,
Humming gay little songs, getting gladder,
I shall come back to Earth; and like that –
On a roof I'll turn into a cat.

I shall live with a nice little girl
In her small, pink, clean bedroom, and curl
Up and purr, gently purr, like as not...
But nobody will know about what.

ИГОРЬ ВЛАДИМИРОВИЧ ЧИННОВ

р. 1914

А может быть, все же – спасибо за это:
За нежность туманно-жемчужного света,
За свежесть дождем всколыхнутого сада,
За первые знаки – уже – листопада.

Спасибо, что облако меркнет и тает
Над этой в закат улетающей стаей,
И розовый свет приближается к морю...
Ну, что же, спасибо. Да разве я спорю...

1957

* * *

О Воркуте, о Венгрии (– о чем?)
О Да́хау и Хирошиме...
Да, надо бы – как огненным мечом,
Стихами грозными, большими.

Ты думаешь о рифмах – пустяках –
Ты душу изливаешь – вкратце,
Но на двадцатый век тебе в стихах
Не удается отозваться.

И если отзовешься – лишний труд:
Не будет отзвука на отзвук.
Стихи, стихи – их даже не прочтут.
Так пар уходит в зимний воздух.

И все-таки – хотя десятком строк,
Словами нужными, живыми...
Ты помнишь, есть у Пушкина 'Пророк':
О шестикрылом серафиме.

1958

IGOR VLADIMIROVICH CHINNOV
b. 1914

But, nevertheless, let me say thanks all right
For such gentleness in the misty, pearl light,
For freshness of gardens awakened by rain,
For first signs (already) of leaf-fall again,

And thanks that the cloud darkens, melting to run
Above flocks of birds flying into the sun,
This last rosy light stretching over the bay...
Well, thanks. But I never argue anyway.

★   ★   ★

About Hungary, Vorkuta... (what else?)
Dachau... Hiroshima, of course...
O yes, one should – as with a fiery sword –
In awe-inspiring, noble verse.

You think about the trifles – such as rhymes;
You distill what is in your soul.
The poetry you write cannot respond
To this century as a whole.

And if it should, so what? You fail again:
No echoes from this echo spread.
The vapor vanishes in winter air,
And poems, poems won't be read.

And yet, with maybe even just ten lines
Where words are needed, living things...
Remember, Pushkin has a *Prophet* poem
About a seraph with six wings.

ДМИТРИЙ ИОСИФОВИЧ КЛЕНОВСКИЙ
(КРАЧКОВСКИЙ)
р. 1892

СЛЕД ЖИЗНИ

Люблю читать на первом снеге
   Скупые заячьи следы.
Смотри: здесь был он на ночлеге,
   Тут уходил он от беды,

Там он сидел, прижавши уши,
   Водя усами на ветру,
А здесь неторопливо кушал
   С березки сладкую кору.

И на душе тепло и славно,
   И я, не отрывая глаз,
Читаю этот своенравный,
   Наивный заячий рассказ,

И думаю: быть может Кто-то
   Моих неизгладимых лет
С такой-же милою заботой
   В моей душе читает след.

И все, что мне цвело так дивно,
   Так пело сердцу и уму,
Такой-же повестью наивной
   Наверно кажется Ему!

1945

DMITRI IOSIFOVICH KLENOVSKY
(KRACHKOVSKY)
b. 1892

FOOTPRINT OF LIFE

When the first snow falls, I enjoy
    Seeing a rabbit's scattered tracks.
Look! Here is where he spent the night,
    And here he ran from fierce attacks!

Here he sat down and dropped his ears,
    Moving his moustache in the breeze.
And here he took his time to eat
    The sweet bark from these slim birch trees.

My soul expands with pleasant warmth;
    And keeping my eyes focused so,
I read this willful, naive tale
    About a rabbit on the snow.

And then I ponder: perhaps Someone
    Reads in my soul the footprints there
Of all my nonerasable
    Years with the same kind, gentle care.

And all that flowered wondrously,
    Filled my heart and mind to the brim,
Probably seems to be the same
    Kind of naive story to Him.

ИВАН ЕЛАГИН
(ИВАН ВЕНЕДИКТОВИЧ МАТВЕЕВ)
р. 1918

Уже последний пехотинец пал,
Последний летчик выбросился в море.
А на путях дымятся груды шпал
И проволока вянет на заборе.

Они молчат – свидетели беды.
И забывают о борьбе и тлене
И этот танк, торчащий из воды,
И этот мост, упавший на колени.

Но труден день очнувшейся земли.
Уже в портах ворочаются краны,
Становятся дома на костыли...
Там города залечивают раны.

Там будут снова строить и ломать.
А человек идет дорогой к дому.
Он постучится – и откроет мать.
Откроет двери мальчику седому.

1945

IVAN ELAGIN
(IVAN VENEDIKTOVICH MATVEYEV)
b. 1918

The last foot soldier has already fallen;
The last pilot chuted into the sea.
On railroad tracks the piled-up ties are smoking;
The wire of fences withers rustily.

This tank that sticks its steel out of the water,
This broken bridge, kneeling upon its knees...
They now are silent – these who saw the horror,
And they forget the fight and war's disease.

But Earth's wakening day is full of labor;
The cranes in harbors start to turn once more,
The houses hoist themselves up on their crutches...
The cities treat and heal each open sore.

Here they will build, and break again, rebuilding,
While down the road to his home walks someone.
He'll knock – and his mother will come to open, –
She'll open the doors to her gray-haired son.

Мне незнакома горечь ностальгии.
Мне нравится чужая сторона.
Из всей – давно оставленной – России
Мне нехватает русского окна.

Оно мне вспоминается доныне,
Когда в душе становится темно –
Окно с большим крестом посередине,
Вечернее горящее окно.

1960

I've never let those homesick-longings find me;
I like this alien land. And I avow
That of the Russia I left long ago behind me,
I only miss a Russian window now.

It's always in my memory, returning
When darkness in my soul begins to toss:
There is that window in the twilight, burning,
A window flashing out, framed, one big cross.

НИКОЛАЙ МОРШЕН
(НИКОЛАЙ НИКОЛАЕВИЧ МАРЧЕНКО)
р. 1917

У МАЯКА

Здесь на юг пролетают птицы,
Обгоняя случайный шквал.
Здесь с разбегу волна дробится
В горьковатую пыль у скал.

Здесь прибой потрясает гривой,
Словно вздыбленный белый конь.
Здесь ночами во мгле бурливой
Зажигает маяк огонь.

Но, привычные к тьме безлюдья,
Не понявши зачем и как,
Перелетные птицы грудью
Ударяются о маяк.

И крылатое, став свинцовым,
Исчезает в морской пыли.
.   .   .   .   .

Вдалеке благодарным ревом
Откликаются корабли.

1948

NIKOLAI MORSHEN
(NIKOLAI NIKOLAYEVICH MARCHENKO)
b. 1917

NEAR THE LIGHTHOUSE

When the birds travel south, they fly here –
Overtaking a casual squall.
With a running jump waves break high here
Into pungent spray at the cliff wall.

Here the flood shakes its mane, all starkness,
Like a wild-rearing horse of white;
Here at night in the stormy darkness
The lighthouse throws its circling light.

But grown used to dark desolation
And not grasping the why and how,
Transient birds in their night migration
Break their breasts gainst the lighthouse now.

And the wingèd becoming leaden
Disappear in the sea-dust banks.
.   .   .   .   .   .
Far away, ships, responding, deaden
The deep night with a roar of thanks.

IV

POETRY AND REVOLUTION

МАКСИМИЛИЯН АЛЕКСАНДРОВИЧ ВОЛОШИН
(КИРИЕНКО)
1877-1932

ГОЛОВА MADAME DE LAMBALLE
(4 сентября 1792 г.)

Это гибкое, страстное тело
Растоптала ногами толпа мне,
И над ним надругалась, раздела...
И на тело
Не смела
Взглянуть я...
Но меня отрубили от тела,
Бросив лоскутья
Воспаленного мяса на камне...

И парижская голь
Унесла меня в уличной давке.
Кто-то пил в кабаке алкоголь,
Меня бросив на мокром прилавке...
Куафер меня поднял с земли,
Расчесал мои светлые кудри,
Нарумянил он щеки мои
И напудрил...

И тогда вся избита, изранена,
Грязной рукой
Как на бал завита, нарумянена,
Я на пике взвилась над толпой
Хмельным тирсом...
                    Неслась вакханалия.
Пел в священном безумьи народ.

MAXIMILIAN ALEXANDROVICH VOLOSHIN
(KIRIENKO)
1877-1932

THE HEAD OF MADAME DE LAMBALLE

(4 September 1792)

On this flexible, passionate body
How the frenzied crowd trampled their feet!
And they stripped it, defiled it and ravished it,
And I didn't
Dare look at
My body...
And then I was chopped off from my body.
They threw the fragments
Of the flaming-red flesh on the stone street.

And the Parisian mob
Took me, carried me off through the jammed streets.
Someone drank alcohol in a tavern
And forgot I was there on the wet bar...
And a hairdresser lifted me up
From the ground, and he combed out my blonde hair,
Took some rouge and colored my cheeks
And used powder...

Having been beaten up and then wounded,
With dirty hands
Rouged as if for a ball, with my hair well-coiffed,
I was raised on a lance high above the crowd
Like an ancient Greek hopbine thyrsus...
$\qquad$ Came the bacchanal.
People sang in a mad, holy trance.

И, казалось, на бале в Версале я...
Плавный танец кружит и несет...
Точно пламя, гудели напевы.
И тюремною узкою лестницей
В башню Тампля, к окну королевы
Поднялась я народною вестницей...

1906, Париж

* * *

Тесен мой мир. Он замкнулся в кольцо.
Вечность лишь изредка блещет зарницами.
Время порывисто дует в лицо.
Годы несутся огромными птицами

Клочья тумана вблизи... вдалеке...
Быстро текут очертанья.
Лампу Психеи несу я в руке –
Синее пламя познанья.

В безднах скрывается новое дно.
Формы и мысли смесились.
Все мы уж умерли где-то давно...
Все мы еще не родились.

(1909)

I thought here was Versailles and a gala ball
Where I whirled, carried off by the dance.
Like a flame how the music kept humming...
And outside of the jail by the narrow stair
To the Queen's window, Temple Tower, coming,
I was raised as the people's own messenger.

1906, Paris

★   ★   ★

My world is narrow. It is locked in a ring.
Rarely, eternity shines in far lightning's flash.
Time blows its squalls in my face. And the years
Hurry like gigantic birds flying past.

Fragments of fog are near by... far away...
Their outlines are billowing rapidly.
I carry Psyche's own lamp in my hand –
Blue flame of knowledge. And now I see

There's a new bottom in every abyss.
Thoroughly intermixed: – thought and form.
We all have died sometime, long long ago...
We all have yet to be born.

Травою жесткою, пахучей и седой,
Порос бесплодный скат извилистой долины.
Белеет молочай. Пласты размытой глины
Искрятся грифелем, и сланцем, и слюдой.

По стенам шифера, источенным водой,
Побеги каперсов; иссохший ствол маслины;
А выше за холмом лиловые вершины
Подъемлет Карадаг зубчатою стеной.

И этот тусклый зной, и горы в дымке мутной,
И запах душных трав, и камней отблеск ртутный,
И злобный крик цикад, и клекот хищных птиц –

Мутят сознание. И зной дрожит от крика...
И там, – во впадинах зияющих глазниц, –
Огромный взгляд растоптанного Лика.

(1910)

* * *

Двойной соблазн – любви и любопытства...
Девичья грудь и голова пажа,
Лукавых уст невинное бесстыдство,
И в быстрых пальцах пламя мятежа...

В твоих зрачках танцуют арлекины...
Ты жалишь нежно больно, но слегка...
Ты сочетала тонкость андрогины
С безгрешностью порочного цветка.

The bare slope of the winding valley's like a
Hoar-haired and fragrant field of grassy hay.
The spurge is white; the layers of washed clay
Are sparkling with the slate and schist and mica.

Along the walls of shale water has cut up
Are caper-sprouts, dried trunks of olive trees.
And high beyond a hill, Karadag sees
Her lilac peaks turn jagged walls that jut up.

And this dulled heat, mountains in muddied haze,
The stifling grass-smell, rocks' quick-mirrored glaze,
Cicadas' evil cries and prey-birds' screeches

Disturb one's mind. Heat shakes as sounds embrace.
And there: In yawning eye-sockets' deep reaches
There is the great glance of the trampled FACE.

★　★　★

Double temptation: love and curiousness.
A young girl's breast and the head of a page.
Your sly lips' free innocent shamelessness,
And in your swift fingers rebellions rage...

How harlequins are dancing in your eyes...
You sting with tender pain – (a small pain's power)...
And you've combined androgynous subtleties
With the sinlessness of a perverse flower.

С тобой мила печаль земного плена
И верности докучливо ярмо...
Тобой звучат напевы Куперена,
Ты грусть огней на празднествах Рамо.

В твоих глазах зубчатый бег химеры;
Но их печаль теперь поймет ли кто?
Так смотрит вдаль на мглистый брег Цитеры
Влюбленный паж на барке у Ватто.

(1910)

ПОД ЗНАКОМ ЛЬВА

Томимый снами, я дремал,
Не чуя близкой непогоды;
Но грянул гром, и ветр упал,
И свет померк, и вздулись воды.

И кто-то для моих шагов
Провел невидимые тропы
По стогнам буйных городов
Объятой пламенем Европы.

Уже в петлях скрипела дверь
И в стены бил прибой с разбега,
И я, как запоздалый зверь,
Вошел последним внутрь ковчега.

Август 1914 г., Дорнах

With you captive-of-earth is no sad plan,
And yokes of faithfulness do tiresome grow...
You sound in melodies of Couperin;
You are sad lights at the fetes held by Rameau.

But now, who will understand such sadness if
Your eyes show the jagged flight of a chimera?
Thus, in Watteau – the hot page in a skiff
Looks toward the far, fogged coastline of Cythera.

UNDER THE SIGN OF LEO[1]

I dozed – tormented by my dreams,
Not sensing the bad weather close.
But thunder spoke and winds came down.
All light went out, the waters rose.

And someone drew for me a path,
Invisible as my steps came
Through squares of violent cities of
A Europe circled in by flame.

The door was creaking every hinge;
The flood beat at the walls and roared.
And I, a lagging animal,
Entered the ark – the last aboard.

August 1914, Dornach

ПЕТЕРБУРГ

пось Бальмонту

Над призрачным и вещим Петербургом
Склоняет ночь край мертвенных хламид.
В челне их два. И старший говорит:
'Люблю сей град, открытый зимним пургам,
На тонях вод, закованных в гранит.
Он создан был безумным Демиургом.
Вон конь его и змей между копыт:
Конь змею – "сгинь!", а змей в ответ: "Resurgam!"
Судьба империи в двойной борьбе:
Здесь бунт, – там строй; здесь бред, – там клич судьбе.
Но вот сто лет в стране цветут Рифейской
Ликеев мирт и строгий лавр палеотр'...
И глядя вверх на шпиль Адмиралтейский,
Сказал другой: 'Вы правы, граф де Местр.'

8 февраля 1915, Париж

РЕЙМСКАЯ БОГОМАТЕРЬ

Vue de trois-quarts, la Cathédrale de Reims évoque une grande figure de femme, agenouillée, en prière.

Rodin

В минуты грусти просветленной
Народы созерцать могли
Ее – коленопреклоненной
Средь виноградников Земли.
И всех, кто сном земли недужен,
Ее целила благодать,
И шли волхвы, чтоб увидать

PETERSBURG

to Balmont

Night drops the hem of her dead cloak above
The phantom-like, prophetic Petersburg.
Two in a boat. The elder speaks, 'I love
This city – open to winter's blizzard.
Forged out of granite, on fishing grounds, it was
Created by a crazy demiurge.
His horse is there. The snake between the hoofs:
The horse, "Be gone!" "Resurgam!", the snake's word.
A two-way fight will set the empire's state:
Revolt – Order. Chaos – A plea to Fate.
But look! This Rhipean land for a century
Has grown Lycius' myrtle, and laurel for palestrae.'
And looking to the spire of the Admiralty,
The other said. 'You're right, my Count de Maistre.'

8 February 1915, Paris

THE RHEIMS MADONNA

*Vue de trois-quarts, la Cathédrale de Reims
évoque une grande figure de femme, agenouillée, en prière.*

Rodin

In minutes of transfigured sadness
All peoples then could contemplate
Her – kneeling
Among the vineyards of the Earth.
All those ill with an earthbound dream
Were cured completely by her mercy.
The Magi walked so they might see

Ее – жемчужину жемчужин.
Она несла свою печаль,
Одета в каменные ткани,
Прозрачно-серые, как даль
Спокойных овидей Шампани.
И соткан был ее покров
Из жемчуга лугов поемных,
Туманных утр и облаков,
Дождей хрустальных, ливней темных.
Одежд ее чудесный сон,
Небесным светом опален,
Горел в сияньи малых радуг,
Сердца мерцали алых роз,
И светотень курчавых складок
Струилась прядями волос.
Земными создана руками,
Она сама была землей –
Ее лугами, и реками,
Ее предутренними снами,
Ее вечерней тишиной.
... И обнажив, ее распяли...
Огонь лизал и стрелы рвали
Святую плоть... Но по ночам,
В порыве безысходной муки,
Ее обугленные руки
Простерты к зимним небесам.

19 февраля 1915, Париж

СВЯТАЯ РУСЬ

Суздаль да Москва не для тебя ли
По уделам землю собирали
Да тугую золотом суму?
В рундуках приданое копили
И тебя невестою растили
В расписном да тесном терему?

Her – the pearl of pearls.
She was forever bearing sadness
Clad in her own stony fabrics,
In transparent-gray like the distance
Of hushed horizons of Champagne.
And her covering was woven
From the pearl of water-meadows,
Misty mornings and from clouds,
Crystal rains and dark downpours.
The wondrous vision of her raiment –
Scorched by a celestial light,
Burned in the shine of small rainbows.
The hearts of scarlet roses glimmered
And the chiaroscuro of the curling folds
Was flowing forth like locks of hair.
Created, carved by earthly hands,
She had become earth herself...
Her fields, her rivers,
Her pre-dawn dreams, her evening silence.
... And then they stripped and crucified her...
The fire licked and arrows tore
The holy flesh... But at night
In a gesture of perpetual pain
Her charred arms stretch toward winter skies.

19 February 1915, Paris

HOLY RUSSIA

Was it not for you – Suzdal and Moscow
Linked the land – grant after grant – together,
Packed into tight bags the gold supplied,
Stored a splendid dowry up in coffers,
And within a narrow, wooden tower,
Painted brightly, reared you as a bride?

Не тебе ли на речных истоках
Плотник-Царь построил дом широко –
Окнами на пять земных морей?
Из невест красой да силой бранной
Не была ль ты самою желанной
Для заморских княжих сыновей?

Но тебе сыздетства были любы –
По лесам глубоких скитов срубы,
По степям кочевья без дорог,
Вольные раздолья да вериги,
Самозванцы, воры да расстриги,
Соловьиный посвист да острог.

Быть Царевой ты не захотела –
Уж такое подвернулось дело:
Враг шептал: развей да расточи,
Ты отдай казну свою богатым,
Власть – холопам, силу – супостатам,
Смердам – честь, изменникам – ключи.

Поддалась лихому подговору,
Отдалась разбойнику и вору,
Подожгла посады и хлеба,
Разорила древнее жилище
И пошла поруганной и нищей
И рабой последнего раба.

Я ль в тебя посмею бросить камень?
Осужу ль страстной и буйный пламень?
В грязь лицом тебе ль не поклонюсь,
След босой ноги благословляя, –
Ты – бездомная, гулящая, хмельная,
Во Христе юродивая Русь!

19 ноября 1917 г., Коктебеля

Was it not for you – by rivers' sources
He, Carpenter-Czar, had built a spacious
House with windows on the earth's five seas?
With your military strength and beauty
Were you not of brides the one most wanted
For the sons of princely families?

But from youth you liked free, open spaces,
Wooden monasteries deep in forests,
Felons and the Robber-Nightingale's
Whistling, the ascetics' chains, pretenders,
Unfrocked monks, the trackless lands of nomads
In the stretching steppes, prisons and jails.

You did not want to remain the Czar's – no,
And the chance was much too good to miss it:
'Scatter! Squander!', spoke the enemy.
'Give the rich your wealth, the slaves your power,
Give the foe your strength, the serfs your honor.'
The fiend whispered, 'Give traitors your keys'.

So you listened to the evil counsel,
Gave yourself to burglars, thieves and scoundrels,
Burned your towns and crops and would not save
This, your ancient home. And from this wasteland
You went out – embarrassed and a beggar
As the least slave of the lowest slave.

Dare I cast a stone at you? And *shall* I
Censure your wild flame, fed with such passion?
Shan't I bow to you (if that sufficed),
Down before you with my face in mud and
Bless the print of your bare foot? You homeless,
Wanton, drunken Russia – fool in Christ!

19 November 1917, Koktebel

СЕВЕРОВОСТОК

Да будет благословен приход твой –
Бич Бога, Которому я служу, и не мне
останавливать тебя.

Слова Св. Лу, архиепископа
Труаского, обращенные к Атилле

Расплясались, разгулялись бесы
По России вдоль и поперек –
Рвет и крутит снежные завесы
Выстуженный Северовосток.

Ветер обнаженных плоскогорий,
Ветер тундр, полесий и поморий,
Черный ветер ледяных равнин,
Ветер смут, побоищ и погромов,
Медных зорь, багровых окаемов,
Красных туч и пламенных годин.

Этот ветер был нам верным другом
На распутье всех лихих дорог –
Сотни лет мы шли навстречу вьюгам
С юга вдаль на северовосток.
Войте, вейте, снежные стихии,
Заметая древние гроба.
В этом ветре вся судьба России –
Страшная, безумная судьба.

В этом ветре – гнет веков свинцовых,
Русь Малют, Иванов, Годуновых –
Хищников, опричников, стрельцов,
Свежевателей живого мяса –
Чертогона, вихря, свистопляса –
Быль царей и явь большевиков.

Что менялось? Знаки и возглавья?
Тот же ураган на всех путях:
В комиссарах – дух самодержавья,
Взрывы революции – в царях.

NORTHEAST

May your arrival be blessed, Scourge of the
God Whom I serve. I cannot stop you.
St Loup, Archbishop of Troyes, to Attila

Devils have their fling and they are dancing...
Over, over Russia how they go!
Now the cold northeaster... tearing, prancing,
Twirling, whirling up curtains of snow.

Wind of high, barren plateaus,
Wind of tundras, swamps and coasts,
Black wind of the ice-packed plains,
Wind of riot, slaughter and pogroms,
Of copper dawns, crimson horizons,
Of reddened clouds and fiery years.

This same wind has been our comrade
At the forks of every ill-starred road.
For a hundred years we've faced this blizzard
As from south to far northeast we strode.
Howl and sweep, O snowy elements,
Covering old graves unceasingly...
In this wind... the total fate of Russia,
Terrible and insane destiny.

In this wind... the yoke of leaden centuries:
Russia of Maliutas, Ivans, Godunovs,
Streltsi, predators, Oprichniks,
Flayers of our flesh, of devil-chasers,
Of great hurricanes and of hell-raisers –
Past of Czars, the Now of Bolsheviks.

What was changing? Merely signs and labels.
Same wind on all roads: In commissars
One could find the autocratic spirit;
Revolutions burst out in the Czars.

Вздеть на виску, выбить из подклетья,
И швырнуть вперед через столетья
Вопреки законам естества –
Тот же хмель и та же трын-трава.

Ныне ль, даве ль? – все одно и то же:
Волчьи морды, машкеры и рожи,
Спертый дух и одичалый мозг,
Сыск и кухня Тайных Канцелярий,
Пьяный гик осатанелых тварей,
Жгучий свист шпицрутенов и розг,
Дикий сон военных поселений,
Фаланстер, парадов и равнений,
Павлов, Аракчеевых, Петров,
Жутких Гатчин, страшных Петербургов,
Замыслы неистовых хирургов
И размах заплечных мастеров,
Сотни лет тупых и зверских пыток,
И еще не весь развернут свиток,
И не замкнут список палачей:
Бред разведок, ужас чрезвычаек –
Ни Москва, ни Астрахань, ни Яик
Не видали времени горчей.

Бей в лицо и режь нам грудь ножами,
Жги войной, усобьем, мятежами –
Сотни лет навстречу всем ветрам
Мы идем по ледяным пустыням –
Не дойдем... и в снежной вьюге сгинем,
Иль найдем поруганный наш храм –
Нам ли весить замысел Господний?
Все поймем, все вынесем любя –
Жгучий ветр полярной Преисподней –
Божий Бич, – приветствую тебя!

1920 г., Коктебель
Перед приходом советской
власти в Крым

Hanged upon the rack, chased from the cellar,
Hurled ahead across the centuries,
Violating all the laws of Nature . . .
Same old nonsense, same old frenzied sprees.

Now or as before? It's all the same:
Muzzles made-for-wolves, and grotesque masks,
Stuffy air, the brain gone savage, grillings,
Kitchen of the Secret Chancellories,
Drunken whoops of creatures run amok,
Flamed whistling of whips (the floggings, whippings),
Phalansteries, parades and formations
Of Pauls, Arakcheyevs and of Peters,
Gruesome Gatchinas, vile Petersburgs,
Plans of furious surgeons,
And the sweep of torture-masters . . .
Hundred years of blunt and beastlike tortures,
And the scroll's not rolled out to the end,
And the list of hangmen is not finished.
Raves of The Intelligence, terror from Special Bureaus . . .
Neither Moscow, Astrakhan nor Yaik
Ever saw a worse, more bitter time.

Slap us in the face and knife our breasts,
Burn with wars, discord, revolts, arrests . . .
Hundred years we've faced this wind so wild,
We've walked this icy plain and do not know
If we'll reach . . . or die in blustering snow
Or will find our temple, now defiled.
Should we ever doubt the plans of God?
We'll bear all with love. (We'll learn all too.)
Burning wind, wind from a polar hell,
Scourge of God – I welcome you.

1920, Koktebel
Before the arrival of the
Soviets in Crimea

КРАСНАЯ ВЕСНА

Зимою вдоль дорог валялись трупы
Людей и лошадей, и стаи псов
Въедались им в живот и рвали мясо.
Восточный ветер выл в разбитых окнах,
А под окном стучали пулеметы,
Свистя, как бич, по мясу обнаженных
Мужских и женских тел. Весна пришла,
Зловещая, голодная, больная.
Глядело солнце в мир незрячим оком.
Из сжатых чресл рождались недоноски –
Безрукие, безглазые. Не грязь,
А сукровица поползла по скатам,
Под талым снегом обнажились кости,
Подснежники мерцали точно свечи,
Фиалки пахли гнилью, ландыш – тленьем,
Стволы дерев, обглоданных конями
Голодными, торчали непристойно,
Как ноги трупов. Листья и трава
Казались красными, а зелень злаков
Была опалена огнем и зноем.
Лицо природы искажалось гневом
И ужасом.

            А души вырванных
Насильственно из жизни – вились в ветре,
Носились по дорогам в пыльных вихрях,
Безумили живых могильным хмелем
Неизжитых страстей, неутоленной жизни,
Плодили мщенье, панику, заразу.
Зима была в тот год Страстной неделей,
И красный май сплелся с кровавой Пасхой.
Но в ту весну Христос не воскресал.

21 апреля 1920 г., Симферополь

RED SPRING

Along the roads in winter the cadavers
(People and horses) lay. And packs of dogs
Were eating at their bellies, tearing flesh.
The east wind howled within the shattered windows,
And down below the sill machine guns rattled,
Whistling like a whip on flesh of naked
Male and female bodies. The spring came,
Hungry and sick and sinister.
The sun looked at the world with sightless eye,
As from the tightened loins freaks were born
Without their arms, without their eyes. Not mud
But lymph crawled down along the slopes.
The bones were bared beneath the melted snow,
Anemones were glimmering like candles,
Violets reeked mold, and lilies of the valley
Smelled of rot. Tree trunks gnawed round by horses
(Hungry ones) protruded obscenely
Like legs of stiff cadavers. Leaves and grass
Seemed to be red. And the green of the grain
Was scorched completely by the fire and heat.
The face of Nature was deformed by wrath
And terror.   And the souls of those torn out
Of life by violence whirled in the wind,
Hurried along the roads in clouds of dust,
Maddened the living with a tomb-like frenzy
Of passion not all-lived, of life not satisfied, –
And increased vengeance, panic, epidemics.
The winter was the Passion Week that year
And red May woven with a bloody Easter.
But that spring Christ did not rise up again.

21 April 1920, Simferopol

ТЕРРОР

Собирались на работу ночью. Читали
Донесения, справки, дела.
Торопливо подписывали приговоры.
Зевали. Пили вино.
С утра раздавали солдатам водку.
Вечером при свече
Вызывали по спискам мужчин, женщин.
Сгоняли на темный двор,
Снимали с них обувь, белье, платье,
Связывали в тюки.
Грузили на подводу. Увозили.
Делили кольца, часы.
Ночью гнали разутых, голодных,
По оледенелой земле,
Под северовосточным ветром
За город, в пустыри.
Загоняли прикладами на край обрыва,
Освещали ручным фонарем.
Полминуты работали пулеметы.
Приканчивали штыком.
Еще не добитых валили в яму.
Торопливо засыпали землей.
А потом с широкою русскою песней
Возвращались в город, домой.
А к рассвету пробирались к тем же оврагам
Жены, матери, псы.
Разрывали землю, грызлись за кости,
Целовали милую плоть.

(1921)

TERROR

In the night – would gather for work. They would read through
Certificates, cases, reports.
With a hasty hand they signed their decisions.
They yawned. They drank wine.
In the morning they passed out vodka to soldiers;
In the evening by candlelight
They would call out the lists – men and women.
They herded them to the dark yard.
They took off all footwear, underwear, clothing
Which they tied into bundles, then
Loaded onto a cart. And took away.
They divided the watches and rings.
At night they would drive them barefoot and hungry
Over the icy ground.
In the northeast wind, out of town to the fields
They would prod them with gun butts to reach the ravine
Lighted them up with lanterns.
For half-a-minute the machine guns would clatter.
Finished them with bayonets.
Those still alive were shoved into a hole
Which they quickly filled with earth.
And then with a broad Russian song ringing
They returned to the city – home.
And at dawn – dogs, wives and mothers
Stole out for the same ravine.
They dug the ground, fought over bones
And kissed the beloved flesh.

НА ДНЕ ПРЕИСПОДНЕЙ

Памяти А. Блока и Н. Гумилева

С каждым днем все диче и все глуше
Мертвенная цепенеет ночь.
Смрадный ветр, как свечи, жизни тушит.
Ни позвать, ни крикнуть, ни помочь.
Темен жребий русского поэта:
Неисповедимый рок ведет
Пушкина под дуло пистолета,
Достоевского на эшафот.
Может быть, такой же жребий выну,
Горькая детоубийца – Русь,
И на дне твоих подвалов сгину,
Иль в кровавой луже поскользнусь,
Но твоей голгофы не покину,
От твоих могил не отрекусь.
Доканает голод или злоба, –
Но судьбы не изберу иной:
Умирать, так умирать с тобой
И с тобой, как Лазарь, встать из гроба.

Ноябрь 1921, Феодосия, в больнице

ON THE BOTTOM OF HELL

To the memory of A. Blok and N. Gumilev

As each day becomes more wild, more lonely,
So the dead night freezes all about.
Stinking wind blows out our lives like candles.
You can't help. You can't call. You can't shout.
Gloomy is the lot of Russian poets:
Fate, inscrutable, has led the great
Pushkin straight before a pistol's muzzle,
Dostoyevsky to the scaffold's gate.
Maybe my drawn lot points such an ending...
(O, my Russia! Cruel infanticide!)
And I'll perish on a basement bottom
Or I'll slip in blood a puddle wide.
But I'll not abandon your Golgotha
Or disclaim the graves of these who've died.
Whether hunger or foul play's my finish,
I'll not choose another course for us:
I die... I shall die with you and *with* you
Rise up from the grave like Lazarus.

November 1921, Theodosia, in a hospital

ГОТОВНОСТЬ

Я не сам ли выбрал час рожденья,
Век и царство, область и народ,
Чтоб пройти сквозь муки и крещенье
Совести, огня и вод?

Апокалиптическому зверю
Вверженный в зияющую пасть,
Павший глубже, чем возможно пасть,
В скрежете и в смраде – верю.

Верю в правоту верховных сил,
Расковавших древние стихии,
И из недр обугленной России
Говорю: 'Ты прав, что так судил.'

Надо до алмазного закала
Прокалить всю толщу бытия.
Если ж дров в плавильной печи мало –
Господи! – вот плоть моя.

Ноябрь 1921, Феодосия

READINESS

Did not I myself choose my own birthday,
Kingdom, people, place, the Age entire?
To endure pain, torture, three baptisms:
Those of conscience, water, fire?

Thrown into the yawning mouth and lathers
Of the Beast of the Apocalypse,
Fallen so deep that I think none dips
Deeper in the crunching stench that gathers,

I believe the Supreme Force is right
Letting loose old elements long shackled.
From the bowels of Russia, charred and crackled,
I say you're correct though recondite.

All the layered depths of our existence
Must be made diamond-red-hot afresh.
If there's not enough wood in the furnace,
Then – God – here's my flesh.

November 1921, Theodosia

ВЛАДИМИР ВЛАДИМИРОВИЧ МАЯКОВСКИЙ
1893-1930

А ВЫ МОГЛИ БЫ?

Я сразу смазал карту будня,
плеснувши краску из стакана;
я показал на блюде студня
косые скулы океана.
На чешуе жестяной рыбы
прочел я зовы новых губ.
А вы
ноктюрн сыграть
могли бы
на флейте водосточных труб?

(1913)

НЕСКОЛЬКО СЛОВ ОБО МНЕ САМОМ

Я люблю смотреть, как умирают дети.
Вы прибоя смеха мглистый вал заметили
за тоски хоботом?
А я –
в читальне улиц –
так часто перелистывал гроба том.
Полночь
промокшими пальцами щупала
меня
и забитый забор,
и с каплями ливня на лысине купола
скакал сумасшедший собор.
Я вижу, Христос из иконы бежал,
хитона обветренный край
целовала, плача, слякоть.

VLADIMIR VLADIMIROVICH MAYAKOVSKY
1893-1930

AND COULD YOU?

Then sousing color from the glass,
I smudged the map of everyday;
I showed where on the jelly dish
the ocean's slanted cheekbones lay.
Upon the scales of the tin fish
I have read new lips sounding off.
And you, could you
play a nocturne
upon the flute
of an eaves trough?

A FEW WORDS ABOUT MYSELF

I like to watch children dying.
Do you note, behind the proboscis sighing,
the vast, vague waves of the laughter's foam?
But I –
in the reading room of the streets –
have so often leafed through the coffin tome.
Midnight
with drenched fingers was groping
me
and the battered fence,
and the crazy cathedral was galloping
in drops of downpour on the cupola's bald head.
I have seen Christ flee from an icon
and the mud in tears kiss
the wind-blown fringe of his chiton.

Кричу кирпичу,
слов исступленных вонзаю кинжал
в неба распухшего мякоть:
'Солнце!
Отец мой!
Сжалься хоть ты и не мучай!
Это тобою пролитая кровь моя льется дорогою дольней.
Это душа моя
клочьями порванной тучи
в выжженном небе
на ржавом кресте колокольни!
Время!
Хоть ты, хромой богомаз,
лик намалюй мой
в божницу уродца века!
Я одинок, как последний глаз
у идущего к слепым человека!'

1913

НИЧЕГО НЕ ПОНИМАЮТ

Вошел к парикмахеру, сказал – спокойный:
'Будьте добры, причешите мне уши.'
Гладкий парикмахер сразу стал хвойный,
лицо вытянулось, как у груши.
'Сумасшедший!
Рыжий!' –
запрыгали слова.
Ругань металась от писка до писка,
и до-о-о-о-лго
хихикала чья-то голова,
выдергиваясь из толпы, как старая редиска

1913

I shout at the bricks,
stabbing the dagger of raving words high
into the pulp of the swollen sky:
'Sun!
My father!
At least have mercy and don't torture me!
This, my blood you spilled, flows down this bottom road.
This is my soul,
tatters of a torn cloud
in a burnt-out sky
on the rusted cross of the belfry!
Time!
Lame icon-painter,
you at least will gild my countenance
for a freak age to have enshrined!
I am as lonely as the last good eye
of a man on his way to the blind!'

THEY DON'T UNDERSTAND A THING

I entered the barbershop and said softly:
'Would you be kind, please, and comb out my ears?'
The smooth-slick barber immediately bristled;
his face dropped, long as a pear's.
'Crazy!
Clown!'
Words started jumping, abuse flew round wiggling,
Squeak after squeak in a manner most maddish,
and for a lo-o-o-ong time
there, the head of somebody giggling
bobbed in the crowd like an old radish.

А ВСЕ-ТАКИ

Улица провалилась, как нос сифилитика.
Река – сладострастье, растекшееся в слюни.
Отбросив белье до последнего листика,
сады похабно развалились в июне.

Я вышел на площадь,
выжженный квартал
надел на голову, как рыжий парик.
Людям страшно – у меня изо рта
шевелит ногами непрожеванный крик.

Но меня не осудят, но меня не облают,
как пророку, цветами устелят мне след.
Все эти, провалившиеся носами, знают:
я – ваш поэт.

Как трактир, мне страшен ваш Страшный Суд!
Меня одного сквозь горящие здания
проститутки, как святыню, на руках понесут
и покажут Богу в свое оправдание.

И Бог заплачет над моею книжкой!
Не слова – судороги, слипшиеся комом;
и побежит по небу с моими стихами подмышкой
и будет, задыхаясь, читать их своим знакомым.

1914

AND YET

The street caves in like the nose of a syphilitic.
The river is lust oozing out like one's spit.
The gardens spread in June, are obscene, sybaritic
and have thrown off their undies' last leafy bit.

I come out into the square
and I put on my head
the burnt city block like a wig of red.
People in terror. The unchewed shout
within my mouth wiggles its legs out.

But I'll not be condemned; I'll not be overpowered.
My footprints will be (like a prophet's) beflowered.
All those with the caved-in noses know it:
I'm – your poet.

Your last judgment terrifies me like a saloon!
I alone will be carried through the burning commune
by whores like a holy thing of adoration
they will show to God as their vindication.

And over my little book God will cry!
Not words, it is shudders that gooseflesh portends.
He will run with my poems in His hands through the sky
and, all-out-of-breath, read them to His friends.

СКРИПКА И НЕМНОЖКО НЕРВНО

Скрипка издергалась, упрашивая,
и вдруг разревелась
так по-детски,
что барабан не выдержал:
'Хорошо, хорошо, хорошо!'
А сам устал,
не дослушал скрипкиной речи,
шмыгнул на горящий Кузнецкий
и ушел.
Оркестр чужо смотрел, как
выплакивалась скрипка
без слов,
без такта,
и только где-то
глупая тарелка
вылязгивала:
'Что это?'
'Как это?'
А когда геликон –
меднорожий,
потный,
крикнул:
'Дура,
плакса,
вытри!' –
я встал,
шатаясь полез через ноты,
сгибающиеся под ужасом пюпитры,
зачем-то крикнул:
'Боже!'
Бросился на деревянную шею:
'Знаете что, скрипка?
Мы ужасно похожи:
я вот тоже

VIOLIN: POCO AGITATO

The violin had worn out her nerves begging
and suddenly burst into tears –
so like a child
that the drum could not bear it anymore:
'All right. All right. All right.'
But he got tired,
did not listen to the end of the violin's speech,
sneaked into Kuznetsky's light
and slipped out of sight.
The orchestra watched, was noncommittal
as the violin wept herself out
without words,
without rhythm.
And then somewhere
a silly cymbal
clashed,
'What is it?
What's with 'em?'
And the bass horn,
copper-faced,
wet with sweat,
bellowed,
'Stupid.
Ninny,
dry your tears!'
Unsteadily,
I stood and climbed up where the sheet music sat,
the music racks bending with their fears.
For some reason I yelled,
'God!'
I rushed to the wooden neck:
'You know what, violin,
we are more similar than odd.
I too

ору –
а доказать ничего не умею!'
Музыканты смеются:
'Влип как!
Пришел к деревянной невесте!
Голова!'
А мне – наплевать!
Я – хороший.
'Знаете что, скрипка?
Давайте –
будем жить вместе!
А?'

1914

ХОРОШЕЕ ОТНОШЕНИЕ К ЛОШАДЯМ

Били копыта.
Пели будто:
– Гриб.
Грабь.
Гроб.
Груб. –

Ветром опита,
льдом обута,
улица скользила.
Лошадь на круп
грохнулась,
и сразу
за зевакой зевака,
штаны пришедшие Кузнецким клешить,
сгрудились,
смех зазвенел и зазвякал:
– Лошадь упала! –
– Упала лошадь! –

shout
and cannot prove one thing!'
The musicians laughed,
'He's in!
He's come to his wooden bride.
Smart one!'
But I spit at their words;
I'm kind.
'You know what, violin?
Let's live
side by side.
Hmm?'

TREATING A HORSE WELL

Horseshoes were beating
a song precise:
'Grit.
Grab.
Groan.
Gruff.'

By the wind eaten,
shod by ice,
the street was gliding.
Down on its butt
a horse crashed,
and at once
idler after idler
on Kuznetsky who came ringing his cloche-trouser bell
formed a crowd.
Laughter started to clang and collide there:
A fallen horse?
A horse fell!

Смеялся Кузнецкий.
Лишь один я
голос свой не вмешивал в вой ему.
Подошел
и вижу
глаза лошадиные...

Улица опрокинулась,
течет по-своему...

Подошел и вижу –
за каплищей каплища
по морде катится,
прячется в шерсти...

И какая-то общая
звериная тоска
плеща вылилась из меня
и расплылась в шелесте.
'Лошадь, не надо.
Лошадь, слушайте –
чего вы думаете, что вы их плоше?
Деточка,
все мы немножко лошади,
каждый из нас по-своему лошадь.'
Может быть
– старая –
и не нуждалась в няньке,
может быть, и мысль ей моя казалась пошла́,
только
лошадь
рванулась,
встала на ноги,
ржанула
и пошла.
Хвостом помахивала.
Рыжий ребенок.

All Kuznetsky was laughing,
howling itself hoarse,
but one voice did not, mine alone.
I came closer
and I saw
the eyes of the horse...

The street flowed inverted
in a way of its own.

I came and I saw
big drops falling always
down the line of its muzzle
to hide in the hair...

And an animal longing,
common to all of us,
poured in splashes from me
and spread out there.
'Horse, don't
Listen, horse.
Don't think you are worse than those men are!
Baby,
we are all partly horse;
each of us is a horse in some manner.'
Perhaps, being old,
she did not need an advisor,
perhaps my idea seemed banal in a way,
but my words
seemed
to raise her
feet; she stood up, neighed
and went away.
The red-haired child
swished her tail

Пришла веселая,,
стала в стойло.
И все ей казалось –
она жеребенок,
и стоило жить,
и работать стоило.

(1918)

ПРОЩАНЬЕ

В авто,
            последний франк разменяв.
– В котором часу на Марсель? –
Париж
        бежит,
                провожая меня,
во всей
        невозможной красе.
Подступай
            к глазам,
                        разлуки жижа,
сердце
    мне
        сантиментальностью расквась!
Я хотел бы
            жить
                и умереть в Париже,
Если б не было
                такой земли –
                            М о с к в а .

1925

and went home gay.
Back in her stall,
feeling young, she thought toil
was well worth the doing,
and life worth it all.

FAREWELL

In a taxicab
        having changed my last franc:
'What time's the next train to Marseille?'
With impossible beauty
        seeing me off
            from each bank
Paris and her Seine
        are running away.
Come
    to my eyes,
        wash of separation.
Sissy
    my heart
        till it's mawkish!
I would like
      to live
        and die a Parisian
If there were no
      such place
         as Moscow.

6 МОНАХИНЬ

Воздев
      печеные
           картошки личек,
черней,
     чем негр,
          не видавший бань,
шестеро благочестивейших католичек
влезло
     на борт
          парохода 'Эспань'.
И сзади
    и спереди
         ровней, чем веревка.
Шали,
    как с гвоздика,
             с плеч висят,
а лица
    обвила
        белейшая гофрировка,
как в пасху
      гофрируют
          ножки поросят.
Пусть заполнится годами
            жизни квота –
стоит
    только
        вспомнить это диво,
раздирает
     рот
       зевота
шире Мексиканского залива.
Трезвые,
    чистые,
        как раствор борной,

6 NUNS

With small baked-potato
    faces
      looking up,
blacker
   than negroes
      who have never used soap,
six pious Catholic sisters
climb the Espagne's
     gangplank
       and board the boat.
Their fronts
   and backs
      as straight as a string,
their habits
    hang from their shoulders
        as from pegs,
and their faces
    are haloed
      by the whitest frills
like the trimmings
    at Easter
      on little pigs' legs.
If only
  I remember
    this marvel
when my time is ripe
     and I'm the next to go,
a yawn
   will rip open
     my mouth
wider than the Gulf of Mexico.
Temperate
    antiseptic –
      like boric acid.

вместе,

эскадроном, садятся есть.

Пообедав, сообща

скрываются в уборной.

Одна зевнула –

зевают шесть.

Вместо известных

симметрических мест,

где у женщин выпуклость, –

у этих выем:

в одной выемке –

серебряный крест,

в другой – медали

со Львом

и с Пием.

Продрав глазенки

раньше, чем можно, –

в раю

(ужо!)

отоспятся лишек, –

оркестром без дирижера

шесть дорожных

вынимают

евангелишек.

Придешь ночью –

сидят и бормочут.

Рассвет в розы –

бормочут, стервозы!

И днем,

и ночью, и в утра, и в полдни

сидят

и бормочут,

дуры господни.

Если ж

день

чуть-чуть

помрачнеет с виду,

A squad,
> they sit down to eat – all
>> at once.

Having eaten,
> they hide in a toilet.

One yawns;
> five yawn in response.

Instead of symmetrical
> places where women

should have curves – they have caves,
>> which do not satisfy us.

In one cave there
> is a silver cross;

in another – medals
> with Leo and Pius.

In Paradise
> (Someday!)
>> they will sleep overtime,

but, still sleepy-eyed,
> and as early as possible,

like an orchestra without a conductor,
now they take out
> six pocket
>> Gospels.

You meet them at night.
They pray all right.
The dawn spreads its roses –
they pray, holy moses!
At night,
> at day, mornings and noons,

they sit
> and they pray –
>> the lord's buffoons.

And if
> the day
>> grows a
>>> little darker,

сойдут в кабину,
                12 галош
наденут вместе
                    и снова выйдут,
и снова
        идет
            елейный скулеж.
Мне б
    язык испанский!
                    Я б спросил, взъяренный:
– Ангелицы,
            попросту
                    ответ поэту дайте –
если
    люди вы,
            то кто ж
                    тогда
                        воро́ны?
А если
    вы вороны,
                почему вы не летаете?
Агитпропщики!
                не лезьте вон из кожи.
Весь земной
            обревизуйте шар.
Самый
        замечательный безбожник
не придумает
                кощунственнее шарж!
Радуйся, распятый Иисусе,
не слезай
        с гвоздей своей доски,
а вторично явишься –
                    с ю д а
                        не суйся –
все равно:
1925   повесишься с тоски!

they go down to their cabin,
                    get out twelve galoshes.
    put them on together
                    and go out again,
    and again
            they continue
                        their unctuous hogwashes.
    Would
        I could
            speak Spanish!
                        I would ask in rage:
    'Angelitas,
            give this poet
                        a simple reply.
    If you
        are people,
                    then who
                        are crows?
    And if
            you are crows,
                    why don't you fly?'
    Propagan-Com!
                    Here's your dish.
    Though you search
                    all earth and nature
    the greatest
                atheist couldn't
    find a more profane
                    caricature.
    Crucified Jesus, rejoice!
    Don't get off
                of the nails on your tree;
    at your second coming
                    keep your nose
                            out of here,
    or you'll hang yourself
                    from ennui!

БРУКЛИНСКИЙ МОСТ

Издай, Кулидж,
радостный клич!
На хорошее
        и мне не жалко слов.
От похвал
      красней,
          как флага нашего материйка,
хоть вы
    и разъюнайтед стетс
            оф
Америка.
Как в церковь
     идет
        помешавшийся верующий,
как в скит
    удаляется,
       строг и прост, –
так я
   в вечерней
      сереющей мерещи
вхожу
    смиренный, на Бруклинский мост.
Как в город
     в сломанный
         прет победитель
на пушках – жерлом
        жирафу под рост –
так, пьяный славой,
      так жить в аппетите,
влезаю,
    гордый,
       на Бруклинский мост.
Как глупый художник
       в мадонну музея

BROOKLYN BRIDGE

Hey, Coolidge boy,
make a shout of joy!
When a thing is good
              then it's good.
Blush from compliments
              like our flag's calico,
even though you're
            the most super-united states
                      of
America.
Like the crazy nut
          who goes
              to his church
or retreats
        to a monastery
             simple and rigid –
so I
    in the gray haze
            of evening
humbly
      approach
         the Brooklyn Bridge.
Like a conqueror
         on cannons with muzzles
                  as high as a giraffe
jabbing into a broken
          city besieged,
so, drunk with glory,
          alive to the hilt,
I clamber
      proudly
         upon Brooklyn Bridge.
Like a stupid painter
         whose enamored eyes pierce

вонзает глаз свой,
                     влюблен и остр,
так я,
         с поднебесья,
                 в звезды усеян,
смотрю
            на Нью-Йорк
                   сквозь Бруклинский мост.
Нью-Йорк
            до вечера тяжек
                   и душен,
забыл,
         что тяжко ему
               и высо́ко,
и только одни
            домовьи души
встают
         в прозрачном свечении окон.
Здесь
       еле зудит
              элевейторов зуд.
И только
         по этому
            тихому зуду
поймешь –
        поезда
           с дребезжаньем ползут,
как будто
        в буфет убирают посуду.
Когда ж,
        казалось, с под речки на́чатой
развозит
       с фабрики
           сахар лавочник, –
то,
     под мостом проходящие мачты

a museum Madonna
                    like a wedge.
    So from this sky,
                    sowed into the stars,

    I look at New York
                    through Brooklyn Bridge.

New York,
            heavy and stifling
                        till night,
    has forgotten
                what makes it dizzy
                            and a hindrance,
    and only
            the souls of houses
    rise in the transparent
                        sheen of windows.
Here the itching hum
                of the 'el'
                        is hardly heard,
    and only by this
                hum,
                    soft but stubborn,
    can you feel the trains
                    crawl
                        with a rattle
    as when dishes
                are jammed into a cupboard.
    And when from
                below the started river
    a merchant
                transports sugar
                            from the factory bins –
    then
            the masts passing under the bridge

размером
            не больше размеров булавочных.

Я горд
      вот этой
            стальною милей,
живьем в ней
           мои видения встали, –
борьба
      за конструкции
               вместо стилей,
расчет суровый
          гаек
             и стали.
Если
      придет
           окончание света –
планету
     хаос
          разделает влоск,
и только
        один останется
              этот
над пылью гибели вздыбленный мост,
то,
    как из косточек,
             тоньше иголок,
тучнеют
      в музеях стоящие
             ящеры,
так
    с этим мостом
          столетий геолог
сумел
     воссоздать бы
          дни настоящие.

are no bigger
        in size
                than pins.
I'm proud
        of this
                mile of steel.
In it my visions
                are alive and real –
a fight
        for structure
                instead of arty 'style',
the harsh calculation
            of bolts
                and steel.
If the end
        of the world
                comes –
and chaos
        wipes out
                this earth
and if only this
        bridge
                remains
rearing over the dust of death,
then
        as little bones,
                thinner than needles,
clad with flesh,
                standing in museums,
                        are dinosaurs, –
so from this
        bridge
                future geologists
will be able
        to reconstruct
                our present course.

Он скажет:
        – Вот эта
                стальная лапа
соединяла
        моря и прерии,
отсюда
        Европа
            рвалась на Запад,
пустив
      по ветру
           индейские перья.
Напомнит
      машину
            ребро вот это –
сообразите,
      хватит рук ли,
чтоб, став
      стальной ногой
            на Мангетен,
к себе
    за губу
        притягивать Бру́клин?
По проводам
        электрической пряди –
я знаю –
      эпоха
        после пара –
здесь
    люди
      уже
        орали по радио,
здесь
    люди
      уже
        взлетали по аэро.

They will say:
                    – this
                              paw of steel
joined seas,
                    prairies and deserts,
from here,
              Europe
                        rushed to the West,
scattering
              to the wind
                          Indian feathers.
This rib here
                reminds us
                          of a machine –
imagine,
              enough hands, enough grip
while standing,
                  with one steel leg
                              in Manhattan
to drag
          toward yourself
                          Brooklyn by the lip!
By the wires
              of electric yarn
I know this
              is
                  the Post-Steam Era.
Here people
              already
                        yelled on the radio,
here people
              already
                      flew by air.

Здесь
     жизнь
         была
              одним – беззаботная,
другим –
       голодный
            протяжный вой.
Отсюда
       безработные
в Гудзо́н
       кидались
            вниз головой.
И дальше
       картина моя
              без загвоздки
по струнам-канатам,
            аж звезды к ногам.
Я вижу –
     здесь
         стоял Маяковский,
стоял
     и стихи слагал по слогам. –

Смотрю,
       как в поезд глядит эскимос,
впиваюсь,
       как в ухо впивается клещ.
Бруклинский мост –
да . . .
     Это вещь!

1925

For some
    here was life
        carefree,
           unalloyed.
For others
    a prolonged
        howl of hunger.
From here
    the unemployed
jumped headfirst
      into
        the Hudson.
And finally
    with clinging stars
          along the strings of cables
my dream comes back
      without any trouble
and I see –
    here
      stood Mayakovsky,
here he stood
    putting
      syllable to syllable.
I look,
    as an eskimo looks at a train,
I dig into you,
      like a tick into an ear.
Brooklyn Bridge.
Yes,
    you've got something here.

СТИХИ О РАЗНИЦЕ ВКУСОВ

Лошадь
  сказала,
    взглянув на верблюда:
'Какая
  гигантская
    лошадь-ублюдок.'
Верблюд же
  вскричал:
    'Да лошадь разве ты?!
Ты
  просто-напросто –
    верблюд недоразвитый.'
И знал лишь
  бог седобородый,
что это –
  животные
    разной породы.

1928

ПАРИЖАНКА

Вы себе представляете
    парижских женщин
с шеей разжемчуженной,
    разбриллиантенной рукой...
Бросьте представлять себе!
    Жизнь – жестче –
у моей парижанки
  вид другой.

LINES ABOUT DIFFERENCE OF TASTE

Looking at a camel,
                  a horse
                          made a crack:
'A gigantic horse
                  with a bad humpback!'
And the camel
                cried out:
                        'You're a horse? Oh, no,
You are simply
                a camel's
                      embryo.'
And only God
                with a gray beard knew
That these
              were animals
                      of a different crew.

LA PARISIENNE

You always picture
                  Parisian women,
heads flashing diamonds,
                        necks – pearl on pearl...
Cut the picture!
                Life
              is hard;
my Parisienne
              is a different girl.

Не знаю, право,
           молода
                  или стара она,
до желтизны
           отшлифованная
                     в лощеном хамье.
Служит
      она
          в уборной ресторана –
маленького ресторана –
                  Гранд-Шомьер.
Выпившим бургундского
                может захотеться
для облегчения
           пойти пройтись.
Дело мадмуазель
             подавать полотенце,
она
     в этом деле
           просто артист.
Пока
      у трюмо
          разглядываешь прыщик,
она,
      разулыбив
            облупленный рот,
пудрой попудрит,
            духами попрыщет,
подаст пипифакс
          и лужу подотрет.
Раба чревоугодий
          торчит без солнца,
в клозетной шахте
          по суткам
              клопея,
за пятьдесят сантимов!
          (по курсу червонца

Rubbed to yellow-
    ness
      among polished boors,
  whether young or old,
      I couldn't tell,
         you see.
She has a job
    at *La Grande Chaumière*
a small restaurant,
     (in the W.C.).

To take a walk
    and relieve oneself
is natural
   after some Burgundy.
Mademoiselle's job
    is to offer towels,
which she does
    with consummate
       artistry.
While you check
    a pimple
      in the looking glass,
she, with smiling
    lips
     full of cracks,
pats you with powder,
      sprays on perfume,
wipes up the puddle,
     gives you pipifax.
A slave of gluttons,
    a bedbug, she sticks
in this restroom shaft
     without sun, stale and wan.
For fifty centimes
    (our rate of exchange

с мужчины
        около
               четырех копеек).
Под умывальником
               ладони омывая,
дыша
        диковиной
               парфюмерных зелий,
над мадмуазелью
              недоумевая,
хочу
      сказать
            мадмуазели:
– Мадмуазель,
          ваш вид,
              извините,
                  жалок.
На уборную молодость
               губить не жалко вам?
Или
    мне
        наврали про парижанок,
или
      вы, мадмуазель,
            не парижанка.
Выглядите вы
        туберкулезно
            и вяло.
Чулки шерстяные...
           Почему не шелка?
Почему
      не шлют вам
           пармских фиалок
благородные мусью
            от полного кошелька? –
Мадмуазель молчала,
        грохот наваливал

about
            four kopecks)
                        per man.
Washing my hands
                        in a lavatory bowl,
inhaling the wonders
                        of the perfume's
                                    spell
and puzzled by
                        the mademoiselle's presence,
I'd like
            to say
                        to the mademoiselle:
Mademoiselle,
                        excuse me,
                                    but you look pathetic.

Isn't it a shame
                        you waste your youth in 'MEN'?
Either I
            was misled
                        about Parisiennes
or you,
            Mademoiselle,
                        are no Parisienne.
You look
            tubercular
                        and flaccid.
Wool stockings . . .
                        No silks then?
Why aren't you given
                        violets
                                    from Parma
by appreciative,
                        moneybagged
                                    gentlemen?
She gave no answer.
                        The roar above

на трактир,
　　　　　на потолок,
　　　　　　　　　на нас.
Это,
　　　кружа
　　　　　веселье карнавалово,
весь
　　　в парижанках
　　　　　　　　гудел Монпарнас.
Простите, пожалуйста,
　　　　　　　за стих раскрежещенный
и
　　за описанные
　　　　　　вонючие лужи,
но очень
　　　трудно
　　　　　в Париже
　　　　　　　женщине,
если
　　женщина
　　　　　не продается,
　　　　　　　　а служит.

1929

СТИХИ О СОВЕТСКОМ ПАСПОРТЕ

Я волком бы
　　　　　выгрыз
　　　　　　　бюрократизм.
К мандатам
　　　　почтения нету.
К любым
　　　чертям с матерями
　　　　　　　　　катись
любая бумажка.
　　　　　Но эту...

rolled into the cafe,
down,
onto us gents.
This was Montparnasse
and a carnival,
full of Parisiennes
and exuberance.

Excuse me for gnashing
my teeth too much,
And for the stinking puddles
I made
in my verse,
but, believe me,
life is hard
for a woman
in Paris...
if she doesn't
sell
herself,
but works.

A POEM ABOUT MY SOVIET PASSPORT

I would gnaw out
red tape
like a wolf.
Show papers, no;
respect, none.
Other documents
may go straight
to the devil
and all mothers,
but not this one...

По длинному фронту
                купе
                        и кают
чиновник
        учтивый
                движется.
Сдают паспорта,
                и я
                        сдаю
мою
        пурпурную книжицу.
К одним паспортам –
                улыбка у рта.
К другим –
                отношение плевое.
С почтеньем
        берут, например,
                        паспорта
с двухспальным
                английским левою.
Глазами
        доброго дядю выев,
не переставая
                кланяться,
берут,
        как будто берут чаевые,
паспорт
        американца.
Не польский –
        глядят,
                как в афишу коза.
На польский –
        выпяливают глаза
в тугой
        полицейской слоновости –
откуда, мол,
        и что это за

Along the long line
                    of cabins
                              and compartments
a polite official
                    moves in this direction.

All hand him their passports
                              and I
                                        give him my
purple booklet
                    for inspection.
For some passports –
                              there's a look down his nose.
For others
          a smile broadly written.
Yet for others,
                    for instance,
                                        respect
for the double-bedded
                              Leo from Britain.
Eating
          the kind uncle with his eyes,
with such bowing that
                              he may disjoint his hips,
he takes
          the passports
                              of Americans
as if they were tips.
He looks
          at the Poles'
                              like a goat at a sign.
At the Poles'
                    his eyes bulge in a blind
bureaucratic
                    idiocy –
as if saying:
                    what's this? And where did you find

географические новости?
И не повернув
            головы качан
и чувств
        никаких
            не изведав,
берут,
      не моргнув,
            паспорта датчан
и разных
       прочих
          шведов.
И вдруг,
      как будто
          ожогом,
              рот
скривило
       господину.
Это
     господин чиновник
             берет
мою
     краснокожую паспортину.
Берет –
      как бомбу,
         берет –
            как ежа,
как бритву
       обоюдоострую,
берет
     как гремучую
          в 20 жал
змею
     двухметроворостую.
Моргнул
      многозначаще
          глаз носильщика,

this geographical novelty?
Never showing
          emotion,
never turning
        his cabbage
            head without brains,
never blinking an eye,
          he just takes
              the passports of the Swedes
and all
     other
        Danes.
And suddenly,
       as if a burn
           made
             the gentleman's
mouth
   distort –
this
   is Mister Official
         taking
my red-skinned
        piece of passport...
As if it
     were a porcupine,
           as if it
             were a bomb;
a razor-like
     super-sharp blade,
like a seven-foot
       twenty-fang
           venomous snake
rattling
     a cannonade.
The redcap
     winks
        significantly:

хоть вещи
            снесет задаром вам.
Жандарм
        вопросительно
                смотрит на сыщика,
сыщик
        на жандарма.
С каким наслажденьем
                    жандармской кастой
я был бы
        исхлестан и распят
за то,
        что в руках у меня
                    молоткастый,
серпастый
        советский паспорт.
Я волком бы
            выгрыз
                бюрократизм.
К мандатам
        почтения нету.
К любым
        чертям с матерями
                    катись
любая бумажка.
                Но эту...
Я
    достаю
        из широких штанин
дупликатом
            бесценного груза.
Читайте,
        завидуйте,
                я –
                    гражданин
Советского Союза.

1929

he will carry
         your bags for free.
The inspector
         and a detective
                  exchange glances
bruskly
         and questioningly.
What joy it would be
                  for this coppers' clique
to nail me and whip me
                  and crush me,
because my hands hold
                  the hammer-and-sickledhood

of a passport
         of Soviet Russia!
I would gnaw out
         red tape
                  like a wolf.
Show papers, no;
         respect, none.
Other documents
         may go straight
                  to the devil
and all mothers
         but not this one...
So
    I take it
         from my wide pants
as a symbol
         of precious weight.
Read it
         with envy:
                  I'm a citizen

of the Soviet State.

Уже второй должно быть ты легла
В ночи Млечпуть серебряной Окою
Я не спешу и молниями телеграмм
Мне незачем тебя будить и беспокоить
как говорят инцидент исперчен
любовная лодка разбилась о быт
С тобой мы в расчете и не к чему перечень
взаимных болей бед и обид
Ты посмотри какая в мире тишь
Ночь обложила небо звездной данью
в такие вот часы встаешь и говоришь
векам истории и мирозданию!

1930

Past one o'clock. You must have gone to bed.
Night's Milky Way flows like a silver stream.
No rush. I'll not wake you, bothering your head
With lightning telegrams to crush your dream.
As they say, that's the end of the story,
The boat of love has smashed against life's reefs.
We are quits and we don't need an inventory
Of our mutual hurtings, insults and griefs.
And see how the world lies in quietness
The sky pays Night with a rash of stars from its purse.
In hours like these, one gets up to address
All Time and History and Universe!

СЕРГЕЙ АЛЕКСАНДРОВИЧ ЕСЕНИН
1895-1925

Там, где капустные грядки
Красной водой поливает восход,
Клененочек маленький матке
Зеленое вымя сосет.

1910

* * *

Сохнет стаявшая глина,
На сугорьях гниль опенок.
Пляшет ветер по равнинам,
Рыжий ласковый осленок.

Пахнет вербой и смолою.
Синь то дремлет, то вздыхает.
У лесного аналоя
Воробей псалтырь читает.

Прошлогодний лист в овраге
Средь кустов – как ворох меди.
Кто-то в солнечной сермяге
На осленке рыжем едет.

Прядь волос нежней кудели,
Но лицо Его туманно.
Никнут сосны, никнут ели
И кричат Ему: 'Осанна!'

1914

SERGEI ALEXANDROVICH ESENIN
1895-1925

There, where the sunrise is sprinkling
Water of red where the cabbage bed sits,
The small maple nuzzling his mother
Impatiently sucks her green tits.

* * *

Snow gone, mounds of clay are drying,
Mold of mushrooms on the foothills.
On the plains the wind is dancing –
Like a gentle small red donkey.

Smells of pine and pussy willow...
Heaven sometimes sighs – and dozes.
And a sparrow reads his psalter
At the pulpit of the forest.

In the draw the leaves of last year
Heap like copper in the bushes.
Someone wearing sunny kaftan
Rides upon the small red donkey.

His hair *is* as soft as raw flax,
But His face is sadly clouded.
Pine trees, fir trees bow before Him
And shout out to him, 'Hosanna!'

ПЕСНЬ О СОБАКЕ

Утром в ржаном закуте,
Где златятся рогожи в ряд,
Семерых ощенила сука,
Рыжих семерых щенят.

До вечера она их ласкала,
Причесывая языком,
И струился снежок подталый
Под теплым ее животом.

А вечером, когда куры
Обсиживают шесток,
Вышел хозяин хмурый,
Семерых всех поклал в мешок.

По сугробам она бежала,
Поспевая за ним бежать...
И так долго, долго дрожала
Воды незамерзшей гладь.

А когда чуть плелась обратно,
Слизывая пот с боков,
Показался ей месяц над хатой
Одним из ее щенков.

В синюю высь звонко
Глядела она, скуля,
А месяц скользил тонкий
И скрылся за холм в полях.

И глухо, как от подачки,
Когда бросят ей камень в смех,
Покатились глаза собачьи
Золотыми звездами в снег.

1915

A SONG ABOUT A DOG

It was morning, and in the rye-bin,
Where the rows of gold mats were spread,
A dog littered seven puppies,
Seven puppies, brownish-red.

She fondled them until evening
And combed them smooth with her tongue,
While the light snow melted beneath her
Where her warm belly hung.

But when night came and the chickens
Were speckling their roosting rack,
Out came her grim-faced owner
And put all seven in a sack.

She went running over the snowdrifts,
Trying to match his pace...
And for a long, long time shudders
Shook the unfrozen water's smooth face.

When she wearily dragged her feet back,
Licking the wet from her side,
She thought the moon over the cottage
Was one of her pups that had died.

And gazing high, whining loudly,
She stared at the blue sky until
The thin moon slid on and vanished
In the fields behind the hill.

And, softly, as if someone, while jesting,
Had thrown her a stone — even so
Tears now rolled down from her dog-eyes
Like golden stars into the snow.

ПЕСНЬ О ХЛЕБЕ

Вот она, суровая жестокость,
Где весь смысл – страдания людей!
Режет серп тяжелые колосья,
Как под горло режут лебедей.

Наше поле издавна знакомо
С августовской дрожью поутру.
Перевязана в снопы солома,
Каждый сноп лежит, как желтый труп.

На телегах, как на катафалках,
Их везут в могильный склеп – овин.
Словно дьякон, на кобылу гаркнув,
Чтит возница погребальный чин.

А потом их бережно, без злости,
Головами стелют по земле
И цепами маленькие кости
Выбивают из худых телес.

Никому и в голову не встанет,
Что солома – это тоже плоть!...
Людоедке-мельнице – зубами
В рот суют те кости обмолоть.

И, из мелева заквашивая тесто,
Выпекают груды вкусных яств...
Вот тогда-то входит яд белесый
В жбан желудка яйца злобы класть.

Все побои ржи в припек окрасив,
Грубость жнущих сжав в духмяный сок.
Он вкушающим соломенное мясо
Отравляет жернова кишок.

A SONG ABOUT GRAIN

Here you have the cruelty that's hardest.
Its sole sense is to give people pain.
And like cutting swans below the gullet,
The scythe cuts off heavy heads of grain.

Our field long has shaken with the shudder
That the usual August morning leaves.
Everywhere the bound, yellow cadavers:
Straw that's lying tied-up into sheaves.

Placed, as if on catafalques, on wagons,
They are taken to the barn's crypt there.
The driver respects the funeral custom
Barking like a deacon at the mare.

And then carefully and without anger
Heads down, on the earth, they're spread about.
Come the threshers . . . From the skinny bodies
All their tiny bones are beaten out.

It does not occur to anybody
That the straw is also flesh and mind!
And those bones are pushed into the open-
Mouthed cannibalistic mill to grind.

From fermenting dough from that farina,
Heaps of fine foods – as an aftermath . . .
This is when the whitish poison enters
The stomach's jug to lay eggs of wrath.

These rye-beatings colored in the surplus,
Reapers' cruelty pressed into good juice,
It poisons the millstones of the innards
Of all those who eat the straw's produce.

И свистит по всей стране, как осень,
Шарлатан, убийца и злодей...
Оттого что режет серп колосья,
Как под горло режут лебедей.

1921

*　*　*

Не жалею, не зову, не плачу,
Все пройдет, как с белых яблонь дым.
Увяданья золотом охваченный,
Я не буду больше молодым.

Ты теперь не так уж будешь биться,
Сердце, тронутое холодком,
И страна березового ситца
Не заманит шляться босиком.

Дух бродяжий, ты все реже, реже
Расшевеливаешь пламень уст.
О, моя утраченная свежесть,
Буйство глаз и половодье чувств.

Я теперь скупее стал в желаньях,
Жизнь моя? иль ты приснилась мне?
Словно я весенней гулкой ранью
Проскакал на розовом коне.

Все мы, все мы в этом мире тленны,
Тихо льется с кленов листьев медь...
Будь же ты навек благословенно,
Что пришло процвесть и умереть.

1922

And the con-man, murderer and robber
Whistle like autumn across the plain...
Since – like cutting swans below the gullet –
The scythe cuts off heavy heads of grain.

★　★　★

I have no regrets, retreats or weepings.
Smoke from white apple trees: all will go.
Gripped as I am by the gold of withering,
I will not be young again, I know.

Heart of mine, touched by the chill already,
You will not be beating anymore.
And the calico birches will never
Coax me to walk barefoot as before.

Less and less the spirit of a gypsy
Stirs my lips into some flaming fire.
O, all gone, my lost-forever freshness,
Wild eyes, floods of feelings and desire.

Now I grow more tame in my ambitions.
Life, were you dreams and no other thing,
Where I galloped by on a pink stallion
Through the echo-filled mornings of Spring?

We are transitory in this world.
Copper leaves from maple trees drift by...
So let all of us be blest forever:
All things that come here to bloom and die.

Да! Теперь решено. Без возврата
Я покинул родные поля.
Уж не будут листвою крылатой
Надо мною звенеть тополя.

Низкий дом без меня ссутулится,
Старый пес мой давно издох.
На московских изогнутых улицах
Умереть, знать, судил мне Бог.

Я люблю этот город вязевый,
Пусть обрюзг он и пусть одрях.
Золотая дремотная Азия
Опочила на куполах.

А когда ночью светит месяц,
Когда светит... чорт знает как!
Я иду, головою свесясь,
Переулком в знакомый кабак.

Шум и гам в этом логове жутком,
Но всю ночь напролет, до зари,
Я читаю стихи проституткам
И с бандитами жарю спирт.

Сердце бьется все чаще и чаще,
И уж я говорю невпопад:
'Я такой же, как вы, пропащий,
Мне теперь не уйти назад.'

Низкий дом без меня ссутулится,
Старый пес мой давно издох.
На московских изогнутых улицах
Умереть, знать, судил мне Бог.

1922-1923

I've decided, now, to abandon
My home fields which I no more shall see.
And the poplars will no longer rustle
Their winged foliage above over me.

The low house will crouch lower without me;
My old dog has been long gone by now.
It seems God has me destined to perish
On the cold, crooked streets of Moscow.

I like this calligraphed, knitted city,
Be it run-down and flimsy on sight.
Asia, all golden and dozing,
Lies asleep on the cupolas' height.

And whenever the moon shines at night-time,
When it shines ... (God-be-damned, what a moon!)
With head drooped, I go into the alley
To the friendly, familiar saloon!

There's a hubbub in this hellish tavern,
But I stay there as night staggers on,
Reading prostitutes part of my poems,
Guzzling vodka with bandits till dawn.

And my heart beats still faster and faster,
And I already ramble and roar:
'I'm a lost one – like you; I'm a lost one,
And I cannot go home anymore.'

The low house will crouch lower without me;
My old dog has been long gone by now.
It seems God has me destined to perish
On the cold, crooked streets of Moscow.

Сыпь, гармоника. Скука... Скука...
Гармонист пальцы льет волной.
Пей со мной, паршивая сука,
Пей со мной.

Излюбили тебя, измызгали –
Невтерпеж.
Что ж ты смотришь так синими брызгами?
Иль в морду хошь?

В огород бы тебя на чучело,
Пугать ворон.
До печенок меня замучила
Со всех сторон.

Сыпь, гармоника. Сыпь, моя частая.
Пей, выдра, пей.
Мне бы лучше вон ту, сисястую, –
Она глупей.

Я средь женщин тебя не первую...
Не мало вас,
Но с такой вот, как ты, со стервою
Лишь в первый раз.

Чем больнее, тем звонче,
То здесь, то там.
Я с собой не покончу,
Иди к чертям.

К вашей своре собачьей
Пора простыть.
Дорогая, я плачу,
Прости... прости...

1923

Shoot, accordion! Boredom, O boredom...
Fingers ripple like waves of the sea.
Drink with me, lousy wench of a woman,
Come drink with me.

You're worn out from their love and their slobbers;
No patience, not a trace.
Then why are your blue eyes winking at me?
You want a fist in the face?

You belong in a vegetable garden –
A good scarecrow.
You've tormented me clear to my liver
And won't let go.

Shoot, accordion! Shoot, my live one!
And drink, fish, drink and sing!
I would like that one there, the bigtitties,
A stupid ding-a-ling.

You are not the first one – of my women.
O, there were many more.
But this is the first time, believe me,
I've been with such a whore.

Bravo! The more painful, the louder!
If here or there, so what?
I will not hang myself this evening.
Go to the devil, slut.

It is time to cold-shoulder
Your whole dog pack that's here.
I am crying. Forgive me.
Forgive me, dear.

СУКИН СЫН

Снова выплыли годы из мрака
И шумят, как ромашковый луг.
Мне припомнилась нынче собака,
Что была моей юности друг.

Нынче юность моя отшумела,
Как подгнивший под окнами клен,
Но припомнил я девушку в белом,
Для которой был пес почтальон.

Не у всякого есть свой близкий,
Но она мне как песня была,
Потому что мои записки
Из ошейника пса не брала.

Никогда она их не читала,
И мой почерк ей был незнаком,
Но о чем-то подолгу мечтала
У калины за желтым прудом.

Я страдал... Я хотел ответа...
Не дождался... уехал... И вот
Через годы... известным поэтом
Снова здесь, у родимых ворот.

Та собака давно околела,
Но в ту ж масть, что отливом в синь,
С лаем ливисто ошалелым
Меня встрел молодой ее сын.

Мать честная! И как же схожи!
Снова выплыла боль души.
С этой болью я будто моложе,
И хоть снова записки пиши.

THE SON OF MY BITCH

Once again the years swim out from shadow,
And like meadows of daisies they bend.
Today I can clearly remember
The dog that was my childhood friend.

Like the maple that rots neath my window,
My youth rustled away. (How it ran!)
But I still see a girl in a white dress
For whom that dog was mailman.

Not everyone has such dear people,
But she was a song in my throat,
Because she never took from his collar
Any of the letters I wrote.

No, she never ever would read them.
She did not know my script. She was fond
Of dreaming for long times of something
By the snowball bush back of the pond.

I suffered. I wanted an answer...
It did not come. I left. And then
After years brought me fame as a poet,
I'm now back at my home gates again.

That dog has been dead for a long time,
But today I was met by her son –
With the wildest possible barking,
And her color – the same bluish one.

Holy Mary! They look like each other!
And the soul's pain swims out – as before.
And with this pain I seem to feel younger
And like writing letters once more.

Рад послушать я песню былую,
Но не лай ты! Не лай! Не лай!
Хочешь, пес, я тебя поцелую
За пробуженный в сердце май?

Поцелую, прижмусь к тебе телом
И, как друга, введу тебя в дом...
Да, мне нравилась девушка в белом,
Но теперь я люблю в голубом.

1924

I'm glad to hear the past singing.
But don't bark, you! Don't bark! Don't start!
Dog, do you want me to kiss you
For the May you awoke in my heart?

I will kiss you, I'll press you close to me,
And take you home like a good friend would do . . .
Yes, I did like a girl in a white dress,
But I now love a girl all in blue.

БОРИС ЛЕОНИДОВИЧ ПАСТЕРНАК
1890-1960

ПОСЛЕ ДОЖДЯ

За окнами давка, толпится листва,
И палое небо с дорог не подобрано.
Все стихло. Но что это было сперва!
Теперь разговор уж не тот и по-доброму.

Сначала все опрометью, вразноряд
Ввалилось в ограду деревья развенчивать,
И попранным парком из ливня – под град.
Потом от сараев – к террасе бревенчатой.

Теперь не надышишься крепью густой.
А то, что у тополя жилы полопались, –
Так воздух садовый, как соды настой,
Шипучкой играет от горечи тополя.

Со стекол балконных, как с бедер и спин
Озябших купальщиц – ручьями испарина.
Сверкает клубники мороженый клин,
И градинки стелются солью поваренной.

Вот луч, покатясь с паутины, залег
В крапиве, но, кажется, это не на́долго,
И миг недалек, как его уголек
В кустах разожжется и выдует радугу.

1915-1928

586

BORIS LEONIDOVICH PASTERNAK
1890-1960

AFTER THE RAIN

Outside of the window – a mob: bushes crowding.
The sky which had fallen still lies in the lane.
All's quiet (But you should have seen the beginning!)
And now the talk's different and friendly again.

It burst headlong into the garden decrowning
The trees, in a manner haphazard and fast:
The drenching downpour, then the hail, through the conquered
Park, on toward the barns, to the log terrace last.

One can't breathe enough of this strong, heady mixture.
And as to the frail poplar bursting its vein . . .
The air in the garden is like soda water
And plays with the fizz from the poplar tree's pain.

As do thighs and backs of the freezing girl-bathers,
The balcony's windowpanes sweat, and the bed
Of strawberries, chilled, coldly glistens with hailstones
Like kitchen salt. Look and see how they're spread.

And look at that sunbeam that falls through the cobweb;
It hides in the nettles (For not long we know).
The moment is near when its coal-glowing ember
Will flare through the bush and flash out a rainbow.

МАРБУРГ

Я вздрагивал. Я загорался и гас.
Я трясся. Я сделал сейчас предложенье, –
Но поздно, я сдрейфил, и вот – мне отказ.
Как жаль ее слез! Я святого блаженней.

Я вышел на площадь. Я мог быть сочтен
Вторично родившимся. Каждая малость
Жила и, не ставя меня ни во что,
В прощальном значеньи своем подымалась.

Плитняк раскалялся, и улицы лоб
Был смугл, и на небо глядел исподлобья
Булыжник, и ветер, как лодочник, греб
По липам. И все это были подобья.

Но как бы то ни было, я избегал
Их взглядов. Я не замечал их приветствий.
Я знать ничего не хотел из богатств.
Я вон вырывался, чтоб не разреветься.

Плыла черепица, и полдень смотрел,
Не смаргивая, на кровли. А в Марбурге
Кто, громко свища, мастерил самострел,
Кто молча готовился к Троицкой ярмарке.

Желтел, облака пожирая, песок,
Предгрозье играло бровями кустарника,
И небо спекалось, упав на кусок
Кровоостанавливающей арники.

В тот день всю тебя, от гребенок до ног,
Как трагик в провинции драму Шекспирову,
Носил я с собою и знал назубок,
Шатался по городу и репетировал.

MARBURG

I'd shudder. And I'd catch on fire, then go out.
I trembled. I had just made a proposal,
But it was too late. I'd backed down. Here was 'no'.
I'm sad for her tears! I'm more happy than saints are.

I came to the square. And they could take me for
A person reborn. Each detail, every trifle
Was living and (paying no mind to me here)
Was rising in all of its farewell importance.

The sidewalk was scorching; the head of the street
Was dusky. The cobblestones looked and were hostile
With heaven – the wind like a rower, rowed on
Through the linden trees. Each of these was a symbol.

But be it whatever it was, I turned eyes
Away from each glance, did not notice each greeting.
I did not desire any part of such wealth.
I wanted out so not to burst into crying.

The roof-tiles were floating; the mid-day looked on
Even without blinking at roofs. And in Marburg
Were some, whistling loud, hard at work on cross-bows;
And some fixed themselves for the fair . . . Whitsun Sunday.

The sand had grown yellow – swallowing clouds.
The pre-storm had played with the eyebrows of bushes
And the sky coagulated when it fell
On the patches of blood-stopping arnica tincture.

I bore all of you (from your head to your feet)
That day like a tragic actor in a province
With some play by Shakespeare – and knew you by heart,
And wandered around town, rehearsing you always.

Когда я упал пред тобой, охватив
Туман этот, лед этот, эту поверхность
(Как ты хороша!) – этот вихрь духоты –
О чем ты? Опомнись! Пропало. Отвергнут.

Тут жил Мартин Лютер. Там – братья Гримм.
Когтистые крыши. Деревья. Надгробья.
И все это помнит и тянется к ним.
Все – живо. И все это тоже – подобья.

Нет, я не пойду туда завтра. Отказ –
Полнее прощанья. Все ясно. Мы квиты.
Да и оторвусь ли от газа, от касс, –
Что будет со мною, старинные плиты?

Повсюду портпледы разложит туман,
И в обе оконницы вставят по месяцу.
Тоска пассажиркой скользнет по томам
И с книжкою на оттоманке поместится.

Чего же я трушу? Ведь я, как грамматику,
Бессонницу знаю. Стрясется – спасут.
Рассудок? Но он – как луна для лунатика.
Мы в дружбе, но я не его сосуд.

Ведь ночи играть садятся в шахматы
Со мной на лунном паркетном полу.
Акацией пахнет, и окна распахнуты,
И страсть, как свидетель, седеет в углу.

И тополь – король. Я играю с бессонницей.
И ферзь – соловей. Я тянусь к соловью.
И ночь побеждает, фигуры сторонятся,
Я белое утро в лицо узнаю.

1915-1956

When I had collapsed before you, having then
Embraced all this fog, all this ice, all this surface,
(How lovely you are!) all this strong stifling wind,
Where was I? Wake up! It's all over. Forget it.

Here lived Martin Luther. There – the Brothers Grimm
The roofs look like claws. All these trees – And the tombstones.
This landscape remembers and stretches toward them.
It – lives! And all this is also a symbol.

No. I won't go there tomorrow. I find
Rejection greater than farewell. Clear. We're even!
Can I leave these shop-windows and these gaslights?
And what happens now to me, old slabs and pebbles?

Fog will spread a blanket out soon everywhere
And they'll put a moon into my two framed windows;
And longing, a passenger, will slip past books;
With one in her hands she'll sit down on a sofa.

Well, what do I fear? My insomnia I know
As I know my grammar. I'm safe if it happens.
And reason? A moon for a sleepwalking man.
Oh yes, we are friends, but I am not its vessel.

The nights stop and sit down to play chess with me
Upon a parquet floor that's flooded with moonlight.
The smell of acacia, windows opened wide ...
And passion, a witness who grays in the corner.

The poplar's my king. With insomnia I play,
And the nightingale is my queen. I stretch toward her
And then the night wins and the figures step back
And I recognize the face of the white morning.

ПАМЯТИ ДЕМОНА

Приходил по ночам
В синеве ледника от Тамары.
Парой крыл намечал,
Где гудеть, где кончаться кошмару.

Не рыдал, не сплетал
Оголенных, исхлестанных, в шрамах.
Уцелела плита
За оградой грузинского храма.

Как горбунья дурна,
Под решеткою тень не кривлялась.
У лампады зурна,
Чуть дыша, о княжне не справлялась.

Но сверканье рвалось
В волосах, и, как фосфор, трещали.
И не слышал колосс,
Как седеет Кавказ за печалью.

От окна на аршин,
Пробирая шерстинки бурнуса,
Клялся льдами вершин:
Спи, подруга, – лавиной вернуся.

1917

* * *

Душистою веткою машучи,
Впивая впотьмах это благо,
Бежала на чашечку с чашечки
Грозой одуренная влага.

IN MEMORY OF 'THE DEMON'

Used to come after dark
In the glacier's blue from Tamara.
With paired wings used to mark
Where the nightmare should start or stop humming.

Never sobbed. Nor entwined
Although wounded and bare-armed and much scarred.
The slab's kept safe behind
The stone fence in a Georgian churchyard.

Ugly as a hunchback,
His dark form neath the grill did no winces.
The zurná, breathing slack,
By the lamp did not ask about the princess.

But the sparks glittered hot
In his hair, snapping, crackling like phosphor.
And the giant did not
Hear the Caucasus graying for sorrow.

Two feet down from the sill,
He swore by the iced peaks, 'Sleep, my darling'.
(Fingering his burnoose still)
'As an avalanche I'll be returning.'

* * *

O swaying with wet, fragrant branches
And drinking such bliss in the warm,
Dark evening, from calyx to calyx
A raindrop ran, dazed by the storm.

На чашечку с чашечки скатываясь,
  Скользнула по двум, – и в обеих
Огромною каплей агатовою
  Повисла, сверкает, робеет.

Пусть ветер, по таволге веющий,
  Ту капельку мучит и плющит.
Цела, не дробится, – их две еще
  Целующихся и пьющих.

Смеются и вырваться силятся
  И выпрямиться, как прежде,
Да капле из рылец не вылиться,
  И не разлучатся, хоть режьте.

1917

СЛОЖА ВЕСЛА

Лодка колотится в сонной груди,
Ивы нависли, целуют в ключицы,
В локти, в уключины – о, погоди,
Это ведь может со всяким случиться!

Этим ведь в песне тешатся все.
Это ведь значит пепел сиреневый,
Роскошь крошеной ромашки в росе,
Губы и губы на звезды выменивать!

Это ведь значит обнять небосвод,
Руки сплести вкруг Геракла громадного,
Это ведь значит века напролет
Ночи на щелканье славок проматывать!

1917

And rolling from calyx to calyx,
   It slipped along two, and it clung
To both. As a gigantic agate
   It sparkled, shy there where it hung.

The wind blowing through the spiraea
   May torture and flatten that drop.
The couple will never be parted
   Nor their kissing and selves-drinking stop.

They laugh, strain and try to be separate,
   To straighten out and start anew.
The drop cannot fall from the pistil,
   And a knife could not cut them in two.

RESTING OARS

A boat is rocking in my drowsy chest;
Willows bend low kissing my collarbone,
Elbows and oarlocks. O wait, rest!
All this could happen to anyone!

Well, in a song everyone loves this too.
And we might add lilac ashes, the strange
Richness of daisies crushed down in the dew,
Lips and more lips – for the stars in exchange.

This means embracing the vast firmament,
Touching your hands around huge Hercules ...
This then means squandering nights for the blent
Song of the nightingales ... through centuries.

УРОКИ АНГЛИЙСКОГО

Когда случилось петь Дездемоне, –
А жить так мало оставалось, –
Не по любви, своей звезде она, –
По иве, иве разрыдалась.

Когда случилось петь Дездемоне
И голос завела, крепясь,
Про черный день чернейший демон ей
Псалом плакучих русл припас.

Когда случилось петь Офелии, –
А жить так мало оставалось, –
Всю сушь души смело и свеяло,
Как в бурю стебли с сеновала.

Когда случилось петь Офелии,
А горечь грез осточертела,
С какими канула трофеями?
С охапкой верб и чистотела.

Дав страсти с плеч отлечь, как рубищу,
Входили, с сердца замираньем,
В бассейн вселенной, стан свой любящий
Обдать и оглушить мирами.

1917

ГРОЗА, МОМЕНТАЛЬНАЯ НАВЕК

А затем прощалось лето
С полустанком. Снявши шапку,
Сто слепящих фотографий
Ночью снял на память гром.

ENGLISH LESSON

When it came time to sing for Desdemona,
So little life to live remaining,
She did not sob to mourn her love, her star...
But only for the willow, willow.

When it came time to sing for Desdemona
And she began – her song, restraining,
The darkest demon saved for her dark day
A psalm of stream-beds, weeping, flowing.

When it came time to sing – for Ophelia,
So little life to live remaining,
Her dried soul was caught up and borne away
Like stems in storms from haystacks blowing.

When it came time to sing – for Ophelia,
Worn-out from dreams bitterly waning,
What trophies filled her arms when she sank down?
Wild celandine and pussy willow.

And dropping passion like a rag, hearts pounding,
They plunged into that vast pool, straining
Their loving bodies toward the universe,
Stunning their naked selves with worlds.

THUNDERSTORM
(INSTANTANEOUS FOREVER)

Then the summer said goodbye to
The train-stop. And doffing hat the
Thunder (for a keepsake) took a
Hundred blinding snaps that night.

Меркла кисть сирени. В это
Время он, набрав охапку
Молний, с поля ими трафил
Озарить управский дом.

И когда по кровле зданья
Разлилась волна злорадства,
И, как уголь по рисунку,
Грянул ливень всем плетнем,

Стал мигать обвал сознанья:
Вот, казалось, озарятся
Даже те углы рассудка,
Где теперь светло, как днем!

1917

★　★　★

Рояль дрожащий пену с губ оближет.
Тебя сорвет, подкосит этот бред.
Ты скажешь: милый! – Нет, – вскричу я, – нет!
При музыке?! – Но можно ли быть ближе,

Чем в полутьме, аккорды, как дневник,
Меча в камин комплектами, погодно?
О, пониманье дивное, кивни,
Кивни, и изумишься! – ты свободна.

Я не держу. Иди, благотвори.
Ступай к другим. Уже написан Вертер,
А в наши дни и воздух пахнет смертью:
Открыть окно, что жилы отворить.

1918

Lilac clusters darkened. By new
Armfuls, plucked from meadows at the
Time, the lightning flashed and look! A
Public building loomed in light!

Waves of evil laughter splashing
Spread along the building's roof and
Like charcoal on drawings, torrents
Poured down, banged against the fence.

Then the crumbling mind was flashing:
'All is bright!' It seemed the truth, and
Bright the brain . . . even those corners
Where light now is day-intense.

★   ★   ★

The trembling piano will lick foam from its mouth:
Delirium – which makes your knees give way
Will lift you. You'll say 'Darling', and 'No', I'll shout,
'While playing music?' But can we be, say,

Closer than in twilight throwing chords
Into the fireplace like a diary
Set, year on year. Oh, great awareness, nod,
Nod and you'll be astonished! – You are free.

I won't hold you. Go. Do your charity.
Go elsewhere. *Werther* can't be written again:
In our times even air smells death to me.
Opening a window is like opening a vein.

Так начинают. Года в два
От мамки рвутся в тьму мелодий,
Щебечут, свищут, – а слова
Являются о третьем годе.

Так начинают понимать.
И в шуме пущенной турбины
Мерещится, что мать – не мать,
Что ты – не ты, что дом – чужбина.

Что делать страшной красоте,
Присевшей на скамью сирени,
Когда и впрямь не красть детей?
Так возникают подозренья.

Так зреют страхи. Как он даст
Звезде превысить досяганье,
Когда он – Фауст, когда – фантаст?
Так начинаются цыгане.

Так открываются, паря
Поверх плетней, где быть домам бы,
Внезапные, как вздох, моря.
Так будут начинаться ямбы.

Так ночи летние, ничком
Упав в овсы с мольбой: исполнься,
Грозят заре твоим зрачком.
Так затевают ссоры с солнцем.

Так начинают жить стихом.

1919

So Life begins! When almost two,
They leave the nurse for melody...
They chirp, they babble – and then words
Will soon appear before they're three.

So they begin to understand!
And in the churning turbine's roar
Mother does not seem mother. You,
Not you; home, not home anymore.

What should that awesome beauty do
Which on the lilac bench awaits –
If not to carry children off?
Suspicion thus originates...

And fears increase. How dare a star
Be past the arc his arms take in
When he's a dreamer and a Faust?
And this is how gypsies begin.

So – oceans, sudden like a sigh
Hover above the fences where
The houses are supposed to be.
And so – iambics begin there.

So, summer nights fall, prone, to pray
In fields of oats: fulfill each one,
Threaten the dawn with your eye's ray.
So – they start quarrels with the sun.

So – they live poetry this way.

Здесь будет все: пережитое
В предвиденьи и наяву,
И те, которых я не стою,
И то, за что средь них слыву.

Шумит прибой, и неизменно
Ложится за волной волна,
И их следы смывает пена
С песчаных куч, как письмена.

Еще ты здесь, и мне сказали,
Где ты сейчас и будешь в пять,
Я б мог застать тебя в курзале,
Чем даром языком трепать.

Ты б слушала и молодела,
Большая, смелая, своя,
О человеке у предела
От переростка муравья.

Есть в опыте больших поэтов
Черты естественности той,
Что невозможно, их изведав,
Не кончить полной немотой.

В родстве со всем, что есть, уверясь,
И знаясь с будущим в быту,
Нельзя не впасть к концу, как в ересь,
В неслыханную простоту.

Но мы пощажены не будем,
Когда ее не утаим.
Она всего нужнее людям,
Но сложное понятней им.

1931

All will be here: what I have lived through: –
Hoped for, seen through, what took place,
And those – of whom I am not worthy
And what I mean to them – my case.

The tide is roaring: never changing,
Wave after wave falls on the strand.
Their tracks are washed away like letters
By foam that floods the piles of sand.

You are still here – and someone told me
Where you are, where you'll be at five.
I could have caught you in the Kursaal –
Not wagged the idlest tongue alive.

And you would hear, you would grow younger,
Courageous, big, my confidant...
About man at the highest limits
From the out-growing of an ant.

There are in the lives of great poets
Traits of complete naturalness.
And having sensed it there, one cannot
But end in all silence, speechless.

And feeling near to all things, greeting
In daily life what-is-to-be,
At last one cannot help but falling
Into a rare simplicity.

But if we do not keep it hidden,
No mercy will be shown us here...
It's what is needed most – but people
Do find complexities more clear.

О, знал бы я, что так бывает,
Когда пускался на дебют,
Что строчки с кровью – убивают,
Нахлынут кровью и убьют!

От шуток с этой подоплекой
Я б отказался наотрез.
Начало было так далеко,
Так робок первый интерес.

Но старость – это Рим, который
Взамен турусов и колес
Не читки требует с актера,
А полной гибели всерьез.

Когда строку диктует чувство,
Оно на сцену шлет раба,
И тут кончается искусство,
И дышат почва и судьба.

1931

ВЕТЕР

Я кончился, а ты жива.
И ветер, жалуясь и плача,
Раскачивает лес и дачу.
Не каждую сосну отдельно,
А полностью все дерева
Со всею далью беспредельной,
Как парусников кузова
На глади бухты корабельной.
И это не из удальства
Или из ярости бесцельной,
А чтоб в тоске найти слова
Тебе для песни колыбельной.

(1946-1953)

O, had I known at my beginning
When I was making my debut,
That lines so full of blood can murder,
Can gush from your throat, and kill you.

Then I'd have said 'no' resolutely
To jokes with such an undercoat –
The first interest was unpretentious
And the beginning so remote.

But age is like a Rome demanding
Not silly babbling with each breath,
Not merely 'reading' from an actor
But nothing less than total death.

A slave is sent to the arena
When passion writes a line that's great.
Then art has reached its limit – leaving
Instead the breathing earth and fate.

WIND

I have died, but... you still live on.
And the wind, crying and complaining,
Is rocking house and forest, straining
Not every pine tree, singly bending,
But all the trees together, one
With unlimited space extending.
They rock like hulls of sailboats on
A harbor's mirrored surface, spending
Themselves in no bravado fun
And with no senseless fury blending,
But so – to find, in longing, spun
Words for your lullaby unending.

ХМЕЛЬ

Под ракитой, обвитой плющом,
От ненастья мы ищем защиты.
Наши плечи покрыты плащом,
Вкруг тебя мои руки обвиты.

Я ошибся. Кусты этих чащ
Не плющом перевиты, а хмелем.
Ну так лучше давай этот плащ
В ширину под собою расстелем.

(1946-1953)

АВГУСТ

Как обещало, не обманывая,
Проникло солнце утром рано
Косою полосой шафрановою
От занавеси до дивана.

Оно покрыло жаркой охрою
Соседний лес, дома поселка,
Мою постель, подушку мокрую
И край стены за книжной полкой.

Я вспомнил, по какому поводу
Слегка увлажнена подушка.
Мне снилось, что ко мне на проводы,
Шли по лесу вы друг за дружкой.

Вы шли толпою, врозь и парами,
Вдруг кто-то вспомнил, что сегодня
Шестое августа по старому,
Преображение Господне.

HOPBINES

Neath a willow the ivy winds round,
We have found a safe place in bad weather.
And my two arms around you are wound,
And one cape shields our shoulders together.

I am wrong. It is hopbines and not
Ivy lacing the brush of these bushes.
Well then, hush, we shall spread on this spot
The raincape very wide underneath us.

AUGUST

As it had promised, not deceiving,
The sun pierced through morning and ran
As one bright slanted stripe of saffron
Across the drapes to the divan.

It covered with its heated ochre
The nearby woods, homes in the place,
My bed – and even my wet pillow, –
A patch of wall by the bookcase.

And I remembered why the pillow
Was slightly moist. That very eve
I dreamed you all came through a forest,
One after one – to see me leave.

You came in crowds, in pairs and singly,
And then someone was heard to say:
It is, old style, the sixth of August,
The Lord's Transfiguration Day.

Обыкновенно свет без пламени
Исходит в этот день с Фавора,
И осень, ясная как знаменье,
К себе приковывает взоры.

И вы прошли сквозь мелкий, нищенский,
Нагой, трепещущий ольшаник
В имбирно-красный лес кладбищенский,
Горевший, как печатный пряник.

С притихшими его вершинами
Соседствовало небо важно,
И голосами петушиными
Перекликалась даль протяжно.

В лесу казенной землемершею
Стояла смерть среди погоста,
Смотря в лицо мое умершее,
Чтоб вырыть яму мне по росту.

Был всеми ощутим физически
Спокойный голос чей-то рядом.
То прежний голос мой провидческий
Звучал, нетронутый распадом:

'Прощай, лазурь преображенская
И золото второго Спаса.
Смягчи последней лаской женскою
Мне горечь рокового часа.

Прощайте, годы безвременщины.
Простимся, бездне унижений
Бросающая вызов женщина!
Я – поле твоего сраженья.

Usually a light that's flameless
Comes from Tabor this day each year,
And autumn draws eyes to her beauty –
An omen, marvelously clear.

And you passed through the tiny, trembling,
Bare and beggared alders into
The graveyard's red-as-ginger forest
Which burned like pressed-out cookies do.

Importantly the great sky neighbored
With those tall, calmed-down tops of trees;
The distance for some time had echoed
With sounds of roosters' reveilles.

Death stood like some state land-surveyor
Amidst the trees in that stilled place
And scrutinized me for my grave size,
While looking in my lifeless face.

And everybody heard it really –
The quiet words of one nearby:
My former, clairvoyant voice was speaking
Which no decay can falsify.

'Farewell, blue of Transfiguration
And second Savior Day's rich gold.
Soften for me with woman's kindness
The bite this last sad hour can hold.

Farewell, years of prolonged stagnation.
And you, woman, let's say goodbye –
You who challenged humiliation!
I am your battlefield and cry.

Прощай, размах крыла расправленный,
Полета вольное упорство,
И образ мира, в слове явленный,
И творчество, и чудотворство.'

(1946-1953)

ЗИМНЯЯ НОЧЬ

Мело, мело по всей земле
Во все пределы.
Свеча горела на столе,
Свеча горела.

Как летом роем мошкара
Летит на пламя,
Слетались хлопья со двора
К оконной раме.

Метель лепила на стекле
Кружки и стрелы.
Свеча горела на столе,
Свеча горела.

На озаренный потолок
Ложились тени,
Скрещенья рук, скрещенья ног,
Судьбы скрещенья.

И падали два башмачка
Со стуком на пол.
И воск слезами с ночника
На платье капал.

И все терялось в снежной мгле
Седой и белой.
Свеча горела на столе.
Свеча горела.

Farewell, spread of the wings out-straightened,
The free stubbornness of pure flight,
The word that gives the world its image,
Creation: miracles and light.'

WINTER NIGHT

It snowed and snowed across the land,
Where'er one turned.
A candle burned upon a stand;
A candle burned.

Like summer swarms of gnats which flew
Into the flame,
Snowflakes swept from the yard up to
The windowframe.

The blizzard etched the glass with grand
Whorls; spears were ferned.
A candle burned upon a stand;
A candle burned.

Two shadows on the ceiling tossed,
Then stilled to wait.
The arms were crossed, the legs were crossed –
And so was fate.

And two small slippers fell and plopped
The floor with stress.
The candle shed wax tears which dropped
Onto a dress.

All vanished in that snow-dark strand,
Gray-haired and white.
A candle burned upon a stand,
A candle bright.

На свечку дуло из угла,
И жар соблазна
Вздымал, как ангел, два крыла
Крестообразно.

Мело весь месяц в феврале,
И то и дело
Свеча горела на столе,
Свеча горела.

(1946-1953)

★　★　★

Во всем мне хочется дойти
До самой сути:
В работе, в поисках пути,
В сердечной смуте.

До сущности протекших дней,
До их причины,
До оснований, до корней,
До сердцевины.

Все время схватывая нить
Судеб, событий,
Жить, думать, чувствовать, любить,
Свершать открытья.

О, если бы я только мог,
Хотя отчасти,
Я написал бы восемь строк
О свойствах страсти.

A corner draft caused flickerings,
And fever of
Temptation raised like angel wings
A cross above.

All February snow swept, and
As each day turned,
A candle burned upon a stand...
A candle burned.

*   *   *

I want to find the essence of
All things, each part:
In work, in groping for a way,
In turmoiled heart.

To touch the core of days now gone,
Past never known,
To know the roots, foundation, cause,
To touch the bone.

And always grasp the thread of acts
And destinies.
To live, feel, think, and love, to make
Discoveries.

O, if only I could write down
Even just eight
Good lines about passion and tell
Its every trait.

О беззаконьях, о грехах,
Бегах, погонях,
Нечаянностях впопыхах,
Локтях, ладонях.

Я вывел бы ее закон,
Ее начало,
И повторял ее имен
Инициалы.

Я б разбивал стихи как сад.
Всей дрожью жилок
Цвели бы липы в них подряд –
Гуськом, в затылок.

В стихи б я внес дыханье роз,
Дыханье мяты,
Луга, осоку, сенокос,
Грозы раскаты.

Так некогда Шопен вложил
Живое чудо
Фольварков, парков, рощ, могил
В свои этюды.

Достигнутого торжества
Игра и мука –
Натянутая тетива
Тугого лука.

Лето 1956

About sins, chases, races and
Unthoughtfulness,
About elbows, about palms and
Lawlessnesses.

I would deduce its law and find
Its starting flame,
I would repeat initials of
Its every name.

I would plan verses like a park.
Their veins meanwhile
Trembling, lindens would bloom in them,
File after file.

I'd bring the breath of roses, mint
Into this verse
And meadows, sedge and haying, with
The thunder's curse.

So once Chopin put this alive
Miracle of
Folwarks, park, groves and graves into
Etudes we love.

And all the play and suffering
Of triumphs so
Achieved is like the pulled-back string
Of a tight bow.

Summer 1956

Быть знаменитым – некрасиво.
Не это подымает ввысь.
Не надо заводить архива,
Над рукописями трястись.

Цель творчества – самоотдача,
А не шумиха, не успех.
Позорно, ничего не знача,
Быть притчей на устах у всех.

Но надо жить без самозванства,
Так жить, чтобы в конце концов
Привлечь к себе любовь пространства,
Услышать будущего зов.

И надо оставлять пробелы
В судьбе, а не среди бумаг,
Места и главы жизни целой
Отчеркивая на полях.

И окунаться в неизвестность
И прятать в ней свои шаги,
Как прячется в тумане местность,
Когда в ней не видать ни зги.

Другие по живому следу
Пройдут твой путь за пядью пядь,
Но пораженья от победы
Ты сам не должен отличать.

И должен ни единой долькой
Не отступаться от лица,
Но быть живым, живым и только,
Живым и только до конца.

Лето 1956

To be famous is unbecoming –
This does not raise one to the heights.
One should not start an archive, trembling
Over the manuscript's delights.

Creation's aim is a self-giving –
Not success with applause. Not quips
Nor big to-do which (Shame!) mean nothing:
Legend on everybody's lips.

One should live with no pretensions,
So one attracts – in the long run –
To oneself the love of expanses
And hears the future calling one.

And one should leave gaps – not on paper–
But in one's destiny instead,
And mark the margins with the places
And parts where a whole life is read.

And to submerge into the unknown
And hide one's steps neath covering –
As in a fog a space is hidden
Till one cannot see anything.

And all the live footsteps of others,
Inch after inch, will walk your street.
But you yourself should not distinguish
A victory from a defeat.

And you must not – by one small portion
Even – renounce your face, my friend.
But be alive, that's all that matters,
Alive and living – to the end.

Summer 1956

ЕВА

Стоят деревья у воды,
И полдень с берега крутого
Закинул облака в пруды,
Как переметы рыболова.

Как невод, тонет небосвод,
И в это небо, точно в сети,
Толпа купальщиков плывет:
Мужчины, женщины и дети.

Пять-шесть купальщиц в лозняке
Выходят на берег без шума
И выжимают на песке
Свои купальные костюмы.

И, на подобие ужей,
Ползут и вьются кольца пряжи,
Как будто искуситель-змей
Скрывался в мокром трикотаже.

О, женщина, твой вид и взгляд
Ничуть меня в тупик не ставят.
Ты вся, как горла перехват,
Когда его волненье сдавит.

Ты создана как бы вчерне,
Как строчка из другого цикла,
Как будто не шутя во сне
Из моего ребра возникла.

И тотчас вырвалась из рук
И выскользнула из объятья,
Сама – смятенье и испуг
И сердца мужеского сжатье.

Лето 1956

EVE

The trees stand at the water's edge,
And mid-day from a steep bank then
Throws down the clouds into the pond,
Like billowed seines of fishermen.

The firmament sinks like a net,
And as into a net, into
This sky a crowd of bathers swim:
Men, women, children – in the blue.

And from the willows five or six
Women come out – perfectly mute.
And each onto the sandy bank
Wrings out her dripping bathing suit.

And similar to grass snakes, rings
Of clothing crawl and twist and flee.
As if the tempting serpent now
Was hiding in the wet jersey.

O, woman, your look and your glance
Do not bewilder me one bit.
You all are like lumps in my throat
When some excitement contracts it.

You are created – a quick draft –
Like some line from my poetry,
As if (sincerely) in a dream
You sprang out of this rib of me...

And tore yourself out of my hands
And left my embrace at the start,
Being yourself – abashed, afraid, –
The tightening of a male heart.

Summer 1956

ДУША

Душа моя, печальница
О всех в кругу моем,
Ты стала усыпальницей
Замученных живьем.

Тела их бальзамируя,
Им посвящая стих,
Рыдающею лирою
Оплакивая их,

Ты в наше время шкурное
За совесть и за страх
Стоишь могильной урною,
Покоящей их прах.

Их муки совокупные
Тебя склонили ниц.
Ты пахнешь пылью трупною
Мертвецких и гробниц.

Душа моя, скудельница,
Все, виденное здесь,
Перемолов, как мельница,
Ты превратила в смесь.

И дальше перемалывай
Все бывшее со мной,
Как сорок лет без малого,
В погостный перегной.

(1957)

MY SOUL

My soul, you are a mourner
Of all where I survive.
You are a mausoleum
Of those tortured alive.

And you embalm their bodies,
Give them the poems you sire
With dedications – grieving
Them with a sobbing lyre.

You, in an age so hoggish,
For conscience and for fear,
Stand as a grave's urn holding
Their ashes always near.

And all their total sufferings
Have bowed you with their thrust.
You smell of morgues and graveyards
And of cadaver dust.

My soul, charnel house even,
All that you see, you still
Make into one great mixture
Grinding it like a mill.

So keep on grinding all things
That have happened to me –
These nearly forty years – to mulch
For the cemetery.

НИКОЛАЙ АЛЕКСЕЕВИЧ КЛЮЕВ
1887-1937

Не верьте, что бесы крылаты, –
У них, как у рыбы, пузырь,
Им любы глухие закаты
И моря полночная ширь.

Они за ладьею акулой,
Прожорливым спрутом плывут;
Утесов подводные скулы –
Геенскому духу приют.

Есть бесы молчанья, улыбки,
Дверного засова, и сна...
В гробу и в младенческой зыбке
Бурлит огневая волна.

В кукушке и в песенке пряхи
Ныряют стада бесенят.
Старушьи, костлявые страхи –
Порука, что близится ад.

О, горы, на нас упадите,
Ущелья, окутайте нас!
На тле, на воловьем копыте
Начертан громовый рассказ.

За брашном, за нищенским кусом
Рогатые тени встают...
Кому же воскрылья с убрусом
Закатные ангелы ткут?

(1912)

NIKOLAI ALEKSEYEVICH KLUYEV
1887-1937

Don't think that the demons are wingèd,
For they have a bladder like fish.
They're fond of mute, desolate sunsets,
And the ocean's expanse at midnight.

They swim after boats like a shark-pack.
The cheek bones of rocks undersea
Are shelter for their hellish spirits,
As if they were greedy octopi.

They're demons of smile and of silence,
Of sleep, of the bolt on the door...
In grave – also in baby cradle
There they seethe – in their own fiery wave.

The flocks of the small demons gather
In cuckoos, in a spinning song..
The bony fears of the old women
Guarantee us that Hell is quite close.

O, Mountains, fall down here upon us!
And gorges, come cover us up!
A thundery tale has been written
On an aphis and hoof of an ox.

At feasts, at the meal of a beggar,
Horned shadows rise up everywhere...
For whom, then, do angels at sunset
Weave their paradise hems and kerchiefs?

Галка-староверка ходит в черной ряске,
В лапотках с оборой, в сизой подпояске,
Голубь в однорядке, воробей в сибирке,
Курица ж в салопе – клеваные дырки.
Гусь в дубленой шубе, утке ж на задворках
Щеголять далося в дедовских опорках.

В галочьи потемки, взгромоздясь на жердки,
Спят, нахохлив зобы, курицы-молодки;
Лишь петух-кудесник, запахнувшись в саван,
Числит звездный бисер, чует травный ладан.

На погосте свечкой теплятся гнилушки,
Доплетает леший лапоть на опушке,
Верезжит в осоке проклятый младенчик...
Петел ждет, чтоб зорька нарядилась в венчик.

У зари нарядов тридевять укладок...
На ущербе ночи сон куриный сладок:
Спят монашка-галка, воробей-горошник...
Но едва забрезжит заревой кокошник –
Звездочет крылатый трубит в рог волшебный:
'Пробудитесь, птицы, пробил час хвалебный!
И пернатым брашно, на бугор, на плесо,
Рассыпает солнце золотое просо!'

(1913)

Old Believer jackdaw – walks in his black cassock,
In bast shoes with frills and warm blue sash around him.
The dove's in a caftan, the sparrow in a fur coat;
The hen wears a smockfrock with pecked holes all through it.
The goose in a tanned fur; the duck in the barnyard
Likes to flaunt grandfather's pair of clumsy brogans.

Having safely roosted, when the dark is crow-black,
The pullets are sleeping – with their crops all tufted.
The soothsayer rooster wraps his shroud still tighter,
Counts the beads of stars and feels the grasses' incense.

Graveyard: rotten wood there – glimmers like a candle,
The wood goblin makes a bast shoe near the forest,
And a cursed baby in the sedge is screeching...
Cocks wait for the dawn to trim its bright corona.

O, the dawn has many chests of festive dresses...
When the night is ending, chicken's sleep is sweetest.
The nun jackdaw sleeps; the pea-thief sparrow's sleeping...
But hardly the kokoshnik of the dawn starts rising
When the winged star-gazer blows his horn of magic:
'Wake up, birds, the hour of praise now is striking!
And the sun is strewing on the hills and rivers
Golden millet, a feast for all those who have feathers!'

Пашни буры, межи зелены,
Спит за елями закат,
Камней мшистые расщелины
Влагу вешнюю таят.

Хороша лесная родина:
Глушь да поймища кругом!...
Прослезилася смородина,
Травный слушая псалом.

И не чую больше тела я,
Сердце – всхожее зерно...
Прилетайте, птицы белые,
Клюйте ярое пшено!

Льются сумерки прозрачные,
Кроют дали, изб коньки,
И березки – свечи брачные
Теплят листьев огоньки.

1914

*   *   *

Осинник гулче, ельник глуше,
Снега туманней и скудней.
В пару берлог разъели уши
У медвежат ватаги вшей.

У сосен сто́рожки вершины,
Пахуч и бур стволов янтарь.
На разопрелые низины
Летит с мошнухою глухарь.

Fields are brown with such green borders;
Sunset sleeps behind the firs.
And the rocks have mossy fissures
Where the springtime's moisture stirs.

My wooded homeland is pleasant:
Backwoods, meadows, ail around!
And the currant sheds a few tears
Hearing grass's psalm-like sound.

I no longer feel my body,
For my heart is sprouting grain.
Come, come flying, all you white birds!
Peck the millet I contain!

The transparent dusk is flowing,
Hiding land, roof-ridges, eaves.
And the birch trees' nuptial candles
Glimmer with the lights of leaves.

★　★　★

Aspens are vibrant, firs more muted,
The snow is slight and foggy here,
And in the steam of lairs the lice-packs
Have chewed the bear-cubs on the ear.

The pine tops are on guard and ready.
Their trunks' resin fragrant and brown.
The wood-grouse with a craw is flying
To where the soppy sloughs lie down.

Бреду зареющей опушкой, –
На сучьях пляшет солнопек.
Вон, над прижухлою избушкой
Виляет беличий дымок.

Там коротают час досужий
За думой дед, за пряжей мать...
Бурлят ключи, в лесные лужи
Глядится пней и кочек рать.

1914

★ ★ ★

Как гроб епископа, где ладан и парча
Полуистлевшие смешались с гнилью трупной,
Земные осени. Бурее кирпича
Осиновая глушь. Как склеп, ворам доступный,
Зияют небеса. Там муть, могильный сор,
И ветра-ключаря гнусавый разговор:
'Украден омофор, червонное кадило,
Навек осквернена святейшая могила:
Вот митра – грязи кус, лохмотья орлеца...'
Земные осени унылы без конца.
Они живой зарок, что мира пышный склеп
Раскраден будет весь, и без замков и скреп
Лишь смерти-ключарю достанется в удел.
Дух взломщика, Господь, и туки наших тел
Смиряешь Ты огнем и ранами войны,
Но струпья вновь мягчишь бальзамами весны,
Пугая осенью, как грозною вехой,
На росстани миров, где сумрак гробовой!

(1917)

I stroll the dawn-lit edge of forest,
The sun, dancing in branches, tags...
And there above a shadowed cottage
Smoke, looking like a squirrel, wags.

Grandfather thinking, mother spinning
Pass idle hours without a care.
Brooks bubble; hosts of trunks and hummocks
Look in the forest puddles there.

★   ★   ★

The autumns of the earth are like a bishop's grave
Where incense and brocade – half-rotten, mix and set in
With the cadaver's mold. The aspen backwoods wave,
Browner than any brick. Like some crypt thieves can get in,
The sky is yawning wide. There – lees, the trash of cold
Graves, and the twangy talk, the sexton wind's endeavor:
'The omophorion and censer of pure gold
Are stolen; the most sacred grave profaned forever:
A miter – lump of dirt, the eagle-rug rags curled.'
The autumns of the earth are sad unendingly...
They are the living pledge the rich crypt of the world
Is stolen piece by piece – and without lock and key
Will be only received by the sacristan death.
Oh Lord, you pacify – with fire and wounds of war –
The spirit of the thief, the fats our bodies store;
But you soften the scabs with balms of Spring's fresh breath
And scare us with the fall – as with some dread landmark
At crossroads of the worlds where the graves' dusk is dark.

Аннушке Кирилловой

Эта девушка умрет в родах...
Не в догад болезной повитухе,
Что он был давяще-яр в плечах
И с пушком на отроческом брюхе,

Что тяжел и сочен был приплод –
Бурелом средь яблонь белоцветных...
Эта девушка в пространствах межпланетных
Родит лирный солнечный народ.

Но в гробу, червивом как валежник,
Замерцает фосфором лобок.
Огонек в сторожке и подснежник –
Ненасытный девичий зрачок.

Есть в могилах роды и крестины.
В плесень – кровь и сердце – в минерал.
Нянин сказ и заводи перины
Вспенит львиный рыкающий шквал.

И в белках заплещут кашалоты,
Смерть – в моржовой лодке эскимос...
Эту девушку, душистую как соты,
Приголубит радужный Христос.

(1917)

to Annushka Kirillova

This young girl will die in childbirth soon ...
And the sickly midwife doesn't know
That he pressed his shoulders hard to her
With fuzz on his boyish groin below,

That the fruit was heavy and like sap –
Windfall midst white blooming apple trees.
This girl in some interplanetary space,
Will birth radiant men of melodies.

In the grave – wormy as the windfalls are –
Her pubes will shine, like phosphorus.
And the girl's greedy eyes are like
White snowdrops, or lodges' lights for us.

In the grave are baptisms and births –
Blood to mold and heart to mineral.
Wet-nurse tales and ponds of feather beds
Foam up from the roaring lion squall.

In the whites of eyes sperm whales will splash.
In a walrus boat is death, eskimo iced ...
And this girl, fragrant as honeycomb,
Will be cared for by the rainbow-Christ.

ПУТЕШЕСТВИЕ

'Я здесь', – ответило мне тело, –
Ладони, бедра, голова, –
Моей страны осиротелой
Материки и острова.

И, парус солнечный завидя,
Возликовало Сердце-мыс:
'В моем лазоревом Мадриде
Цветут миндаль и кипарис.'

Аорты устьем красноводным
Плывет Владычная Ладья;
Во мгле, по выступам бесплодным
Мерцают мхи да ягеля.

Вот остров Печень. Небесами
Над ним раскинулся Крестец.
В долинах с желчными лугами
Отары пожранных овец.

На деревах тетерки, куры,
И души проса, пухлых реп.
Там солнце – пуп, и воздух бурый
И лучам бесчувственен и слеп.

Но дальше путь, за круг полярный,
В края Желудка и Кишок,
Где полыхает ад угарный
Из огнедышащих молок.

Где салотопни и толкуши,
Дубильни, свалки нечистот,
И населяет гребни суши
Крылатый, яростный народ.

JOURNEY

'I am here' – replied the body
The thighs, the head, the palms, each hand,
And all the continents and islands
Which makes up my own orphaned land.

The promontory heart exalted
When suddenly one bright sail loomed:
'In my Madrid, Madrid so azure,
The almond trees and cypress bloomed!'

By the Aorta's reddened delta
The Sovereign Bark floats in the stream.
On barren mounds there in the darkness,
The mosses and the lichens gleam.

Here is the island, Liver. Over
It like sky does the Sacrum sweep.
In valleys with the green gall meadows
There are flocks of devoured sheep.

On their trees are grouse and chickens
And souls of millet – turnips too.
There is the navel-sun. The brown air
Is blind to each beam shining through.

The road leads past the polar circle
To Stomach and to Guts entire
Where such a fumy hell is blazing
From many milks that spit out fire.

Where the rendering plant and foundry,
Where tanneries and dump yard stand,
And where wingèd violent masses
Inhabit crests of the dry land.

О, плотяные Печенеги,
Не ваш я гость! Плыви, ладья,
К материку любви и неги,
Чей берег ладан и кутья!

Лобок – сжигающий Марокко,
Где под смоковницей фонтан
Мурлычет песенку востока
Про Магометов караван.

Как звездоточностью пустыни
Везли семь солнц – пророка жен –
От младшей Евы, в Месяц Скиний,
Род человеческий рожден.

Здесь Зороастр, Христос и Брама
Вспахали ниву ярых уд,
И ядра – два подземных храма
Их плуг алмазный стерегут.

Но и для солнечного мага
Сокрыта тайна алтарем...
Вздыхает судрожно бумага
Под ясновидящим пером.

И возвратясь из далей тела,
Душа, как ласточка в прилет,
В созвучий домик опустелый
Пушинку первую несет.

(1917)

O I am not your guest, pagans
Of flesh! Sail, sail, my boat (though crude)
To the continent of love and joy
Where the coast is incense and holy food.

The pubes is Morocco burning
Where neath fig trees a fountain can
Purr out its oriental singing
About Mohammed's caravan:

How through the star-flow of the desert
Came seven suns – the prophet's wives;
From Eve, the youngest – in the holy
Month – all the human race arrives.

Here Zoroaster, Christ, and Brahma
Plowed fields of fervid members. How
Two cannon balls, underground temples,
Keep watch over their diamond plow!

But also for the sun's own Magus
The altar hides the mystery...
And neath the pen's clairvoyant scratching
The paper sighs shudderingly.

Returning from the body's spaces,
The soul, a swallow homeward-bound,
Is bringing the first downy feather
Into the empty house of sound.

СЕРГЕЙ МИТРОФАНОВИЧ ГОРОДЕЦКИЙ
р. 1884

ВЕСНА
(Монастырская)

Звоны-стоны, перезвоны,
Звоны-вздохи, звоны-сны.
Высоки крутые склоны,
Крутосклоны зелены.
Стены выбелены бело:
Мать-игуменья велела!
У ворот монастыря
Плачет дочка звонаря:

– Ах ты, поле, моя воля,
Ах, доро́га дорога́!
Ах, мосток у чиста поля,
Свечка чиста четверга!

Ах, моя горела ярко,
Погасала у него.
Наклонился, дышит жарко,
Жарче сердца моего.

Я отстала, я осталась
У высокого моста,
Пламя свечек колебалось,
Целовалися в уста.

Где ты, милый, любызанный,
Где ты, ласковый такой!
Ах, пары весны, туманы!
Ах, мой девичий спокой!

SERGEI MITROFANOVICH GORODETSKY

b. 1884

SPRING

(THE CLOISTERS)

Bells ring, moaning, re-intoning,
Tolling sighs, extolling dreams.
Hills are high and overgrown in
Green; with green each sloping gleams.
Walls have a fresh white exterior:
Orders from Mother Superior!
And the sexton's daughter waits –
Crying at the convent's gate.

Ah, fields! Spaces! Breathing-places!
Ah, a way that winds away!
Ah, small bridge in open spaces!
Candle of Maundy Thursday!

Ah, my candle burning higher...
His was down to its last part.
Near me his breath was a fire
Even hotter than my heart.

I loitered behind, I loitered
At the high bridge till you came.
There we kissed. And the adroiter
Candles shook with open flame.

O kind, kissed one, one for dreaming!
Where are you? Why do you stay?
Ah! The mists of springtime steaming!
Ah! My peace of yesterday!

637

Звоны-стоны, перезвоны,
Звоны-вздохи, звоны-сны.
Высоки крутые склоны,
Крутосклоны зелены.
Стены выбелены бело.
Мать-игуменья велела
У ворот монастыря
Не болтаться зря!

1906

НАКАЗ

Прорвись огнем ума сквозь грохот,
Сосредоточься и пойми:
Настала новая эпоха,
Ты стал последним меж людьми.

И все, что знал ты, что проведал
Сквозь шум мечты и дебри книг,
Лежит едва заметным следом
И жалко просит: зачеркни!

Немногое лишь пригодится,
И многое уснет в глуби.
И сам ты должен раздвоиться
И одного себя убить.

Другому же себе ребенком
Велишь ты в новый мир войти...
Как больно в этом мире звонком
Глазам, ослепшим взаперти!

1928

Bells ring, moaning, re-intoning,
Tolling sighs, extolling dreams.
Hills are high and overgrown in
Green; with green each sloping gleams.
Walls have a fresh white exterior.
Orders from Mother Superior:
No loitering from this date
At the convent gate.

INSTRUCTION

Let your Mind's fire break through the roaring,
Just concentrate, forget the past
And try to grasp that a new era
Has come; you're now the least, the last.

And all you knew, all you discovered
In your books' jungles, your dream's shout
Lies as a trace that's hardly noticed
And asks sadly to be crossed out!

So few things will be thought worth using
And many, many will sleep deep!
You'll have to split yourself in two parts,
And kill the self you cannot keep.

And you will tell the half remaining:
Enter your new world, child; it's yours!
But this sun's brilliance is so painful
For eyes which have gone blind indoors.

КЛИО

Она стоит с улыбкою лукавой
И держит свиток в мраморных руках,
Внося в анналы жизнь, и смерть, и славу,
Мелькающие средь людей в веках.

И скучно ей, ничуть не виноватой
В судьбе рабов, вождей, племен и рас.
Но вот мудрец кудряво-бородатый
Недавно улыбнулся ей, Карл Маркс.

Она сошла проворно с пьедестала:
'Прошу! Влезайте! Я ведь так устала
Записывать, не зная что к чему!

В музеях и библиотеках
Найду приют! А судьбы человека
Разгадывать не девичью уму!'

1962

CLIO

She stands there with a sly expression, smiling,
Holding a huge scroll in her marble hands.
She notes life, death, and fame in her compiling,
Records all time, all people in all lands.

And she (who's not to blame) gets bored and weary
With fates of slaves, chiefs, races, patriarchs.
But recently a curly-bearded, cheery
Wise man smiled up at her – a Karl Marx.

She stepped down swiftly from the pedestal:
'I beg you! Come up! I'm so tired of all
This writing, not knowing what links the chain!

In the museums and the libraries
I'll find a home. But human destinies
And their untangling aren't for a girl's brain.'

НИКОЛАЙ НИКОЛАЕВИЧ АСЕЕВ
1889-1963

Когда земное склонит лень,
выходит стенью тени лань,
с ветвей скользит, белея, лунь,
волну сердито взроет линь,

И чей-то стан колеблет стон,
то, может, пан, а может, пень...
Из тины тень, из сини сон,
пока на Дон не ляжет день.

А коса твоя – осени сень, –
ты звездам приходишься родственницей.

1916

СИНИЕ ГУСАРЫ

I

Раненым медведем
                мороз дерет.
Санки по Фонтанке
                летят вперед.
Полоз остер –
            полосатит снег.
Чьи это там
           голоса и смех?
'Руку
      на сердце свое
             положа,
я тебе скажу:
             ты не тронь палаша!

NIKOLAI NIKOLAYEVICH ASEYEV
1889-1963

When loneliness bends over all,
A languid doe sighs on an isle;
From linden trees glides one white owl;
Wave's lawn is furrowed by an eel;

Is that a man? Why does he moan?
Somebody stands? Or just a stone?
From naught comes night, from sky's dome – dreams
Till dawn lights up the Don with gleams.

And the fall is foil to your hair;
You are sister to stars on heaven's stair.

BLUE HUSSARS

I

The frost is clawing
               like a wounded bear;
sleighs along Fontanka
               split the icy air.
The runners are sharp,
               they cut the snow.
Whose are those voices
               laughing so?
'I tell you
        the truth
               and cross my heart:
don't put on your sword,
               do not take part.

Силе такой
　　　　　становясь поперек,
ты б хоть других –
　　　　　　　　не себя –
　　　　　　　　　　　поберег!'

II

Белыми копытами
　　　　　　лед колотя,
тени по Литейному –
　　　　　　　дальше летят.
'Я тебе отвечу,
　　　　　　друг дорогой, –
гибель нестрашная
　　　　　　в петле тугой!
Позорней и гибельней
　　　　　　　в рабстве таком,
голову выбелив,
　　　　　стать стариком.
Пора нам состукнуть
　　　　　　клинок о клинок:
в свободу –
　　　　сердце мое
　　　　　　влюблено!'

III

Розовые губы,
　　　　　витой чубук.
Синие гусары –
　　　　пытай судьбу!
Вот они,
　　　не сгинув,
　　　　　　не умирав,
снова собираются
　　　　　в номерах.
Скинуты ментики,
　　　　ночь глубока,

Too strong a power
                   to resist.
You should spare
                 the others –
                       though *you* insist.'

II

White horses' feet
                 beat the ice and the sleet
and the two proceed
                 on Liteiny Street.
'Here is my answer
                 for you, my friend.
I'm not afraid
                 of a noose for my end.
More shameful and deadly
                 when your head is white
to be an old man
                 who lacked guts to fight.
Blade against blade:
                 our destiny.
My heart
             is in love
                 with liberty.'

III

Red-blooded lips,
                 long curling pipe...
Blue hussars,
             the time is ripe.
They did not perish,
                 nor did they die.
They're again
             at the inn
                 and they are high.
It's late at night,
             let's feel at home.

ну-ка – вспеньте-ка
                полный бокал!
Нальем и осушим
                и станем трезвей:
'За Южное братство,
                за юных друзей!'

IV

Глухие гитары,
                высокая речь . . .
Кого им бояться
                и что им беречь?
В них страсть закипает,
                как в пене стакан:
впервые читаются
                строфы 'Цыган' . . .
Тени по Литейному
                летят назад.
Брови из-под кивера
                дворцам грозят.
Кончена беседа.
                Гони коней!
Утро вечера –
                мудреней.

V

Что ж это,
          что ж это,
                  что ж это за песнь?!
Голову
          на руки белые
                свесь.
Тихие гитары,
                стыньте, дрожа:
синие гусары
                под снегом лежат!

1926

Pelisses off
          – mugs full of foam,
let's pour and drink
                  as sober men should:
for our young friends
                 and the Southern Brotherhood.

IV

Muted guitars,
               high speeches soar . . .
Whom should they fear,
                   what should they care for?
Their passion seethes
                like the foaming steins;
they're the first to read
                  The Gypsies' lines.
On Liteiny two
              hurry home they guess.
Under shakos – eyes
                leer at palaces.
Conversation's through;
                   whip the horses, right?
Morning is more
              wise than the night!

V

What kind
        of song
               is this we've read?
Let your heart
           sink down
               and hang your head.
Soft guitars, tremble,
              but freeze when you know
that blue hussars lie
             beneath the snow.

ПЕСНЬ О ГАРСИА ЛОРКЕ

Почему ж ты, Испания,
                в небо смотрела,
Когда Гарсиа Лорку
                увели для расстрела?
Андалузия знала,
              и Валенсия знала, –
что ж земля
              под ногами убийц не стонала?!
Что ж вы руки скрестили
              и губы вы сжали,
когда песню родную
              на смерть провожали?
Увели не к стене его,
              не на площадь, –
увели, обманув,
              к апельсиновой роще.
Шел он гордо,
              срывая в пути апельсины
и бросая с размаху
              в пруды и трясины;
те плоды
              под луною
              в воде золотели
и на дно не спускались,
              и тонуть не хотели.
Будто с неба срывал
              и кидал он планеты, –
так всегда перед смертью
              поступают поэты.
Но пруды высыхали,
              и плоды увядали,
и следы от походки его
              пропадали.

A SONG ABOUT GARCIA LORCA

Noble Spain, why did you
               turn your head to the sky
when Garcia Lorca
          was taken to die?
Andalusia, Valencia,
           all must have known
of the murderers' feet,
            then why didn't Earth moan?
Why did you fold your arms,
             keep your lips nicely taut
when you saw your own song
             march away to be shot?
And not to a wall,
          to a square did they go,
but they tricked him and took him
              where oranges grow.
He walked proudly along,
           picking off the ripe fruit,
hurling them into ponds,
           into marshes en route.
And the moon
        made them shine
            in the water like gold;
they did not want to sink
           to the bottom's dark cold.
And he plucked down the planets
             and he hurled them too –
but this is what poets
          before death always do.
The grove ponds dried up;
           the fruit withered small,
and the prints of his feet
          could not be seen at all.

А жандармы сидели,
                 лимонад попивая
и слова его песен
             про себя напевая.

1956-1957

And the soldiers sat sipping
>   their bright orangeade,
humming the words
>   of the songs he had made.

ИЛЬЯ ЛЬВОВИЧ СЕЛЬВИНСКИЙ
р. 1899

ПИСЬМО

Мамоч-ка мил-дорогая
Я. Вас. Люблю.
Баушка мил-дорогая
Больше я буду

Я уже знаю буквы
Скоро мне шесть
Они наверно подарят куклу
А у меня есть

Уже больше нету места
Цлую всех вас
Эта палка и бубликов десять
Значит-мильон раз

У нас есть один мальчик
Он очень ухий
А есть который другой мальчик
Незабудущая вас
Кука.

1921

ВОР

Вышел на арапа. Канает буржуй.
А по пузу – золотой бамбер.
'Мусью, сколько время?' – Легко подхожу...
Дзззызь промеж роги... – и амба.

Только хотел было снять часы –
Чья-то шмара шипит: 'Шестая.'
Я, понятно, хода. За тюк. За весы.
А мильтонов – чортова стая.

ILYA LVOVICH SELVINSKY
b. 1899

LETTER

Dear Mummy my darling
I. Love. You.
Gran – my darling
I will right more to

I no the alfa bet already
I'll be six pretty soon
A doll is what there gonna get me
And I already got

Theres no more room
I kis all of you
This stick and ten donuts
A million times, I do

There is little boy here
The biggest ears you ever saw
And there is that another boy –
      Never forgetting you, dear
      Kuka.

THIEF

I came out to pull a job.
Here comes a square – and dig
That gold watch on his gut. 'Hey, Man,
You got the time?' I get near . . .

I only wanted to take his watch.
Some smart-ass hisses, 'The fuzz!'
Sure I scrammed. Behind a bale and a scale.
Cops are devils in a pack.

Подняли хай: 'Лови – ' – 'Держи!...'
Елки зеленые: бегут напротив...
А у меня, понимаешь ты, шанец жить, –
Как петух недорезанный, сердце колотит.

Заскочил в тупик: ни в бок, ни черта.
Вжался в закрытый сарай я...
Вынул горячий от живота
Пятизарядный шпайер:

– Нну-ну! Умирать – так будем умирать.
В компании таки да веселее.
Но толпа как поперла в стороны, в мрак
И построилася в целую аллею.

И я себе прошел, как какой-нибудь ферть,
Скинул джонку и подмигнул глазом:
– 'Вам сегодня не везло, мадамочка Смерть?
Адью до следующего раза!'

1922

БРОНЗА

Маленький пупс-карапузик,
Весь изогнувшись и выпятив пузико,
Расставив ножки с пухлыми коленками,
Стоял и пипикал на стенку,
Стараясь повыше вскинуть
Золотистую струйку длинную.

А девочка со вздернутым ротиком
В шубке, шитой на кроте,
Удивленно следила глазами круглыми
За этим мальчишкой смуглым.

They start yellin': 'Stop him, catch him!'
Oh, Christ ... They're coming my way ...
You see, I wanta live; my heart
Beats like a rooster that won't die.

This blind alley – no sides, no out.
... Against a locked warehouse
I pull out my five-shooter,
All warm from my gut.

Oh well – You gotta die sometime:
With company it's best.
The crowd jammed side-streets, into the dark,
And formed a lengthy lane.

And I passed through – a slippery king –
Took off my cap and winked:
Today, no luck, sweet Madame Death,
So long till next we meet.

BRONZE

The little chubby boy bent
Back and bulged his paunch and went,
Spreading his legs with pudgy knees.
He stood and pee'd against the wall,
Trying hard to get
The long gold stream higher yet.

And the girl with an upturned mouth who wore
A moleskin fur coat stopped to explore:
Her round eyes followed with astounding joy
This dark-skinned little boy.

Она ничего не понимает...
Но уже из упрямства женственного,
Присев, чтобы видеть лучше,
Кричит на всякий случай:
'Ай-ияй... Ай-и-яй...
Мошеенство, мошенство!'

1920

ЧЕРЕПАХА

Черепаха на базаре Хакодате
На прилавке обессиленно лежит.
Рядом высятся распиленные латы,
Мошкара над обессиленной жужжит.

Миловидная хозяюшка степенно
Выбирает помясистее кусок:
– Отрубите мне, прошу, за пол-иены
Этот окорок или вот этот бок.

И пока мясник над ухом у калеки
Смачно крякает, топориком рубя, –
Черепаха только суживает веки,
Только втягивает голову в себя.

Отработавши конечности до паха,
Принимается торговец за живот,
Но глядит, не умирает черепаха...
Возмутительно живучая – живет!

Здесь, читатель мой, кончается сюжет,
Никакого поучения тут нет.
Но конечно же я не был бы поэтом,
Если б мысль моя закончилась на этом.

1932, Хакодате

She knows nothing as yet: how, why...
She crouches – to see better, yes,
And out of female captiousness,
Already – she shouts, repeating
'Ay – Ay – Ay – Ay – Ay – Ay
You are cheating. You are cheating.'

TURTLE

In a Hakodate market on the counter
Lies a turtle that fatigue has overcome.
Near it heaps a pile of shells which have been sawed-up;
And around its bleeding, swarms of midges hum.

Picking out a piece that seems to her more meaty,
The attractive shopper says with a staid air,
'Will you please chop off for me a half-a-yen's worth
Of this hump of ham or of that side-flank there?'

While the butcher with his little ax stands chopping,
He grunts with relish above the cripple's ear.
But the turtle only narrows more its eyelids,
Only pulls its head into itself, asmear.

Having lopped off all the legs up to the groin,
Now the butcher starts work on the belly's hill.
But the turtle doesn't die. It still is living...
And, outrageously tenacious, looks on still!

Here, my reader, is the ending of my story,
And there is no moral here as an adjoint.
But, of course, I wouldn't be much of a poet,
If my thinking stopped at this important point.

1932, Hakodate

ТАНЕЦ В КАФЕ 'БЕЛЫЙ БАЛ'

Она выходит на эстраду. Танец
Возник не сразу. Mademoiselle
Сперва прошлась подробно, как газель,
Вдруг падает и тут на шею тянет
Угольник своего колена. Вдруг
Она описывает полукруг,
Как бы изображенная Матиссом,
И рушится в сплошной супрематизм,
Где нет уж

           ни лица,

                 ни ног,

                       ни рук,
А только брызги пламенности. Вдруг
Остановилась. Ноет и трепещет.
А публика ей бурно рукоплещет.
Особенно визжал какой-то тип:
– Как хороша! Какие руки, плечи!
А бедра? Феерический изгиб!

А я подумал, сын своей России:
'Нескромные не могут быть красивы.'

1935, Париж

AT A DANCE IN THE CAFE

She comes out on the stage. The dance does not
Spring up immediately. The mademoiselle
First makes a detailed walk like a gazelle
And then falls down, pulling up to her neck
The angle of her knee. Then – like a shot –
She arcs a semi-circle, a release
Which moves like one depicted by Matisse –
Collapsing in an absolute abstraction
Where there's
    no face
      no legs
        no arms
           but action:
Only splashes of fire. And then a pause.
She's stopped! She seems to tremble and to whine
As her caught public storms her with applause.
One character screamed out with special verve:
'How beautiful! What shoulders! What divine
Arms, thighs! And like a fairy's – every curve!'

And I, a son of Russia, thought: – horrible!
What is immodest can't be beautiful.

1935, Paris

ДЕКРЕТИРОВАННЫЙ ЗАЯЦ
Басня

Однажды лев собрал зверей
И объявил, не заикаясь,
Что, мол, отныне всех сильней
    Считаться будет заяц.
Пошел Зайчишка в лес
И ну плясать да петь!
Но тут с березы слез
    Медведь.
– С дороги! – пискнул Заяц. – Идиот!
    Или не видишь, кто идет? –
Медведь захохотал! (Ну, право же, смешно!)
Он так хватил косого среди смеха,
Что от того осталось лишь пятно
    И не осталось даже меха.
Но с дуба вдруг Совы раздался вещий глас:
– Поплатишься ты за бестактность эту:
    Ведь Заяц был сильней всех нас
    Согласно львиному декрету.
Лев объявил о том, собрав лесную знать.

Заплакал тут Медведь: – О небо...
Откуда же я мог про Зайца это знать?
    Ведь я-то на собрании-то не был!

1936, Берлин

A RABBIT MADE STRONG BY DECREE
A FABLE

The Lion once gathered the beastly throng.
And he decreed, without a stuttering habit,
That from now on the one most strong
    Would be simply – the Rabbit.
The little Rabbit went into the wood,
And there was dancing, there was singing there!
But from where a birch tree stood
    Climbed down a Bear.
'Get out of my way,' the Rabbit squeaked, 'You dummy!
    Don't you see who's coming?'
The Bear guffawed ('How ludicrous and grim!')
He whacked the bunny in the midst of laughter
And not one spot was left of him
    – Not even any fur thereafter.
But from an oak the Owl raised up a fuss
With its prophetic voice, 'You'll rue this blunder.
    The Rabbit was the strongest among us,
    According to the Lion's law we're under.
He told us when we met, the wood's aristocracy.'

And here the Bear began to cry – repeating
'O heaven, how could I know about the Rabbit? See,
    I wasn't at the meeting.'

1936, Berlin

ТРАГЕДИЯ

Говорят, что композитор слышит
На три сотни звуков больше нас,
Но они безмолвствуют иль свищут,
Кляксами на ноты устремясь.

Может быть, трагедия поэта
В том, что основное не далось:
Он поет, как птица, но при этом
Слышит, как скрипит земная ось.

1958

НАТЮРМОРТ

Разрежь арбуз – петушьи гребни
Ярятся сочной сердцевиной;
Когда он свеж – в нем дух целебный,
А если вял – оттенок винный;
Сизеют пузырьки морозца
Меж семечек, торчащих сором.
Но не считай, что все тут просто:
Зажмурься – и задышишь морем.

1960

TRAGEDY

It is sometimes said the ear of a composer
Hears three hundred more sounds than our ears can gauge.
But either they all are silent or they whistle,
Rushing as ink-blots onto the music page.

And perhaps the tragedy of any poet
Is that the main thing is NOT made known. He speaks,
He sings like a bird but throughout all the singing,
He is hearing how Earth on her axis creaks.

STILL LIFE

Cut the watermelon: the rooster's
Comb burns bright with a juicy center;
When it is fresh – the wholesome flavor,
And when it's stale – the wine aroma.
Between the seeds sticking like rubbish
The frost glows with its blue-gray bubbles.
But don't think all things here are simple.
Just squint your eyes; you'll breathe an ocean.

НИКОЛАЙ СЕМЕНОВИЧ ТИХОНОВ
р. 1896

ДАВИД

... Марата нет...

Париж перетолпился у окна.
– Художник, ты позолотишь нам горе,
Он с нами жил, оставь его для нас –
И смерть Давид надменно переспорил.

Зелено-синий мягкий карандаш
Уже с лица свинцового не стравишь,
Но кисть живет, но кисть поет: – отдашь!
Того возьмешь, но этого оставишь!

И смолкнул крик и топот площадей...
Триумф молчанья нестерпимо жуток.
– Какую плату хочет чудодей?
– Я спать хочу, без сна я трое суток.

Он говорит, усталость раздавив,
Но комиссары шепчутся с заботой:
– Добро тебе, – но, гражданин Давид,
Зачем рука убийцы патриота?

– Шарлотта – неразумное дитя,
И след ее с картины мною изгнан,
Но так хорош блеск кости до локтя,
Темновишневой густотой обрызган.

1919

664

NIKOLAI SEMENOVICH TIKHONOV
b. 1896

DAVID

... Marat is dead ...

Then all Paris came crowding to your window,
'You, artist, will put gilt upon our grief;
He lived with us, leave him with us forever.'
David outargued death – beyond belief.

One can't unsketch the greenish-blue soft crayon
With which his leaden face is lightly lined.
But the brush lives, it sings: You'll give him back, Death!
You'll take that one; you'll leave this one behind.

The square's shouting and trampling has subsided ...
Uncanny silence: who can bear this phase?
'What pay does such a wonder-worker want now?'
'I want to sleep. I've not slept for three days.'

Crushing his tiredness, thus he spoke. But worried,
Hushed commissars among themselves implore:
'Good for you, Citizen David, but tell us
What is the arm of his knifer there for?'

'Charlotte was an unreasonable child. I simply
Left out the traces of her which I might have shown.
But this brilliance of bone up to the elbow
Is so good, sprinkled by its thick, dark-cherry tone.'

ПЕСНЯ ОБ ОТПУСКНОМ СОЛДАТЕ

Батальонный встал и сухой рукой
Согнул пополам камыш:
'Так отпустить проститься с женой,
Она умирает, говоришь?

Без тебя винтовкой меньше одной, –
Не могу отпустить. Погоди:
Сегодня ночью последний бой.
Налево кругом – иди!'

... Пулемет задыхался, хрипел, бил,
И с флангов летел трезвон,
Одиннадцать раз в атаку ходил
Отчаянный батальон.

Под ногами утренних лип
Уложили сто двадцать в ряд.
И табак от крови прилип
К рукам усталых солдат.

У батальонного по лицу
Красные пятна горят,
Но каждому мертвецу
Сказал он: 'Спасибо, брат!'

Рукою, острее ножа,
Видели все егеря,
Он каждому руку пожал,
За службу благодаря.

Пускай гремел их ушам
На другом языке отбой,
Но мертвых руки по швам
Равнялись сами собой.

BALLAD OF A SOLDIER ON FURLOUGH

The battalion commander stood up and broke
A reed with his dry hand:
'So you want to say goodbye to your wife
She is dying, you understand.

I cannot let you go, not now;
Without you there is one less gun.
Our last battle will be tonight.
To the left! About face! Go, son!'

... The machine guns choked, barked, grew hoarse,
And the flanks filled with blades' chimes.
The desperate battalion advanced
And attacked eleven times.

In the morning, neath lindens lay a row
Of one-hundred-and-twenty men –
And tobacco stuck to the blood
On the hands of the soldiers then.

The battalion commander had a rash
On his face, burning spots of red.
But he spoke in a grateful tone,
'Thank you, brother!' to each one of the dead.

All the soldiers saw him when
With a hand more sharp than a knife,
He shook every dead man's hand
And thanked him for his help and life.

Though another tongue's retreat
Still was sounding in their dreams,
The soldiers aligned themselves
With their hands along their seams.

'Слушай, Денисов Иван!
Хоть ты уж не егерь мой,
Но приказ по роте дан,
Можешь итти домой.'

Умолкли все – под горой
Ветер, как пес, дрожал.
Сто девятнадцать держали строй,
А сто двадцатый встал.

Ворон сорвался, царапая лоб,
Крича, как человек.
И дымно смотрели глаза в сугроб
Из-под опущенных век.

И лошади стали трястись и ржать,
Как будто их гнали с гор,
И глаз ни один не смел поднять,
Чтобы взглянуть в упор.

Уже тот далеко ушел на восток,
Не оставив на льду следа,
Сказал батальонный, коснувшись щек:
'Я, кажется, ранен. Да!'

1922

'Listen, Ivan Denisov,
The orders had been given before;
You may go home now to your wife,
Though you are my soldier no more.'

The wind trembled below the hill
Like a dog. All was hushed, in repose.
One-hundred-nineteen men stayed in line
But the one-hundred-twentieth arose...

(Bumping his head, a raven flew up
With a screech full of human woe.)
... and like smoke, like smoke, eyes looked out
Through closed eyelids across the snow.

The horses began to shake and to neigh,
As if driven too close to a cliff,
And no living soul dared to lift his eyes
But just stood there, strangely stiff.

One went away over ice, over snow,
To the east – leaving no footprints' trace;
The battalion commander said, touching his cheeks:
'Yes, I think I've been wounded some place.'

Женщина в дверях стояла,
В закате с головы до ног,
И пряжу черную мотала
На черный свой челнок.

Рука блеснет и снова ляжет,
Темнея у виска,
Мотала жизнь мою, как пряжу,
Горянки той рука.

И бык, с травой во рту шагая,
Шел снизу в этот дом,
Увидел красные рога я
Под черным челноком.

Заката уголь предпоследний,
Весь раскален, дрожал.
Между рогов – аул соседний
Весь целиком лежал.

И сизый пар, всползая кручей,
Домов лизал бока,
И не было оправы лучше
Косых рогов быка.

Но дунет ветер, леденея,
И кончится челнок,
Мелькнет последний взмах, чернея,
Последней шерсти клок...

Вот торжество неодолимых
Простых высот.
А песни что? Их тонким дымом
В ущелье унесет.

1938-1940

A woman standing in the doorway;
In sunset – head to feet.
Winding black yarn on her black shuttle,
She watched the sun retreat.

Her hand, in shadow at her temple,
Would flash and lie down then;
That mountaineer's quick hand was winding
My life like yarn again.

An ox, munching on grass, was going
To this house from below;
And underneath the jet black shuttle,
I saw his red horns show.

The last coals of the sun were trembling;
Dying, they seemed forlorn.
And all of the neighboring village
Lay in between the horns.

And up the slope – dove-blue mist, crawling,
Licked houses' sides, roofs, rocks . . .
There was no better frame made for it
Than curved horns of that ox.

But ice-sharp winds will start their blowing,
The shuttle end its strain,
The last gesture will flash and darken
The tuft of the last skein . . .

Here is the triumph that unvanquished,
Simple heights forge.
And what are poems? Thin smoke, carried
Into a gorge.

ЭДУАРД ГЕОРГИЕВИЧ БАГРИЦКИЙ
(ДЗЮБИН)
1895-1934

ПТИЦЕЛОВ

Трудно дело птицелова:
Заучи повадки птичьи,
Помни время перелетов,
Разным посвистом свисти.

Но, шатаясь по дорогам,
Под заборами ночуя,
Дидель весел, Дидель может
Песни петь и птиц ловить.

В бузине, сырой и круглой,
Соловей ударит дудкой,
На сосне звенят синицы,
На березке зяблик бьет.

И вытаскивает Дидель
Из котомки заповедной
Три манка – и каждой птице
Посвящает он манок.

Дунет он в манок бузинный, –
И звенит манок бузинный, –
Из бузинного прикрытья
Отвечает соловей.

Дунет он в манок сосновый,
И свистит манок сосновый, –
На сосне в ответ синицы
Рассыпают бубенцы.

EDUARD GEORGIEVICH BAGRITSKY
(DZYUBIN)
1895-1934

THE BIRD-CATCHER

A bird-catcher's job takes practice:
Learn the habits of the birds,
Know the time of their migrations,
Duplicate their different calls.

But as he roams down the roadways,
Spending a night by a fence,
Diedel is happy, Diedel does
Sing his songs and catch his birds.

Nightingales jug-jug their song-pipes
In the moist, round elder bush;
Titmice twitter in a pine tree;
Finches warble in a birch.

Diedel then pulls out precisely
From his precious haversack
Three lures, and to each bird singing
He now dedicates a lure.

He blows on a lure of elder,
And the lure of elder sings.
And within the elder bushes
Soon a nightingale replies.

He blows on a lure of pine wood,
And the lure of pine wood rings.
In the pine a titmouse twitters,
Scattering its tiny bells.

И вытаскивает Дидель
Из котомки заповедной
Самый легкий, самый звонкий
Свой березовый манок.

Он лады проверит нежно,
Щель певучую продует, –
Громким голосом береза
Под дыханьем запоет.

И, заслышав этот голос,
Голос дерева и птицы,
На березе придорожной
Зяблик загремит в ответ.

За проселочной дорогой,
Где затих тележный грохот,
Над прудом, покрытым ряской,
Дидель сети разложил.

И пред ним, зеленый снизу,
Голубой и синий сверху,
Мир встает огромной птицей,
Свищет, щелкает, звенит.

Так идет веселый Дидель
С палкой, птицей и котомкой
Через Гарц, поросший лесом,
Вдоль по рейнским берегам.

По Тюрингии дубовой,
По Саксонии сосновой,
По Вестфалии бузинной,
По Баварии хмельной.

Diedel then pulls out precisely
From his precious haversack
This, the smallest and most ringing –
The lure whittled out of birch.

He checks all the stops most gently,
Blows into the singing hole,
And beneath his breath the birch wood
Sings out in a high-pitched voice.

And when hearing that voice singing,
That voice of both tree and bird,
From the roadside's slender birches
A finch warbles his loud song.

On beyond the country byways,
Where the din of carts is mute,
Over a pond thick with duckweed,
Diedel has put out his nets.

Many shades of blue above him,
Green below him, and the world
Is a giant bird before him,
Warbling, trilling, full of song.

Happy Diedel thus goes walking
With a stick, a bird, a pack...
Through the Harz, the thick-grown forest,
By the green banks of the Rhine...

Through Thuringia with oak trees,
Through Saxonia with pines,
Through Westphalia's elder bushes,
Through Bavaria's hopbines.

Марта, Марта, надо ль плакать,
Если Дидель ходит в поле,
Если Дидель свищет птицам
И смеется невзначай?

1918

КОНТРАБАНДИСТЫ

По рыбам, по звездам
   Проносит шаланду:
Три грека в Одессу
   Везут контрабанду.
На правом борту,
   Что над пропастью вырос:
Янаки, Ставраки,
   Папа Сатырос.
А ветер как гикнет,
   Как мимо просвищет,
Как двинет барашком
   Под звонкое днище,
Чтоб гвозди звенели,
   Чтоб мачта гудела:
– Доброе дело!
   Хорошее дело!
Чтоб звезды обрызгали
   Груду наживы:
Коньяк, чулки
   И презервативы...

Ай, греческий парус!
   Ай, Черное море!
Ай, Черное море...
   – Вор на воре.

.   .   .   .

Martha, Martha, should you cry tears
Because Diedel walks the fields,
Because your dear Diedel whistles
To the birds – and laughs perchance?

THE SMUGGLERS

Among fish, among stars
   A fishing boat sneaks
To Odessa with contraband,
   Manned by three Greeks.
Hanging over the starboard
   Where the chasm is near us:
Yanaki, Stavraki
   And Papa Satyros.
Look how the wind whoops
   And comes howling ker-whap,
Ramming into the bilge
   A raucous whitecap!
Let the mast hum,
   Let the nails ring:
'It's a good business,
   It's a good thing!'
Let the stars splatter
   Their cargo all stacked up:
Cognac, stockings,
   And prophylactics...

Ay, Greek sail!
   Ay, Black Sea that heaves!
Ay, ay, Black Sea...
   Full of thieves!
  .   .   .   .

Двенадцатый час –
Осторожное время.
Три пограничника!
Ветер и темень.
Три пограничника,
Шестеро глаз,
Шестеро глаз
Да моторный баркас...
Три пограничника!
Вор на дозоре!
Бросьте баркас
В басурманское море,
Чтобы вода
Под кормой загудела:
– Доброе дело!
Хорошее дело!
Чтобы по трубам,
В ребра и винт,
Виттовой пляской
Двинул бензин.

Ай, звездная полночь!
Ай, Черное море!
Ай, Черное море!
– Вор на воре!

.   .   .   .

Вот так бы и мне
В налетающей тьме
Усы раздувать,
Развалясь на корме,
Да видеть звезду
Над бушпритом склоненным,
Да голос ломать
Черноморским жаргоном,
Да слушать сквозь ветер,
Холодный и горький,

Close to midnight,
    Time to watch out.
Three men from the coast guard!
    Wind and darkness about.
Three men from the coast guard,
    Six eyes, sharp and steady,
Six eyes, sharp and steady,
    And a motorboat ready.
Three men from the coast guard!
    And a thief in sight!
Launch the craft:
    It's a bad sea, all right!
So let the stern
    Hear the water sing:
'It's a good business,
    It's a good thing!'
Like St Vitus' dance
    Let the gasoline brew
Through the pipes to the ribs
    And the speeded-up screw.

Ay, starry midnight!
    Ay, Black Sea that heaves!
Ay, Ay, Black Sea...
    Full of thieves!

    .   .   .   .

I wish I were there
    In the stern's gust of black,
Moustache flicked by the wind,
    And sprawled on my back.
Seeing a star
    On the bent bowsprit hang,
Breaking my jaws
    With the Black Sea slang.
Hearing the wind bring
    Bitter cold to cut us

Мотора дозорного
        Скороговорки!
Иль правильней, может,
        Сжимая наган,
За вором следить,
        Уходящим в туман...
Да ветер почуять,
        Скользящий по жилам,
Вослед парусам,
        Что летят по светилам...
И вдруг неожиданно
        Встретить во тьме
Усатого грека
        На черной корме...

Так бей же по жилам,
        Кидайся в края,
Бездомная молодость,
        Ярость моя!
Чтоб звездами сыпалась
        Кровь человечья,
Чтоб выстрелом рваться
        Вселенной навстречу,
Чтоб волн запевал
        Оголтелый народ,
Чтоб злобная песня
        Коверкала рот, –
И петь, задыхаясь,
        На страшном просторе:
Ай, Черное море,
        Хорошее море!...

1927

And the patrol engine's
   Rapid staccatos!
Or perhaps it's better
   To grasp a gun
And to watch the fog
   Where a thief may run...
And to feel the wind
   Slipping through my veins
After chasing sails
   Flying heaven's plains...
And come face to face
   In a sudden turn
With a moustached Greek
   On a black stern.

So pulse through the veins,
   Rush to the sides,
My homeless youth,
   My frenzy! My tides!
And let my human blood
   Rain like stars and disperse;
Let me spurt like a shot
   To meet the universe!
Let the shameless waves,
   A singing throng,
Also twist my lips
   With a wicked song!
On this awesome expanse
   Let me sing breathlessly:
Ay, Ay, Black Sea
   You're a damn good sea!...

НИКОЛАЙ АЛЕКСЕЕВИЧ ЗАБОЛОЦКИЙ
1903-1958

ДВИЖЕНИЕ

Сидит извозчик как на троне,
из ваты сделана броня,
и борода, как на иконе,
лежит, монетами звеня.
А бедный конь руками машет,
то вытянется, как налим,
то снова восемь ног сверкают
в его блестящем животе.

(Декабрь 1927)

ФИГУРЫ СНА

Под одеялом, укрощая бег,
фигуры сна находит человек.

Не месяц – длинное бельмо
прельщает чашечки умов;
не звезды – канарейки ночи
блестящим реют многоточьем.
А в темноте – кроватей ряд,
на них младенцы спят подряд;
большие белые тела
едва покрыло одеяло,
они заснули как попало:
один в рубахе голубой
скатился к полу головой;
другой, застыв в подушке душной,
лежит сухой и золотушный,
а третий – жирный как паук,

682

NIKOLAI ALEKSEYEVICH ZABOLOTSKY
1903-1958

MOTION

With armor made of padded cotton,
the coachman sits as on a throne;
his beard, as one upon an icon,
lies ringing with the coins' tone.
And then the poor horse waves its arms,
and now it stretches like a catfish,
and yet again eight long legs shine
out of his glittering belly.

(December 1927)

PATTERNS OF SLEEP

Man discovers patterns for his sleep,
taming his race beneath the blanket heap.

No moon: an eye's long cataract
to which small cups of minds react.
Not stars: canary birds of night
making their shining, dotted flight.
And in the dark – bed after bed
in which babies sleep as though dead;
the blankets only partially
cover their big, white bodies, sprawled
out in their sleep chaotically.
One of them in a blue nightshirt
lobs his head into the floor's dirt;
another, dry and scrofulous,
in stifling pillows makes no fuss;
a third – fat, like a spider – swirls

683

раскинул рук живые снасти,
храпит и корчится от страсти,
лаская призрачных подруг.

А там – за черной занавеской,
во мраке дедовских времен,
старик-отец, гремя стамеской,
премудрости вкушает сон.
Там шкаф глядит царем Давидом –
он спит в короне, толстопуз;
кушетка Евой обернулась –
она – как девка в простыне.
И лампа медная в окне,
как голубок веселый Ноев, –
едва мерцает, мрак утроив,
с простой стамеской наравне.

(Март 1928)

ИВАНОВЫ

Стоят чиновные деревья,
почти влезая в каждый дом;
давно их кончено кочевье –
они в решетках, под замком.
Шумит бульваров теснота,
домами плотно заперта.

Но вот – все двери растворились,
повсюду шопот пробежал:
на службу вышли Ивановы
в своих штанах и башмаках.
Пустые гладкие трамваи
им подают свои скамейки;
герои входят, покупают
билетов хрупкие дощечки,

the tackles of his arms. And sliding,
Snoring and passionately writhing,
he hugs imaginary girls.

And there – behind a murky curtain,
in his ancestral dark and dank,
partaking of a dream of wisdom,
old Father makes his chisel clank.
The wardrobe looks like good King David,
pot-bellied, crown on in his sleep;
the sofa has turned into Eve;
she's like a wench in a bed-sheet.
And Noah's gay dove on the sill
(the copper lamp) with its pale glimmer
makes all the darkness three times dimmer
and the plain chisel's partner still.

(March 1928)

THE IVANOVS

Official trees stand, limbs extended
into each house along the block.
Their nomad life has long been ended;
now they are caged and under lock.
The narrow streets grumble and groan,
constricted by the houses' stone.

But suddenly – all doors were opened
and there were whispers everywhere:
the Ivanovs appear in doorways,
leaving for work in pants and shoes.
The empty and smooth streetcar coaches
proffer them polished benches there;
our great heroes come in and purchase
small, fragile ticket-boards as fare.

сидят и держат их перед собой,
не увлекаясь быстрою ездой.

А мир, зажатый плоскими домами,
стоит, как море, перед нами,
грохочут волны мостовые,
и через лопасти колес –
сирены мечутся простые
в клубках оранжевых волос.
Иные – дуньками одеты,
сидеть не могут взаперти:
ногами делая балеты,
они идут. Куда итти,
кому нести кровавый ротик,
кому сказать сегодня 'котик',
у чьей постели бросить ботик
и дернуть кнопку на груди?
Неужто некуда итти?!

О, мир, свинцовый идол мой,
хлещи широкими волнами
и этих девок упокой
на перекрестке вверх ногами!
Он спит сегодня – грозный мир,
в домах – спокойствие и мир.

Ужели там найти мне место,
где ждет меня моя невеста,
где стулья выстроились в ряд,
где горка – словно Арарат,
повитый кружевцем бумажным,
где стол стоит, и трехэтажный
в железных латах самовар
шумит домашним генералом?

О мир, свернись одним кварталом,
одной разбитой мостовой,

They sit and hold them in front of their nose,
most unconcerned how fast the streetcar goes.

Pressed by flat houses swelling their dull chorus,
the world moves like a sea before us.
The pavement waves are roaring, gushing...
And through the paddle-wheels we stare
at simple sirens busy rushing
in tangles of their orange hair.
Some others dress like silly Sallys,
cannot stay home the whole day so
they lift their legs around in ballets
as off they go. 'But where to go?
Who gets this small red mouth, this beauty?
Today who will I call my cutie?
By whose bed will I toss my bootee
and unbutton my blouse?' O, no,
really – is there no place to go?!

O world, my idol made of lead,
swash your wide waves as you emboss roads,
and give these ladies rest instead –
with their legs raised up at the crossroads!
The sinister world sleeps today,
the houses find peace here to stay.

Will my true place, my celebrating,
be found where such a bride is waiting,
where lined-up chairs stand stiff and pat,
and cupboards look like Ararat –
embellished with fine lace shelf-paper,
and tables, where the three-storied gaper
in iron armor, the samovar,
grunts like a chamber pot amok?

O world, shrink to one city block,
to one section of broken street,

одним проплеванным амбаром,
одной мышиною норой,
но будь к оружию готов:
целует девку – Иванов!

1928

О С Е Н Ь

Когда минует день и освещение
Природа выбирает не сама,
Осенних рощ большие помещения
Стоят на воздухе, как чистые дома.
В них ястребы живут, вороны в них ночуют,
И облака вверху, как призраки, кочуют.

Осенних листьев ссохлось вещество
И землю всю устлало. В отдалении
На четырех ногах большое существо
Идет, мыча, в туманное селение.
Бык, бык! Ужели больше ты не царь?
Кленовый лист напоминает нам янтарь.

Дух Осени, дай силу мне владеть пером!
В строенье воздуха – присутствие алмаза.
Бык скрылся за углом,
И солнечная масса
Туманным шаром над землей висит
И край земли, мерцая, кровянит.

Вращая круглым глазом из-под век,
Летит внизу большая птица.
В ее движенье чувствуется человек.
По крайней мере, он таится
В своем зародыше меж двух широких крыл.
Жук домик между листьев приоткрыл.

to one bespattered barn with stock,
to even one mouse-hole retreat,
but be prepared to take up arms:
A wench is in Ivanov's arms!

AUTUMN

When Day is at an end and Nature
Itself does not select the lighting seen,
The big rooms of the autumn groves are standing
Out in the open like houses swept clean.
Hawks live in them; at night they give crows bed.
And clouds like phantoms migrate overhead.

The substance of the autumn leaves has shriveled
And covered up the land. In the background
A large, four-legged animal is walking
Into the blurred village – making a mooing sound.
Bull! Bull! Weren't you a king once, you who grieve?
One thinks of amber seeing maple leaves.

O spirit of Autumn, give me strength to describe you!
The structure of the air suggests a diamond here.
The bull went 'round the corner.
The sinking misty sphere,
The mass of sun, hovers with fiery limb
And blazes as it bloodies the earth's rim.

Rolling its round eyes underneath its eyelids,
A good-sized bird flies down below.
And as it moves, one senses that here Man is present –
At any rate, in embryo;
Between the two wide wings he seems to be concealed.
A beetle half-opens his leaf-house in the field.

Архитектура Осени. Расположенье в ней
Воздушного пространства, рощи, речки,
Расположение животных и людей,
Когда летят по воздуху колечки
И завитушки листьев, и особый свет, –
Вот то, что выберем среди других примет.

Жук домик между листьев приоткрыл
И, рожки выставив, выглядывает,
Жук разных корешков себе нарыл
И в кучку складывает,
Потом трубит в свой маленький рожок
И вновь скрывается, как маленький божок.

Но вот приходит ветер. Все, что было чистым,
Пространственным, светящимся, сухим, –
Все стало серым, неприятным, мглистым,
Неразличимым. Ветер гонит дым,
Вращает воздух, листья валит ворохом
И верх земли взрывает порохом.

И вся природа начинает леденеть.
Лист клена, словно медь,
Звенит, ударившись о маленький сучок.
И мы должны понять, что это есть значок,
Который посылает нам природа,
Вступившая в другое время года.

1932

The architecture of Autumn. The right arrangement
In it of streams and groves – and of air space,
The distribution of the animals and people
When through the air small, whirling circles chase,
And whorls of leaves, with the specific light to mix –
Let's choose, from all the rest, these characteristics.

A beetle half-opens his leaf-house in the field;
Antennae out, he looks about awhile.
The beetle digs himself some roots and puts them
Into a pile.
He blows into his little trumpet then;
And, like a little god, he vanishes again.

But now here comes the wind. What used to be transparent,
Pure, shining, dry, clean and dimensional –
Becomes gray, murky, hazy and unpleasant,
Hard to distinguish. The wind mixes all:
Drives smoke, twirls air, stacks heaps of leaves, grows louder,
Explodes Earth's crust in dusty powder.

And gradually Nature turns into icy things.
A loose maple leaf rings
Like copper – as it hits a twig, now crystalline.
And we must understand that this is but a sign
Which Nature sends crisply for us to hear
That it begins another time of year.

СТАРАЯ АКТРИСА

В позолоченной комнате стиля ампир,
Где шнурками затянуты кресла,
Театральной Москвы позабытый кумир
И владычица наша воскресла.

В затрапезе похожа она на щегла,
В три погибели скорчилось тело.
А ведь, Боже, какая актриса была
И какими умами владела!

Что-то было нездешнее в каждой черте
Этой женщины, юной и стройной,
И лежал на тревожной ее красоте
Отпечаток Италии знойной.

Ныне домик ее превратился в музей,
Где жива ее прежняя слава,
Где старуха подчас удивляет друзей
Своевольем капризного нрава.

Орденов ей и званий немало дано,
И она пребывает в надежде,
Что красе ее вечно сиять суждено
В этом доме, как некогда прежде.

Здесь картины, портреты, альбомы, венки,
Здесь дыхание южных растений,
И они ее образ, годам вопреки,
Сохранят для иных поколений.

И не важно, не важно, что в дальнем углу,
В полутемном и низком подвале,
Бесприютная девочка спит на полу,
На тряпичном своем одеяле!

THE OLD ACTRESS

In a fine gilded room done in Empire style,
Where the period armchairs are roped off with cord,
The forgotten idol of Moscow's theater,
And our own sovereign, has been freshly restored.

She is like a goldfish in her everyday clothes,
And her body is bent like a round barrel's staves.
But O, Lord! What an actress she once used to be!
And what minds she once ruled over, all gladly slaves!

There was something that came not from this world in such
A young, well-shaped woman, like she was, one would guess.
And there lay on her beauty (disturbingly great)
The imprint of Italian provocativeness.

Her small house has turned into a museum now,
Where her earlier glory still bubbles and brims,
Where the old woman sometimes surprises her friends
With the willfulness of her capricious, odd whims.

The state gave many medals and honors to her,
And she lives keeping one hope ablaze:
That her beauty will shine in this house evermore
As it did in her younger and luminous days.

Here are paintings and portraits, old albums and wreaths;
Here are plants from the South with their exotic breath.
Though time ticks off the years, they will keep well-preserved
Her young image for all people after her death.

And no matter, no matter that in the half-dark
And cramped basement in one remote part of the house,
A homeless, little girl is asleep on the floor
On a blanket of rags – curled up like a mouse.

Здесь у тетки-актрисы из милости ей
Предоставлена нынче квартира.
Здесь она выбивает ковры у дверей,
Пыль и плесень стирает с ампира.

И когда ее старая тетка бранит,
И считает, и прячет монеты,
О, с каким удивленьем ребенок глядит
На прекрасные эти портреты!

Разве девочка может понять до конца,
Почему, поражая нам чувства,
Поднимает над миром такие сердца
Неразумная сила искусства!

1956

The old actress, her aunt, out of good charity,
Gave her these quarters which could be her private room.
In return she's to shake all the rugs at the door
And wipe off dust and mold from each Empire heirloom.

And when her aunt counts coins and hides them away,
Reprimands her, and bruskly starts to moralize,
The child looks at the beautiful portraits, and O,
The amazement and fairyland-glow in her eyes!

Can this girl ever grasp it, completely: why, why,
Though it staggers our feeling, why, why is the heart
Elevated, translated all over the world
By the strange and unreasonable power of Art?

ВАСИЛИЙ ДМИТРИЕВИЧ АЛЕКСАНДРОВСКИЙ
1897-1934

МЫ

На смуглые ладони площадей
Мы каждый день расплескиваем души,
Мы каждый день выходим солнце слушать
На смуглые ладони площадей...

Что горячее: солнце или кровь?
Оно и мы стоим на вечной страже,
Но срок придет – и мы друг другу скажем,
Что горячее: солнце или кровь...

Мы пьем вино из доменных печей,
У горнов страсти наши закаляем,
Мы, умирая, снова воскресаем,
Чтоб пить вино из доменных печей...

У наших девушек бездонные глаза,
В голубизну их сотни солнц вместятся,
Они ни тьмы, ни блеска не боятся...
У наших девушек бездонные глаза...

На смуглые ладони площадей
Мы каждый день расплескиваем души,
Мы каждый день выходим солнце слушать
На смуглые ладони площадей...

1921

VASILY DMITRIEVICH ALEXANDROVSKY
1897-1934

WE

Upon the dark-skinned palms of city squares,
Each day we spill our souls with everyone;
Each day we come to listen to the sun
Upon the dark-skinned palms of city squares.

Which is more hot: the sun or our own blood?
Both, it and we, are ever sentinels,
But time comes quick, and then one of us tells
Which is more hot – the sun or our own blood.

We drink our wine from fiery furnaces,
And we temper our passions at the forges;
We die, but ultimately Death disgorges
Us, so we drink our wine from furnaces.

There is no bottom to our young girls' eyes;
In their blue – scores of suns find room to dance.
They fear neither the dark nor radiance...
There is no bottom to our young girls' eyes.

Upon the dark-skinned palms of city squares,
Each day we spill our souls with everyone;
Each day we come to listen to the sun
Upon the dark-skinned palms of city squares.

АЛЕКСЕЙ КАПИТОНОВИЧ ГАСТЕВ
1882-1941

МЫ РАСТЕМ ИЗ ЖЕЛЕЗА

Смотрите! – Я стою среди них: станков, молотков, вагранок и горнов и среди сотни товарищей.

Вверху железный кованный простор.

По сторонам идут балки и угольники.

Они поднимаются на десять сажен.

Загибаются справа и слева.

Соединяются стропилами в куполах и, как плечи великана, держат всю железную постройку.

Они стремительны, они размашисты, они сильны.

Они требуют еще большей силы.

Гляжу на них и выпрямляюсь.

В жилы льется новая железная кровь.

Я вырос еще.

У меня самого вырастают стальные плечи и безмерно сильные руки. Я слился с железом постройки.

Поднялся.

Выпираю плечами стропила, верхние балки, крышу.

Ноги мои еще на земле, но голова выше здания.

Я еще задыхаюсь от этих нечеловеческих усилий, а уже кричу:

– Слова прошу, товарищи, слова!

Железное эхо покрыло мои слова, вся постройка дрожит нетерпением. А я поднялся еще выше, я уже наравне с трубами.

И не рассказ, не речь, а только одно, мое железное, я прокричу:

'Победим мы!'

(1918)

ALEKSEI KAPITONOVICH GASTEV
1882-1941

WE GROW OUT OF IRON

Look! Here I stand: among lathes, hammers, furnaces and forges – among hundreds of comrades.

There are iron-forged spaces above me.

Girders and angle-bars on the sides,

Rising seventy-five feet,

Bending right and left.

They are tied to the cupola rafters, and like a giant's shoulders, support the whole, iron frame.

They are impetuous, sweeping, strong.

They require a still greater strength.

I look at them and I stand straighter.

New iron blood pours into my veins.

And I'm growing taller.

Steel shoulders and immeasurably strong arms grow out from me. I merge with the building's iron.

Then I stretch myself.

With my shoulders I push out the rafters, the highest girders and the roof.

My feet are still on the ground, but my head is above the building.

I'm out of breath from this superhuman effort, but I'm already shouting:

'I ask for the floor, Comrades! For the floor!'

The iron echo has drowned my words; the whole structure is trembling with impatience. And I've risen still higher, I'm even with the smokestacks.

And I'm going to shout – not a story, not a speech, but one single iron phrase:

'The victory will be ours!'

ПЕТР ВАСИЛЬЕВИЧ ОРЕШИН
1887-1943

РЖАНОЕ ВЫМЯ

Бог, Небо, Ангелы – тяжелый груз.
Тяжелый груз на человечьих спинах.
Его я сбросил, больше не согнусь, –
Пусть гром гремит в заоблачных вершинах.

В весенних грозах, в каждом красном дне
Легко дышать без груза и без ноши.
Тот груз в угоду старине
Я не хочу возить, как лошадь!

Другая радость в Мире есть:
Родиться и забыть себя и имя.
И в стадо человеческое влезть,
Чтобы сосать одно ржаное вымя!

Страдать, спасать, – кого, зачем, кому? –
Одно корыто всем, и вздох ко вздоху.
Чудесен Мир, но одному
От скуки можно в нем подохнуть!

1923

PETER VASILYEVICH ORESHIN
1887-1943

THE RYE UDDER

God, Heaven, Angels – a tremendous burden,
A heavy load upon the human back.
I've thrown it off. I won't bend any longer.
And let the thunder in the high clouds crack.

Throughout each red-red day, in spring's warm showers,
Breathing is easy when the weight's offcast.
I do not want to carry such a cargo,
Like some packhorse merely to please the past.

Another joy exists within this World:
To be born, to forget self and one's name,
To get into the human herd, in order
To suck one rye udder, no other aim!

To suffer, to save – whom, what for, and for whom?
One trough for all, sighs grouped fraternally...
The World is wondrous, but one individual,
Alone in it, can croak from dry ennui!

ПАВЕЛ АЛЕКСАНДРОВИЧ РАДИМОВ
р. 1887

ПОЙЛО

Всякая дрянь напихалася за день в большую лоханку:
   Тут кожура огурцов, корки, заплесневший хлеб;
В желтых помоях, из щей образуемых с мыльной водою,
   Плавает корнем наверх вялый обмусленный лук;
Рядом лежит скорлупа, и ошметки от старой подошвы,
   Сильно намокнув в воде, медленно идут ко дну.
Всклянь налилася лоханка, пора выносить поросятам:
   В темном они катухе подняли жалобный визг.
Старая баба Аксинья, в подтыканной кверху понёве,
   Взявши за ушки лохань и понатужась, несет.
Вылила вкусное пойло она поросятам в корыто.
   Чавкают, грузно сопят, к бабе хвосты обратив.

(1924)

PAVEL ALEXANDROVICH RADIMOV
b. 1887

SLOP

All kinds of garbage got shoved through the day in the big catch-all
bucket;
Here is a cucumber peel, bread crumbs and old moldy bread;
And in the yellow slop made from the cabbage soup and soapy water
One flabby, slobbery onion with its roots floats on top.
Next to it lie shells of eggs, and the scraps of some worn leather shoe-
soles,
Soaked up with water, settle down to the depths of the pail.
With bucket full to the brim, it is time for the little pigs' feeding.
In the dark pigpen they grunt, chanting their loud, plaintive squeals.
And the old woman, Axinia, with long skirts tucked up, takes the
bucket
Right by the ears, and she strains – struggling to carry it out.
She dumps the good, tasty slop in the trough, and the pigs push in –
crowding,
Heavily puffing; with tails turned toward the woman, they champ.

ПАВЕЛ НИКОЛАЕВИЧ ВАСИЛЬЕВ
1910-1937

СЕСТРА

В луговинах по всей стране
Рыжим ветром шумят костры,
И, от голода осатанев,
Начинают петь комары.

На хребтах пронося траву,
Осетры проходят на юг,
И за ними следом плывут
Косяки тяжелых белуг.

Ярко-красный теряет пух
На твоем полотенце петух.
За твоим порогом – река;
Льнут к окну твоему облака,

И поскрипывает, чуть слышна,
Половицами тишина.

Ой, темно иртышское дно!
Отвори, отвори окно!

Слушай, как водяная мышь
На поемах грызет камыш.
И спокойна вода, и вот
Молчаливая тень скользнет:
Это синие стрелы щук
Бороздят лопухи излук,
Это всходит вода ясней
Звонкой радугой окуней!

PAVEL NIKOLAYEVICH VASILYEV
1910-1937

SISTER

Bonfires rustle like red-haired wind
In the grass fields across the land,
And mosquitoes begin to sing
Like a hungry devils' band.

The white sturgeon head toward the south,
Bits of grass still stuck to their backs.
And the heavy beluga schools
Swim to follow their watery tracks.

The pert rooster on your towel's lawn
Somehow loses his bright red down.
There's a river by your door still,
And clouds nuzzle your window sill.

And the silence squeaks, hardly heard
With the floor boards your feet have stirred.

O, the bottom of Irtysh is dark!
Open, open the window! Hark!

How the muskrat gnaws at and feeds
On the water-meadow reeds.
And the water is quiet but
Silent shadows through it now cut:
The blue arrows of pikes; their ends
Furrow burdocks of river bends;
This is water rising more bright
In the basses' rainbow of light.

Твой родной, постаревший дом
Пахнет медом и молоком.
Я приветствую этот кров
За мычанье пестрых коров,
За густой его палисад,
За сырой его аромат.
Наступил нашей встречи срок,
Дай мне руки, я не остыл,
Пусть махорки моей дымок
Синь взойдет, как тогда всходил.

Горячей шумит разговор...
Вот в зеленых мхах и лугах
Юность мчится во весь опор
На крутых степных лошадях.
По траве, по корявым пням
Юность мчится навстречу нам!

Первобытной листвой пыля,
Шатаются пьяные тополя,
Всходит рыжею головой
Раньше солнца подсолнух твой.
Осыпая горячий пух,
С полотенца кричит петух...

1930

Your own native and aged home
Smells of milk and of honeycomb.
I say, Welcome, sheltering house,
With your mooing of piebald cows,
Your front garden grown thick with plants,
And your heady and moist fragrance.
Now's the moment: here we both stand,
Not much older; give me your hand.
My tobacco smoke will rise blue
As it always used to do.

Conversation hums, more alive...
Look! Youth races riding full course
Through green meadows and mossy fields
On the fastest, strong steppeland horse.
By rough tree-stumps and grasses, thus –
Youth comes rushing onward toward us.

Spreading dust with their primal leaves,
Every drunken, tall poplar weaves.
Your sunflower with red hair spun
Rises daily before the sun.
Shedding feathers like any fowl,
The pert rooster crows on the towel.

ВИЛЬГЕЛЬМ АЛЕКСАНДРОВИЧ ЗОРГЕНФРЕЙ
1882-1938

НАД НЕВОЙ

Поздней ночью над Невой,
В полосе сторожевой,
Взвыла злобная сирена,
Вспыхнул сноп ацетилена.

Снова тишь и снова мгла.
Вьюга площадь замела.

Крест вздымая над колонной,
Смотрит ангел окрыленный
На забытые дворцы,
На разбитые торцы,

Стужа крепнет. Ветер злится.
Подо льдом вода струится.

Надо льдом костры горят.
Караул идет в наряд.
Провода вверху гудят:
Славен город Петроград!

В нише темного дворца
Вырос призрак мертвеца,
И погибшая столица
В очи призраку глядится.

А над камнем, у костра,
Тень последнего Петра —
Взоры прячет, содрогаясь,
Горько плачет, отрекаясь.

WILHELM ALEXANDROVICH SORGENFREI
1882-1938

ALONG THE NEVA

In the guarded area
By the Neva late at night
The malicious siren howled,
And acetylene flared white.

Then silence and darkness there
As the blizzard swept the square.

His cross raised above a column,
A winged angel looks down, solemn,
At forgotten palaces,
At wood-pavement's brokenness.

Sharper frost. Angry wind blowing.
Neath the ice – water is flowing.

On the ice the fires burn;
Patrols make rounds and return.
Wires hum overhead for us:
Petrograd is marvelous!

In the dark palace's niche
A dead man's ghost seems to rise,
And the perished capital
Looks into the phantom's eyes.

At the fires, hiding his glance,
Peter's form above the stones.
He is crying and denying,
Shuddering his bitter moans.

Ноют жалобно гудки.
Ветер свищет вдоль реки.

Сумрак тает. Рассветает.
Пар встает от желтых льдин,
Желтый свет в окне мелькает.
Гражданина окликает
  Гражданин:

  – Что сегодня, гражданин,
   На обед?
  Прикреплялись, гражданин,
   Или нет?

  – Я сегодня, гражданин,
   Плохо спал:
  Душу я на керосин
   Обменял.

От залива налетает резвый шквал,
Торопливо наметает снежный вал –
Чтобы глуше еще было и темней,
Чтобы души не щемило у теней.

1920

Whistles whine their plaintive scream.
The wind sings along the stream.

Night is palling. Dawn comes crawling.
Yellow ice-blocks steam, and then
Yellow light from windows falling
Greets one citizen who's calling,
   'Citizen!

      Citizen, what cooks today
        In the pot?
      Citizen, have you signed up
        Yet or not?'

      'Citizen, last night I slept
        Bad; I mean
      I traded off my soul for
        Kerosene.'

Now a playful squall comes blowing from the bay,
Sweeping up a wall of snow upon its way –
So that all is darker, more forsaken then,
So the souls of shadows will not ache again.

ПАВЕЛ ГРИГОРЬЕВИЧ АНТОКОЛЬСКИЙ
р. 1896

ШЕКСПИР

Он был никто. Безграмотный бездельник.
Стратфордский браконьер, гроза лесничих,
Веселый друг в компании Фальстафа.
И кто еще? Назойливый вздыхатель
Какой-то смуглой леди из предместья.

И кто еще? Комедиант, король,
Седая ведьма с наговором порчи,
Венецианка, римский заговорщик –
Иль это только сыгранная роль?

И вот сейчас он выплеснет на сцену,
Как из ушата, эльфов и шутов,
Оденет девок и набьет им цену
И оглушит нас шумом суматох.

И хватит смысла мореходам острым
Держать в руках ватаги пьяных банд,
Найти столетью тот туманный остров,
Где гол дикарь, где счастлив Калибан.

И вот герой, забывший свой пароль,
Чья шпага – истина, чей враг – король,
Чей силлогизм столь праведен и горек,
Что от него воскреснет бедный Йорик, –
Иль это недоигранная роль?

(1930)

PAVEL GRIGORYEVICH ANTOKOLSKY
b. 1896

SHAKESPEARE

He was nobody. An illiterate loafer.
A Stratford poacher, trouble for the rangers,
A gay friend whenever he was with Falstaff.
And what else? An importunate, young swooner
Of one certain dark lady from the suburbs.

What else? Comedian. A king. A tart,
Grayed witch whose evil incantations purr.
A Venice maid. A Rome conspirator.
Or is he only acting out a part?

He'll spill onto the stage in just a trice,
As from a wooden pail, jesters and elves;
He'll dress his wenches up and raise their price;
He'll stun you with the noise of many selves.

Sharp navigators with the sense to see
Will hold in hand drunk fools on mischief bent
And find that fogged isle for this century –
A savage, naked; Caliban, content.

And here's a hero: password lost. A friend
Whose foe: the king; whose sword: Truth to defend;
Whose syllogism: so righteous and bitter
That poor Yorick will rise from death's lean litter –
Or is this role not played out to the end?

ВАДИМ ГАБРИЭЛЕВИЧ ШЕРШЕНЕВИЧ
1893-1942

Каждый раз
Несураз-
    ное брякая,
Я в спальню вкатившийся мотосакош;
Плотносложенным дням моя всякая
фраз-
    а
Раз-
    резательный нож.

Я зараз-
    ой дымлюся от крика чуть,
Весь смешной, как соитье машин;
Черпаками строчек не выкачать
Выгребную яму моей души.

Я молюсь на червонную даму игорную,
А иконы ношу на слом,
И похабную надпись заборную
Обращаю в священный псалом.

Незастегнутый рот, как штанишек прорешка;
И когда со лба полночи пот звезды,
Башка моя служит ночлежкой
Всем паломникам в иерусалим ерунды.

И на утро им грозно я в ухо реву,
Что завтра мягчее чем воск,
И тащу продавать на Сухареву
В рай билет, мои мышцы и мозг.

VADIM GABRIELEVICH SHERSHENEVICH
1893-1942

When like a nut
I mut-
    ter some absurdity,
I'm a motorcycle on a bedroom raid:
Every phrase of mine crisply
cut-
s
my well-jut-
ted-together days
As would a keen paper knife's blade.

Funny and absurd, like engines copulating,
I but
    smoke with infection from a shout, slightly, so l-
ines of my verse, the dippers, cannot empty
The garbage dump of my soul.

I carry icons to the junkyard
And give the queen of hearts prayerful reverence.
And I fashion a holy psalm
From the obscene scrawl on the fence.

My unbuttoned mouth like the fly of my trousers.
When a star's sweat drips from midnight's face,
For pilgrims en route to the Jerusalem of nonsense
My noodle serves as an all-night stopping-place.

And next morning I forcibly roar in their ears
That tomorrow's soft wax we can mold from the start,
And I'll peddle my ticket to paradise,
Brains and muscles at Sukharev flea-mart.

Вот вы помните: меня вы там встретили,
Так кричал, что ходуном верста:
– 'Принимаю в починку любовь, добродетели,
– 'Штопаю браки и веру в Христа!'

. . . . . .

И работу окончив обличительно тяжкую,
После с людьми по душам бесед,
Сам себе напоминаю бумажку я
Брошенную в клозет.

Июнь 1919

Well, of course you remember, you saw me there,
Shouting loud till signs threatened to hurt you:
'I put patches on marriages, on faith in Christ,
I accept for repair love and virtue!'

.   .   .   .

After frank conversations with all kind of men,
Having finished soul-searching toil at it,
I think I resemble a thin piece of paper
Thrown into the toilet.

June 1919

АНАТОЛИЙ БОРИСОВИЧ МАРИЕНГОФ
1897-1962

Твердь, твердь за вихры зыбим,
Святость хлещем свистящей нагайкой
И хилое тело Христа на дыбе
Вздыбливаем в Чрезвычайке.

Что же, что же, прощай нам грешным,
Спасай, как на Голгофе разбойника, –
Кровь Твою, кровь бешено
Выплескиваем, как воду из рукомойника.

Кричу: 'Мария, Мария, кого вынашивала! –
Пыль бы у ног твоих целовал за аборт!...'
Зато теперь: на распеленутой земле нашей
Только Я – человек горд.

1918

ANATOLY BORISOVICH MARIENHOF
1897-1962

We lift the heavens, the heavens by the ears;
We whip holiness to please us.
In Cheka torture-chambers we put on the rack
The sickly body of Jesus.

Well, what of it? Forgive us sinners,
As you did the thief on Golgotha's tree.
As if it were water from a washstand,
We spill your blood furiously.

'Mary, Mary,' I shout, 'See what you bore!
He would kiss your feet gladly if you had aborted Him then!'
But today: in our unswaddled land
Who are the proud ones? Only men!

МАРИЯ МИХАЙЛОВНА ШКАПСКАЯ
1891-1952

Было тело мое без входа и палил
его черный дым. Черный враг чело-
вечьего рода наклонялся хищно над
ним.

И ему, позабыв гордыню, отдала
я кровь до конца за одну надежду о
сыне с дорогими чертами лица.

(1921)

MARIYA MIKHAILOVNA SHKAPSKAYA
1891-1952

My body had no entrance, and the black
smoke was scorching me. He bent, preying
upon my body – the black foe of humanity.
I forgot my pride and I gave him – all my
blood till the last drop had run... only for
the hope of bearing my own lovely-featured
son.

НИНА ХАБИАС
(КОМАРОВА)

Телом скатанная как валенок
Головы мосол между ног
Вышиб любовь на заваленку
Сапожищем протоптанный кот
Довольно колеса белок
Аркане шею тянуть
Над отопленном спермой телу
Креститель поставил свечу
У меня все места поцелованы
Выщипан шар живота
Как на скачках язык оторван
Прыгать барьеры зубам
О кляняйтесь мне совнаркомы
Священник и шимпанза
Я славнейшая всех поэтессин
Шафрана Хебеб Хабиас

1921

NINA HABIAS
(KOMAROVA)

Rolled my body felt-like
Between legs lump of head
Kicked love out the cellar
Cat boot-worn trod
Down with rat races
Pulling broken horse
John Baptist lights tapers
Over body's semen warmth
All places kissed
Belly globe plucked
As on runs tongue ripped
Hurdles the teeth jumped
Worship me Communist leaders
Trinity and chimpanzoo
I'm the best of all skirt-poets
Saffrona Habeeb Habias

ДАНИИЛ ИВАНОВИЧ ХАРМС

(случай на железной дороге)

Как то бабушка махнула
и тотчас же паровоз
детям подал и сказал:
пейте кашу и сундук.
Утром дети шли назад.
Сели дети на забор
и сказали: вороной
Поработай, я не буду,
Маша тоже не такая
Как хотите может быть
мы залижем и песочек
то что небо выразило
вылезайте на вокзале
здравствуй здравствуй Грузия
как нам выйти из нее
мимо этого большого
не забора – ах вы дети –
выростала палеандра
и влетая на вагоны
перемыла не того
кто налима с перепугу
оградил семью волами
вынул деньги из кармана
деньги серые в лице.

ну так вот, а дальше прели
все супа – сказала тетя
все чижи – сказал покойник
даже тело опустилось
и чирикало любезно,
но зато немного скучно
и как будто бы назад.

DANIEL IVANOVICH KHARMS

(a railroad happening)

Once when Grandma moved her hand
the train stopped immediately
for the children – and it said,
'drink your porridge and valise'.
In the morning they came back.
Children sat down on the fence
and they said, 'You, raven-horse,
You may work but I will not,
Mary's not like that at all
As you like it and perhaps
it's all right; we'll lick the sand
something that the sky expressed
here's the station, let's get off
hello Georgia! hello Georgia!
how can we get out of here?
Simply go on past the big one –
o you children – not the fence
there a polyandra grew
and alighting on the cars
she kept scrubbing the wrong man
who surrounded out of fright
one catfish with seven oxen
he took money from his pockets
Money pale gray in the face.

well that's that, and so they simmered
all the soups – the old aunt said
all the sparrows – said the dead man
and the body sank down lower
with a chirping that was pleasant
but a little boring too
moving backward – as it seemed.

дети слушали обедню
надевая на плечо
мышка бегала в передник
раздирая два плеча

а грузинка на пороге
все твердила. А грузин
перегнувшись под горою
шарил пальцами в грязи.

(1926)

children went to hear a mass
putting it upon a shoulder
mousey ran into an apron
tearing shoulders all apart

Georgian woman on the threshold
kept repeating. Georgian man
by the hill was bending over
groped for something in the mud.

V

SOVIET POETRY

ВЕРА МИХАЙЛОВНА ИНБЕР
р. 1890

ТАК БУДЕТ

Закономерно, чередою длинной
Пройдут года.
И в город-сад асфальтово-пчелиный
Сольются города.

В нем будут розы на стеклянных крышах,
Но мы – увы, –
Его уж не увидим, не услышим,
Ни я, ни вы.

Но все же так легко себе представить,
И вам и мне,
Зеленый город в солнечной оправе
В ничьей стране.

Там памятник на площади крылатой
Поставлен так,
Что солнце сыплет золото заката
На бронзовый пиджак.

Туда приходят маленькие дети,
Счастливые на вид,
И улыбаются в закатном свете
Тому, кто там стоит.

И мать, подняв ребенка на ступени
И за лучом следя,
Негромко произносит: 'Это Ленин,
Мое дитя.'

1925

VERA MIKHAILOVNA INBER
b. 1890

IT WILL COME TO PASS

Inevitably, years will pass by, filing –
A long, long row.
Into one garden city, asphalt beehive,
All cities will grow.

Beautiful roses planted on glass roof-tops
Will flourish, too.
But we – alas! – will neither see nor hear it;
Not I, nor you.

Despite all this, it's easy to imagine
This city and
Its greenery, framed in sunlight's brilliance,
In all men's land.

There'll be a statue centered in a certain
Square's octagon,
Constructed so the sunset's gold spills, streaming
Onto the jacket's bronze.

All kinds of little children go there, happy,
Mindless of care.
Glowing, they send their smiles in the rich sunset
To him who towers there.

A mother lifts her baby to the stone steps
And watching sunbeams piled
Above them utters softly, 'This is Lenin,
My child.'

731

САМУИЛ ЯКОВЛЕВИЧ МАРШАК
1887-1964

1616-1949

Я перевел Шекспировы сонеты.
Пускай поэт, покинув старый дом,
Заговорит на языке другом,
В другие дни, в другом краю планеты.

Соратником его мы признаем,
Защитником свободы, правды, мира.
Недаром имя славное Шекспира
По-русски значит: потрясай копьем.

Три сотни раз и тридцать раз и три
Со дня его кончины очертила
Земля урочный путь вокруг светила,
Свергались троны, падали цари...

А гордый стих и в скромном переводе
Служил и служит правде и свободе.

1949

МИНИСТР ПО ДЕЛАМ РАЗОРУЖЕНЬЯ

Благочестив миролюбивый Стассен,
Но в сущности весьма огнеопасен.
В его петлице – пальмовая ветка,
Но он сидит на бомбах, как наседка,
И в этом интересном положенье
Рассматривает план разоруженья.

(1956)

SAMUEL YAKOVLEVICH MARSHAK
1887-1964

1616-1949

I've translated the final Shakespeare sonnet.
So let the poet leaving now his dear
Old home start speaking in another year,
Another tongue, in this part of the planet.

We know him as a fellow warrior here:
Defender of truth, peace and freedom. On its
Own feet, in Russian, that great name of honor,
'Shakespeare', means (and not by chance) shake a spear.

Three hundred times, thirty and three this sphere
Called Earth has spun in its predestined manner
Around the sun since it heard his death knell;
Some thrones were overturned and some kings fell . . .

His proud verse – even in translations' shell –
Served and still serves both truth and freedom well.

A MINISTER OF THE DISARMAMENT CONFERENCE

Peace-loving Stassen who appears so pious
Is most inflammable and could well fry us.
He wears an olive branch in his lapel,
But sits on bombs like some hen doing well
In her present condition. Still he can
Consider any disarmament plan.

РАБОТА В САДУ

Речь – зимостойкая семья.
  Я, в сущности, мичуринец.
  Над стебельками слов – моя
  упорная прищуренность.

Другим – подарки сентября,
грибарий леса осени;
а мне – гербарий словаря,
лес говора разрозненный.

То стужа ветку серебрит,
то душит слякоть дряблая.
Дичок привит, и вот – гибрид!
Моягода, мояблоня!

Сто га словами поросло,
И после года первого –
уже несет плодыни слов
счасливовое дерево.

1935

ЧЕРЕЗ ТРИСТА...

Я увидал корабль,
              который плыл
без весел, без винта и без ветрил,
я увидал аэроплан без крыл,
который тихо в воздухе парил.

SEMYON ISAAKOVICH KIRSANOV
b. 1906

WORK IN THE GARDEN

Language – a winterhardy class.
    At heart I'm a Michurin man.
    Working with stems and stalks of words,
    I'm a stubborn squinturian.

    I like herbariums of speech,
    Vocabulary's scattered grove.
    Some like September's berriums,
    Mushroomiums – Fall's treasure-trove.

    Frost kills the twigs with silver stings;
    Slush chokes them in a miry snare.
    My grafting grows; a hybrid shows: –
    My mapple tree – my junipear.

    Acres have sprouted with my words.
    After a year's anxiety
    Lingtwistic lemelons appear –
    The crop of my plum-happy tree.

AFTER THREE HUNDRED...

I saw a ship,
        floating and sailing through
The seas without an oar, or sail, or screw;
I saw an airplane without wings which flew
And hovered lightly in the highest blue.

И я привык
            смотреть со стороны
на странные явления вдали,
на мчащегося около Луны
искусственного спутника Земли.

Я пью необычайное вино,
но – виноградом не было оно,
ем белый хлеб,
                не росший никогда,
искусный синтез мысли и труда.

Чиста, как небо,
                новая земля,
и наш граненый дом из хрусталя,
но мало в нем знакомых и родных,
лишь ты одна –
            последняя из них.

Нам каждому уже по триста лет,
но мы еще не мыслим о конце,
и ни морщинки ни единой нет
ни на моем,
            ни на твоем лице.

Хвосты ракет за тучами скользят,
их водят электронные умы...
Скажи,
        тебе не хочется назад
в двадцатый век, где прежде жили мы?

Где надо было землю корчевать,
под бомбами в землянках ночевать,
пилить дрова и хлебом дорожить,
и только там
            хотелось жить и жить...

(1962)

I've grown accustomed
                    from my sideline site
To seeing far and strange events balloon
Upon Earth's artificial satellite
As it speeds ever closer to the moon.

I drink a glass of this unusual wine
But it was never grapes upon a vine;
I eat white bread –
                    which never grew as grain:
A clever synthesis of brawn and brain.

All this new world of ours
                          is pure like sky
As our jeweled crystal house can verify,
But so few friends and relatives have passed
Through it. And you alone,
                          you are the last.

Both you and I are three-hundred years old,
And we're not thinking yet about the end.
There's not a single wrinkle to behold –
Either on my face
                    or on yours, my friend.

The tails of rockets tag behind the clouds,
And electronic minds move them . . .
                                    Tell me,
Wouldn't you like to go back, if allowed,
Back there, into the twentieth century,

Where we once lived, where we cleared off the land,
Where we sawed firewood, valued our bread and
Spent nights in dugouts as bombs poured till dawn?
And only there
              we wanted to live on and on and on.

ВАСИЛИЙ ИВАНОВИЧ ЛЕБЕДЕВ-КУМАЧ
1898-1949

ПЕСНЯ О РОДИНЕ

Широка страна моя родная,
Много в ней лесов, полей и рек.
Я другой такой страны не знаю,
Где так вольно дышит человек!

От Москвы до самых до окраин,
С южных гор до северных морей,
Человек проходит как хозяин
Необъятной родины своей!
Всюду жизнь и вольно и широко,
Точно Волга полная, течет.
Молодым – везде у нас дорога,
Старикам – везде у нас почет.

Широка страна моя родная, и т.д.

Наши нивы глазом не обшаришь,
Не упомнишь наших городов,
Наше слово гордое 'товарищ'
Нам дороже всех красивых слов.
С этим словом мы повсюду дома,
Нет для нас ни черных, ни цветных,
Это слово каждому знакомо,
С ним везде находим мы родных.

Широка страна моя родная, и т.д.

За столом никто у нас не лишний,
По заслугам каждый награжден.
Золотыми буквами мы пишем
Всенародный Сталинский закон.

VASILY IVANOVICH LEBEDEV-KUMACH
1898-1949

SONG ABOUT OUR MOTHERLAND

O, my homeland is a spacious country:
Streams and fields and forests full and fair.
I don't know of any other country
Where a man can breathe a freer air!

> All the way from Moscow to the border,
> Southern peaks to northern oceans' foam
> Man can walk and feel that he's the owner
> Of this boundless motherland and home.
> Here our life can flow as freely, broadly
> As the Volga – brimming and unchecked.
> Here the young will always have a roadway
> And the old will always have respect.

O, my homeland is a spacious country, etc.

> One can't see the end of fields that are rich
> Or recall all names of towns we've heard,
> But one proud word that we say, 'Tovarich',
> Means much more than any other word.
> With this word we are at home all places
> And this word we always comprehend:
> There are no more black or colored races,
> For with it – the whole world is your friend.

O, my homeland is a spacious country, etc.

> There is none unwelcome at our table;
> He who merits it gets his reward.
> We now write in golden strokes the stable
> Law of Stalin in a calm accord.

739

Этих слов величие и славу
Никакие годы не сотрут:
Человек всегда имеет право
На ученье, отдых и на труд!

Широка страна моя родная, и т.д.

Над страной весенний ветер веет,
С каждым днем все радостнее жить,
И никто на свете не умеет
Лучше нас смеяться и любить.
Но сурово брови мы насупим,
Если враг захочет нас сломать.
Как невесту, родину мы любим,
Бережем, как ласковую мать!

Широка страна моя родная, и т.д.

1935

These words have a greatness and a glory
Which the years cannot mar or molest:
Every man has these rights in his story:
He may work, may study and may rest.

O, my homeland is a spacious country, etc.

O, the spring wind blows across our homeland,
What a joy to be alive today!
And no one wherever he may roam can
Laugh and love in any better way.
But we'll frown our eyebrows most severely
If a foe should want to cause our fall –
Like our bride, we love our homeland dearly;
Like our mother we'll save her from all.

O, my homeland is a spacious country, etc.

АЛЕКСАНДР ТРИФОНОВИЧ ТВАРДОВСКИЙ
р. 1910

Отцов и прадедов примета, –
Как будто справдилась она:
Таких хлебов, такого лета
Не год, не два ждала война.
Как частый бор, колосовые
Шумели глухо над землей.
Не пешеходы – верховые
Во ржи скрывались с головой.
И были так густы и строги
Хлеба, подавшись грудь на грудь,
Что, по пословице, с дороги
Ужу, казалось, не свернуть.
И хлеба хлеб казался гуще,
И было так, что год хлебов
Был годом клубней, землю рвущих,
И годом трав в лугах и пущах,
И годом ягод и грибов.
Как будто все, что в почве было, –
Ее добро, ее тепло –
С великой щедростью и силой
Ростки наружу выносило,
В листву, в ботву и колос шло.
В свой полный цвет входило лето,
Земля ломилась, всем полна...
Отцов и прадедов примета, –
Как будто справдилась она:

Гром грянул – началась война...

1942

ALEXANDER TRIFONOVICH TVARDOVSKY
b. 1910

Father's, Grandfather's superstition
Seems to have proved itself quite true:
The war did not wait one year, two –
With such a summer, such fruition.
The grain crops, like a thick pine forest,
Rustled their hush across the land;
The men on foot, even on horseback,
Were hidden by the rye's tall stand.
And all the grains, bent breast to breast,
Kept crowding with their heads' full load;
That old saying applied: a grass snake
Had no place to get off the road.
Each field seemed thicker than its neighbors;
That great year for grain was the best
Also for grasses in the meadows
And the woods, for earth-tearing tubers
And for the berries and mushrooms.
As if everything in the earth,
The soil's goodness and its warmth
With such abundance and such strength
Pushed to the outside air the blooms,
Sprouts, heads, ears, foliage and plumes.
Summer was set for full fruition.
The earth burst with plenty and plan...
Father's, Grandfather's superstition
Seemed to have proved quite true for man:

The thunder cracked; the war began.

В пилотке мальчик босоногий
С худым заплечным узелком
Привал устроил на дороге,
Чтоб закусить сухим пайком.

Горбушка хлеба, две картошки –
Всему суровый вес и счет.
И, как большой, с ладони крошки
С великой бережностью – в рот.

Стремглав попутные машины
Проносят пыльные борта.
Глядит, задумался мужчина.
– Сынок, должно быть сирота?

И на лице, в глазах, похоже, –
Досады давнишняя тень.
Любой и каждый все про то же,
И как им спрашивать не лень.

В лицо тебе серьезно глядя,
Еще он медлит рот открыть.
– Ну, сирота. – И тотчас: – Дядя,
Ты лучше дал бы покурить.

1943

The barefoot boy in service headgear
With a small bundle on his back
Halts alongside the road – to open
His dry rations for a quick snack.

A crust of bread and two potatoes –
He weighs and counts out with great care
The total contents – and like grown-ups,
He mouths the crumbs remaining there.

And now the trucks, their sides dust-layered,
Come rushing by in a convoy.
A man looks thoughtfully down at him:
Hey there, are you an orphan, boy?

The eyes in the boy's face are kindled
As his pet peeve again is fired: –
They all, they all, they ask the same thing.
Always! Don't they ever get tired?

He looks into your face ... and opens
His mouth – half-waiting even yet:
Yeah, I'm an orphan. (And then) Mister,
Come on, give me a cigarette ...

К ПОРТРЕТУ

Глаза, опущенные к трубке,
Знакомой людям всей земли.
И эти занятые руки,
Что спичку с трубкою свели.
Они крепки и сухощавы,
И строгой жилки вьется нить.
В нелегкий век судьбу державы
И мира им пришлось вершить.

Усов нависнувшею тенью
Лицо внизу притемнено.
Какое слово на мгновенье
Под ней от нас утаено?
Совет? Наказ? Упрек тяжелый?
Неодобренья горький тон?
Иль с шуткой мудрой и веселой
Сейчас глаза поднимет он?

1950-1952

TO A PORTRAIT OF STALIN

His eyes look downward at the pipe –
Well-known to people of all lands –
And now a match and that pipe meet
United by his busy hands.
They are both firm and lean; there winds
A prominent thread of a vein.
They've had to rule our destiny...
And Earth's in this age of such strain.

His face's lower part is dark
With the moustache's hanging shade.
What words are hidden there from us,
For just a moment's pause delayed?
Advice? An order? Strong reproach?
A disapproval in harsh cloak?
Or will he raise his eyes right now
With some judicious, funny joke?

МИХАИЛ ВАСИЛЬЕВИЧ ИСАКОВСКИЙ
р. 1900

СЛОВО К ТОВАРИЩУ СТАЛИНУ

Оно пришло, не ожидая зова,
Пришло само – и не сдержать его...
Позвольте ж мне сказать Вам это слово,
Простое слово сердца моего.

Тот день настал. Исполнилися сроки.
Земля опять покой свой обрела.
Спасибо ж Вам за подвиг Ваш высокий,
За Ваши многотрудные дела.

Спасибо Вам, что в годы испытаний
Вы помогли нам устоять в борьбе.
Мы так Вам верили, товарищ Сталин,
Как, может быть, не верили себе.

Вы были нам оплотом и порукой,
Что от расплаты не уйти врагам.
Позвольте ж мне пожать Вам крепко руку,
Земным поклоном поклониться Вам.

За Вашу верность матери-отчизне,
За Вашу мудрость и за Вашу честь,
За чистоту и правду Вашей жизни,
За то, что Вы – такой, какой Вы есть.

Спасибо Вам, что в дни великих бедствий
О всех о нас Вы думали в Кремле,
За то, что Вы повсюду с нами вместе,
За то, что Вы живете на земле.

1945

MIKHAIL VASILYEVICH ISAKOVSKY
b. 1900

A WORD TO COMRADE STALIN

I cannot stop it. It came by itself.
It came without any call on my part.
So please allow me to tell You these words,
These simple words that rose up from my heart.

The day arrived. The time is now fulfilled.
At last the earth has found its peace again.
So I thank You for Your supreme exploit,
For Your great labors You have done for men.

Thank You – that through the years of our ordeal –
You helped us hold ground till the fight was through.
Though our belief in ourselves may have dimmed,
Comrade Stalin, we never doubted You.

You were our strength and guarantee the foe
Would not escape his punishment somehow.
So please allow me, Sir, to shake Your hand
Firmly – and bow before You this low bow.

For Your faithfulness to our Motherland,
For Your wisdom and honor, for the star
Of purity and truth of Your own life,
For Your being the great man that You are.

Thank You – that in those greatly troubled days –
In the Kremlin You thought about *our* worth,
That You are present everywhere with us,
That You live on this planet we call Earth.

СТЕПАН ПЕТРОВИЧ ЩИПАЧЕВ
р. 1899

ОБ 'ЭВОЛЮЦИИ' (ПРОСТИТЕ ЗА КАВЫЧКИ)

Снова думы мои об одном.
Все не вечно, все в природе переменится.
Сыплет листья береза за окном,
Милая моя современница.
Остановки движению нет.
И земля совсем иной когда-то станет вся;
Даже русского неба цвет
Лишь в глазах потомков останется;
Гор иных не найдут и следа,
Звездный ковш и тот исчезнет в звездной замети, —
Но семнадцатый год и тогда
Не сотрется в народной памяти.

STEPAN PETROVICH SHCHIPACHEV
b. 1899

ABOUT 'EVOLUTION' (FORGIVE MY QUOTES)

Once again this thought absorbs me:
Nothing's stable in nature, nothing will abide.
My dear contemporary, the birch tree,
Sheds its leaves outside.
Motion cannot be stopped.
The whole earth, someday, will look differently,
And the color of the Russian sky
Will remain only in the eyes of our posterity.
Where mountains are now, none will be seen;
Even the Big Dipper will be lost in the stars' blizzarding scene.
But in the memory of man – one thing
Will endure even then: nineteen-seventeen.

МАРГАРИТА ИОСИФОВНА АЛИГЕР
р. 1915

О КРАСОТЕ

По всей земле, во все столетья,
великодушна и проста,
всем языкам на белом свете
всегда понятна красота.

Хранят изустные творенья
и рукотворные холсты
неугасимое горенье
понятной людям красоты.

Людьми творимая навеки,
она понятным языком
ведет рассказ о человеке,
с тревогой думает о нем
и неуклонно в жизни ищет
его прекрасные черты.

Чем человек сильней и чище,
тем больше в мире красоты.

И в сорок пятом, в сорок пятом
она светила нам в пути
и помогла моим солдатам
ее из пламени спасти.

Для всех людей, для всех столетий
они свершили подвиг свой.
И этот подвиг стал на свете

MARGARITA IOSIFOVNA ALIGER
b. 1915

ON BEAUTY

Through all the world, through all the ages,
both simple and magnanimous
Beauty, speaking to this bright planet,
stays understandable to us.

The mouth-to-mouth, the folk-, creations
and handmade canvases likewise
preserve and present to the people
Beauty's pure flame which never dies.

Created to endure forever,
it tells with clear simplicity
the story of Man's life and actions,
thinks of him with anxiety,
and looks for his beautiful features
in life with an unswerving plan.

And this world gains a greater beauty
if stronger, purer is the man.

We had the chance along our pathway
in forty-five, in forty-five,
and my soldiers rescued this Beauty
from flame and kept it still alive.

For all ages and for all people
they did their deed of noble worth,
and this deed became an example

примером красоты земной.
И эта красота бездонна,
и безгранично ей расти.

Прощай, Сикстинская мадонна!
Счастливого тебе пути!

1955

also of Beauty on this earth.
And this Beauty grows without limits,
and it will never have an end.

Adieu, goodbye, Sistine Madonna!
Have a happy trip, old friend!

ОЛЬГА ФЕДОРОВНА БЕРГГОЛЬЦ
р. 1910

ВОЗВРАЩЕНИЕ

Вошли – и сердце дрогнуло ... Жестоко
Зияла смерть, безлюдье, пустота ...
Где лебеди? Где музы? Где потоки?
С младенчества родная красота?

Где наши люди – наши садоводы,
Лелеявшие мирные сады,
Где их благословенные труды
На счастье человека и природы?

И где мы сами – прежние, простые,
Доверчиво глядевшие на свет?
Как страшно здесь ... Печальней и пустынней
Селения, наверно, в мире нет.

... И вдруг в душе, в ее немых глубинах,
Опять звучит надменно и светло:
'Все те же мы: нам целый мир чужбина,
Отечество нам Царское Село ...'

25 января 1944 г., Пушкин

OLGA FYODOROVNA BERGHOLZ
b. 1910

RETURN

We enter – and our shocked hearts shudder ... Cruel
Death, desolation, emptiness yawn here ...
Where are the swans ... and brooks? Where are the muses?
The beauty that from childhood we've held dear?

Where are the gardeners? Where are the people
Who used to cherish peaceful parks like this?
There is no sign of any blessed labor
For man and nature's benefit and bliss?

And where are we ourselves – we former, simple
Ones who viewed the world in a trusting way?
How fearful it is here! ... I'm sure no sadder,
Lonelier place exists on Earth today.

... And suddenly the haughty and bright echoes
From mute depths in our soul again outflow:
'We're still the same; we're aliens in the whole world;
Our home is always Tsarskoe Selo ...'

25 January 1944, Pushkin

ОБЕЩАНИЕ

... Я недругов смертью своей не утешу,
Чтоб в лживых слезах захлебнуться могли.
Не вбит еще крюк, на котором повешусь.
Не скован. Не вырыт рудой из земли.
Я встану над жизнью бездонной своею,
Над страхом ее, над железной тоскою...
Я знаю о многом. Я помню. Я *смею*.
Я тоже чего-нибудь страшного стою...

1952

PROMISE

... I won't give my enemies that consolation:
My death – hypocritically to deplore.
The hook where I'd hang myself is not yet driven,
Not yet forged. Not dug out from the earth as ore.
I'll rise over all of my bottomless life,
The terrors, the whole iron anguish I knew.
I know of so much. I remember. I *dare*.
I deserve some terrible destiny too.

КОНСТАНТИН МИХАЙЛОВИЧ СИМОНОВ
р. 1915

УБЕЙ ЕГО

Если дорог тебе твой дом,
Где ты русским выкормлен был,
Под бревенчатым потолком
Где ты, в люльке качаясь, плыл;
Если дороги в доме том
Тебе стены, печь и углы,
Дедом, прадедом и отцом
В нем положенные полы;
Если мил тебе бедный сад
С майским цветом, с жужжанием пчел
И под липой сто лет назад
В землю вкопанный дедом стол;
Если ты не хочешь, чтоб пол
В твоем доме немец топтал,
Чтоб он сел за дедовский стол
И деревья в саду сломал...

Если мать тебе дорога,
Тебя выкормившая грудь,
Где давно уже нет молока,
Только можно щекой прильнуть;
Если вынести нету сил,
Чтобы немец, ее застав,
По щекам морщинистым бил,
Косы на руку намотав,
Чтобы те же руки ее,
Что несли тебя в колыбель,
Немцу мыли его белье
И стелили ему постель...

CONSTANTINE MIKHAILOVICH SIMONOV
b. 1915

KILL HIM

If your house means a thing to you
Where you first dreamed your Russian dreams
In your swinging cradle, afloat
Beneath the log ceiling beams.
If your house means a thing to you
With its stove, corners, walls and floors
Worn smooth by the footsteps of three
Generations of ancestors.
If your small garden means a thing:
With its May blooms and bees humming low,
With its table your grandfather built
Neath the linden – a century ago.
If you don't want a German to tread
The floor in your house and chance
To sit in your ancestors' place
And destroy your yard's trees and plants...

If your mother is dear to you
And the breast that gave you suck
Which hasn't had milk for years
But is now where you put your cheek;
If you cannot stand the thought
Of a German's doing her harm,
Beating her furrowed face
With her braids wound round his arm.
And those hands which carried you
To your cradle – washing instead
A German's dirty clothes
Or making him his bed...

Если ты отца не забыл,
Что качал тебя на руках,
Что хорошим солдатом был
И пропал в карпатских снегах,
Что погиб за Волгу, за Дон,
За отчизны твоей судьбу;
Если ты не хочешь, чтоб он
Перевертывался в гробу,
Чтоб солдатский портрет в крестах
Немец взял и на пол сорвал
И у матери на глазах
На лицо ему наступал...

Если ты не хочешь отдать
Ту, с которой вдвоем ходил,
Ту, что долго поцеловать
Ты не смел, – так ее любил, –
Чтобы немцы ее живьем
Взяли силой, зажав в углу,
И распяли ее втроем
Обнаженную на полу,
Чтоб досталось трем этим псам,
В стонах, в ненависти, в крови,
Все, что свято берег ты сам,
Всею силой мужской любви...

Если ты не хочешь отдать
Немцу, с черным его ружьем,
Дом, где жил ты, жену и мать,
Все, что Родиной мы зовем, –
Знай: никто ее не спасет,
Если ты ее не спасешь.
Знай: никто его не убьет,
Если ты его не убьешь.
И пока его не убил,
То молчи о своей любви,
Край, где рос ты, и дом, где жил,
Своей родиной не зови.

If you haven't forgotten your father
Who tossed you and teased your toes,
Who was a good soldier, who vanished
In the high Carpathian snows,
Who died for your motherland's fate,
For each Don and each Volga wave,
If you don't want him in his sleeping
To turn over in his grave,
When a German tears his soldier picture
With crosses from its place
And before your own mother's eyes
Stamps hobnailed boots on his face.

If you don't want to give away
Her you walked with and didn't touch,
Her you didn't dare even to kiss
For a long time – you loved her so much,
And the Germans cornering her
And taking her alive by force,
Crucifying her – three of them
Naked, on the floor; with coarse
Moans, hate, and blood, –
Those dogs taking advantage of
All you sacredly preserved
With your strong, male love...

If you don't want to give away
To a German with his black gun
Your house, your mother, your wife –
All that's yours as a native son –
No: No one will save your land
If you don't save it from the worst.
No: No one will kill this foe,
If you don't kill him first.
And until you have killed him, don't
Talk about your love – and
Call the house where you lived your home
Or the land where you grew up your land.

Если немца убил твой брат,
Если немца убил сосед, –
Это брат и сосед твой мстят,
А тебе оправданья нет.
За чужой спиной не сидят,
Из чужой винтовки не мстят.
Если немца убил твой брат, –
Это он, а не ты, солдат.
Так убей же немца, чтоб он,
А не ты, на земле лежал,
Не в твоем дому чтобы стон,
А в его по мертвом стоял.
Так хотел он, его вина –
Пусть горит его дом, а не твой,
И пускай не твоя жена,
А его пусть будет вдовой.
Пусть исплачется не твоя,
А его родившая мать,
Не твоя, а его семья
Понапрасну пусть будет ждать.

Так убей же хоть одного!
Так убей же его скорей,
Сколько раз увидишь его,
Столько раз его и убей!

июль 1942 г.

If your brother killed a German,
If your neighbor killed one too,
It's your brother's and neighbor's vengeance,
And it's no revenge for you.
You can't sit behind another
Letting him fire your shot.
If your brother kills a German,
He's a soldier; you are not.
So kill that German so he
Will lie on the ground's backbone,
So the funeral wailing will be
In *his* house, not in your own.
He wanted it so – It's his guilt –
Let *his* house burn up, and his life.
Let *his* woman become a widow;
Don't let it be *your* wife.
Don't let *your* mother tire from tears;
Let the one who bore him bear the pain.
Don't let it be yours, but his
Family who will wait in vain.

So kill at least one of them
And as soon as you can. Still
Each one you chance to see!
Kill him! Kill him! Kill!

July 1942

ЛЕОНИД НИКОЛАЕВИЧ МАРТЫНОВ
р. 1905

На побережье после бури
Твоих камней я слышу хруст,
О, море, море, лучший в мире
Художник-абстракционист.
И не участвую я в споре,
В дискуссии весьма пустой:
Что ты изобразило, море,
На гальке этой или той.

10 марта 1962 г.

LEONID NIKOLAYEVICH MARTYNOV
b. 1905

I hear the crunch of your beach pebbles,
Now that the storm takes a recess;
O sea, sea, you are the unrivaled
Painter of abstract canvases.
I do not enter the discussion,
Which seems pointless: I do not care,
Sea, what picture you have depicted
On this small stone or that one there.

10 March 1962

ЛЕВ ОЗЕРОВ
(ЛЕВ АДОЛЬФОВИЧ ГОЛЬДБЕРГ)
р. 1914

На берегу морском лежит весло
И больше говорит мне о просторе,
Чем все огромное сверкающее море,
Которое его на берег принесло.

LEV OZEROV
(LEV ADOLFOVICH GOLDBERG)
b. 1914

An oar is lying on the coastal sand;
It tells me more about expanse and motion
Than the entire, enormous, brilliant ocean
Which brought it in and tossed it on the land.

БОРИС АВРАМОВИЧ СЛУЦКИЙ
р. 1919

ФИЗИКИ И ЛИРИКИ

Что-то физики в почете,
что-то лирики в загоне.
Дело не в сухом расчете,
дело в мировом законе.

Значит, что-то не раскрыли
мы,
        что следовало нам бы!
Значит, слабенькие крылья –
наши сладенькие ямбы.
И в пегасовом полете
не взлетают наши кони...
То-то физики в почете.
То-то лирики в загоне.

Это самоочевидно.
Спорить просто бесполезно.
Так что – даже не обидно,
а, скорее, интересно
наблюдать, как, словно пена,
опадают наши рифмы
и величие
        степенно
отступает в логарифмы.

1959

BORIS AVRAMOVICH SLUTSKY
b. 1919

PHYSICS AND POETRY

Looks like physics is in honor,
Looks like poetry is not.
It's not dry figures that matter;
Universal law, that's what.

It means that we failed in something,
Something,
           which was ours to do!
It means that our cute iambics
Had weak wings and hardly flew.
Unlike Pegasus, our horses
Do not soar nor even trot...
That's why physics is in honor,
That's why poetry is not.

Any argument is pointless,
But even if there is one:
It is nothing so dismaying;
Rather it's amusing fun
To observe the foam-like falling
Away of our rhymes and rhythms
And to watch how greatness
                        staidly
Retreats into logarithms.

ЕВГЕНИЙ АЛЕКСАНДРОВИЧ ЕВТУШЕНКО
р. 1933

ВЕРЛЕН

Мне гид цитирует Верлена,
Париж рукою обводя,
так умиленно,

      так елейно
под шелест легкого дождя.
И эти строки невозвратно
журчат, как звездная вода...
'Мосье,

    ну как,

         звучит приятно?'
Киваю я:

      'Приятно... Да...'
Плохая память у Парижа,
и, как сам бог теперь велел,
у буржуа на полках книжных
стоит веленевый Верлен.
Приятно,

     выпив джина с джусом
и предвкушая крепкий сон,
вслух поцитировать со вкусом...
Верлена чтить –

     хороший тон!
Приятно, да?

     Но я припас вам
не вашу память,

     а свою.
Был вам большая неприятность
Верлен.

   Я вас не узнаю.

EVGENY ALEXANDROVICH EVTUSHENKO
b. 1933

VERLAINE

Encircling Paris with his hand
the guide is quoting from Verlaine,
so sweetly
       and so unctuously,
under the rustling of light rain,
and these lines irrevocably
ripple with starry liquidness...
'Monsieur,
      tell me,
           does it sound nice?'
I nod and say,
       'It's pleasant... yes...'
Paris has a bad memory,
and, as god himself might command,
upon the big bourgeois bookshelves
the vellum Verlaine volumes stand.
While one awaits a heavy sleep,
it's pleasant,
      after juice and gin
to quote aloud lines with delight...
Verlaine is great; –
        Verlaine is 'in'.
It's pleasant, yes?
      But I've got news:
my memory
      is different.
I don't know you.
      The live Verlaine,
he was your big embarrassment.

Он не укладывался в рамки
благочестиво лживых фраз,
а он прикладывался к рюмке
и был безнравственным для вас.
Сужу об этом слишком быстро?
Кривитесь вы...
              Приятно, да?
Убило медленным убийством
его все это, господа.
Его убило все, что било
насмешками из-за угла,
все, что моралью вашей было,
испепеляющей дотла.
Вы под Верлена выпиваете
с набитым плотно животом.
Вы всех поэтов убиваете,
Чтобы цитировать потом!

1960, Париж

РАЗГОВОР С АМЕРИКАНСКИМ ПИСАТЕЛЕМ

'Мне говорят –
           ты смелый человек.
Неправда.
           Никогда я не был смелым.
Считал я просто недостойным делом
унизиться до трусости коллег.

Устоев никаких не потрясал.
Смеялся просто над фальшивым,
                    дутым.
Писал статьи.
           Доносов не писал.
И говорить старался
              все, что думал.

He did not fit the framework of
the pious lies you love to chew.
He bent the bottle much too much;
he was too scandalous for you!
I am too quick to judge, n'est-ce pas?
You make a face...
                              It's pleasant, no?
And all this, my dear gentlemen,
killed him – though the killing was slow.
He died from all your snide remarks,
your innuendoes' hidden slash
and from your code of morals which
ignites, then burns one to an ash.
Now you drink listening to Verlaine
with stretched-tight stomachs, finely fed.
You kill all poets so you can
quote them long after they are dead.

1960, Paris

CONVERSATION WITH AN AMERICAN WRITER

They tell me:
                         you are a courageous man.
That's not correct.
                         I've never been courageous,
but crawling – as my fellow-writers can –
for me seemed simply too low and outrageous.

Subversiveness is not one of my fortes.
I saw the blown-up fraud,
                              mocked it and fought:
wrote articles,
                    did not write police reports;
I simply tried
              to say the things I thought.

Да,
   защищал талантливых людей,
клеймил бездарных,
      лезущих в писатели,
но делать это, в общем, обязательно,
а мне твердят о смелости моей.
О, вспомнят с чувством горького стыда
потомки наши,
     расправляясь с мерзостью,
то время,
    очень странное,
       когда
простую честность
     называли смелостью . . .'

1960, Нью Йорк

ПРОДАВЩИЦА ГАЛСТУКОВ

Когда окончится работа,
бледна от душной суеты,
с лицом усталого ребенка
из магазина выйдешь ты.

Веселья горькое лекарство
спасать не может без конца.
Дневное нервное лукавство
бессильно схлынуло с лица.

Вокруг весна и воскресенье,
дома в огнях и голосах,
а галстуки на карусели
все кружатся в твоих глазах.

И в туфельках на микропоре
сквозь уличную молодежь
идешь ты мимо 'Метрополя',
отдельно, замкнуто идешь.

Yes,
> I defended those whose talent shone;
I panned the fakes,
> > the mediocre writing.
But isn't that what usually is done?
And so my 'bravery' bears much reciting.
O, when our sons make short work of all trash,
they will remember
> > with a bitter shame
this strange,
> > bizarre time,
> > > when a simple flash
of honesty
> > had 'courage' as its name.

1960, New York

A TIE SALESGIRL

When you have finished your day's work
(pale from the stifling human storm –
and with the face of a tired child)
you then leave the department store.

The bitter pills of gaiety
in the long run are bound to fail,
the day's hectic diplomacy
retreats, exhausted, from your face.

Houses are full of voices, lights...
It's Sunday everywhere – and Spring,
but in your eyes the carousel
is that on which the neckties spin.

You pass young people on the street,
on shoe soles made of micropore.
Shut off from their world, by yourself,
you walk on past the Metropole.

И чемоданчик твой овальный
(замок раскроется вот-вот),
такой застенчиво печальный,
качаясь, улицей плывет.

И будет пригородный поезд,
и на коленях толстый том,
и приставаний чьих-то пошлость,
и наконец-то будет дом.

Но в тихой маленькой Перловке
соседки шумные опять,
и просьбы, просьбы о перлоне,
который надо им достать.

Заснешь, и лягут полутени
на стены, на пол, на белье,
а завтра будет понедельник.
Он – воскресение твое.

Цветы поставишь на клеенку,
и свежесть дом заполонит,
и улыбнешься ты клененку,
который под окном стоит.

Ударит ветер теплых булок,
забьют крылами петухи,
жесть загремит, и прыгать будут
в пыли мальчишек пятаки.

И в смеси зелени и света,
и в добрых стуках топора,
во всем – щемящие приметы
того, что не было вчера.

(1962)

And your small, oval-shaped valise
(which may at any time unlock)
shyly and sadly swings along –
floating through every city block.

Then there'll be a suburban train –
reading a thick book on your lap;
somebody makes a pass at you,
and finally you're home at last.

In quiet, small Perlovka all
your neighbors will for the umpteenth
time loudly speak of the perlon
that they request you to obtain.

You'll fall asleep; half-shadows hit
the walls, the floor, your lingerie...
Tomorrow will be Monday – and
your Sunday – your one day that's free.

You'll put flowers on the oilcloth,
and they will make your room smell fresh;
you'll smile at the small maple tree
outside your window like a friend...

The wind from warm bread strikes your nose;
the roosters flap their wings and drum;
the tin goes clash – and copper coins
of little boys jump in the dust.

The mixing of such green with light,
the kindly cuttings of the ax –
all are heart-rending signs of things
which weren't here yesterday as facts.

АНДРЕЙ АНДРЕЕВИЧ ВОЗНЕСЕНСКИЙ
р. 1932

Сидишь беременная, бледная.
Как ты переменилась, бедная.

Сидишь, одергиваешь платьице,
И плачется тебе, и плачется...

За что нас только бабы балуют
И губы, падая, дают.

И выбегают за шлагбаумы,
И от вагонов отстают?

Как ты бежала за вагонами,
Глядела в полосы оконные...

Стучат почтовые, курьерские,
Хабаровские, люберецкие...

И от Москвы до Ашхабада,
Остолбенев до немоты,

Стоят, как каменные, бабы,
Луне подставив животы.

И поворачиваясь к свету
В ночном быту необжитом –

Как понимает их планета
Своим огромным животом...

ANDREI ANDREYEVICH VOZNESENSKY
b. 1932

You're pale and pregnant sitting here.
And, O, how much you've changed, my dear.

You tug your skimpy dress and try
To keep from crying, crying, cry...

But why do you girls spoil us all
And give us your lips as you fall

And run past railroad-crossing bars
And get left by the fast train's cars?

You ran with them along the rails;
The windows streaked by rapidly.

They chug – the passengers, the mails –
Bound for Khabarovsk... Lubertsy...

And from Moscow to Ashkabad
The girls still stand like stone, rough-hewn,

In speechlessness along the road
With bellies bending to the moon.

This planet this unlived-in night
Is slowly turning toward that light,

And through its own big belly swell
Can understand these women well.

ТОРГУЮТ АРБУЗАМИ

Москва завалена арбузами.
Все дышит волей без границ.
И веет силой необузданной
От возбужденных продавщиц.

Палатки. Гвалт. Платки девчат.
Хохочут. Сдачею стучат.

Ножи и вырезок тузы.
Держи, хозяин, не тужи!

Кому кавун?
Сейчас расколется! –
И так же сочны и вкусны
И милицейские околыши
И мотороллер у стены.

Сентябрьский воздух свеж на вкус
И так же звонок, как арбуз.

И так же весело и свойски,
Как те арбузы у ворот,
Земля мотается
В авоське
Меридианов и широт!

(1958)

THEY SELL WATERMELONS

Moscow is heaped with watermelons –
Exuding space without restraint.
And the excitement of saleswomen
Carries a stirring, untamed strength.

Tents. Kerchiefs of girls. All din,
Laughs, clinks of small coins coming in.

Knife blades, cut-outs shaped like an ace.
You've made it, Buster, feed your face.

Who wants one?
They're dead ripe, delicious! Men,
They'll tease your taste; they bulge with juice!
So do the hat-bands of militiamen;
Parked motor scooters even rejoice.

September air tastes fresh and round
As any watermelon sound.

As friendly and as care-forgetting
As watermelons each girl sells –
The earth sways
In the tote-bag netting
Of longitudes and parallels.

ГОЙЯ

Я – Гойя!
Глазницы воронок мне выклевал ворог, слетая на поле нагое.

Я – горе.

Я – голос
Войны, городов головни на снегу сорок первого года.

Я – голод.

Я – горло
Повешенной бабы, чье тело, как колокол, било над площадью
голой…
Я – Гойя!

О грозди
Возмездья! Взвил залпом на Запад – я пепел незваного гостя!
И в мемориальное небо вбил крепкие звезды –
Как гвозди.

Я – Гойя.

(1959)

GOYA

I am Goya!
The foe gouged eye-sockets with bombs and grenades which go to the
                                        bare ground gliding.
I am grief.

I am the glow
Of the charred towns engulfed in the '41 snow with the groans of a
                                        great famine growing.
I am gore.

I am the gullet
Of a wench on the gallows whose body is a bell above the city-square
                                        tolling...
I am Goya!

O, grapes
Of revenge! With a salvo I hurled the gray ashes of unwelcome guests
And I drove solid stars into the sky's memorial crest –   [to the west!
Like nails.

I am Goya!

СТРИПТИЗ

В ревю
            танцовщица раздевается дуря...
Реву?...
Или режут мне глаза прожектора?

Шарф срывает, шаль срывает, мишуру.
Как сдирают с апельсина кожуру.

А в глазах тоска такая, как у птиц.
Этот танец называется 'стриптиз'.

Страшен танец. В баре лысины и свист,
Как пиявки,
            глазки пьяниц налились.
Этот рыжий, как обляпанный желтком,
Пневматическим исходит молотком!
Тот, как клоп, –
            апоплексичен и страшон.
Апокалипсисом воет саксофон!

Проклинаю твой, Вселенная, масштаб,
Марсианское сиянье на мостах,
Проклинаю,
            обожая и дивясь.
Проливная пляшет женщина под джаз!...

'Вы Америка?' – спрошу, как идиот.
Она сядет, сигаретку разомнет.

'Мальчик, – скажет, – ах, какой у вас акцент!
Закажите мне мартини и абсент.'

1961

STRIP TEASE

On stage
        there's a dancing girl who strips until she's bare...
Do I rage?...
Or do these strong tears come from the floodlights' glare?

Scarf she takes off, shawl she shakes off, all the shine –
Tinsel that she peels off like an orange rind.

In her eyes a melancholy lies, – unease
Such as birds have. This dance is called a strip tease.

And the dance is fearful. Whistles and bald tops
In the club.
        And, like leeches, small drunk eyes go pop:
This red-haired man, his face dabbed as with egg-yolks,
Tires himself like an air-hammer's up-down strokes!
That grotesque bedbug –
                whom apoplexy grips.
And the saxophone howls an apocalypse!

O, I curse your scale and scope, O universe,
And the Martian sheen on bridges.
                Yes, I curse –
While adoring, admiring your razzmatazz.
This cascading woman gyrating to jazz!...

'You America?' I'll ask like an idiot.
She'll sit down and fidget with her cigarette.

'Boy,' she will say, 'where'd you get that crazy accent?
Would you buy me a martini or absinthe?'

Сирень похожа на Париж,
горящий осами окошек.
Ты кисть особняков продрогших
серебряную шевелишь.

Гудя нависшими бровями,
страшон от счастья и тоски,
Париж,
     как пчелы,
          собираю
в мои подглазные мешки.

(1964)

Paris is like a lilac bloom
where wasps of windows burn with luster,
and so you move the silver cluster
of trembling mansions as a plume.

Humming with hanging eyebrows there, as
nostalgia and joy terrorize,
like honeybees
                    I gather
                              Paris –
into the bags beneath my eyes.

ЕВГЕНИЙ МИХАЙЛОВИЧ ВИНОКУРОВ
р. 1925

ПТИЦЫ

Что означает это пенье птичье?
Гремит, звенит, поет ночная мгла.
То песнь, наверно, звездному величью?
То космосу бескрайнему хвала?

А может, то совсем не песнь,
                                                    а просто
Так, разговор про разные дела –
Что скоро утро, что, мол, нынче росно,
Что вот, мол, дескать, червяка нашла...

1953

*   *   *

Прозванье
Дала себе
Каждая нация
В согласии с главной
Чертой:
Англия – доброй,
Прекрасною – Франция,
А Русь называлась
Святой...

1957

EVGENY MIKHAILOVICH VINOKUROV
b. 1925

BIRDS

What do birds say when they sing? Any sense?
Night's full of sounds that swell, blend and disperse.
Are they paeans to stars' magnificence?
Or hymns to the unbounded universe?

Or maybe they're not songs at all,
                     but, say,
Talks about many things, in different terms.
Like: Morning's coming. The dew's thick today.
Or: Look here, all you birds,
                  I found some worms...

         ★   ★   ★

Each nation
Has given itself
Its own epithet;
To carry its essence,
The aim:
For England – a 'merry old'
For France – a 'beautiful'
And 'holy' was once
Russia's name...

СОВЕСТЬ

Можно жить безмятежно, условясь
Зло считать для удобства добром,
Но что делать тому,
               чья совесть
Все нежданно поставит ребром?
Что тут делать, когда в человеке
О приходе своем возвестит,
Пусть случайно, пусть в кои-то веки,
Словно трубы архангелов,
                   стыд?
Стыд людской –
          бог жестокий,
                 старинный!
Через рощи, скрывая кинжал,
Он в одеждах безумных Эриний
За мятущейся жертвой бежал.
И хоть годы летели, он все же
Человека врасплох настигал –
Среди битвы,
           с любимой на ложе,
На пиру поднимавшим бокал.
Я не ведаю большего чуда!
Совесть наша доныне темна.
Я не знаю, откуда, откуда
В человеке возникла она.
Совесть – миру навеки награда.
Вечно жить ей – глуши не глуши.

Удивляться не низости надо,
А безмерным высотам души!

1957

CONSCIENCE

One can have peace of mind by agreeing,
For convenience, to call evil good.
But then what should one do,

                one whose conscience
Unexpectedly unmasks its hood?
What to do here when shame comes arriving
In a man, telling him why it came?
Accidentally, eventually, may it happen –
Like the trumpets of angels –

            that shame!
Human shame,

        the great god,

            cruel, ancient,
Used to run through the groves with the blade
Of its dagger hid, dressed like mad Furies,
For its victim who trembled, afraid.
And though years flew by, it still pursued him,
Caught him when he expected it least:
Midst a battle,

        in bed with his woman,
Or while raising a glass at a feast.
I don't know of a miracle greater!
Even now it's an unexplained plan.
I don't know from what place came our conscience,
Where it originated in man.
Choked or not, it will live on forever;
It's Earth's lasting reward for all plights.

One should marvel not at the soul's baseness
But, instead, at its measureless heights.

В сапогах огромного размера,
Я вошел на цыпочках в музей . . .
Грозная Милосская Венера
Поднялась в беспомощности всей.

. . . Я прошел немало верст в пехоте,
Путь был труден.
                              Боже упаси!
Грязь такая осенью – шагнете,
И сапог останется в грязи.

Девушки лукавы и румяны
В госпиталях были тыловых,
Тонкие и сложные романы
Заводил я с многими из них.

У меня неловкая манера –
Я гашу цыгарку о каблук . . .
Ты стоишь, высокая Венера,
Выше моих радостей и мук:

'Вот я вся –
                    что значу и что стою,
Вот я вся –
                    как будто ото сна,
Страшная своею простотою,
Как волна,
                    легко вознесена.'

1957

Wearing my enormous boots, I entered
The museum – walking on tiptoes...
The redoubtable Venus de Milo
There in all her helplessness arose.

... I had covered miles while in the army:
Infantry, the hard way.
                          God forbid!
There was always so much mud each autumn;
You'd step; your feet stayed stuck in the mud.

Girls in those rear-area hospitals
Were sly and with rosy cheeks. And I
Had complex and subtle love relations
With many of them in passing by.

I know I possess a clumsy manner –
I put cigarettes out on my heel...
You are standing tall, Venus, much taller
Than any joy and suffering I might feel:

'Here is all of me –
                          my worth and meaning.
Here is all of me –
                          as from a sleep,
Fearful in my simpleness, emerging
Like a wave – O, lightly lifted up.'

Крестились готы.
                    В водоем до плеч
Они входили с видом обреченным.
Но над собой они держали меч,
Чтобы кулак остался некрещеным.
Быть должен и у кротости предел,
Что б заповедь смиренья ни гласила...
И я кулак бы сохранить хотел.
Я буду добр. Но в нем пусть будет сила.

1961

*   *   *

Цирк не люблю: вон тот сидит в пальто,
А тот жует, покуда, напрягая
Все силы, крутит смертное сальто
Девчонка в высоте,
                        полунагая.

Мне пляж постыл:
                        вон тот острит, а тот,
Под тентом развалясь, глядит с зевотой,
Как к морю зябко женщина идет,
По синеве блистая позолотой.

Я злюсь в кино: тот спит, а этот пьян.
Болтают. Иль хихикают несмело.
А женщина стоит во весь экран, –
Обнажено ее святое тело.

1961

The Goths were being baptized.
>   They looked doomed
Going into the stream up to their shoulders...
But up above their heads their own swords loomed;
Their fists were unbaptized to all beholders.
Humility should have its limits too,
Whatever 'meek Commandment' comes along...
And I should like to keep my fist in view.
I shall be kind. But let *it* still be strong.

*   *   *

I don't like circuses: this one sits in
An overcoat and that one chews, while vaulting
With all her strength, a girl begins her spin
Down from the heights,
>   half-naked, somersaulting.

I'm fed up with the beach:
>   this one rants, raves
His wit... and that one neath the canvas, yawning,
Eyes the girl, freezing, walking toward the waves,
Shining her gold against the sea's blue awning.

I'm mad at movies: this one sleeps and that
One's drunk. They chat... or giggle their shy chorus.
A woman stands up, filling all the flat
Screen with her holy body – bare before us.

БЕЛЛА АХАТОВНА АХМАДУЛИНА
р. 1937

Ах, мало мне другой заботы,
обременяющей чело, –
мне маленькие самолеты
все снятся, не пойму с чего.
Им все равно, как сниться мне:
то, как птенцы, с моей ладони
они зерно клюют, то в доме
живут, словно сверчки в стене.
Иль тычутся в меня они
носами глупыми – рыбешка
так ходит возле ног ребенка,
щекочет и смешит ступни.
То подле моего огня
они толкаются и слепнут,
читать мне не дают, и лепет
их крыльев трогает меня.
Или глаза открою – в ряд
все маленькие самолеты,
как маленькие Соломоны,
все знают и вокруг сидят.
Еще придумали – детьми
ко мне пришли и со слезами,
едва с моих колен слезали,
кричали: 'На руки возьми!'
Прогонишь – снова тут как тут.
Вот стыд какой – из блеска ваксы,
кося белком, за мной, как таксы,
тела их долгие плывут.

Что ж, он навек дарован мне –
сон жалостный, сон современный,
и в нем ручной, несоразмерный
тот самолетик в глубине?

BELLA AKHATOVNA AKHMADULINA
b. 1937

Oh! All these headaches pressing their pains
into my forehead! Here's one now:
I dream and I see tiny airplanes,
but can't understand why or how.
They don't care how they join my dreaming:
they peck grain from my palm like chicks,
or live in my house like the crickets
inside the wall constantly drumming.
Or nip me with each stupid nose
the way a fish does at the loafing
legs of some child and gets him laughing
by tickling him upon the toes.
Or elbow me around my hearth,
squinting their eyes, dazed in their clutter,
stopping my reading... and the prattle
of their young wings touches my heart.
Or – when I open my eyes wide –
in one long row are all of them,
sitting like little Solomons,
knowing all things and looking wise.
They come to me with tears and noise,
with some new brainstorm, just like children;
they shout, 'Oh! Carry me' until one
can hardly keep them off one's knees.
Shoo-shoo! They're back in nothing flat.
Their eye-whites slant in my shoes' polish;
they dog me like tail-wagging doxies:
their low-hung, long bodies afloat.

This modern dream, dreamt with a sigh,
will it stay with me now forever?
Will my unconscious hear it hover –
Some little plane, tamed, not real-size?

И все же, отрезвев от сна,
иду я на аэродромы
следить огромные те громы,
озвучившие времена.
Пока в преддверье высоты
всесильный действует пропеллер,
я думаю: ты все проверил,
мой маленький? Не вырос ты.
Ты здесь огромным серебром
всех обманул. На самом деле
ты – крошка, ты – дитя, ты еле
заметен там, на голубом.
И вот мерцаем мы с тобой
на разных полюсах пространства.
Наверно, боязно расстаться
тебе со мной, такой большой?
Но там, куда ты вознесен,
во тьме всех позывных мелодий,
пускай мой добрый, странный сон
хранит тебя, о самолетик!

(1963)

And still I walk to the airports,
fresh, wide-awake from my deep sleeping,
and follow airplanes in their sweeping
through our age with tremendous roars.
And at the threshold to those wilds,
that almighty propeller whirring,
I have but one persistent worry:
everything checked out right, my child?
With your impressive silver, maybe
you fooled them all, but, actually,
in that vast blue, you're hard to see;
you're so small, just a child, my baby.
And so we two, you and I, shine
but at two different poles of space;
you hate to leave me, I suppose,
I am so big – and you're so shy.
But in the dark where you are lifted,
where signal-beam melodies play,
may my kind, strange dream keep you lighted
and preserve you, my little plane.

РОБЕРТ ИВАНОВИЧ РОЖДЕСТВЕНСКИЙ
р. 1932

ПЕРЕД НОВЫМ ПРЫЖКОМ

Мы в зале ожидания
живем.
Любой из нас
      все время ждет
           чего-то...
Начальника
у дома ждет шофер,
поигрывая
      ключиком от 'Волги'...
Вот аккуратный старичок в пенсне.
Он ждет.
Он едет в Вологду
        за песнями...
Старуха,
     что-то бормоча о пенсии,
блаженно улыбается во сне...
Безропотного мужа
        ждет
           жена.
Девчонка ждет любви, –
ей очень боязно.
А на девчонку
      смотрит
         старшина,
и у него есть целый час
до поезда...
Ждет поворота лоцман:
скоро
   мель!
Учитель ждет
      решения примеров.

ROBERT IVANOVICH ROZHDESTVENSKY
b. 1932

BEFORE A NEW JUMP...

We live in one perpetual
waiting room.
Each one of us
                    must wait for something always.
A chauffeur
waits for his boss at his home,
and while he waits,
                    plays with the *Volga's* car-keys...
Here is a neat old man who wears pince-nez.
He goes to Vologda for folk-songs;
                                    pensive,
he waits.
And muttering about a pension,
an old woman smiles as she sleeps away...
A wife
        waits for her meek,
                        submissive mate.
A young girl waits for love –
                        afraid.
                            A sergeant
looks at
        the girl.
                    And he also must wait
(another hour) till his train's departure.
A helmsman waits the turn:
shoals –
        in an instant!
A teacher waits
            for problems to be solved;

Ребята
　　　　　ожидают перемены.
Колхозы
ожидают
перемен!...
Над миром гулким
дождь идет с утра.
Над миром гулким –
облаков движение...
Мы ждем.
Мы знаем:
нам уже
　　　　　пора
из зала ожиданий
в зал
свершений...
Мы ждем открытий.
Мы друзей зовем.
Друг другу
　　　　　говорим слова несладкие.
Мы в зале ожидания
живем!
Но руки
　　в ожидании
　　　　　　не складываем!
За нами –
взорванная тишина!
За нами –
　　　　　нашей силы нарастание.
Разбуженная,
ждущая страна.
И целый мир,
　　　　　застывший в ожидании.

8 сентября 1962

the pupils wait
        for
             recess to be called.
Collective farms
wait
for the change!... not distant!...
All morning in this echo-filled world –
rain.
Now in this echo-filled world
clouds are moving...
We wait.
We know
it's time for us
            to range
from waiting room
to rooms
of deeds and doing...
We wait for new discoveries.
We call
our friends. We exchange
                honest words which bite.
We in the waiting room
live! live! But all
during our wait
          we don't sit
             idly by!
Behind us:
shattered silence in our land!
Our strength –
its steady, vast accumulation.
Our waiting and awakened country, and
the whole wide world,
             frozen in expectation.

8 September 1962

ВЛАДИМИР АЛЕКСЕЕВИЧ СОЛОУХИН
р. 1924

Сомнений червь в душе моей гнездится,
Но не стыжусь я этого никак.
Червяк всегда в хороший гриб стремится,
Поганый гриб не трогает червяк!

(1958)

VLADIMIR ALEKSEYEVICH SOLOUKHIN
b. 1924

The worm of doubt has a nest in my soul,
But I am not ashamed of this. No fool,
A worm always likes mushrooms, good and whole;
He does not touch a sickening toadstool.

НОВЕЛЛА НИКОЛАЕВНА МАТВЕЕВА
р. 1934

НАРЦИСС

Кривые корни ивы под уклоном
Мохнатятся, как вытертый канат.
Среди реки, в ее бряцаньи сонном,
Расцвел нарцисс – мой бледнолицый брат.

В мельканьи струй, то синем, то зеленом,
Он день-деньской раскачиваться рад.
Он кажется таким самовлюбленным
Чужим глазам, что с берега глядят.

Но скромен, тих Нарцисса образ ясный.
Легенда лжет. Не слушайте ее!
Нет! Не себя любил Нарцисс прекрасный,
А только отражение свое.

Судить его – не нам, нарциссам суши:
Мы тоже любим родственные души.

21 декабря 1963 г.

NOVELLA NIKOLAYEVNA MATVEYEVA
b. 1934

NARCISSUS

The willow's crooked roots below the slope
Are shaggy like a worn and raggy rope.
The river strums and in its drowsing fuss,
My leafy brother blooms: pale Narcissus.

He's glad to sway the livelong day in such
Bright currents, that flash now with green, now blue.
He seems to love himself so very much –
To all eyes on the banks watching the view.

Narcissus' true image shows no conceit.
The legend lies, mirrors the wrong complexion.
Ignore it. No, Narcissus – handsome, sweet –
Loved not himself, but only his reflection.

We can't judge him: we're all a Narcissus
On dry land – loving other souls like us.

21 December 1963

РИММА ФЕДОРОВНА КАЗАКОВА
р. 1932

КАРТИНА

Еще по-девичьи узки
и угловаты плечи,
но две малинины – соски
пылают, будто печи.

Как дерзко вырубала кисть
игрой любви и риска
ее девическую кисть
в изломе материнства!

Экскурсовод плетет про 'ню',
про вывихи таланта,
а мы прилипли к полотну,
как к вымени телята.

Гудит он где-то далеко,
дерет свое мочало...
А в нас струится молоко,
что всех начал начало!

(1962)

RIMMA FYODOROVNA KAZAKOVA
b. 1932

A PAINTING

Her shoulders – like those of young girls –
Are angular and slender.
Her nipples are two raspberry burls
And glow like a stove's embers.

What play with love and risk! What nerve
The artist showed in sketching
The latent mother in the curve
Of this girl's hand outstretching!

The guide runs on about 'La Nue',
And 'art with misplaced rudder';
We're stuck to the canvas like glue –
Young calves against an udder.

The guy drones – platitudinous,
Bla-bla-ing in the distance
While milk already flows in us –
The sap of all existence.

АНОНИМНЫЕ ПОЭТЫ

I

Евреи хлеба не сеют.
Евреи в лавках торгуют.
Евреи раньше лысеют.
Евреи больше воруют.

Евреи люди лихие,
Они солдаты плохие:
Иван воюет в окопе,
Абрам торгует в райкопе.

Я все это слышал с детства
И скоро совсем постарею,
И все никуда не деться
От крика 'Евреи, евреи!'

Не торговавши ни разу,
Не воровавши ни разу,
Несу в себе, как заразу,
Эту проклятую расу.

Пуля меня миновала,
Чтоб говорилось не лживо:
'Евреев не убивало!
Все воротились живы!'

II

А нам, евреям, повезло.
Не прячась под фальшивым флагом,
На нас без маски лезло зло,
Оно не притворялось благом.

ANONYMOUS POETS

I

Jews don't plant the grain.
Jews sell things in a store.
Jews get bald when young.
Jews steal more.

Jews are a tricky crew.
They make poor soldiers too.
Ivan fights a battle;
Abie hears money rattle.

Ever since my childhood,
I've heard the same old news.
I'll grow old but I won't escape it:
The shouting, 'Jews!' 'Jews!'

I never sold a thing.
I never stole a thing.
But I carry my pedigree
Like a plague that curses me.

Somehow a bullet missed me,
So they talk (This is not a lie):
'Jews were never killed! See!
All of them come back alive!'

II

But we Jews have a certain luck.
When evil came, it wore no hood,
And used no false flag when it struck,
Made no pretensions to be good.

813

Еще не начинались споры
В торжественно-глухой стране,
А мы, припертые к стене,
В ней точку обрели опоры.

(1960)

КЛЮЧ

У меня была комната с отдельным ходом.
Я был холост и жил один.
Всякий раз, как была охота,
Я знакомых к себе водил.

Мои товарищи жили с тещами
И с женами, похожими на тещ, –
То слишком толстыми, то слишком тощими,
Серыми и однообразными, как дождь.

С каждым годом, старея на год,
Рожая то сыновей им, то дочерей,
Жены становились символами тягот,
Статуями нехваток и очередей.

Мои товарищи любили жен,
Они мне говорили все чаще и чаще:
Отчего ты не женишься? Эх ты, пижон!
Что ты понимаешь в семейном счастье?

Мои товарищи не любили жен:
Им нравились девушки с молодыми руками,
С глазами, в которые погружен,
Падаешь, падаешь, падаешь, как камень.

Throughout this solemn, silent land,
With time not ripe yet for debate,
We found the wall where we must stand,
The point for levering our‛fate.

THE KEY

I was a bachelor, – I lived by myself.
I had a room with a private door.
And whenever I got in a certain mood,
I invited a visitor.

My friends lived with their mothers-in-law
And with wives from that same grain ...
Either too fat or else too thin,
Monotonous and gray like rain.

And every year – having aged one year
Bearing kids of either sex.
The wives became statues in long bread lines
And nooses around their necks.

And all my friends loved their wives;
They used to ask me this:
Why don't you marry? You, playboy, you!
What do you know of married bliss?

My friends didn't love their wives;
They liked girls with soft, young hands
And with eyes into which like a stone one falls
And falls and falls and never lands.

Я был брезглив (вы, конечно, помните),
Я глупых вопросов не задавал,
А просто давал им ключи от комнаты –
Они просили, и я давал.

(1960)

*   *   *

Сегодня я ничему не верю –
Глазам – не верю.
Ушам – не верю.
Пощупаю, – тогда, пожалуй, поверю – все без обмана.

Мне вспоминаются хмурые немцы,
Печальные пленные сорок пятого года,
Стоявшие – руки по швам – на допросе.
Я спрашиваю – они отвечают:
– Вы верите Гитлеру? – Нет, не верю.
– Вы верите Герингу? – Нет, не верю.
– Вы верите Геббельсу? – О, пропаганда!
– А мне вы верите? – Минута молчания. –
– Господин комиссар, я вам не верю.
Все пропаганда. Весь мир – пропаганда.

Четыре слога про-па-ган-да
Гудят в моих ушах еще сегодня:
Все – пропаганда. Весь мир пропаганда.
Если бы я превратился в ребенка,
Снова учился в начальной школе,
И мне сказали такое:
Волга впадает в Каспийское море!

I was squeamish (You remember, no doubt)
I didn't ask stupid questions; I knew how to behave ...
I simply gave them the key to my room;
That's what they asked for – and that's what I gave.

        ★   ★   ★

I don't believe a thing today –
I don't believe my eyes.
I don't believe my ears.
But let me touch it, then I'll believe it's true, – maybe.

I remember sullen Germans,
The sad prisoners of nineteen-hundred-forty-five,
Standing – during interrogation – with their hands on their seams.
I asked: – They answered: –
'You believe Hitler?' – 'No, I don't.'
'You believe Goering?' – 'No, I don't.'
'You believe Goebbels?' – 'O, propaganda!'
'And what of me?' – (A brief silence.)
'Mr. Commissar, I don't believe you.
All propaganda. The whole world – propaganda.'

Four syllables: pro – pa – gan – da
Still resound in my ears today:
All propaganda. The whole world – propaganda.
If I were changed to a child once more,
Learning a game in a primary school,
And they told me this:
The Volga flows into the Caspian Sea!

Я бы, конечно, поверил, но прежде
Нашел бы эту самую Волгу,
Спустился бы вниз по течению к морю,
Умылся его водой мутноватой –
И только тогда бы, пожалуй, поверил.

   .   .   .   .   .   .

Лошади едят овес и сено!
Ложь! Зимой сорок восьмого года
Я жил на тощей, как жердь, Украине.
Лошади ели сначала солому,
Потом – худые соломенные крыши,
Потом их гнали в Харьков на свалку.
Я лично видел своими глазами
Суровых, серьезных, почти что важных,
Молча, неспешно бродивших по свалке.
Они ходили, потом стояли,
А после падали и долго лежали.
Умирали лошади не сразу...
Лошади едят овес и сено!
Нет! Неверно! Ложь. Пропаганда.
Все пропаганда. Весь мир пропаганда.

(1960)

I would believe it, of course,
But, first, I would find that Volga,
Would go down that stream to the sea,
Would wash in its turbid water,
And only then would I believe.

. . . . . .

Horses eat oats and hay!
It's a lie. In the winter of forty-eight
I lived in the Ukraine which was thin as a rail.
Horses at first ate straw,
Next – the skimpy straw-roofs,
And then they were herded to Kharkov to the city dump.
I saw them with my own eyes:
Austere, serious, almost important-looking.
Silently, unhurriedly, walking in the dump,
They used to walk, then they used to stand . . .
After which they fell and lay a long time.
And the horses took a while to die . . .
Horses eat oats and hay!
No! It's not true. It's a lie. Propaganda.
All propaganda. The whole world – propaganda.

КРЕМАТОРИЙ

Там кумачем завесив небо комнат
Перистый вепрь выпрыгивает в дым;
Нагие ноги поют в катакомбах,
Перебираемые как лады;
Там загнивающие укрепленья
В коренья превращаются в печи;
Там те, кто убоявшись погребенья,
Багряный погреб предпочли.

1958

ПЬЕСА С ДВУМЯ ПАУЗАМИ
ДЛЯ САКС-БАРИТОНА

Металлический зов в полночь
слетает с Петропавловского собора,
    из распахнутых окон в переулках
    мелодически звякают деревянные часы комнат,
    в радиоприемниках звучат гимны.
Все стихает,
ровный шопот девушек в подворотнях
стихает,
    и любовники в июле спокойны.
    Изредка проезжает машина.
Ты стоишь на мосту и слышишь,
как стихает и меркнет и гаснет
целый город.
    Ночь приносит
    из теплого темно-синего мрака
    желтые квадратики окон
и мерцанье канала.
Играй, играй, Диззи Гиллеспи,
Джерри Маллиган и Ширинг, Ширинг,
в белых платьях, все вы там в белых платьях

CREMATORIUM

Red calico drapes the skies of the rooms,
A cirrus boar jumps out into the smoke,
And naked legs chant in the catacombs
Like buttons an accordion awoke.
There – sinews, which have started rotting, ferment
And work their twisting roots inside this stove.
There is – for those who fear an earth interment –
This brilliant, berry-red burial cove.

A PIECE WITH TWO RESTS FOR THE BARITONE SAX

At midnight a metallic call
floats down from Peter and Paul Cathedral;
        from the wide-opened windows in the alleys
        the wooden clocks in the rooms melodically tick,
        and anthems play on the radios.
Everything calms down,
the even whispers of the girls in the archways
calm down,
        and the lovers in July are cool.
        Occasionally a car drives past.
You stand on the bridge and hear
the whole city calm down, grow dark
and die out.
        Night brings
        small yellow squares of windows
        and the glimmer of the canal
in the warm, deep-blue darkness.
Play, play, Dizzy Gillespie,
Gerry Mulligan and Shearing, Shearing
in white clothes, all of you there in white clothes

и в белых рубахах
на сорок второй и на семьдесят второй улице
там, за темным океаном, среди деревьев,
над которыми с зажженными бортовыми огнями
летят самолеты
за океаном.
Хороший стиль, хороший стиль
в этот вечер.
Боже мой, Боже мой, Боже мой. Боже мой,
что там вытворяет Джерри,
баритон и скука, и так одиноко,
Боже мой, Боже мой, Боже мой, Боже мой,
и звук выписывает эллипсоид, так далеко за океаном,
     и если теперь черный Гарнер
     колотит руками по черно-белому ряду,
все становится понятным.
                              Эррол!
Боже мой, Боже мой, Боже мой. Боже мой,
какой ударник у старого Монка
и так далеко,
за.океаном,
Боже мой, Боже мой, Боже мой,
это какая-то охота за любовью,
     все расхватано, но идет охота,
Боже мой, Боже мой,
это какая-то погоня за нами, погоня за нами,
Боже мой,
кто это болтает со смертью, выходя на улицу,
сегодня утром.
Боже мой, Боже мой, Боже мой, Боже мой,
ты бежишь по улице, так пустынно, никакого шума,
только в подворотнях, в подъездах, на перекрестках,
в парадных, в подворотнях говорят друг с другом,
и на запертых фасадах прочитанные газеты оскаливают заголовки.
Все любовники в июле так спокойны, спокойны. спокойны.

(1964)

and in white shirts
on 42nd and 72nd Streets –
there, across the dark ocean amidst the trees,
over which with signal lights on
airplanes are flying –
across the ocean.
Great style, great style
this night.
My God, my God, my God, my God,
the things Gerry's doing,
baritone and boredom, and it's so lonely.
My God, my God, my God, my God,
and the sounds make an ellipse, so far away, across the ocean,
    and if now the black Garner
    knocks his hands on that black-white row,
everything becomes clear.
                  Errol!
My God, my God, my God, my God,
what a percussionist the old Monk has,
and so far away,
across the ocean.
My God, my God, my God,
it's some kind of hunt for love,
    it's all snatched away, but the hunt goes on,
my God, my God,
it's some kind of chase – after us, a chase after us,
my God,
who's the one chatting with death, coming out on the street
this morning?
My God, my God, my God, my God,
you run along the street, it's empty, no noise,
only in the archways, in the doorways, on the corners,
at the front doors, in the archways, they talk with each other,
and on the locked facades read-through papers grin their head-
All lovers in July are so cool, cool, cool.   [lines.

КОСТЯ БАРАННИКОВ
р. 1924

Пусть всегда будет небо!
Пусть всегда будет солнце!
Пусть всегда будет мама!
Пусть всегда буду я.

1928

KOSTYA BARANNIKOV
b. 1924

Let there always be sky.
Let there always be sun.
Let there always be Mama.
Let there always be me.

NOTES

IN EACH section, the poets are arranged approximately in the order of their discussion in the preface. The order of the individual poet's poems is basically chronological with few exceptions. Dates placed in parenthesis are 'not later than' dates. Dedications to unknown or little-known persons were generally omitted. As to individual poems, our usual practice was to omit any elucidating commentary on the text which could be found in encyclopedias and other reference books and to concentrate on details of Russian life, history and culture which are more or less immediately appreciated by natives but may be stumbling blocks to a Western reader. We tried to avoid obvious comments which abound in Soviet editions of poetry, like: 'Venus is the goddess of love.'

THE TIME OF SYMBOLISM

BALMONT:

The Box: Ah-oo! – a shout Russians exchange in a forest in order not to lose each other; also used by those who are lost.

Lingonberry: Lingonberry – vaccinium vitis idaea. Snowball tree – viburnum opulus.

Hunting: Mole cricket – gryllida vulgaris.

BRYUSOV:

New Syntax: Kemi – the Coptic name for Egypt.

Ilya Repin (1844-1930), probably the most popular name in Russian painting, a conventional realist, an excellent craftsman.

The Joahimstal slag contained uranium ore.

Croesus' son, mute from birth, began to speak when his father was threatened with death.

Jean Metzinger (1883-1956), French painter and one of the first theoreticians of cubism. His book (co-authored with Albert Gleizes), *Du Cubisme*, appeared in 1913 in two Russian translations.

The Russian text refers not to 'abstractionism', but rather to 'suprematism' (1915-1935), the pioneering Russian abstractionist group, headed by Kazimir Malevich (see also 'At a Dance in the Cafe' by Selvinsky).

HIPPIUS:

Petersburg: The ironic epigraph is from Pushkin's *The Bronze Horseman*, the poem which both glorified this beautiful capital built by Peter I on the banks of the Neva River and started the tradition of presenting it as a dark, fantastic, tragic and evil place (see works by Gogol, Dostoyevsky, Merezhkovsky and A. Biely). Russian poets of the twentieth century never tired of giving their own portrayals of this enigmatic and the only really European city in Russia, but, on the whole, they followed Pushkin. So, almost invariably, the 'bronze horseman' (i.e., the equestrian statue of Peter I with a snake underneath, by Étienne Maurice Falconet, 1716-1791), the banks of the Neva or of the city canals, neo-classical architecture, and 'white nights' (i.e., summer nights lighted by the aurora borealis) are the main ingredients of this poetry. See in this book the poems by Annensky, Vyacheslav Ivanov, Voloshin, Gumilev, Mandelstamm, Livshits, Sorgenfrei, Aseyev and some others devoted to St Petersburg (changed in 1914 to Petrograd, and in 1924 to Leningrad). For Hippius this is a city of treachery, violence and blood.

Joy: This magnificent political invective in verse was written in the wake of the October Revolution, only four days after the Communist takeover.

Departure: This poem describes Hippius' flight from Soviet Russia.

ANNENSKY:

Ennui: It may help the reader to understand the poem if he knows that the flowers and the figures described by the poet are on the wallpaper of a bedridden man's room.

The word, 'ennui', is one of our attempts to render the Russian *toská*, which we also translated on other occasions as 'longing', 'yearning', 'boredom', 'melancholy', 'anguish', 'depression', 'tedium', 'homesickness', and even 'Angst'.

Pace: This statue by Bartolo Modolo stands in Catherine Park of Tsárskoe Seló (Tsar's Village), a town which is forty minutes by train from St Petersburg and which used to be a summer residence of

Russian rulers. Annensky was a school superintendent there from 1896 to 1906. And, among the poets represented in this book, Gumilev, Akhmatova and Klenovsky also lived in Tsárskoe Seló. But the town's most glorious connection with Russian poetry is the fact that Pushkin went there to school in 1811-1817. In 1937 it was renamed Pushkin. The statue's broken-off nose was restored by the Soviets.

Petersburg: See note to 'Petersburg' by Hippius. When Annensky mentions Swedes, he refers to the Northern War of 1700-1721 fought during the reign of Peter I. In his presentation of St. Petersburg, Annensky emphasizes its unreality and accursedness (both frequent themes in Russian literature).

My Angst: This poem is a result of Annensky's discussion of the essence of love with the poet, Mikhail Kuzmin; it was also his last poem: eighteen days after writing it, he died of heart failure on the steps of the Tsárskoe Seló station in St Petersburg.

V. IVANOV:

Taormina: Ivanov's own note to this poem is: 'On identification of Dionysus with Sun cf. Lobeck, *Aglaophamus*, 296.498; Welcker, Gr[iechische] Götterl[ehre] I, 411; Sam Wide, *Lakonische Culte*, 161.' It may seem gratuitous and trivial, but this sonnet happened to be translated at Mount Etna, Iowa.

Narcissus: Lyaeus, another name for Bacchus (Dionysus – god of Nysa).

Nomads of Beauty: The epigraph is from a novel, written by V. Ivanov's first wife, Lydia Zinovieva-Hannibal.

To the Translator: This poem might be considered the epigraph to this entire anthology.

Sphinxes over the Neva: The two statues were brought to St Petersburg from Egypt. They face each other on the Neva quay in front of the Academy of Arts. For V. Ivanov they are a sign that St Petersburg is a city of mysteries where polarities come together.

'Winter, winter, your name is orphanhood': Sonnet IX from the series of twelve entitled 'Winter Sonnets', which were written during the winter of 1919, the time of hunger and deprivation following the Revolution.

'*These tangling dolphins brought a bivalve out*' and
'*The hunchbacked captives thrown into the clear*':
Sonnets V and VI of the nine 'Roman Sonnets' written when
V. Ivanov left Russia and saw the Eternal City again. His own notes
to these two sonnets, respectively, follow: (1) 'The famous Russian
painter, Alexander Ivanov, who worked in Rome for a long time,
was Gogol's frequent guest at the via Sistina' [The fountain is, of
course, Il Tritone on Piazza Barberini]. (2) 'The fountain "delle
Tartarughe" whose figures were created in 1585 by the Florentine
sculptor, Taddeo Landini, evokes in one's memory the poetic world
of Lorenzo the "Magnificent".'
    July: This is the title for a whole series of poems comprising the
July portion of V. Ivanov's poetry diary for 1944.
    '*The chiton that the flame consumes hugs him*': This sonnet III of
the sonnet sequence entitled 'De profundis amavi' was finished by
V. Ivanov one day before his death.

BLOK:
    '*A girl was singing in the church's choir*': Holy Doors is the middle
entrance in the iconostasis leading into the sanctuary in a Russian
church.
    '*On the Field of Kulikovo*': The title of the five-poem cycle, of
which this is the first. In 1380, Russians defeated the Tartars in the
battle at Kulikovo, which, though not decisive, was the first blow to
the 'Tartar Yoke' which lasted for more than two centuries. For
Blok, the battle of Kulikovo was a mystical, ever-recurring event.
The idea of the Eternal Feminine which dominated practically the
entire lyrical output of Blok went through successive stages and was,
at first, The Beautiful Lady (see 'Poet'), then a streetwalker with
otherworldly features (see 'The Stranger'). Here it is Blok's native
country.

BIELY:
    To my Friends: This is a prophetic poem. Biely actually died
twenty-seven years later of a sunstroke.
    To Asya: Biely 'orchestrated' this poem so that all stressed vowels

in each stanza are identical (in the original, 'a' and 'o' in stanzas 1 and 2, respectively).

Spirit: As much of Biely's late work, this poem is based on anthroposophic theories.

POST-SYMBOLISTS

KUZMIN:

'*When they say to me, "Alexandria"*,'
'*I don't know how it happened*' and
'*Am I not like an apple tree*':
From Kuzmin's cycle of poems (later a book) entitled *Songs of Alexandria*.

'*I tried to breathe a soul into*': Uses, as its basis, the apocryphal story about the child Jesus making live doves out of clay.

Chodowiecki: Daniel Nikolaus Chodowiecki (1726-1801) famous German engraver-illustrator, whose gentleness and lightness of touch remind one of Kuzmin himself.

'*Faustina*': One of Kuzmin's 'Gnostic poems'. The name of Faustina, the wife of Antoninus Pius, is still visible on the temple in the Roman Forum, just opposite the Palatine.

'*Venice*': Jacque Cazotte (1719-1792) wrote a novel, *Le Diable Amoureux*.

A Message: The second Tamara (the *Firebird*) is the famous Tamara Karsavina, ballerina who danced the *Firebird*.

The End of the Second Volume: Pavlovsk, another former imperial summer residence, not far from St Petersburg, with palaces, villas and parks. Emelyan Pugachev (1742-1775), the leader of the famous Cossack rebellion in 1773-1775.

The First Thrust: The first episode of Kuzmin's poetic story of homosexual love, *The Trout Breaks the Ice*, divided into twelve 'thrusts' which mark the successive stages of the affair. Karl Bryullov (1799-1852), Russian romantic painter whose huge canvas, 'The Last Days of Pompei', made him famous, but his most appealing and typical works are his Italianate portraits of Russian aristocratic ladies.

GUMILEV:

'*You are dazed by the roar and the trampling*': Its Russian title is

Introduction, and it is a poetic preface to Gumilev's book of African poems, *The Tent*.

The Worker: This poem, often now considered prophetic (Gumilev was executed by a 'proletarian' government), actually has to do with World War I and presents a German worker. Dvina, a river flowing into the Baltic Sea.

The Lost Streetcar: In its St Petersburg background, this poem adds St Isaac's Cathedral to the inevitable 'Bronze Horseman'. The Empress mentioned is Catherine II.

AKHMATOVA:

Pushkin: Pushkin seems to be one of Russian poets' favorite subjects (in addition to St Petersburg, ennui and the Muse). Here he is presented as a student at the *lycée* in Tsárskoe Seló (where Akhmatova spent her young years, too), reading one of his then favorite French poets, Viscount de Parny (1753-1814). For other Pushkin poems or poetical references see Parnok, Mandelstamm, Tsvetayeva, Aseyev, Zabolotsky, Chinnov, G. Ivanov.

He Did Love . . .: Akhmatova writes here about Gumilev, her first husband.

Cabaret Artistique: Akhmatova later dropped this title, but we decided to restore it to help the English-language reader in visualizing this New Year's party scene in the famous artistic night club, *The Stray Dog*, where walls were painted by Sergei Sudeikin (1882-1946).

'*Faded flag on the customs building*': A scene from Akhmatova's childhood when she spent the summers in Crimea near Sevastopol.
'*I would rather shout out . . .*,'
'*Was this why I used to carry*' and
'*You will no more be alive*':
Poems where Akhmatova used the form of a folksong, or, more precisely, of the *chastushka*, a popular street-song.

'*When in a suicidal anguish*': Akhmatova's famous poetic statement of her refusal to emigrate from Revolution-torn Russia.

MANDELSTAMM:

'*The hoofs of horses keep recalling*': A Russian *dvornik* (apartment house caretaker), opening the house gate for the poet returning home late after a party or a theatrical performance, evokes ancient times in his mind.

'*Upon a wide sled full of fateful litter*': In this complex poem the real Tsarevich Dmitri, murdered in Uglich in 1591, and the pretender, who later appeared using his name, are merged into one person. With this is interwoven the theme of the 'third Rome' – the popular political theory of the Muscovite period of Russian history that Moscow is the third Rome (i.e., the real spiritual center of Christianity now that Rome and Constantinople, for different reasons, have been disqualified). 'And there will be no fourth one', as one of those theorists put it.

'*I'm cold . . .*': Petropolis is Mandelstamm's name for St Petersburg.

'*Brothers, let's glorify the twilight of freedom*': Marks Mandelstamm's cautious acceptance of the Communist revolution.

Ariosto: Mandelstamm probably means it figuratively: Ariosto was not born in Ferrara. The last line of the poem is the cliché ending of Russian fairytales.

'*We exist in a country . . .*': Mandelstamm's satire of Stalin, which brought about his arrest and exile to a concentration camp. Stalin's 'Osset' chest (whatever Mandelstamm meant by this) is changed by us into a Georgian (Gruzian) one.

'*Do not compare . . .*': Was written in a concentration camp.

KHLEBNIKOV:

Occasional ungrammatical strangeness in our translations of Khlebnikov is intentional; it is an attempt to reproduce some characteristics of Khlebnikov's primitivist style.

'*All rest, all air, all flutter*': In the final lines, Khlebnikov's pacifist ideas are mixed with his bizarre linguistics. The reference to the 'law of the sword' has to do with the so-called 'internal declension', where a change of one vowel brings about a radical change in meaning. One of Khlebnikov's favorite examples was that *mech* (sword), the tool of death, thus is transformed into *myach* (playing ball).

SEVERYANIN:

Champagne Polonaise: Though we spell Escamillo correctly in our translation, we keep the misspelling in the original, as characteristic of the poet.

LIVSHITS:

The Warmth: Livshits' ambitious attempt to apply the principles of avantgarde painting to poetry. The 'canvas' balances 'the warmth' of a yellow-lighted interior, with a housekeeper rummaging in a chest of drawers and a child about to fall asleep in his bed, and the cold of the winter-night landscape seen through the window. Livshits aimed at dislocating ('shifting') the reality, without, however, distorting the relationship between its elements. He transforms the chest into an executed African ('an aberration of the first degree', according to Livshits) and decomposes the white of the blizzard outside into the seven colors of the spectrum (thus a peacock tail – which is 'an aberration of the second degree'). The blizzard sweeps through southern Russia steppelands where there are many mounds (skulls of the buried warriors).

Fontanka Canal and *Kazan Cathedral*: These are Livshits' architectural poems from his St Petersburg cycle. Columbus egg: Columbus is said to have been able to make an egg stand by simply crushing one end of it.

GNEDOV:

Poem of the End: This was a favorite of the audiences. According to some contemporaries, Gnedov 'recited' it by being tensely silent for a minute or two; others say that he made a gesture resembling a cross.

ZENKEVICH:

Rows of Meat: A *zolotnick* is an old Russian measure of weight (4.26 grams), used before the introduction of the metrical system.

PARNOK:

'*No grain will sprout . . .*': Parnok refers here to the well-known romantic elegy of Pushkin beginning in Russian with the words, *Nenastnyi den' potukh*. As emotion accumulates towards the end, Pushkin interrupts the poem twice with lines of dots, then marks the appearance of jealousy with 'But if' (*No esli*) after which dots finish the poem.

POETRY AND EXILE

KHODASEVICH:

In the Suburbs: This depicts the environs of Berlin.

Before the Mirror: Ostánkino was a famous estate of the Counts Sheremetev near Moscow.

G. IVANOV:

'*Along the street . . .*': The epigraph is from an obscure comedy, *Coryon*, by the greatest Russian playwright of the eighteenth century, Denis Fonvizin.

'*The music is transformed into a flower*': Toward the end, Ivanov plays with a quotation from the poem, 'I come out, alone, to the road', by the great romantic poet of nineteenth-century Russia, Mikhail Lermontov. We were unable to reproduce the play on words: 'Tuman . . Taman' (Fog . . . Taman) of the original, where Taman is the title of one part of Lermontov's famous novel, *A Hero of our Time*.

TSVETAYEVA:

'*Your name . . .*' and '*For a beast . . .*': From the cycle addressed to Alexander Blok, the poet worshipped by Tsvetayeva.

The Don: Glorifies the White resistance to the Communists in the Russian Civil War.

'*Larger than organs . . .*': Refers or alludes, in addition to the *Song of Songs*, also to Borodin's opera, *Prince Igor*, gypsy songs, Pushkin's ballad about the ancient Russian prince, Oleg, and to Russian epics.

ODOYEVTSEVA:

'*He said goodbye . . .*': The Summer Park is the famous park in St Petersburg adjacent to the Neva.

NABOKOV:

The two translations are by Mr Nabokov himself and were done by him at Lake Garda in May, 1965.

'*What is the evil deed I have committed*': This begins with a parody of Pasternak's poem (printed against the poet's wishes), 'Nobel Prize', and ends with Nabokov's own version of '*Exegi monumentum*'.

CHINNOV:

Vorkuta is the place in Russia's North (Republic of Komi) with some of the greatest concentration camps; Hungary is mentioned with reference to the Hungarian revolution of 1956. 'The Prophet' is Pushkin's famous and overinterpreted poem, which ends with God's command to the prophet to go and 'burn human hearts with words'.

POETRY AND REVOLUTION

VOLOSHIN:

'*The bare slope of the winding valley . . .*': Karadag is a mountain in Crimea.

Petersburg: Count Joseph de Maistre (1754-1821) the brilliant French ultramontanist writer and one of the most magnificent reactionary ideologists of all time, lived in St Petersburg in 1803-1817 as Sardinian ambassador. His company is perhaps Peter Chaadayev (1794-1856), one of the most original Russian thinkers and the author of *Philosophical Letters*.

Rhipean land: here stands for Russia. Rhipaei montes was the classical name for the Urals.

Holy Russia: Suzdal and Moscow were the grand duchies of Vladimir-Suzdal before the fourteenth century and of Moscow after that century, respectively, and were important centers in the formation of Russia. The Carpenter-Czar is Peter I. Wooden monasteries are those of Old Believers hiding in remote areas from government persecution. 'The nightingale whistle' of the original has both the connotations of the Robber-Nightingale, the epic monster who killed people with his whistle, and of the Russian brigands and outlaws who lived in the forests and signaled each other with whistles. Esenin uses the same whistle image at the end of his *Song about Grain* (below), where the whistle also has the overtones of the howling of wind along the Russian plains. Of course, any translation would miss the lexical and melodic echoes of old songs present in *Holy Russia*.

Northeast: This poem is even more filled with historical names, facts and allusions than the previous one, so that we were forced to omit some of them in translation to avoid lengthy explanations (e.g., about 'military settlements'). Most of these details illustrate the chaos, cruelty and violence of Russian history. Among them are names of tyrannical and/or mad rulers, such as Ivan the Terrible (1530-1584), Peter I (1672-1725) and Peter III (1728-1762), Paul I (1754-1801); of their ferocious henchmen, such as Maliuta Skuratov (d. 1572), head of the dreaded Oprichniks, and General Aleksey Arakcheyev (1769-1834); and of the terror-striking secret police organs from the Secret Chancellory organized in 1718 by Peter I to Special Bureau (Cheka) created by Lenin in 1917. Often there is no boundary between persecutors and victims, as in the case of the Tsar's troops, the Streltsi, whose brutal destruction by Peter I in 1698 was only the end to their century-long history full of their own brutality and violence. Astrakhan (a city at the Volga delta) and Yaik (the old name of the Ural River) allude to the well-known Cossack and peasant uprisings led by Stepan Razin (1667-1671) and Emelyan Pugachev (1773-1775), respectively, in which the cruelty of the rebels matched that of their final suppressors. The name of Gatchina, a city near St Petersburg, alludes to inhuman military discipline under Paul I, who lived there for many years.

On the Bottom of Hell: Gumilev was executed by Soviet authorities; Blok died in madness, starvation and disillusionment.

MAYAKOVSKY:

And Could You?: By 'the tin fish', Mayakovsky means signboards of fish shops.

Violin: Kuznetsky is a street in Moscow.

Six Nuns: Prop-com (*agitprop*) – before 1934, local Communist political-indoctrination sections, whose job was also antireligious propaganda.

Brooklyn Bridge: Mayakovsky mistook the East River for the

Hudson. 'Constructions instead of styles' refers to Mayakovsky's fight for technologically oriented, utilitarian art in contradiction to 'arty' styles.

'*Past one o'clock* . . .': Probably Mayakovsky's last poem, hastily jotted down in his notebook.

ESENIN:

'*There, where the sunrise* . . .': We are certain Esenin cheated when he dated this little masterpiece 1910, probably to show, possibly to fake, his precociousness. His other poetry dating from this time is extremely unoriginal and inept. The recent Russian editions of Esenin, nevertheless, uncritically accept this date.

PASTERNAK:

Marburg: Pasternak studied philosophy in Marburg under Professor Hermann Cohen in 1912. It was there that, after he was rejected by a girl to whom he proposed, he quit philosophy and became a poet.

In Memory of the Demon: *The Demon* is a long romantic poem by Lermontov about the love of a Lucifer-like Spirit of Evil for a mortal Caucasian princess. The action takes place in Georgia (Gruzia), Caucasus. The zurna is a Caucasian musical wind instrument.

'*All will be here* . . .': This is one of the cycle of introductory poems to Pasternak's book, *The Second Birth*, where the poet tries very hard to understand and accept socialism. This is reflected in the lines about 'man at the highest limits/from the outgrowing of an ant'.

Hopbines: The Russian title has a double meaning: *khmel'* means both 'hopbines' and 'intoxication'. The tone of the poem is restrained, but the man and woman in it kiss each other at least seven times without Pasternak mentioning it. Count the sucking 'shch' sounds in the original; compare this also with the preceding 'O swaying with wet, fragrant branches' in which raindrops kiss each other in the same way. The device of describing processes and facts by sounds is part of Pasternak's futurist background and was frequently used by him.

August: The Second Saviour Day is the popular name for Transfiguration Day which is 6 August, according to the Old Style (Julian

Calendar), which is 19 August, according to the New Style (Gregorian Calendar). There are three Saviour Days in August.

Winter Night: This is the poem about the candle Yuri Zhivago sees in the window while passing the apartment on Kamergersky Street which figures prominently in the novel.

'I want to find the essence of . . .': Folwark – estate or farm in Polish areas.

My Soul: Pasternak's requiem for his friends lost during the time of Stalin.

KLUYEV:

'Old believer jackdaw': According to peasant superstition, the infant drowned by its mother because it was born out of wedlock is eternally damned.

Kokoshnik – old Russian female headgear.

Journey: Unless Kluyev has something else in mind, this is an anatomical impossibility: when erect, man's sacrum is not located above his liver.

GORODETSKY:

Spring: This poem made Gorodetsky famous and, though very prolific, he never matched this early success and remained a poet of one poem. During the Maundy Thursday (in Russian, Pure Thursday), preceding Good Friday, people hold burning candles while twelve excerpts from the Gospels are read at the vespers. It used to be customary to try to bring the burning candle home from the church without extinguishing it on the way.

ASEYEV:

'When loneliness bends over all': Aseyev's early attempt to apply Khlebnikov's theories of 'internal declension'.

Blue Hussars: The Hussars in this St Petersburg picture are conspirators and later participants in the Decembrist revolt of 1825. The main societies were the Northern and the Southern ones.

Song about Garcia Lorca: It is interesting to note that Aseyev and/ or his colleagues never publicly reproached Russia for sending their fellow poets, Mandelstamm, Kluyev and Livshits, to jails and concentration camps where they met death.

SELVINSKY:

Rabbit Made Strong by Decree: This fable could apply to many cases during the time of Stalin, e.g., when everyone was made to understand that Lebedev-Kumach (see his *Song about our Motherland*) was seriously to be considered a major poetic force. Selvinsky, whom Stalin disliked as a poet, had all reasons to feel bitter about it. The date and place are perhaps camouflage, trying officially to pass it as a satire of literary conditions in Hitler's Germany.

TIKHONOV:

David: The famous canvas in Brussels doesn't show any Charlotte Corday. Perhaps Tikhonov had some earlier version in mind or simply was mistaken.

ZABOLOTSKY:

Patterns of Sleep: 'Like dead' is the translators' license which, we hoped, was in the spirit of the original. Though it logically contradicts the situation (the sleeping boys symbolize New Life), it is nonsensically Zabolotskian in effect.

The Ivanovs: 'But suddenly all doors were opened' is a parodic quotation from Pushkin's *Eugene Onegin*.

VASILYEV:

Sister: Irtysh – a tributary of the Ob in Siberia.

SHERSHENEVICH:

'*When like a nut*': 'Ticket to Paradise' alludes to Dostoyevsky's *Brothers Karamazov* where Ivan returns his ticket to Paradise in protest against the human sufferings God permits in the world.

SOVIET POETRY

KIRSANOV:

Work in the Garden: Ivan Michurin (1855-1935), Russian horticulturist. His theories on hybrids were officially supported during the Stalin era.

LEBEDEV-KUMACH:

Song about our Motherland: 'Law of Stalin' is the Soviet Constitution from which the poet quotes (the lines about rights).

ALIGER:

On Beauty: Soviet soldiers may or may not have saved the Sistine Madonna from fire, but they certainly continued saving it for ten years, during which time the painting remained in Russia.

BERGHOLZ:

Return: About Tsárskoe Seló and Pushkin: see notes to Annensky's *Pace* and Akhmatova's *Pushkin*. The poem portrays the park after being ravaged by the Germans in World War II. The quoted lines are from Pushkin's famous school reunion poem, written in 1825 ('October 19').

Promise: This bitter poem is an excellent example of desk-drawer poetry. Bergholz published it only in 1964. Her husband, the well-known Soviet poet, Boris Kornilov, like many, disappeared in the purges of the 1930s.

MARTYNOV:

'*I hear the crunch*': This is a cautiously independent opinion on Soviet discussions of Western abstract art, which is still officially condemned in the USSR.

EVTUSHENKO:

A Tie Salesgirl: 'Micropore' is a type of gum rubber from which soles are made. Perlon is a synthetic fabric similar to nylon.

VOZNESENSKY:

Strip Tease: Voznesensky must be speaking about an artificial absinthe such as Pernod, because serving real absinthe has been illegal in the United States for many years.

AKHMADULINA:

'*O! All these headaches . . .*': 'Doxies' has a new meaning these days. Pet shop owners, along with their customers, use it when referring to dachshunds.

ROZHDESTVENSKY:

Before a New Jump: 'Volga' in this poem describes a Russian make of automobile.

ANONYMOUS POETS:

The names of the three poets who wrote these poems are known to us, but, for various reasons, we do not choose to divulge them. Some of these poets are well-known, some completely unknown; some young, some not so young. Also for various reasons, all these poems belong to underground poetry.

'*I don't believe a thing today*': 'The Volga flows into the Caspian Sea' and 'Horses eat oats and hay' are common currency, statements of obvious facts, used ironically. They come from a Chekhov story wherein a schoolteacher dictates them to his pupils.

KOSTYA BARANNIKOV:

'*Let there always be sky*': A four-year-old child composed these lines in 1928. Now everybody in Russia knows this little poem as a song.

DATE DUE

FEB 21 '72			
FEB 21 '73			
FEB 20 '73			